THE LAND THAT LOST ITS HEROES

THE FALKLANDS THE POST-WAR AND ALFONSÍN

JIMMY BURNS

BLOOMSBURY

First published 1987
Copyright © 1987 by Jimmy Burns

Bloomsbury Publishing Ltd, 4 Bloomsbury Place, London WC1A 2QA

British Library Cataloguing in Publication Data

Burns, Jimmy
The land that lost its heroes: the
Falklands, the post-war and Alfonsín.
1. Falkland Islands War, 1982——Influence
2. Argentina——Politics and government——
1983–
I. Title
982'.064   F2849.2

ISBN 0-7475-0002-9

PICTURE CREDITS

The author and publishers are grateful to the following for permission to reproduce
copyright black and white photographs: Fox Photos, 13; Keystone Press Agency Ltd,
1, 3; and Popperfoto, 2, 4, 5, 6, 7, 8, 9, 10, 11, 12, 14, 15, 16, 17, 18.

Designed by Newell and Sorrell Design Ltd
Printed by Butler & Tanner Ltd,
Frome and London

Five years on from the Falklands War, Jimmy Burns is in a unique position to place that historic confrontation in perspective. He was the only full-time British foreign correspondent to remain in Argentina after covering the war. He gives the first detailed account of the military planning of the invasion, exposing not only the hidden motives and nature of Argentina's military regime, but also the pitifully inadequate reactions of both British diplomacy and intelligence.

Here is the first detailed account of the junta's secret military alliance with Qadafi, and of how Margaret Thatcher deliberately chose to ignore evidence of this alliance for fear of upsetting Britain's commercial relationship with Libya. Burns exposes the duplicity of other Western nations and the international banking community and provides shocking evidence of Argentine naval attempts to sabotage British warships in Gibraltar. He gives a vivid account of the end of the military regime, the debt crisis and the return to democracy under the leadership of anti-military Raul Alfonsín.

A clear observer, an assiduous researcher and an objective analyst, Jimmy Burns has brought vital, previously murky information to light. His outstanding book will cause political discomfort to some – and new understanding to many.

TO KIDGE

CONTENTS

ILLUSTRATIONS

INTRODUCTION

This book is the result of journalistic good luck: of being in the right place at the right time. My posting as the Argentine correspondent of the *Financial Times* began just after Christmas 1981 in the grill room of the Carlton Tower Hotel in London. An Argentine Embassy official, enthusiastic because my newspaper had at last decided to show more than passing interest in the backwoods of Latin America by opening up several new bureaux there, urged me to look forward to an affluent and tranquil life in Argentina. I would eat huge steaks on a daily basis, drink tea with my British compatriots in the Anglo-Argentine community, see good opera, ride horses across the *pampa* and, if I still had the time to work, observe his great country being guided towards democracy 'some time in the distant future' under the enlightened and responsible pro-Western rule of General Leopoldo Galtieri and his military junta.

Such a picture fitted perfectly with the somewhat romantic vision of Argentina I had formed from the writings of nineteenth-century British travellers, which provide an essential source of reference for the country's history. However, they seemed to contradict the horror of human rights violations on a massive scale which Argentine exiles had told me about in London and Madrid. They also were not borne out by my impressions once I arrived in Buenos Aires. The steaks, tea, opera and horses were all there in abundance. But so were the beggars, the black market in foreign exchange, a practically worthless local currency, phones which would not work, abandoned motor-ways which went nowhere, and an underlying violence and regimentation of public attitudes made manifest in the brutality of the police, the absence of debate on any issue, and the identical clothes worn according to social class. The part of the city where we had our first flat was called Villa Freud because there were so many people seeking help from psychoanalysts with their sense of frustration about the present and lack of hope for the future.

Three months after I arrived, the Galtieri junta invaded the Falkland Islands. Between 1982 and 1986 I experienced the war from the Argentine end, reported the subsequent collapse of the military regime, and watched the first firm foundations of democracy being laid by President Raul Alfonsín. Argentina – the land of infinite promise in the early part of this century which fifty years ago had had a *per capita* income greater than Sweden's and Australia's and a foreign trade larger than Canada's – chalked up in the four and a half years I was there an inflation rate of over 1,000 per cent and a foreign debt of fifty billion dollars, before once again looking hopefully towards the future, on the basis of Mr Alfonsín's bold promise of a New Argentina and a hundred years of democracy.

Research for this book in June 1982 was stimulated initially by a sense of revenge for the past. I was determined to focus on the background to the war – its military planning and the motivation of the junta – thus recreating the real story I had missed in the first, somewhat confused, three months of my posting. But the longer I stayed in Argentina the more I realised that the run-up to the war – important as it was in exposing not just the nature of military rule but also the diplomatic failings of the Thatcher government – could only be properly understood within a wider historical context. Thus this book looks back through Argentina's military history to the Perón years and the repression which followed the 1976 coup. It also examines the country's transition to democracy after the Falklands War and looks forward to the likely problems facing not just Mr Alfonsín but a future British government over the Falklands issue. The emphasis is primarily analytical, explaining the nature of Argentine militarism and the implications of democracy for Argentina's development as a nation and its impact on the Falklands issue.

While the Falklands War is central, I have not attempted to give a blow-by-blow account of military and diplomatic events as there is already an extensive bibliography on the subject both in Argentina and Britain. Argentina's own official investigations into the military conduct of the war – carried out by the military themselves – threw up very little of substance that was not already known. Essentially the information focused on logistical questions such as the lack of adequate preparation for the war and the failure of interservice co-operation. Little attention was paid to the chronology of events leading up to the invasion, the political aspect of the decision to invade and pursue a total war, the military's relations with the kelpers and the way the junta took advantage of the good faith of its own people and international opinion by manipulating public opinion and dangerous secret alliances. By concentrating on these little-known aspects of the Argentine campaign I hope to have provided fresh insights and revelations which are crucial to an overall assessment of the Falklands War five years on.

I have also avoided consciously a profound discussion of the rights and wrongs of Argentina's claims to the islands. In November 1985 an Argentine historian claimed that the only certain fact about the early history of the islands was that they were discovered neither by an Englishman nor by an Argentinian but by a Dutchman.[1] Sebald de Weert, an adventurous naval captain sighted them on 16 January 1600. Thereafter Dutch cartographers included them in their maps for the first time, naming them the 'Sebald Islands'. Most Argentines, however, do not have any real sense of who discovered them and prefer to believe that Amerigo Vespucci, in the service of the Spanish crown, saw them in 1502, ninety years before a British navigator, John Davis, thought he did. There seems little doubt that an Englishman, John Strong – a sea captain from Plymouth – physically set foot on the islands in 1690. And yet discovery does not come into the 'Malvinas equation'. For over a century successive Argentine governments have argued that discovery alone has never been accepted by international law as the foundation of sovereignty. What makes discovery the key to any claim is occupation and settled administration, it is argued. Argentina declared sovereignty to the Falklands by inheritance from Spain in 1820 and administered the islands for the next thirteen years. The Argentine belief that Britain's reassertion of its claim by military seizure in 1833 was an illegal occupation of Argentine territory has been accepted as an absolute truth by successive Argentine generations of whatever race, creed or political sympathy ever since.

Argentina's claim may not lack juridical persuasiveness but does not in itself explain the Falklands War. There are numerous other countries in the world whose territorial claims to a piece of allegedly illegally seized territory go back as far as Argentina's and which have nevertheless not been resolved by conflict. Indeed, as has been noted, 'If all nations reopened 150-year-old claims whenever they felt strong enough, the world would be a bloodier place than it is.'[2] Before the Falklands invasion few Argentines had contemplated regaining the islands by any other means than diplomacy. In the early twentieth century not even the considerable economic and commercial influence which Britain wielded in Argentina prevented Argentine officials from raising the issue of the 'Malvinas'.[3] Even from 1964 onwards, when the Radical government of Arturo Illia first stepped up its efforts to attract international attention to the island question at the United Nations, the emphasis was on regaining the islands through negotiation.

This political attitude was mirrored in the reactions of ordinary Argentines. Before 1982 there is no record of a single major demonstration in support of the seizure of the islands, and even the occasional attacks on British property within Argentina and two symbolic landings of civilian Argentine planes on the Falklands were the work of small groups of extremists only.[4] And yet to say, as some commentators have, that before Galtieri there was never any intention in the inner councils of any Argentine government to use force to reclaim the islands is not borne out by the facts. I hope to have provided sufficient evidence to show that a serious attempt by Argentina to invade the islands was considered during the Second World War and that a secret landing of troops took place in the 1960s. That both occasions were planned by a restricted group of military officers without the knowledge of the vast majority of the Argentine nation suggests that a key explanation for the invasion of the Falklands in 1982 can be found in the militarised nature of Argentine political culture. The limited number of Argentines who bothered to go and stay on the islands before 1982, to find out about the way of life of the inhabitants and the prospects for economic development, appears to confirm Dr David Rock's suggestion that for Argentina the Malvinas were 'less important in themselves than as a nationalist myth'.[5]

I have concentrated only on the main economic themes running through the Falklands War, the post-war period and Alfonsín's government, since a wider and more detailed account of Argentine economic history, so important for understanding the country's fragility as a nation, has been published by Dr Rock and Dr George Philip.[6] I have highlighted the junta's use of torture and murder as a manifestation of a political system, although readers wishing more details can turn to John Simpson and Jana Bennett[7] or Argentina's own official investigation into the 'disappeared', which has been published in English as well as Spanish.[8] Joseph Page's biography of Perón and Eduardo Crawley's no less weighty *A House Divided*[9] fill in the few remaining gaps on the Perón years. By examining the Falklands War and its aftermath within the context of Argentine political history I hope to have made a similarly useful contribution to a better understanding of the war and the country.

Although my book is principally drawn from the raw material I gathered while working in Buenos Aires as a daily newspaper journalist, I have tried to avoid writing an instant history or a simple collection of published articles. Both during and after the conflict I conducted detailed interviews with many of the main political and military protagonists, including two Economy Ministers, numerous soldiers, from conscripts to Generals, and President Alfonsín himself. Although I was not sent to the Falklands Islands during the war (British journalists in Argentina were banned from going there by the junta), I made a point of visiting them in 1984 to gather additional material for this book. To establish the effect the war had had on the kelpers seemed to me almost more relevant to the future of the Falklands debate than any account of the Argentine occupation. I discovered that cause and effect were virtually inseparable and influenced island attitudes towards the new Argentina of Alfonsín. Both during and after the war I also made a point of bearing in mind British perspectives and research on the subject. Although objectivity is an unattainable virtue in journalism I take comfort from having being accused of being partisan by both sides involved in the Falklands dispute. During the military regime I was arrested twice on unfounded allegations of spying and subjected to constant intimidation, including a death threat which forced me to leave Argentina for a week in April 1983, on the first anniversary of the invasion. On the day British troops walked into Port Stanley after the surrender of General Menéndez, an anonymous phone call from London informed me that I was an 'Argie bastard'. On the Falklands a number of kelpers looked on me suspiciously as an 'agent' from Buenos Aires. I am, I hope, what I am, half British and half Hispanic (Scottish father, Spanish mother) without a particular racial axe to grind.

If, after experiencing the years 1982–6 in Argentina, I did not have my own views I would be a strange fish indeed – and none too honest. I share the views of British colleagues who have noted the inherent dangers for world peace represented by competing sovereignty claims.[10] These twin nationalisms are the preserve of rulers not people. My final chapter is both a summary and a plea for the future. I began to write this book in an attempt to overcome some of the prejudice and forgetfulness that has set in as the war has faded into the past – although the nearer the date of the fifth anniversary the more danger there seemed of increased prejudice rather than forgetfulness.

The fishing dispute between the two countries which blew up towards the end of 1986 superficially revolved around the issue of conservation of fishing stocks in the south Atlantic. However, it soon became clear that the dispute had very little to do with fish and almost everything to do with sovereignty. Britain's decision to extend its fishing zone around the islands was a response to what it saw as an encroachment on its territorial rights by Argentina. In 1986 Argentina signed several bilateral agreements with third-party countries and stepped up its naval patrols in the area. It accused Britain of using the fishing dispute to revive an ultra-nationalist 'Falklands factor' in the run-up to a general election.

By exploring the political culture that generated the war on the Argentine side and looking at the changes brought about by Alfonsín, I hope to dissuade voters and decision-makers from even contemplating a second round. Half-way through Alfonsín's six-year presidential term, the direction and attitudes of Argentina's nascent democracy seemed fragile and confused. And yet even at this short range Alfonsín deserves a place in the history books as a political maverick who steered his country through the collective catharsis of the post-war period. Through some unprecedented decisions, he shed new light on previously unquestioned institutions, not least the military, forcing them to justify themselves within a Latin American democratic context. Therein lies the highly charged political drama of contemporary Argentina – a nation in search of a new identity which it still has not found, the land that lost its heroes.

Various people have been helpful while I was writing this book. My thanks must go first and foremost to María-Laura Avignolo, whose courage and professionalism during the Falklands War and during the period I was based in Buenos Aires distinguished her as one of Argentina's leading journalists. It was thanks to her that I was initially granted access to several high-ranking sources when we began jointly researching the background to the War in the latter half of 1982 and the first few months of 1983. Details of the secret submarine landing on the Falklands in 1966 in Chapter I and some of the background to the invasion in Chapters 3 and 4 were based on interviews we conducted together, as was the Argentine view on the sinking of the *General Belgrano* as reported in the final chapter. María-Laura was also instrumental in providing some of the raw material on Argentina's Libyan connection which I checked against my own British sources as reported in Chapter 5. For all this I am indebted to my friend and colleague in difficult times. Thanks too to the editor of the *Financial Times*, Geoff Owen, for sending me to Buenos Aires in the first place and for giving me the necessary time to write. Throughout my time in Argentina both Robert Graham and Hugh O'Shaughnessy, the Latin American editors of the *Financial Times* and the *Observer* respectively, were constant sources of inspiration. They also offered helpful suggestions on the book, along with David Stephen, David Joy, Andrew Graham-Yooll, Tricia Feeney of Amnesty International, Nicholas Tozer and my father, Tom Burns. Numerous Argentine friends and contacts were also helpful during the four and a half years I was in Buenos Aires. Federico Massot, Robert Guareschi, Eduardo de la Fuente, Juan Carlos Torre, Emilio Mignone, Juan and Silvia Fink, Juan Edwardo Fleming, Celia Szusterman, Andrés Federman and Diana Tussie all tried to give me an understanding of their country, although we did not always agree. Many government officials in Buenos Aires and London provided background advice. It has been a great pleasure to be one of Bloomsbury's first authors, and I would like to thank Liz Calder, and Caroline Dawnay, whose early help was invaluable. Liz Cowen was always diligent and patient with her editing. I would also like to thank the staffs of the libraries at the Institute of Latin American Studies, the Royal Institute of International Affairs (Chatham House) in the press cuttings library, the *Financial Times* and the *Observer*. On the personal front I am indebted to Antony Beevor for finding me a place to work, and to Cassandra Jardine for her constant good cheer. Last, but by no means least, many many thanks to Kidge, Julia and Miriam – my wife and daughters – who suffered my bad moods and helped me to survive.

J. B.
London, November 1986

1
A NATION IN ARMS

'Those who cannot remember the past are condemned to repeat it.'

George Santayana

To the outside world watching the World Cup in Mexico City in June 1986 it seemed that history was repeating itself. The match between England and Argentina was being preceded by the kind of virulent jingoism that normally leads to war. Indeed, as far as sectors of the Fleet Street press were concerned, battle had already commenced: 'Mexico Alerts 5,000 Troops', warned one headline; 'Argies, Here We Come', screamed another. The mood was perhaps best symbolised by a cartoon showing Mrs Thatcher dressed in military fatigues and instructing the English team on how to advance like a Task Force.

In Argentina, sentiment had reached fever pitch among the *barras bravas* – the country's equivalent of the Liverpool football supporter – nationalist in the extreme and always ready to be exploited for political ends. The 'shirtless ones', whom Juan Perón had brought into the country's political life and whom the military had adopted, boarded their planes for Mexico pledging revenge for their dead brothers on the 'Malvinas' and burning English flags as they went. As it turned out, however, the match proved the most peaceful of the whole World Cup series. When it was finished the players shook hands with each other and the government in Buenos Aires defused any suggestion of a new war. 'The Malvinas will be won through diplomacy not on the football pitch,' was the official comment. It seemed that a new Argentina was in the making – Maradona, not the *barras bravas*, had won.

Late in March 1982 the local English-language newspaper the *Buenos Aires Herald* described Argentina's looming clash with Britain over the Falkland Islands as an 'attempt to combine an Italian opera with a very British Ealing comedy'. And so it seemed to most of the outside world. The Italian opera was played out by an assortment of scrap-metal merchants, tin-pot dictators, with names like Galtieri and Perón, and an Oxford-educated Foreign Minister with a funny limp and a penchant for tweed jackets, called Costa Méndez. The Ealing comedy had the British military establishment and Parliament immersed in the most heated debate since

Suez over a group of islands in the South Atlantic which the majority of English schoolboys had never heard about and which the *Financial Times* dismissed in an editorial as of no strategic, political or economic value.

The opera had its *mise en scène* in South Georgia, one of the Falkland Islands dependencies but over 900 miles further east from Port Stanley across the South Atlantic. Until recently it had been administered from the Falklands capital, but in fact there was very little to administer. The only inhabitants had been twenty-two members of the British Antarctic Survey, quietly engaged in geological and scientific research. Several hundred sea-lions made up the island's indigenous population. On 19 March the geologists and the sea-lions were joined by the scrap-metal merchants from Buenos Aires singing the Argentine national anthem and raising the blue and white flag on an improvised flag pole. The occasion was reported to Rex Hunt, the portly Governor of the Falkland Islands. Diplomatic exchanges ensued, marines were sent on board a boat belonging to the Royal Navy and, on the morning of 2 April, several thousand Argentine troops landed on the Falklands. The combination of opera and comedy had given way to war.

In the five years that have elapsed since the end of the conflict, much has been written about its possible causes and in the process history has become to some extent mythologised by piecemeal evidence and partisan analysis. On the Argentine side historiography is already taking a potentially dangerous turn: the anti-militarism and self-criticism shared in the immediate aftermath of the War is giving way to a revisionist theory, which seeks to explain the War simply in terms of Britain's diplomatic intransigence and Argentina's own deep-rooted collective sentiment about the justice of the 'Malvinas' cause. And yet this view of history as a series of patient diplomatic efforts on the back of a noble patriotic objective distorts the nature of Argentine society and the run-up to the Falklands War. For the invasion was exclusively planned and executed by military men with the precision of a coup; the event reflected their attitudes and their sense of their own importance as the pillars of the State. Far from being a historic revindication, the landing on the islands was the realisation of a well-tested military exercise which exploited nationalist sentiment for political ends.

In July 1982 Mrs Thatcher announced the appointment of a committee of Privy Councillors under the chairmanship of Lord Franks with the following terms of reference:

To review the way in which the responsibilities of Government in relation to the Falkland Islands and their dependencies were discharged in the period leading up to the Argentine invasion of the Falkland Islands on 2 April 1982, taking into account all such factors in previous years as are relevant; and to report.[1]

The 'relevance' was, however, judged only from 1965, the year in which the dispute between Argentina and Britain was judged to have been publicly discussed for the first time at the United Nations. Ignored was the fact that twenty years before this a group of Argentine Generals had first drawn up a plan of military action for the islands, which in its resolution contrasted with the lukewarm diplomatic efforts not only of the time but also of the previous 122 years – the period since Britain had first taken the islands by force. Recent evidence has emerged in Argentina confirming that in 1942 officers of the élite military academy in Buenos Aires had received instructions from the government to study the feasibility of an invasion of the islands. After weeks of analysis the officers concluded that such an invasion could be carried out with ease.[2] Three years later the Argentine War Ministry issued instructions for the invasion. That orders were reversed on this occasion was not for lack of will but because of the unexpected turn of events on the world stage. The military government which had supported Germany was surprised by an Allied victory that overnight divided the world stage between East and West.

Even without this precedent, the Franks Report, in the context of its own terms of reference, now looks terribly out of touch with the reality of Argentina's political culture. The committee drew much evidence from Foreign Office and Ministry of Defence files on the military government of General Juan Carlos Onganía. His years of rule (1966–70) have gone down in official Falklands history as a time when considerable progress was made in resolving the Falklands dispute thanks to the signing of a communications agreement linking the Argentine mainland with the islands. The Franks Report does mention an incident in September 1966 in which a group of left-wing Perónist trade unionists hijacked a plane in Patagonia and landed it on the islands by force. However, Operation Condor was a piece of amateur dramatics which temporarily aroused nationalist sentiment but was promptly denied by the military government.

Far more important was an operation that took place a few weeks later which has remained undetected to this day by British intelligence and by the Argentine civilian population. Just before Christmas 1966 a small US-built submarine leased to the Argentine navy and called the *Santiago del Estero* broke off from an exercise near the Patagonian coast and headed south-east towards the Falklands. The absence of the submarine was noticed when the other vessels participating in the exercise returned to port. The navy's official explanation was that the *Santiago* had stayed behind to patrol the shallow waters near the mainland off the seaside resort of Mar del Plata. So tight was the security net thrown up around the *Santiago* that only Admiral Varela, the Navy Commander-in-Chief, Admiral Boffi, the Fleet Commander, and Captain González Llanos, the submarine's chief officer, knew about its true mission. As far as British and US intelligence were concerned, Argentina's annual naval exercise was proceeding as usual, both below and above surface.

Within three days the *Santiago del Estero* had slipped quietly and undetected into Falklands waters some forty kilometres north of Port Stanley. Just after sunset Captain Llanos ordered the operation to get underway. About fifteen marines climbed into rubber craft and began paddling with silent speed towards the beach a few hundred yards away. Their mission was to use the available twelve hours of darkness at that time of year to survey the beach and its surroundings as a site for a possible future landing. But, from the moment they had covered their first few yards, the marines found themselves confounded by the elements. A strong current took both craft off course and they spent most of the rest of the night trying to regroup on shore. Miraculously the current abated and both groups managed to head back to their submarine before first light forced it to submerge again.

The marines reported that, as expected, they had landed on a part of the island which had neither islanders living nearby nor British marine look-out posts (the British marine contingent had been reinforced from six men to forty as a result of Operation Condor). There was, however, no certainty that they had not been detected and reported. A cautious commander would have now ordered the mission to abort, but the Argentine marines, like the British SAS, admit 'no limits to what determined men can achieve'.[3] For the crew of the *Santiago* this was a high-point in their careers which they were not prepared to throw away. As one officer involved in the operation later recalled during the research for this book, 'It was really a very moving experience. We can spend most of our lives looking at maps and carrying out mock exercises, and yet here we were at last doing something for real, something concrete.'[4] So Captain Llanos decided to give it a second try. After spending a further day submerged, the *Santiago* surfaced again the next night and the two craft were set back down into the water. This time some determined rowing took the contingent of marines to the planned rendezvous without further mishap and the group spent the rest of the night unmolested. For over four hours they inspected the beach, measured distances and probed the nearby countryside for tracks before returning to their submarine.

The mission appears to have had two specific aims: firstly reconnaissance of a beach that could, if and when needed, be used for an eventual military operation. A contingency plan was then already in the books of the military, although political differences between Varela and Onganía appear to have held up its execution. Secondly, the navy wanted to test British intelligence and their own capacity to keep a secret. The mission succeeded on both fronts.

When history repeats itself it tends to become farce, and yet the Argentine recovery of the Falkland Islands sixteen years later smacked of *déjà vu*. The preparations for the invasion of 2 April depended on secrecy for their success; when the invasion finally got under way the entire exercise nearly collapsed when a craft carrying the first troops was swept off course by the currents. Significantly the man entrusted with the planning and overall execution of the invasion, Admiral Lombardo, had in 1966 served as the second officer on the *Santiago del Estero*.[5] Thus the limited exercise of 1966 laid the ground for a far more ambitious military project without firing a shot. The very fact that the exercise had taken place at all confirmed in the minds of an emerging generation of naval officers the vulnerability of the islands and the ease with which Argentine troops could do with them what they willed. More important, it pointed to a key weakness in Britain's commitment to the islands – her own early warning system. Franks never admitted it but the evidence leaves little doubt: British intelligence had grossly misjudged the meaning of military life in Argentina. Diplomatically there was a communications agreement. But the motor of events was confused, divided, and unpredictable – in short the most complex and potentially dangerous of all worlds.

The officers of the *Santiago del Estero*, like the plotters of the Falklands invasion, belonged to a society that had moulded itself over the years round the belief that Argentines owed their nationhood to their military heroes. It is a highly selective view of history which has nevertheless had a potent effect on the country's political life. 'This is a country which is formed by Generals, liberated by Generals, led by Generals and today claimed by Generals,' General

Juan Perón told the Buenos Aires Military Academy in 1950. And this was a sentiment which, before the Falklands conflict, moved the imagination of generation after generation of Argentines.

Long before Perón there was Don Diego de Mendoza, a leading nobleman of the Spanish court who in 1556 sallied forth with an impressive fleet and 1,500 troops in search of conquest and bounty in the New World. Mendoza landed on the shores of the River Plate estuary only to discover that his dreamed-for El Dorado had sand banks without silver and a huge expanse of prairie populated not by jewelled sun kings but by wild nomadic Indians with a rudimentary culture based on wood totems and animal skin. Besieged by the tribes and abandoned by their mother country the *conquistadores* were killed one by one; those who survived suffered appalling starvation for which fractricide and cannibalism proved the only remedy.[6]

That the nation's first military exploit was an unmitigated disaster was subsequently suppressed in the national conscience. Of far greater consequence were the exploits of the main protagonists in the struggle for independence from Spain. In 1806 and 1807, the fuse was lit for the country's political emancipation when two British expeditionary forces were routed in and around Buenos Aires. 'The great victory of Buenos Aires', one of the country's Presidents later wrote, 'had a resounding impact on the world, and above all in the hearts of Latin Americans, who were now made conscious of a force which had been previously unknown. They were given a new sense of nationality.'[7] In the process General Santiago Liniers, a renegade Frenchman formerly in the pay of the Spanish army, became Argentina's first military hero.

Even more important than Liniers was General José San Martín, the man who abandoned service in the Spanish army in 1812 and led a revolutionary army of 5,000 men in an epic march across Argentina, over the Andes to Chile and up the Pacific to Peru. To this day there is no government office without a poster or a statue of him, no town or schoolroom unnamed in his honour. In Buenos Aires the 'great liberator's' permanently torch-lit marble mausoleum in the cathedral dwarfs any tribute to a civilian. It also makes Mendoza, tucked away astride a small stone block in one of the capital's least impressive squares almost irrelevant. In the 176 years that elapsed between independence and the Falklands War, historians have dug up some curious facts about San Martín. His plan of conquest was prepared by the British; he wrote political treatises about the dangers of military involvement in politics; he exiled himself to France having abandoned hope in Latin American solidarity. But such details have been brushed aside, leaving intact the picture-book hero crossing the Andes – an effective symbol of Argentina's potential as a great power and of her military glory. This concept was strengthened by the military nature of Argentina's territorial expansion and the formation of the nation state.

Argentina's last international war before the Falklands was fought in 1862 in alliance with Brazil against neighbouring Paraguay. The war was a drawn-out and tragic affair lasting five years, with the initial blaze of jingoistic enthusiasm gradually giving way to domestic resistance to its economic and human costs – Paraguay alone lost half its male population. On the Argentine side it was fought by a hastily put together conscript army of peasants and gauchos. The war left them empty-handed but greatly enriched their General, to the tune of 600,000 cattle, 500,000 sheep, 20,000 horses and more than two million acres of land. With such an ignoble war Argentina gained its northern provinces of Entre Rios and Misiones. Thirteen years later General Roca avenged the spirit of Mendoza. He attacked the Indians who had surrounded the white settlers in Patagonia and put them to the sword. The 'Campaign of the Desert'[8] pitted superior fire power and sheer numbers against the tribes. The subsequent orgy of brutality, alcohol, and disease annihilated Argentina's most ancient culture, but Roca is remembered as a national hero who brought civilisation to the wild lands of the south.

Nineteenth-century British and American history is peopled by military heroes like Roca. That only in Argentina do we find such heroes subsequently being used to justify a succession of military interventions in politics reflects on the weakness of civilian society. In spite of San Martín's 'great liberation', Argentina remained a society in flux with an underdeveloped economic structure vulnerable to the swings of world markets. Tensions developed between a traditional land-owning class, who regarded their large properties simply as a badge of social status, and successive waves of immigrants, socially and racially diverse and having the hope of prosperity as their only common denominator. The feelings of these immigrants, who populated the empty prairies and converted Buenos Aires from a small commercial port into a large unwieldy metropolis were perhaps best summarised in 1905 by the 300 inhabitants of Boado, a small village stuck in the midst of Spain's northern province of Galicia. Accused by the Spanish authorities of being antipatriotic for turning their backs on their poverty-stricken land of coarse grass and granite and offering themselves to the Argentine President, the villagers answered, 'Patriotism consists in eating and giving one's children something to eat.'[9]

Argentina's first constitution in 1853 paved the way for the establishment of Buenos Aires as the capital of a federal State, and a presidential system based around an elected Congress as the basis of the country's political system. But the Congress was initially manipulated by a conservative party linked to the landed groups, which only fuelled the anger of the emerging immigrant middle class. Universal and secret male suffrage (women remained excluded from the political process) was established only in 1912, paving the way for the election victory of the Radical party. This grouping initially helped to interpret the political aspirations of the native-born sons of immigrants who had settled in Argentina after the 1880s. But a combination of overcautious reform, conservative obstructionism and increasing working-class militancy influenced by European anarchist and socialist movements, turned Argentina into a conflict-ridden society in which political argument could be easily generated and where elected congressmen were ill-equipped or unwilling to meet rising expectations.

Compared to the divisions of civilian political society, the Argentine armed forces emerged in the late nineteenth and early twentieth centuries as an increasingly solid institution to which politicians turned to defend their own narrow interests. While the 1953 constitution failed to produce a workable parliamentary system, it did secure the primacy of a national army over the numerous local militias which, under the leadership of provincial governorships, had divided the country after the independence from Spain. The turn of the century witnessed a series of reforms that boosted popular identification with the military establishment, the most important of these being the introduction of universal military service. Introduced in 1905, seven years before universal suffrage, the Riccheri reform provided its own form of participation for the immigrants and the sons of oligarchs alike: one year's service in the army, or two in the navy. From this time on, the enlisted ranks of the Argentine army were to consist of a permanent cadre of citizen-soldiers. As the young conscripts were incorporated, their first act of allegiance was not to Congress, President, or even God, but to 'the flag'. The ceremony symbolised the extent to which the military were becoming the standard-bearers of nationhood.

The military forged an early sense of its own place in society thanks to the influx of German military advisers after 1900. They brought with them all the traditions transmitted to the Reich by the Prussian army. These traditions included social élitism, an emphasis on professional discipline – by which orders were orders whatever their outcome – and a somewhat ambivalent attitude towards what constituted the national good and the defence of the nation. Thus did the Argentine military achieve a sense of corporate identity long before any single political movement. As occurred in Spain in the early twentieth century, the army grew to possess not only a monopoly of physical force but also a disciplined *esprit de corps* which no other social group could rival.

It is perhaps not surprising that the military's first appearance on the political stage coincided with the Riccheri reforms. In an attempt to break the oligarchy's hold on politics, the Radical leader Hipólito Yrigoyen organised a series of military conspiracies around groups of young officers, claiming that persistent electoral fraud had left him with no choice. Legitimate as such conspiracies may have seemed in the eyes of the Radicals, the fact remains that this belated Argentine experiment in the old-fashioned party *pronunciamiento* – so beloved of nineteenth-century Spain – assured the stillbirth of the very democratic system Yrigoyen claimed to cherish so much. These early conspiracies failed, but by 1930 the soldiers had reappeared in the political arena no longer as political mutineers but as active participants in the nation's first ever military coup, which brought the Radicals' first administration to an abrupt end. The support given to the military by large sectors of society indicated that the coup mongers had been absorbed as a political fact of life, as natural to Argentina as Liniers and San Martín.

Between 1930, the year of Argentina's first military coup, and 1982, the year of the Falklands War, the country had a succession of twenty-four Presidents. Of these only thirteen were civilian, although not one civilian government survived without having its constitutionally defined six-year term interrupted by the armed forces. The only elected government to have stayed the course and entered a second term was that of General Juan Perón, and yet no other figure in Argentine political history was more instrumental in strengthening the foundations of a militarised society.[10] Perón's election victory in 1946, far from democratising the military's involvement in politics, legitimised their presence in government. 'I am a soldier like yourselves, with the same preoccupations, the same problems, the same virtues and the same shortcomings because we come from the same school,' Perón told a military banquet in

1949. There were occasions when he would embrace the workers, roll his sleeves up, and say he was a 'shirtless one' like them. But for most of the time Perón wore uniform, subtly eroding the concept of democracy at home and creating a distorted sense of Argentina's place in the world. Such a combination of authoritarianism and nationalism paved the way for the Falklands War. The rising expectations of an increasingly politicised working class combined with an adverse economic climate resulted in Perón being himself toppled in a coup in 1955, but his pervading influence on Argentine politics remained up to and beyond his death in 1974.

It was Perón who brought to Argentina a contemporary meaning to the phrase a nation in arms. On taking power he exaggerated the threat of a Third World War, using this as an excuse for massive military spending and increased internal security. In his first years in government, over 50 per cent of total government expenditure went on the armed forces, a figure far exceeding the combined military expenditures of Chile, Colombia, Peru, Venezuela and Brazil. In 1949 Perón promulgated a law which laid great emphasis on security measures to 'prevent crimes against the nation'. The growing link between geopolitics and domestic politics arose out of a peculiarly militarist interpretation of the world and Argentine society. The interpretation defined by some writers as a 'doctrine of national security' is based on the military's belief that 'they are the true and only valid interpreters of national interests'.[11] The concept, which had an early testing ground in the Fascism of the 1930s, eradicates the distinction between armed forces and nation. Because the potential enemy is perceived to be both abroad and at home, the politics of force can be used in both instances. Ultimately civilian society is conditioned to accept repression as much as it accepts war. This phenomenon found its ultimate expression in the Process of National Reorganisation, the title given by the military to its attempt to justify the continuation of Perónist rule under another guise.

2
THE POLITICS OF REPRESSION

Compared to the bombast and improvisation that had characterised previous military interventions in Argentina, the coup of 24 March 1976 was a streamlined affair – bloodless, serene and quickly executed. The circumstances in which it took place ensured a wide cross-section of civilian support for this latest in a long line of direct military intrusions into Argentina's political system. 'We have been placed on the edge of disintegration and thus the intervention of the armed forces constitutes the only possible alternative in the face of the crisis provoked by a lack of government, and the existence of corruption and complacency,' declared General Jorge Videla, the President and member of the new three-man junta in his first speech to the nation.

Guerrilla violence was claiming victims at a rate of hundreds a month, and the economy was a shambles. Hit by a combination of union unrest and increased costs brought about by the advancing world recession, industry was in a state of virtual paralysis. Inflation was running at an annual rate of 600 per cent and going upwards in a seemingly uncontrollable spiral. At the centre of the stage stood the small, fragile figure of Isabelita Perón, the late General's third wife who had apparently lost her grip on the presidency. Over the previous few months she had temporarily handed over power to the head of the Senate, Italo Luder, officially for 'reasons of health'. In the glass-bowl atmosphere of Buenos Aires, where rumours breed like goldfish, it was said that Isabelita was being slowly poisoned by her personal doctor while the armed forces were preparing the coup. No one wanted to jump to her defence because her image was already so bad.

In Congress, a young woman deputy married to an army officer, called Cristina Guzmán, demanded a legal investigation into allegations that the President had been misappropriating funds from a public charity. The rest of Congress, however, showed itself less than enthusiastic about offering a democratic alternative to Isabelita, which, as provided for by the constitution, could have taken the form of an impeachment and the immediate holding of elections. Nor had Congress as a body made any attempt to check the actions of the armed forces, which in the early 1970s had become involved in an increasingly brutal repression of left-wing guerrillas and their allies using their own troops as well as plain-clothes 'death squads' like the Triple A, acting under the orders of the Welfare Minister, José López Rega.

The public grew to accept the regimentation of their society as the best possible solution to their own social and economic uncertainties. The restructuring of collective consciousness was influenced by the media, which increasingly turned a blind eye to the military's tactics and dramatised the scale of the economic and social crisis. Jacobo Timerman, the then editor of *La Opinión*, the most widely read centre-left daily, was only one of many journalists who, as a result of their frequent meetings with military contacts, concluded that a coup was not only inevitable but also imperative. The popular acceptance of the coup confirmed the ideological redundancy of the large majority of Argentina's political class, and inflated the military's historical perception of themselves as the saviours of the nation.[1]

In reality the coup was the product of cold calculation and a lust for power. It was carried out against the background of a doctrine of national security which had been elaborated over years and refined down to its strategic details from January 1975 onwards. Behind the charade of constitutional government, countless secret meetings between officers had finalised the mechanics not just of the take-over but of the kind of government that would follow. In the last few weeks before the coup, the plotters consulted a generous selection of technocrats willing to act as acolytes. In the end they picked on two for ministerial jobs and kept the others in reserve.

The regime that took charge in March 1976 was the most easily identified as military in a long line of take-overs by the armed forces. At the tip of the pyramid was the three-man junta, representing each of the Commanders-in-Chief. As head of the largest force, the army chief, General Jorge Videla, was also made President but only on the understanding that all executive decisions would be taken by the junta as a whole. The six military posts on the eight-man cabinet were divided up as follows: the army controlled the Ministries of the Interior, and Labour; the navy, the Ministries of Foreign Affairs and Social Affairs; the air force, the Ministries of Justice and Defence. Economy was the only important Ministry to be entrusted to a civilian, but the man put in charge, José Martínez de Hoz, was forced to report regularly to the junta and its senior officers and was constantly forced to modify his policies. The specially created Legal Accessory Council (CAL) completed the government line-up. Roughly similar in make-up to Portugal's Council of the Revolution, the CAL was to draw on those officers regarded as 'legal experts' within the armed forces and act as a faithful legislative watchdog, interpreting not just Argentina's liberal constitution but also the decrees establishing the broad aims of the junta – the Acts of the Process of National Reorganisation. Nothing perhaps better sym- bolised the junta's capacity to confuse terminology than the CAL. The Council set up its offices in the buildings of the banned Congress. The move was a parody of the country's 'liberal tradi- tions'. It was also a crude image of the military's appropriation of the State.

The '33 per cent, 33 per cent, 33 per cent' factor, as the share-out of Cabinet posts between the three services of the armed forces was dubbed (the 1 per cent went to the technocrats), spanned out through all levels of society, effectively militarising it on a scale unpre- cedented in Argentine history. Military officers found a place for themselves on everything from the board of a State bank to the directorship of the national ballet company. In proportion to their size and political influence the army, air force and navy took their share in all the television channels, provincial governorships and State companies. In Buenos Aires, where the majority of the popu- lation live and work, the army took the Ministry of the Interior, the navy the port and customs, and the air force the airports and municipality. Such a physical encirclement of the capital symbolised the grip the military intended to exercise on the nation as a whole. In fact the regimentation of society was facilitated by the large degree of centralisation which already existed in Argentine society. As the principal port of an export-orientated economy, Buenos Aires had for long been the commercial and financial centre of the country. The city's obvious attractions – its situation at the mouth of the River Plate, good climate and its position at the end of Argentina's vast railway network – had by the 1970s concentrated in it almost 40 per cent of Argentina's thirty million population and 60 per cent of its industry. As has been noted in an article by Robert Graham,

> In a country this size, development is distorted by such a high concentration of resources, human and economic, in a tiny portion of the territory. A vicious circle grows up, whereby civil servants, doctors, engineers or teachers do not wish to work elsewhere, companies cannot locate elsewhere and people come from else- where to find opportunity. Thus the dominance of the capital snowballs, its privileges bolstered by the presence of the most politically articulate groups being based here.[2]

The opportunity for exploiting what the Argentine writer Ezequiel

Martínez Estrada called the 'head of Goliath' seemed obvious to the junta that took power in 1976.[3]

Apart from facilitating the repression of political dissidence, centralisation helped the militarisation of the economy. From the outset the junta's first Economy Minister, José Martínez de Hoz, appeared to adopt an orthodox monetarist approach to his country's financial woes. He tightened up on government spending and passed resolutions favouring foreign investment and the reduction of tariff barriers. On an early tour of Europe and the United States Martínez de Hoz – an old Etonian, a graduate of Harvard and a member of one of the richest land-owning families in Argentina – projected an image of class and responsibility which contrasted with the chaotic managers of Isabelita Perón's government. He was nicknamed the 'Wizard of Hoz' by the international banking community, which, awash at the time with petrodollars, was soon pouring funds into the coffers of Argentine banks. The bubbling enthusiasm the foreign business community in Argentina felt for the Minister was conveyed in a full-page advertisement placed in the Argentine national press in New Year 1977 by the local subsidiary of Ford. '1976: Argentina gets back on the right track,' the advertisement proclaimed, '1977: New Year of faith and hope for all Argentines of good will. Ford Motor Company and its staff pledge their participation in the efforts to fulfil the Nation's Destiny. Again Ford give you more.'[4] Ford certainly gave the security forces almost anything they wanted. Ford Falcons without number plates – the favourite cars of the right-wing hit squads under Perón – were incorporated on a massive scale into the machinery of repression. For thousands of Argentines a ride in a Ford Falcon became a passport to torture and execution.

As for Martínez de Hoz, not only was he not quite the gentleman he was made out to be, but, more importantly, this widely acclaimed 'super Minister' was in political terms little more than a paper tiger. Martínez de Hoz has denied that he took any direct part in the military's repression and claims that for most of the time he didn't know what was going on.[5] But about the fairest judgment most Argentines now pass on him is that his obsession with meeting economic targets indirectly led to torture and killings on a massive scale. His freeze on wages emerged not from negotiation between both sides of industry but as a result of the suppression of union activity. Strikes were banned, and the main trade union organisation the General Confederation of Labour (CGT) and its thirty-six main affiliated unions were put under the control of military administrators. Union secretaries and shop stewards were replaced by army officers, and union dues, administrative offices and welfare organisations – traditionally a main source of union funds – placed under a permanent embargo. Workers judged to be too militant were forcefully made redundant or else handed over to the security forces by their managers. Right of appeal, not just for unionists but for any Argentine who felt unfairly treated by the government's economic policies, was circumscribed by the junta's control of the judiciary. Following the 1976 coup, members of the Supreme Court and all federal judges were requested to resign. Some of them were allowed to take up their posts again only after they had taken a solemn oath of allegiance to the Process of National Reorganisation.

Under Martínez de Hoz – the alleged champion of the 'free market' – State intervention in the economy, far from diminishing, grew in a more pervasive and sinister guise than at any time in Argentine history. The military, under the influence of their Prussian education, had first put forward ideas relating the armed forces to a development of a national industry in the 1920s. These ideas were implemented more fully once Perón came to power and significant portions of the economy, including the British-owned railways, were nationalised. Following the coup of 1976, Martínez de Hoz was forced to modify his strategy whenever it was judged to threaten the military's growing involvement in the economy. The public and private sectors thus did not act separately on the whole, but developed a complex system of alliances. The arrangement involved appointing military officers to management boards and establishing a direct link with the regime to ensure favourable pricing and privileged access to credit and markets. Although many small and medium-sized companies went bankrupt and a number of foreign companies such as General Motors were forced to disinvest during the regime of the juntas, private enterprises linked to the militarised economy managed to do lucrative business. One example was BRIDAS, the huge private holding within the oil industry. Well represented by its directors within the military establishment, BRIDAS worked closely with the state oil company, Yacimientos Petrolíferos Fiscales. Although YPF had a monopoly on oil exploration and distribution and power to dictate prices in the industry, BRIDAS survived as one of the richest private companies in Argentina.

The interrelationship between the military and economic power, which effectively prevented the emergence in Argentina of a dynamic capitalist class capable of forcing changes in government policy, came to be particularly pronounced in the Dirección General de Fabricaciones Militares (DGFM), the armed forces' own industrial complex. DGFM had been set up in 1941 when the Allies had begun to consider imposing an arms embargo against Argentina to try and force it into the war against Germany. In response to this pressure nationalist officers urged the development of a domestic arms industry as a guarantee of national sovereignty. By 1976 DGFM's original statutes remained unchanged. These entitled the military to take a leading role in the exploitation of the country's strategic mineral resources and to involve itself in the manufacture of anything judged to be insufficiently developed by the private sector. Under the regime of the juntas DGFM grew to become the most powerful economic group in the country. How this took place has always been kept a closely guarded secret from the public. Nevertheless DGFM, at the height of its influence, had significant shareholdings in twenty-two leading companies. Only nine of these were military plants, producing everything from a hand grenade to a tank. The rest pervaded most areas of the economy including ship-building, construction and petrochemicals.

After the Videla coup, attempts by Martínez de Hoz to turn over DGFM's non-military activities to civilian ownership and management were violently resisted. On the contrary DGFM became a fiefdom of the army, much as Argentina's Atomic Energy Commission became a fiefdom of the navy, and the aerospace industry became a fiefdom of the air force, with privileged access to government subsidies and foreign loans. A detailed breakdown of DGFM's accounts was never published, but in the late 1970s its annual turnover is believed to have exceeded 2·2 billion dollars, equivalent to about 2·5 per cent of the country's Gross National Product (GNP). It was the country's biggest employer with 14,000 people working in its wholly owned companies and another 16,000 in associated enterprises.

In addition to the drain on state resources represented by the military's fiefdoms, Martínez de Hoz also saw his economic strategy undermined by the military's massive spending on arms following the 1976 coup. Official statistics used by the Economy Ministry to forecast the Treasury's annual budgets bore little relation to what was actually being diverted from government resources to boost the military machinery. The three services of the armed forces regarded arms contracts as their exclusive domain – although they were usually negotiated by civilian middle-men – and both for security and political reasons kept civilian technocrats in the Cabinet like Martínez de Hoz ill informed on the subject. The Grand Master of the outlawed Italian Masonic Lodge, Licio Gelli, is understood to have been one of the leading international figures behind some of the junta's more ambitious arms deals.[6] Thanks to Gelli's mediation, Italy was approached by Argentine military officers with a large shopping list, including several Lupo frigates, missile systems and radar equipment. The contract for the frigates was aborted by the Argentine navy chief Admiral Emilio Massera in October 1977 in an outburst of personal pique. During a private visit to Italy to process the contracts Massera was faced with a formal parliamentary protest and a twenty-four-hour strike at the Oto Melara shipyards in Spezia. In the end Massera and Gelli compromised. Argentina looked elsewhere for its frigates but purchased the missile systems and radar equipment.

This was not the first time that Massera is believed to have acted behind Martínez de Hoz's back on a major arms deal. In the run up to the coup, Martínez de Hoz had been convinced during secret talks with the plotters that the military hierarchy would go along with his plans for drastically reducing State spending and channelling resources to productive investment. However, no sooner had Martínez de Hoz been sworn in as Minister than he discovered to his apparent surprise that he had inherited a commitment from the Perón administration he could not renege on. This was a major programme of weapons purchases which had been initialled by Isabelita Perón and Massera.[7] Subsequently Martínez de Hoz's separation from the centre of decision-making on military questions did not prevent him from volunteering to become a conduit for external finance. Official figures for the period 1976–82 suggest that Martínez de Hoz was remarkably successful in reducing his budget deficit as a proportion of GDP and that defence spending was far from spectacular. But budget figures were easily cooked and even then did not reflect the 'special funds' set aside by the military for the recycling of loans in foreign bank accounts.[8] Well before the planning for the invasion of the Falklands got under way, the military resurrected its old war scenarios to justify military spending. Massera's own tough stance on the Malvinas and Argentina's territorial dispute with Chile over the Beagle Channel (which nearly brought the two countries to the brink of war in Christmas 1978), led to an unprecedented arms buying spree. The equipment ordered by the navy included six submarines and four destroyers from West Germany; fourteen Super Etendard fighter planes with Exocet missiles from France; ten Lynx helicopters and two destroyers from Britain and two coastal patrol boats from Israel. The air force ordered forty A-4 Skyhawks and five Chinook helicopters from the United States, and forty-two Daggers from Israel. The army purchased artillery, armoured personnel carriers and missile systems from several countries including Austria, Switzerland and the United States. It is reliably estimated that between 1976 and the beginning of the Falklands War, Argentina may have spent as much as 14·3 billion dollars on arms purchases – the equivalent to a quarter of its total foreign debt.[9]

In retrospect it is interesting to note that Argentina's re-equipment programme was subjected to none of the constraints that the British armed forces were forced to accept during this period. The junta's arms build-up appears to have reached its climax in 1980. As Simon Jenkins and Max Hastings noted, this was the blackest year of all for the British armed forces, 'with a total moratorium on defence contracts, and fuel allocations so severely cut that many ships could not be put out to sea for many months'.[10] Martínez de Hoz was more concerned with maintaining Argentina's financial stability than in the geopolitical ambitions of the military establishment. But much as he would have liked to have been given the powers over defence chiefs enjoyed by British ministers, it was a military regime that he chose to work in, not a parliamentary one. Faced with the intransigence of men like Massera, the Minister could have offered his resignation. Instead he chose to stick to his job for five years at the end of which he was removed by the junta. Martínez de Hoz was neither the first nor the last 'technocrat' to compromise his principles for the greater glory of the military rulers he served.

The military's regimentation of the country's moral attitudes was assured by the junta's control of the Church. The Bishops were allowed to stay in their posts. Any changes in ecclesiastical authority remained, as it had done for most of Argentine history, in the domain of the Episcopal Conference and ultimately of the Vatican. But in the temporal world, a new link between the Church and military authorities for the purpose of 'consultation' was set up within months of the coup under the auspices of the Pastoral Commission. In theory the Commission, made up of moderate Bishops, saw itself as acting not just as a moral watchdog on the government's activities but also as the intermediary between the civilian and military worlds at a time when both the political parties and the unions were banned. In practice, however, the existence of the Commission helped to divert and defuse public protest against the regime on issues like the economy and human rights.

Some politicians would no doubt have protested had they had a voice, but there were few outlets left unlatched by the armed forces.

Within a month of the coup the media were forbidden from informing, commenting or making reference to the tactics employed by the military for dealing with political dissidence without prior consultation with the authorities. With the exception of *La Opinión*, the *Buenos Aires Herald* and *La Prensa*, most newspapers strictly adhered to the new instructions.[11] Newspaper editors were 'invited' to regular meetings with Ministers, junta members and the President himself, at which they were briefed on matters of government policy while at the same time being issued with directives about what should and should not be published. Superficially similar to the 'lobby' system in Western democracies like Britain, the arrangement in the context of Argentina took on a very different aspect. Journalists found themselves willingly surrendering any ethical sense of their profession, and becoming instead essential pawns in the conspiracy of silence from which the regime drew its life blood. There were no checks and balances of investigative journalism to counter the self-censorship. On the contrary journalists who broke the rules found themselves persecuted, forced to go into exile or else risking death. Just in case a particular editor strayed from the official line and did not pass the junta's instructions down to his subordinates, the military strengthened its control on the media by using its secret police to infiltrate many newspapers and news agencies. The agents were not only entrusted with spying on politically suspect journalists but also doubled up as reporters to ensure prominent coverage for the military's version of events.

In the strategically more important world of TV and radio, the junta's control of free expression was even more blatant. The four State-controlled television channels and the bulk of radio stations had their management boards made up of officers with few technical or cultural qualifications but with a good eye and ear for propaganda. The '33 per cent, 33 per cent, 33 per cent' factor was maintained with the army, navy and air force each getting one channel and agreeing to share out the fourth with a token presence of civilians. The extreme television-consciousness of the regime was reflected in the regular appearances of Martínez de Hoz. In one memorable performance, which in Europe and the United States would have provoked horror among programme planners, de Hoz spoke for a mammoth two and a half hours. News slots were given over to military ceremonies and speeches by junta members. This was accompanied by a large dose of light entertainment, designed to underline the junta's self-projected image of surface calm and normality. The viewing public was anaesthetised in other words. Argentina's cultural élite – the best of the country's authors, directors, actors and musicians – were, of course, excluded from the screens. Judged politically suspect, hundreds were placed on an official 'black list' of banned artists. The junta completed its 'cultural revolution' by censoring films and plays, and purging teachers and curricula from the universities and schools. In the streets of Buenos Aires even *The Little Prince* was thrown on to the funeral pyre of 'subversive books'.

The all-pervasive ideological and structural regimentation of Argentine society which was imposed following the 1976 coup was one aspect of the Process of National Reorganisation which distinguished it from previous experiences of military rule in Argentina. Another was the nature and scale of violence used to deal with the political opposition. To a large extent both aspects fed off each other.

At the outset there seemed to be nothing particularly original in the sweeping powers assumed by the junta under the excuse of a state of siege. The ban on political parties and unions, censorship, the introduction of extraordinary powers of search, arrest and detention, the setting up of military tribunals and the introduction of the death penalty for those guilty of terrorist activities, were all measures that had been tried and tested with varying degrees of success in other Third World countries and in Europe. In Argentina's case such measures were only the façade of repression. The brutality of the regime expressed itself in a far more sinister way, in the systematic use of kidnappings, clandestine detentions, torture and execution without trial or record. In the words of author Ernesto Sabato, 'Thus, in the name of national security, thousands upon thousands of human beings, usually young adults or even adolescents, fell into the sinister, ghostly category of the *desaparecidos*, a word (sad privilege for Argentina) frequently left in Spanish by the world's press.'[12]

The method had been used in limited cases by the security forces and extreme right-wing death squads like the Triple A during the Perón government. It was now refined and extended as part of a secretly documented official strategy of repression organised and conducted by members of the armed forces. Regular meetings between high-ranking officers were used to go over lists specially prepared for them by the secret police. The lists, compiled from newspaper cuttings, informants, telephone tappings and photographs, were not just of well-known guerrillas engaged in terrorist activity but of all those men, women and even children regarded as ideologically suspect. The abductions were not haphazard acts but precisely organised operations carried out by specially created 'task groups'. Instead of being trained in the skills of conventional warfare or civic duty, young officers were turned into storm troopers in whom sadism and plunder (houses of the victims were usually emptied of valuables) became indistinguishable from heroism. The ends justified the means, and the junta was convinced that it was purging Argentine society of Marxist revolution and immorality.

Suspects were dragged away often in broad daylight or, if not, at night under bright searchlights from their homes or places of work, others from restaurants, schools, churches, street corners. Quite simply they then disappeared. Inquiries by relatives or friends of the kidnapped victims were met with a wall of silence. The so-called victims, the authorities claimed, simply did not exist. The combination of open repression and secrecy intimidated the population, making it both vulnerable and that much more dependent on the military for its existence. Against the background of censorship, it became impossible to distinguish rumour from fact, a nightmare from a lived experience. It was a situation worthy of Dante's *Inferno* but one which cried out for political and spiritual guidance. And yet the one institution capable of countering the military's distortion of the truth with a moral lead simply joined in the conspiracy.

The night before the 1976 coup, Mgr Adolfo Tortolo, Vicar-General of the armed forces and President of the Argentine Episcopal Conference, held a private meeting with the two leading plotters, General Videla and Admiral Massera.[13] Exactly what was said has been kept a closely guarded secret by both sides, but there is at least circumstantial evidence to suggest that the Argentine hierarchy, jealously protective of its past relationship with the State, warmed to the idea that a junta should take over, given the alleged moral, financial and social disintegration surrounding the government of Isabelita Perón. A pastoral letter issued on 15 May 1976 suggested that murder or abduction for political ends could be considered a sin, but it emphasised that the coup had been carried out for the 'common good'. 'Moreover, we should remember that it would be a mistake to believe', the letter continued, 'that the security forces can act with the purity of action of peacetime when there is already blood on the streets. It is necessary to accept some constraints on our liberties as demanded by the circumstances.'

Between 1976 and 1981, the Episcopal Conference issued four more pastoral letters which similarly condemned the violation of human rights while at the same time implicitly accepting that there was a moral and social justification for the regime. During the same period they sent four private messages to the junta which were kept a closely guarded secret from the public until their publication in a book after the Falklands War. The messages are more specific in their concern about the 'disappeared', but nevertheless still err on the side of compromise. Bishops I have talked to have defended their approach to the issue of human rights. Private messages and diplomatic language, they suggest, were more effective in saving lives than outright confrontation with the authorities. At the same time the Church as an institution could not allow itself to be ident-ified in any way with the left-wing guerrilla groups. The military were always quick to remind a demurring Bishop that the 'terrorists' of the 1960s and 1970s had exercised their early militancy as members of university action groups like Catholic Action and had received the formal blessing of priests linked to the Third World Movement that arose in the wake of Medellín. Members of the Bishops' Conference were even shown videos of interrogation sessions, during which prisoners confessed their links with certain priests.

However numerous the doctrinal and tactical reasons for the attitude of the hierarchy, the Church can only really be judged on results rather than motives. Human rights groups insist that a great many more lives would have been saved had the Church as an institution taken a more forceful and public stand during a period when journalists, trade unionists, judges, lawyers and politicians were silenced by intimidation, proscription and, in many cases, murder. At no time during the military regime did the Church as an institution assume effective leadership of the opposition, as in Chile. On the contrary, it seemed to have no intention of seriously questioning the regime, beyond a token intervention on behalf of some individuals. The human rights group formed by the female relatives of the 'disappeared', the Madres de Plaza de Mayo, has a copious file of letters which members wrote to the Episcopal Conference asking for help and which were never answered. The Madres remember with bitterness how the doors of the cathedral in Buenos Aires were nearly always barred to them, particularly when they tried to escape from the baton charge of the riot police, or the kidnap attempts of the death squads.

By contrast, leading members of the Argentine Church, like the Cardinal Primate of Buenos Aires, Juan Carlos Aramburu, always accepted invitations from the military to attend public functions ranging from march pasts to Te Deums in which the unity of the militarised State achieved its ultimate symbol. In 1980 Aramburu was invited to London along with two Chilean Bishops. The latter took cheap lodgings in the Paddington area and spent much of their time visiting refugees. Aramburu, however, immersed himself in the pomp and security of his Embassy in Belgravia and made a point of avoiding all contact with fellow Argentines who had fled to England for political reasons.

A more blatant collaboration with the regime was practised by military chaplains. They not only provided a theological framework for the use of torture and killings against perceived 'anti-Christs' but also actively acquiesced in the military's actions. One former detainee of the military junta, for example, recalled the visit of one Fr Pelanda López during which a fellow prisoner cried out, 'Father, they are torturing me terribly during interrogations and I beg you to intercede to stop them from torturing me any more.' López replied, 'Well, my son, but what do you expect if you don't co-operate with the authorities interrogating you?'

Perhaps the most notorious case involved Fr Christian von Wermich, as it was recounted by a repentant former police officer who belonged to a 'task force'. The officer recalled how on one occasion he and his colleagues used the butts of their guns to beat two women and a man whom they had taken prisoner. The torture session and the subsequent murder – the three were given lethal injections by a police doctor – were witnessed by Fr von Wermich.

'The priest saw that what had happened had shocked me and spoke to me telling me that what we had done was necessary; it was a patriotic act and God knew it was for the good of the country,' the policeman remembered.[14]

Among the rest of the population, not everyone was a collaborator. The Madres de Plaza de Mayo along with other human rights groups from 1977 onwards defied the complacency of the large majority of Argentines, and consistently pestered the authorities and newspaper editors for information, staging demonstrations when this was not forthcoming. The Madres risked arrest and their own 'disappearance' by conducting a silent protest outside the presidential palace every Thursday. But in the first years of the regime the only civilians who joined them were mainly foreign journalists or diplomats curious for a bit of local colour with which to grace their reports to head office.

Within the Church there was a minority of Bishops, priests and nuns who never pandered to national Catholicism as refined and reinforced through successive authoritarian regimes, but on the contrary laid their lives on the line in defence of social and political justice in the spirit of Vatican II. Many of these men and women were abducted and presumed killed by the security forces. Two Bishops died in 'car accidents'. The survivors of the Catholic Church included three Bishops, Jaime de Nevares of Neuquén, Miguel Hesayne of Viedma, and Jorge Novak of Quilmes; a number of priests, who by virtue of living close to their flocks were able to perceive a less distorted image of the temporal world; and Catholic laymen such as Adolfo Peréz Esquivel, who in 1980 was given the Nobel Prize for Peace for his stand on human rights. In Chapter 9 we shall see how a member of the Radical party, called Raul Alfonsín, was almost alone among politicians at the time in also confronting the regime.

During the early years of the military regime the impact of these courageous individuals on the collective conscience was equivalent to that of small matchlights in a huge dark night. They attracted the attention of the outside world but illuminated little within. The junta was largely successful in impressing a domestic audience with its own moderate attitudes in public and was careful to use open repression selectively (there were no football pitches filled with political prisoners as in Chile), and it contrasted this with the horror stories leaked abroad by survivors and bounced back to Argentina in the form of denunciations by international bodies like Amnesty and the United Nations. It was, the junta insisted, part of a 'foreign-backed' conspiracy designed to undermine the nation.

Such double-think fitted into the context of what the junta, following in the footsteps of Perón, convinced itself was nothing less than a Third World War against the forces of Marxism which had to be fought both at home and abroad. From an early stage in his career as a General, Leopoldo Galtieri had lent himself willingly to the exteriorisation of Argentine military prowess which from a different perspective was nothing more than the export of State terrorism. It was during his posting as the commander of the Second Army Corps in Rosario in 1980 that Galtieri sent a group of army intelligence officers on a secret mission to Mexico City. The officers were under specific instructions to kidnap and kill several high-ranking members of the Montonero guerrilla organisation who were then living in exile. The plan subsequently collapsed when the officers were discovered and revealed publicly, causing a major diplomatic row between Argentina and Mexico. However, the incident never caught the attention of the rest of the world let alone of Britain.[15]

With the evidence of hindsight it is possible to argue that this was one of many tragic omissions in British intelligence assessments before the Falklands conflict. For the incident confirmed Galtieri as a man quite capable of violating international law as a result of his single-minded pursuit of an objective. Instead his inauguration as President was viewed simply as that of a hardline General with strictly pro-western sympathies.

Moreover, evidence has recently come to light showing that such a characteristic was by no means unique to Galtieri. There were many officers of the Process of National Reorganisation who, as a result of what they regarded as their highly successful military campaign against the guerrillas, had an inflated sense of their capacity to act elsewhere. By the early 1980s Argentine officers were exporting their tactics throughout Latin America (actively helping to organise a coup in Bolivia), and in European countries. In Central America, Argentine self-delusions of military grandeur were actively encouraged by the United States. It was a relationship Washington was subsequently to regret bitterly once the Falklands War exposed the logical outcome of the junta's folly.

Right up to and during the Falklands War, the attitude of the majority of Argentines reflected the regimentation of their society. Collaborators fell roughly into two camps: those who shared the view that the end justified the means, and those whose instinct for survival mixed with blind nationalism ensured first silence, and subsequently amnesia. The scenes of widespread euphoria which followed Argentina's World Cup win in 1978 epitomised the regime's success of projecting its double-think. On that occasion the national support of football rather than the national cause of Las Malvinas mobilised the masses to the Plaza de Mayo.

In August 1978, as in April 1982, propaganda and populist stereotype converged. There were a few, very few, Argentines who drew a distinction between the regime and the nation. The image projected by the TV cameras, and witnessed at first hand by foreign sports reporters was of a smiling General Videla and a nation, jubilant and united at his feet. The outside world shuddered as it perceived the flippancy of a nation that could celebrate goals and yet seemingly forget the 'disappearance' of over 9,000 Argentines, but the confusion was greatest among the survivors of the genocide. An exile living in Madrid at the time of that World Cup final has given a vivid description of the emotional schizophrenia of the Argentines:

I saw the final with two compatriots, with an irreconcilable mixture of confused feelings. On the one hand, the immense wish for victory . . . it was football, our national sport, and it was difficult not to get enthusiastic. On the other, a profound disgust with the evidence that the regime had put all its efforts into exploiting the victory. It was like that when we scored the second goal . . . the three of us looked at each other with our eyes wide open and watering, as if we didn't know what to do next until finally we burst out screaming and crying, hugging ourselves on the floor, and crying. Until the final whistle. Afterwards . . . we walked out on to the streets of a Madrid that looked down on us as if we'd gone mad.[16]

Not since the Berlin Olympics of 1936 had sport been so transformed into a political circus. And yet, as the Argentine sociologist Juan José Sebreli has pointed out, the occasion was perfectly consistent with the collective delirium that had periodically gripped the Argentine nation since the 1930 military coup.[17] The ease with which the majority of Argentine society forgot the reality of the repression showed the scope and scale of its regimentation. It would take the invasion of the Falklands to confirm the extent to which such conditioning could be used by the regime to implement its ultimate act of 'heroism'.

3
THE NAVY'S PLOT

Just before Christmas 1981, Argentina appeared fated to be ignored, as it had been for most of its history, by international opinion. The military coup in Poland, the kidnapping of General James Dozier in Italy and the civil war in El Salvador were the key items of interest. The fact that on 22 December an Argentine President called General Roberto Viola had been toppled in a 'palace coup' by his army chief, General Galtieri, hardly drew a mention. In Britain, Fleet Street had geared down for its 'silly season', and Parliament was in recess. At the time the British Ambassador to Buenos Aires, Anthony Williams, reported that the Argentine navy, traditionally the hardest of the services on the Falklands issue, was playing a 'decisive role in the change of Government, which it was likely to maintain in the new junta'. His immediate superiors at the Foreign and Commonwealth Office took the view that the Argentine government could be expected to take a more forceful line of action on the Falklands issue. And yet no one on the British side appears to have considered that an outbreak of hostilities was imminent.

Planned and executed by General Galtieri, the downfall of Viola would not have been possible without the active support of Admiral Jorge Isaac Anaya, the navy chief, who had a personal grudge against Viola. The two men had first crossed swords in the months leading up to the 1976 coup when senior officers from the three branches of the armed forces had laid the initial plans for the toppling of Isabelita Perón. Viola had wanted immediate action; Anaya had urged a tactical delay, arguing that a few more months of Perónist misrule would make it that much easier for the military to appropriate for itself the destiny of the nation. In 1978 the two men were again at loggerheads, with Anaya sharing the navy's deep distrust for Viola's flirtation with the political parties and his insistence that the army should dictate the terms of any future transition to democracy. In a stormy meeting, at which other officers were present, Viola not only mocked Anaya's political judgment but also made a fleeting reference to the navy man's dark skin and his Bolivian background. Anaya never forgot the racist jibe, and spent the next three years looking at ways of restoring his self-respect. By Christmas 1981, Anaya had rediscovered Leopoldo Fortunato Galtieri.

The two men had first known each other at the age of fifteen when they had gone together to military school. They had maintained an easy-going although not particularly profound acquaintance since then. Anaya was content simply to find in Galtieri everything that Viola wasn't. Galtieri was an anti-intellectual, preferring action to words. Without any fixed ideological position of his own he was permeable to other people's influence, all the more so if a particular recommendation coincided with his own ambition to reach the top of the army hierarchy and to go down in history as the most populist President since Perón.

In their history of the Second World War, Peter Calvocoressi and Guy Wint describe Hitler thus:

> He did not have the mind of a statesman but rather was an impresario and improvisor. When a Bismarck imposed himself on events, Hitler imposed himself on people by the fervour of his personality. He was a leader of men first and a framer of policies only a poor second. He was not an original thinker or theoriser but he was adept at picking up ideas which suited him and at taking the opportunities given him by others; he knew how to wait for his chances and how to seize them and he was guided by certain preconceptions. He had a view of history. He was a Manichee, a man who sees the world and its history in terms of black and white.[1]

The character study fits Galtieri almost to perfection and explains his rise to power in the ideologically, morally and politically bankrupt militarised society which reached its apogee following the 1976 coup.

On 9 December 1981 Galtieri and Anaya met for lunch with their respective wives in the main army barracks of Campo de Mayo. The lunch was taken up with earnest discussion about the latest political situation. The main source of concern for both men was the damage being wrought to the prestige of the armed forces by General Viola's mishandling of the economy. Five months earlier the country had experienced its third financial crisis since the 1976 coup. This had involved a major panic on the local foreign exchange markets, which had drained over 300 million dollars from central bank reserves. In November there had been a new run on the peso bringing the depreciation of the local currency for the whole of 1981 to over 600 per cent against the dollar – it set a new record even in Argentina. Financial instability had been accompanied by a deepening recession with high interest rates and a level of indebtedness threatening the survival of an increasing number of companies particularly in manufacturing industry. During the year Gross Domestic Product had fallen by 11·4 per cent, manufacturing output by 22·9 per cent and real wages by 19·2 per cent, stirring the first symptoms of political opposition to the regime since the coup. As early as March 1981 both the Sociedad Rural Argentina (the main farmers' association which represented the richest land-owning families in Argentina) and the main employers' federation, the Union Industrial Argentina (IUA), had spoken out against the growing financial instability, urging the junta to adopt a more forceful medium-term economic strategy.

Even foreign companies like Ford, which, following the coup had been very supportive of the regime, seemed worried. In September 1981 Juan María Courard, the president of Ford's Argentine subsidiary said, 'For months now we've been waiting to see what the government will do. Always waiting. The high interest rates, the most worrying factor, have been discussed at all levels of government, but still nothing has been done to stop them climbing. No industrialist in the world can work with interest rates in excess of 11 per cent a month.'[2]

Rank and file unionists were also beginning to lose their fear. In June the traditionally militant automobile workers had staged a series of stoppages and demonstrations. This was followed a month later by a general-strike call from the newly reconstituted and still outlawed General Confederation of Labour (CGT). Although some CGT leaders were linked to the military, the partially successful strike did 'serve as a point of reference for workers who wanted to fight the dictatorship'.[3] In November, coinciding with the latest financial crisis, a Mass commemorating Argentina's patron saint of work, San Cayetano, was turned into a peaceful protest march of over 50,000 people demanding 'Paz, Pan y Trabajo' ('Peace, Bread and Work'). The junta would have been in even more serious trouble politically had it not been for the ineffectual opposition put up by the main political parties. The Multipartidaria – an *ad hoc* alliance made up of the Perónists, the Radicals and three smaller parties on the centre and left of the political spectrum, called rather half-heartedly for a change in economic policies and the holding of elections. In the words of one of the country's leading columnists, Manfred Schonfeld, the Multipartidaria confrontation with the regime was like 'a mouse taking on a mountain'.[4]

The lunch between Anaya and Galtieri on 9 December 1981 nevertheless appears to have ended with both men sufficiently convinced of the gravity of the situation to toast a change of government within the regime. Galtieri confirmed that, as commander of the army, he had the power of the tanks to thwart any resistance by Viola, although both men seemed convinced that the President would resign without resort to arms. It was to be a palace coup like so many others tested and tried during fifty years of military power. Anaya offered the full political and military support of the navy on the understanding that the navy would be allowed to expand its plans for the occupation not just of South Georgia but also of the Falklands.

Even at this early stage, Galtieri appears to have calculated that the political risk implied by his handing the initiative on the Malvinas to the navy was worth taking. Properly managed, public opinion would accept a successful occupation of the islands as an act not just of the navy but of the military as a whole. Anaya would take the initial kudos, but Galtieri, as President, would reap the ultimate glory. With a bit of luck, Galtieri hoped to stay in power for at least ten years. Both he and Anaya considered the opinions of the air force only belatedly, thus carrying on a military tradition that had relegated the airmen to a secondary role inside the political system. It was not until 29 December that Brigadier Basilio Lami Dozo was informed of the decision to recover the islands before the end of the year. The junta was convinced that the raising of Argentina's blue and white flag in Port Stanley on the 150th anniversary of Britain's 'illegal usurpation' of 'Las Malvinas' would stir nationalist sentiment as much as San Martín's epic crossing of the Andes.

The detailed planning stage for the invasion of the Falklands began in early January 1982. A very restricted 'task group' headed by the commander of the Argentine fleet, Rear-Admiral Juan José Lombardo, and including Brigadier Sigfrido Plessel, one of Lami Dozo's senior advisers, and General Osvaldo García, the commander of the Fifth Army Corps, set up an improvised 'war room' in an annexe of the Navy Club in Buenos Aires – an imposing *fin de siècle* building on the corner of the capital's busiest shopping arcade, the Calle Florida. The setting was soon judged too exposed and the task group moved to the southern port of Puerto Belgrano – a naval reserve where few civilians dared tread.

Codenamed Operation Azul, Lombardo's plan drew heavily on the scenarios developed as part of basic military training ever since 1942, and which had been refined by Anaya himself soon after returning from a posting as naval attaché to London in 1977. The operation would focus on a surprise amphibious landing of not more than 3,000 troops, capable of subduing with a minimum of bloodshed the token contingent of Royal Marines on the islands. Speed would be of the essence, with the Argentines moving quickly to place under arrest the island administration, control the more virulently anti-Argentine among the islanders, and dominate Port Stanley and outlying farms to such an efficient degree as to make protracted armed resistance impossible. Within forty-eight hours, the bulk of the invasion force would withdraw to the Argentine mainland, leaving a military Governor and a token presence of about 500 men to make a symbolic assertion of Argentine sovereignty and await Britain's diplomatic surrender to a *fait accompli*. The only major modification to Anaya's draft plan appears to have involved the islanders. Lombardo's task force drew up a plan of financial compensation to be offered to those kelpers who wished to emigrate once an Argentine administration had been installed. But this was devised as an option rather than a compulsory final solution. The navy had originally planned to remove the entire island population by force so as to leave the islands free for Argentine settlers. Lombardo believed that this would outrage international opinion, and preferred a more flexible arrangement by which a mixed island community would evolve and in which kelpers and Argentines would enjoy equal rights.

From the outset, Lombardo's task group incorporated detailed assessments of the nature of Britain's defence of the islands, the attitudes of individual islanders (a black list of the most anti-Argentine was drawn up), and the diplomatic context in which the invasion would take place.

Early advice came from Vice-Commodore Hector Gilobert, an air force officer who had used his position as chief representative in Port Stanley of the State airline Líneas Aéreas del Estado (LADE) and his excellent English as a cover for four years of persistent intelligence gathering. Gilobert was far from being the perfect spy and does not seem to have been trained as one. He was simply an astute officer who had found little difficulty in absorbing the reality of a small, simple and extremely transparent island community. The marine barracks at Moody Brook on the outskirts of Port Stanley, for example, was throughout his posting run virtually with the openness of a pub. Argentine female teachers were among those who regularly attended the camp's drunken social occasions, when a generous amount of indiscreet information about training and schedules was passed around as freely as beer. As one islander confessed,

If Gilobert or any other Argentine officer wanted to, all he had to do was run up in his car on a Sunday afternoon, photograph the premises, study the layout through a pair of binoculars and send it all back to Buenos Aires. The barracks were always open to the public at weekends so there was no one to prevent this from happening.[5]

Additional information on the islands was provided by Captain Capaglio, skipper of the naval transport ship *Isla de los Estados*. Since 1980 the ship had carried out a series of commercial trips to the islands, transporting food to and from the mainland. Capaglio is believed to have gathered detailed intelligence on the layout of some strategically placed farms, the loyalties of their owners, and of the lack of a military presence on the majority of the beaches and jetties that dotted the islands.

As for British diplomatic intentions, one of the early advisers of the task group appears to have been Rear-Admiral Walter Allara. A former head of Argentina's navy intelligence (SIN), Allara had recently returned from a two-year posting as naval attaché to London. The navy officer had had the good fortune to find virtually the same degree of transparency in Britain as his colleagues had found on the islands. In the English summer of 1981, for instance, Allara had been pleasantly surprised to be invited on board HMS *Invincible*. A few weeks later he returned the compliment by inviting Admiral Sir Henry Leach, the First Sea Lord, to cocktails on board the Argentine naval training ship *Libertad*, which had docked in London. As a result of his regular conversations with British naval personnel, Allara had returned to Argentina convinced that neither the Foreign Office nor Leach regarded the Falklands as a priority issue. Nor did he think that the British suspected an invasion in the near future. On the contrary the recently elected Thatcher government seemed to be somewhat embarrassed by the anti-junta campaign of the human rights groups and anxious to deepen the traditional links between the Royal Navy and Argentina, which in recent years had led to the supply of a generous assortment of equipment and training facilities, including destroyers, communications equipment and helicopters. Some sectors of British industry and of the military establishment could not forgive the Labour government for its refusal in 1978 to receive officially the then navy chief Admiral Massera – a move considered to have been behind Argentina's decision to ditch a planned purchase of British frigates and turn to West Germany instead. During Allara's posting, which coincided with the first years of Mrs Thatcher's premiership, activity seems to have returned to normal at the Argentine navy's 'naval commission' – a group of Argentine naval officers who co-ordinated arms purchases from an office in Vauxhall Bridge Road on the same street – irony of ironies – as one of the offices belonging to MI5. Given such complacency it is hardly surprising that the renewal of military training facilities under the Thatcher government was extended to include junior Argentine naval officers enlisted by SIN.

As important in forging the junta's views on how the world saw Argentina, and therefore in completing the essential diplomatic context motivating the decision to invade the Falklands, were the dealings senior officers had had with the United States.

Traditionally relations between Buenos Aires and Washington had been marked by intense rivalry. Argentine nationalism and her aspirations to be a regional leader often clashed with the US self-perceived role as guardian and imperial master of its strategic reserve south of the Río Grande. Following the Cuban revolution in 1959, however, Argentine and US military officers joined in a community of common interest to fight against what they saw as the threat of Marxist-inspired guerrilla activity spreading throughout Latin America. In the 1960s Argentines began to attend courses at West Point, while US advisers shared the lessons learned in the fight against the Vietcong with a new generation of Argentine soldiers for whom eradicating subversion was more important than defending frontiers.

Contrary to popular legend, the Carter administration brought little more than a hiccup to an otherwise fluid relationship. The US human rights policy coupled with the junta's decision not to support the grains embargo against the Soviet Union produced a great deal of public outrage from Washington. But although the protests of some State Department officials like Pat Derian undoubtedly saved some individuals from joining the list of the disappeared, the military links between the two countries continued more or less unabated.[6]

In 1979, the Argentine navy was invited to participate in UNITAS, a US-organised multi-national naval exercise aimed at co-ordinating support for Western trade routes based on the hypothesis that the Panama Canal was being blockaded. The junta sent word privately to Washington that it was prepared to join the exercise as long as the United States repealed the Kennedy–Humphrey amendment of the Senate, which banned arms sales to countries like Argentina where human rights had been violated. Privately word was sent by the Pentagon that the amendment could not be overturned without risking a major public outcry; there were, however, ways of renewing supplies through more discreet channels. 'During my time in Washington we got everything we asked for,' recalled a senior Argentine naval officer who served as naval attaché during the Carter years.[7] The shopping list included turbines for A-4 Skyhawk fighter planes, electronic equipment for submarines, spare parts for helicopters, and even sensitive material for Argentina's nuclear programme, which was run by an Admiral.

After the duplicity of the Carter years, the junta moved to encounter the open collaboration of Reagan. Since 1977 the Argentine military had given open support to anti-Marxist forces in Central America, providing Somoza with arms in Nicaragua and training death squads in El Salvador, Guatemala and Honduras. They had willingly filled the vacuum left by Carter, gaining a reputation as gallant crusaders once Reagan came to power. The US administration saw in the Argentine military a useful ally which would help them do the work the American military could not at the time do openly without provoking a national outcry over a second Vietnam.[8]

Soon US presidential advisers and generals were making their way to Buenos Aires; the public rhetoric of 'moral persuasion', so beloved of the Carter administration, gave way to a more pragmatic although no more effective policy of 'quiet diplomacy' on the human rights issue; the visitors, who included two senior Reagan advisers, Roger Fontaine and Vernon Walters, meanwhile put the public emphasis on regional security and talked in private more bluntly of the possibility of lifting the arms embargo altogether and crushing the Communists not only in Central America but also in the South Atlantic, where the navy could be called upon to play an increasingly useful role in helping to prevent Soviet incursions.

The Argentine navy's perception of itself as an important player on the South Atlantic stage was also stimulated by US navy chiefs, who never ceased to promote the idea that the annual UNITAS exercise could develop into a more permanent military pact. Following the 1980 exercise, for instance, an Argentine naval attaché was invited to the US headquarters in Norfolk, Virginia. There he was shown a large electronic map of the South Atlantic with flashing lights marking an alleged Soviet submarine base in Angola and suspected back-up bases all the way up the African coast. The Argentine naval officer came away from the meeting convinced that the US had in mind an important strategic role for Latin American countries, in which Buenos Aires could and should be the key.

No less seduced by the Reagan administration was General Galtieri. Trained at West Point, Galtieri's military career had revolved around a loyal respect for his old teachers. Indeed his lack of political sophistication and toughness seemed to make him Washington's 'perfect client-state leader'. As army chief he had visited one of his West Point colleagues, General Edward Meyer, and offered Argentina's full participation in the formation of a peacekeeping force in Sinai in August 1981. Two months later he returned to Washington to give his full support for the US administration's get-tough policy in Central America, gaining in return its tacit approval for his imminent palace coup. President Reagan's national security adviser, Richard Allen, described Galtieri publicly as a man 'possessed of a majestic personality'.[9] By that Christmas, Galtieri in one of his first acts as President had ordered an increase in the funds, military advisers and arms which since 1977 had been making their way to Central America.

US officials have always denied that at any stage the Reagan administration hinted that it would remain neutral in the event of an Argentine invasion of the Falklands as a tacit exchange for Galtieri's generous backing in Central America. What is certain however is that the junta and its 'Malvinas' task group convinced themselves that Washington would not allow itself to become militarily involved in the Falklands. The belief that the United States was capable of allying itself with Argentina against its oldest NATO ally showed the extent to which the militarisation of Argentine society had isolated it from reality. The diplomatic miscalculation, so instrumental in pushing the country towards war, was the product of the military's inflated sense of its own importance.

Against this diplomatic background, in mid-February Lombardo and his team fixed 15 May as a provisional date for the invasion. The fact that the junta had calculated on a minimum international outcry and little if no military response from Britain or the United States meant that Lombardo could ignore detailed logistics: in June the navy was due to receive a delivery of fourteen Superetendards and their accompanying Exocet missiles. Nor did it matter that the Argentine air force was also only half-way through its re-equipment programme with many of its bombs timed for land as opposed to naval targets. An officer later commented on this period:

The fact was that the subject of the recovery of the Malvinas was old hat, discussed on countless occasions in the Military Academies and in the chiefs of staff headquarters. So that, as far as our spirits were concerned, this was just one more operation that was destined to end up in an archive ... very few of us believed that it would ever really take place.'[10]

But higher up the military hierarchy a great deal of importance was attached to Allara's perception of British diplomatic indifference over the Falklands. Although the junta, largely on the insistence of Brigadier Lami Dozo, had in principle agreed that any final decision on the invasion should await the outcome of the latest round of Anglo-Argentine talks scheduled in New York, the navy planners had already begun to look upon Operation Azul with a sense of inevitability.

The New York talks took place on 26 and 27 February. The Argentine delegation was headed by Enrique Ros, a career diplomat with long experience of the Falklands issue. Through a mixture of dedication and opportunism he had managed to suppress in public his dislike for what he regarded as an unnecessary intrusion into foreign policy by his military peers. In private he had gone out of his way to impress on the few people he could trust that he was not a soldier in civilian uniform. But while this may have satisfied Ros's political conscience, it kept him ostracised from the inner circle of decision-makers around which the junta's power revolved. He had gone to New York, unaware that the junta had planned Operation Azul and set a provisional date for the invasion. On the contrary, Ros intended to focus the talks on fixing a timetable for further talks, and the setting up of a commission to streamline contacts between Argentina and Britain. He did not wish to press the British to accept Argentina's territorial claims – detailed discussion of sovereignty would be left for another round of talks.

Ros seriously underestimated the mood of the junta. Anaya was proceeding with the planning of Operation Azul, convinced that the British had agreed to the New York talks simply to waste time as they had always done. Galtieri was only slightly more cautious. He hoped that the talks might produce a commitment from the British to talks about sovereignty within a month and Argentine administration of the islands by the end of the year. Lami Dozo characteristically sat on the fence, prepared to back a military solution if the junta so decided. On 28 February the Argentine and British delegations failed to fix a date for a further meeting, but did agree on the setting up of a commission, to be presided over by Ministers from both countries and with the possible inclusion of the islanders. The commission's task was mutually defined as that of identifying and discussing 'all elements in the dispute' (diplomatic short-hand for an open agenda including sovereignty), and of bringing up specific proposals as to how they might be resolved within an overall settlement. The commission's period of operation would be one year initially, at the end of which Ministers could decide on an extension for further talks.

Ros emerged from the meeting fully satisfied that he had achieved a great deal more than any of his predecessors, and quite willing to accede to the British delegation's request for public restraint. The delegation had argued that such restraint was needed if it was to have any chance of winning support for the commission from MPs and island opinion. It too had emerged in an optimistic frame of mind, believing that it had 'bought three to six months'. Both sides had seriously miscalculated military feelings back in Buenos Aires.[11]

Subsequently the conflict between Ros and the junta surfaced with a vengeance. The conciliatory and vaguely phrased joint communiqué issued in New York was followed by a statement issued by the Foreign Ministry in Buenos Aires insisting on an urgent and prearranged agenda for substantial talks, and the immediate activation of the commission. 'Should this not occur, Argentina reserves the right to terminate the working of this mechanism and to choose freely the procedure which best accords with her interest.' As far as Galtieri and Anaya were concerned the text, prepared on their insistence by Costa Méndez and his first secretary, Gustavo Figueroa, was a masterful stroke of diplomatic wording. Its ambiguity hinted at the junta's real feelings about the dispute without making it explicit that an invasion was planned. It therefore preserved the essential element of secrecy on which Operation Azul was destined to stand or fall.

Costa Méndez followed up the communiqué by getting selected journalists to publish stories insisting that this time round the junta really meant business. A typical Ministry-inspired 'leak' appeared in *La Prensa*, which speculated on a step-by-step plan of action over the next four months beginning with a cut-off of services to the Islands and ending possibly in direct action. Seeking a British reaction, I was informed by the British Ambassador, Anthony Williams, on his return from New York that the British press should not allow itself to be over anxious. Such hysteria was typical of the local media and should not be taken too seriously. The irony of the situation, however, was that the reports understated rather than exaggerated the seriousness of the situation, although neither Costa Méndez himself nor the journalists involved appear to have been aware of this.

On 2 March General Mario Benjamín Menéndez, an officer attached to the Chiefs of Staff, was informed by General Galtieri of his appointment as the future Governor of Las Islas Malvinas. Menéndez later recalled how he was struck dumb at the end of the regular Tuesday briefing at the army headquarters, chaired by Galtieri. It was there that he was informed that a decision had been taken to recover the islands by force. Scarcely pausing for breath, Galtieri then went to insist that the plan should be kept secret. Until further notice, Menéndez was to discuss his appointment only with his Chief of Staff, General José Antonio Vaquero. Galtieri gave Menéndez no further details of Operation Azul. The future Governor was simply told that he would be flown to the islands and take charge of a military detachment of not more than 500 troops.

'Five hundred only?' Menéndez interjected for the first time. 'What about the air force and the navy . . .?'

'Oh, you should look upon the troops as playing the role of military policemen,' Galtieri said, 'and there will be some people from the air force and the navy, maybe a couple of Pucaras, one or two patrol boats . . . just enough to assert our control over juridical waters.'

It was not until the following week, during a further routine briefing at army headquarters, that Menéndez managed to summon up enough courage to express some real doubts about the viability of such an operation. 'Look, my General, it's not that I don't want to carry out my mission. It's a responsibility and a very great honour and I have no intention of resigning. But I just want to ask you one question: what is going to be the international reaction to this at a point in time when Argentina and Britain are still officially negotiating the future of the Islands?'

Galtieri paused momentarily, then stiffened, cleared his throat, and in a voice that cut the air of the room like a sharp knife said, 'Menéndez, that is none of your business . . . it's the junta's problem and no one else's. I just want you to think about being a military Governor.'[12]

Mario Benjamín was the latest in the Menéndez family to be called to lay his heroic stamp on Argentine military history. His cousin, Luciano, had only two years before headed an aborted uprising in the northern city of Córdoba over what he considered to be the increasingly soft approach to politics being adopted by General Videla. His uncle, Benjamín, had tried to overthrow Perón in 1951 to stop what he considered was the emergence of a workers' State. The future Governor of the Malvinas had earned his stars as second in command in the military's campaign against the People's Revolutionary Army (ERP) in the northern sugar province of Tucuman. The ERP was an organisation of middle-class revolutionaries, influenced by Guevara, who believed that the poverty of the sugar workers within the context of the military society could only be solved by armed struggle.

In October 1975, during the government of Isabelita Perón, Tucuman was declared a military zone under General Agdel Vilas. Selected 'war correspondents' were regularly flown into the province in military aircraft to report on 'Operation Independencia' as the campaign was officially dubbed. The military, they were told, were there to liberate the sugar workers from the Marxist yoke. Back in Buenos Aires magazines and newspapers faithfully reported on the heroic actions of the largely conscript army and its success in crushing terrorism. Not reported was Vilas's penchant for 'necklaces'. Arrested suspects had gelignite tied round their necks before being shackled to a jeep and blown up. The luckier victims were herded into a concentration camp near the provincial capital called 'La Escuelita' (the little school), to be tortured. Few came out alive.

While Vilas supervised the repression down in the valley, Menéndez directed the troops up in the hills. His battlefield was a subtropical forest where a few hundred members of the ERP had taken refuge and were finally trapped. They were liquidated one by one, by Pucara ground-attack aircraft strafing them with machine-gun fire and napalm. In an interview following the Falklands War, Menéndez insisted that he didn't consider his seven months in Tucuman as particularly crucial to his career prospects. He denied having ever authorised torture or of personally killing anyone in the way that Vilas is alleged to have done. But that was to be wise after the event. On the Falklands stage, where Menéndez was called upon to play out his final heroic act, professionalism and humanity towards the islanders counted for very little in the war of propaganda relentlessly pursued by the British. The Governor was quickly caricatured by the British media as a tough no-nonsense soldier who had, like his mentor Galtieri, made a name for himself heartlessly murdering young Argentines. The implicit message was that this one-time violator of human rights could hardly be expected to treat the kelpers as humans. Thus Menéndez, chosen by his countrymen to fight a courageous last stand, became in the eyes of the British the epitome of everything that was morally wrong with Argentina.

By March 1982, union unrest because of diminishing real salary levels and lay-offs was increasing and was to reach a climax with a violent demonstration against the government at the end of the month. And yet, although the state of the economy was an important factor behind the junta's decision to contemplate an invasion of the Falklands, its influence on the events which finally led to the outbreak of war should not be exaggerated. Contrary to the widely accepted history of the period, Argentina's economic situation was showing tentative signs of recovery at the end of the first quarter of 1982. Galtieri's Economy Minister, Roberto Alemann, in the short period he had been in office had already proved far more determined than any of his predecessors, particularly in his dealings with the military. His success in bridging the junta's credibility gap was reflected in the stability that had been restored to the financial markets and in the figures showing a reduction in overall public spending. In terms of austerity Alemann himself took the lead by substantially cutting his own staff. He had also gone much further than Martínez de Hoz in announcing his intention to hive off large sectors of the military industrial complex Dirección Nacional de Fabricaciones Militares and letting the military hang on to only those plants used exclusively for military purposes.

The main problem facing Alemann was the enormous foreign debt he had inherited. With high international interest rates and dwindling prices for Argentine agricultural exports, Alemann was finding it difficult to pay the principal and interest falling due on some 35·6 billion dollars owed to the international financial community at the end of 1981. Nevertheless, he had already held a successful first round of talks with Argentina's main creditors at which much of this debt had been restructured and new loans arranged.[13] There was a feeling in the business and banking community that, given time and the support of the military, Alemann might just be able to pull the country through. Such views, however, appear to have carried little weight with the junta, which seems to have been driven towards war by less rational motives than those suggested by their supporters and detractors alike.

4
OPERATION ALPHA

On the day General Menéndez had his appointment as military Governor of the Falklands secretly confirmed, Mr David Joy, Counsellor at the British Embassy in Buenos Aires, received a neatly typed letter from a scrap-metal merchant called Constantino Davidoff. The letter gave formal notification to the British authorities of Mr Davidoff's intention to sail to the island of South Georgia on board the Argentine naval support vessel *Bahía Buen Suceso* on a four-month contract to clear a disused whaling station. The Embassy's response was to ensure that Davidoff was clearly informed that, even though details of the expedition's members had been supplied, it was essential for them to call first at Grytwiken to clear British immigration before proceeding to the whaling station at Leith harbour. Eleven days later, on 20 March, the *Bahía Buen Suceso* was observed by the base commander of the British Antarctic Survey putting ashore a sizeable party composed not just of Mr Davidoff and his workmen but also of military personnel. It was a member of the latter that, on setting foot on South Georgia, raised the Argentine flag.

The Florida Garden, a popular tea-room equidistant from the Foreign Ministry's palace of San Martín and the Navy Club, and right in the heart of the capital's shopping centre, is a regular haunt for young lovers and journalists seeking information. However, on one particular late November afternoon in the approaching heat of the Argentine summer of 1981, neither group appeared to have taken notice of a meeting between five men over coffee, which within four months would set off a chain of events culminating in the junta's private ruling on 26 March to bring forward to 2 April its decision to invade the Falklands.

The men included two high-ranking officials from the Foreign Ministry, two navy Captains and Constantino Davidoff, a young Argentine entrepreneur of Greek extraction, with an eye for a good deal, however bizarre. Davidoff had in his hands a two-year-old contract with the Christian Salvesen shipping firm, reserving to him the right of access to all the equipment belonging to some whaling stations on the South Atlantic island of South Georgia.[1] Over the previous weeks, Davidoff's request for local labour had been turned down by the Governor of the Falkland Islands. The British, although giving him permission officially to exploit the contract, had also turned down a request for transport. The only British ship available in the area at the time was HMS *Endurance*, and this was needed on station for relief of the small contingent of marines then based on the Falkland Islands.

Davidoff had a very different reception from the Argentine authorities. At the Foreign Ministry, he was told that if he brought back the scrap to Argentina he would not have to pay any import duty – South Georgia was after all officially claimed as Argentine territory. Now at the meeting in the Florida Garden, Captain César Trombetta from the navy's Atlantic squadron offered to transport the Greek and an Argentine workforce in the newly commissioned ice-breaker *Almirante Irizar* for absolutely no charge. In accepting, Davidoff appears to have been motivated simply by money, the prospect of a handsome profit now being virtually assured by the additional perks. He seems to have been unaware that by accepting he was becoming an innocent pawn in a more complex and sinister plot.

Trombetta was a veteran of the South Atlantic who five years previously had joined Operation Sol. This was the code name given to an Argentine military landing on Southern Thule, an unoccupied piece of British territory belonging to the South Sandwich group. At the time a formal protest was issued by the Chargé d'Affaires in Buenos Aires, stating that the British government considered the establishment of the alleged scientific station, without prior reference to the British authorities, to be a violation of British sovereignty. However nothing more was done. Accordingly Thule was added to Varela's clandestine mission in 1966 and Allara's intelligence assessments in a growing list of what the Argentine navy regarded as tell-tale signs of Britain's diplomatic indifference and military vulnerability.

By the end of 1981, however, the Argentine navy high command was split over the feasibility of carrying out a repeat performance of Operation Sol on South Georgia. Lombardo, although closely involved in an original contingency plan for South Georgia, had subsequently changed his mind. He felt that the political future of the regime rested on a successful recapture of the Falklands. Any incident in South Georgia ran the risk of alerting the British to a wider plot in the South Atlantic and thus of undermining the secrecy of which Operation Azul would stand or fall. 'Either we do the Falklands or we do South Georgia. But we can't do both,' he warned Anaya.

The Commander-in-Chief told Lombardo not to worry because any plans involving South Georgia had been cancelled until further notice.[2]

In spite of Anaya's reassurances, the reality was very different. By the time he met Davidoff, Trombetta was working independently from Lombardo. As the head of the navy's Antarctic Squadron he was under the direct orders of Admiral Edgardo Otero, the commander of naval operations and transport. Otero was one of the navy's most notorious hardliners. In 1980 he had served as camp commander of the Naval Mechanical School, where hundreds of 'disappeared' were tortured and summarily executed. A fellow officer who served with Otero during that so-called dirty war against left-wing guerrillas recalled later that the Admiral was fond of spectacular actions.

Otero's colleague and close friend was Admiral Eduardo Girling, who in 1981 had succeeded Allara as head of naval intelligence. In that year Otero and Girling became, in theory, respectively eleventh and tenth in the naval hierarchy. In practice, however, Otero used his close links with the intelligence services to increase his influence on Anaya, forming a *de facto* troika of hidden power which ran parallel and often above the officially defined command structure in which Lombardo was number three. By November 1981, Otero and Girling had become the joint Rasputins in Emperor Anaya's court. In the words of one senior officer, the two men had begun to 'fill Anaya's head with ideas'.

The most ambitious of these ideas was an updated contingency plan for South Georgia codenamed Operation Alpha, which envisaged a repeat performance to that on Thule but on a more elaborate scale. Alpha was to take place in two stages: the first would involve the infiltration of Davidoff's workforce with military 'scientists' and a token landing on South Georgia; the second had a carefully selected group of *buzos tacticos* – the navy's crack commando unit – secretly joining the annual resupply trip to Argentina's Antarctic bases, which included a stop-over at Thule. From the South Sandwich Islands, the commandos were to go to South Georgia and establish a more permanent military base from early April onwards. Argentine naval intelligence had information that by then Britain's only military presence in the South Atlantic, HMS *Endurance*, would be on its way to Brazil. Any further military reaction was judged improbable given the onset of the local winter.

At the Florida Garden meeting, Davidoff had expressed his wish to inspect the scrap metal on a preliminary trip before taking the final decision as to whether to take up the option of removing it. This fitted in well with Operation Alpha.

Trombetta, an expert in signals and human intelligence work, saw such a trip as a perfect opportunity to take a closer look at South Georgia and test the likely British reaction prior to the main stage of the operation. On 16 December 1981 Davidoff left Buenos Aires on board the naval ice-breaker *Almirante Irizar*, captained by Trombetta. On the recommendation of his navy peers Davidoff had timed his formal notification of his trip to the British Embassy so that it wouldn't arrive until after the boat's departure. Although this was intended by the navy as an act of provocation, Davidoff himself did not see it this way; unaware of Operation Alpha, he believed that the written permission he had already received from the British authorities approving his contract with Salvesen made further notification superfluous.

Captain Trombetta covered the 1,650-mile passage in four days, maintaining radio-silence throughout, 'A most unusual procedure in a region where ships' captains regularly broadcast weather reports and generally exchange news and feelings.'[3] But on 20 December the *Irizar* was observed by the base commander of the British Antarctic Survey entering South Georgian waters. A message was subsequently sent to London via Port Stanley pointing out that the boat was required by the Dependencies' legislation to obtain entry clearance from the local magistrate at Grytwiken. Instead the *Irizar* made its way twenty miles up the coast to Leith. There Davidoff and a small landing party went ashore and, according to his account, made an inventory and took photographs of a disused whaling station. One of his party commemorated the day of the landing by chalking 20 December on a nearby wall, beneath the slogan 'Las Malvinas son Argentinas'. Then the *Irizar* raised its anchor and headed back towards the Argentine mainland.

On 4 January, over two weeks after the *Irizar* had been sighted, the British Ambassador in Buenos Aires, Anthony Williams, was instructed to deliver a formal protest in the 'strongest terms' against what was regarded as a violation of British sovereignty, and to warn of the undesirable consequences that would follow from a repetition. The Ambassador was to say that if any further attempt was made to land in South Georgia without proper authorisation, the British government reserved the right to take whatever action might be necessary.

In a subsequent meeting with Costa Méndez, the Argentine Foreign Minister, Williams was told that the Ministry knew nothing of the Davidoff expedition and that it would immediately conduct an investigation. The Ambassador agreed to let the matter rest for another four weeks, after which he renewed his protest. On this second occasion the Foreign Ministry ignored him. In fact, unknown to Williams, the Foreign Ministry had known about Davidoff since the previous August, when the Under-Secretary for Foreign Affairs, Enrique Ros, had sent a note to navy headquarters confirming the scrap merchant's interest in securing transport for a trip to South Georgia. The navy had spent the following two months conducting security checks on Davidoff.

What seems to have been more genuine was Costa Méndez's insistence that an investigation would be carried out. Although a contingency plan for South Georgia had been on file at the Foreign Ministry for at least a year as a possible way of giving fresh impetus to the regime's negotiations over the Falklands, it seems to have been put to one side by the time of the Florida Garden meeting. The Foreign Ministry, like Lombardo, appeared to believe that any military incident on South Georgia ran the risk of proving counter-productive. If the Ministry had given its OK to the *Irizar* trip it was because it had no knowledge of Otero's plans and thus regarded it as purely a commercial enterprise. The British protest, however, alerted Costa Méndez to the possibility that the navy was more involved with Davidoff than initially seemed to be the case.

It was not until early in March 1982 that the Argentine Foreign Ministry had gathered sufficient evidence about Operation Alpha. By then, the New York talks had come and gone, the junta had issued its strongly worded communiqué, General Menéndez had been secretly appointed military Governor, and Costa Méndez had embarked on a major diplomatic juggling act aimed at pressurising the British to agree to an early hand-over of sovereignty and convincing his own military superiors to hold back from invading the Falklands. Costa Méndez had no doubts that if Operation Alpha went ahead, any offensive to recover Las Malvinas would be stillborn. In an uncharacteristic show of courage he said as much in a meeting with Rear-Admiral Leopoldo Suárez del Cerro, the head of the joint Chiefs-of-Staff. Del Cerro agreed to pass on the message to Anaya. What motivated Argentina's military rulers from this point on is difficult to establish with total accuracy since the main protagonists have blotted out Operation Alpha from naval history.

One theory is that Anaya was sufficiently unimpressed by Williams's reaction to the *Irizar* incident to assume that Britain's attitude towards the South Atlantic had changed little since the landing on Southern Thule. There was thus no military or diplomatic reaction to worry about. Another is that Anaya did believe in the seriousness of Williams's warning and deliberately chose to ignore it, possibly in the hope that South Georgia would divert Britain's attention away from the main act of Operation Azul.

Motives notwithstanding, there is at least circumstantial evidence to suggest that Operation Alpha did indeed proceed after the *Irizar*'s return to base in January and that the plan to take over South Georgia moved into top gear in the hectic chain of events leading up to the invasion on 2 April.

The Franks Report revealed that on 8 January the skipper of HMS *Endurance*, Captain Barker, reported that he had spoken by radio to Captain Trombetta. The Argentine had told Barker he was *en route* for a base in the Antarctic, although shortly afterwards it became apparent that he was really making his way to Southern Thule. Subsequent information emerging in Buenos Aires confirmed that the *buzos tácticos* commissioned by Otero left soon after the New Year from the southern mainland base of Ushuaia on board the *Bahía Paraíso*, the Argentine navy's newest fleet auxiliary. Before their departure, the commandos, officially attached to the Antarctic mission under the command of Trombetta, were handed secret instructions in a sealed envelope which they were ordered to open only after they had put to sea. The orders confirmed that they were to proceed in late March to South Georgia, where they were to establish a military base in support of the workforce and scientists already there.

Among the *buzos* no one was more enthusiastic about the plan than their commander Lieutenant Alfredo Astiz. In the weeks before the *Bahía Paraíso*'s departure, Astiz had been rapidly assuming the air of a stray dog, moving from one posting to the next and meeting with an increasingly controversial reception. Astiz had been one of the few Argentine officers involved in kidnappings and killings during the repression to have been identified by human rights organisations. Evidence gathered from survivors had allowed human rights lawyers and organisations like Amnesty International to compile a hefty dossier on several of Astiz's 'acts of duty' committed while acting as a naval storm trooper attached to the Naval Mechanical School. The Swedish and French Embassies were among several official bodies that were convinced of Astiz's links with the torture and 'disappearance' of two French nuns and a young Swedish student between 1976 and 1978.

Astiz had subsequently joined naval intelligence, infiltrating human rights organisations in Argentina and groups of exiles in Paris and London. By 1981, stories linking Astiz with human rights violations were regularly appearing in the international press as the most identifiable example of the repression that had occurred within Argentina. In South Africa, Astiz had been forced hastily to cut short a posting as assistant naval attaché when his presence and background were exposed by the local English press. His navy superiors believed it was only a matter of time before a more daring Argentine press exposed him at home, opening up a witch hunt against all those responsible for human rights violations. They did, however, have great regard for Astiz professionally and were not prepared to offer him up as a sacrificial lamb. His involvement in Operation Alpha thus seemed to be the perfect solution in the short term.

In retrospect the sending of Astiz to the South Atlantic appears to have been one of the most ill-conceived decisions made by the junta. Captured by the British, he subsequently provided Whitehall's propaganda machinery with much-needed cannon fodder. To a greater degree than even Menéndez, the 'blond angel of death' – as Astiz had identified himself to his victims – ensured a moral linkage between the invasion of the Falklands and the violation of human rights.

In the context in which the decision was taken, however, the posting was consistent with the nature of Argentina's military society. Accustomed to believing in their own propaganda, by the beginning of 1982 the Argentine armed forces had not shifted an inch from their view that the human rights campaign was a Marxist-inspired initiative prompted by foreign forces opposed to Argentina's crusade in defence of Western values. Otero regarded Astiz as a modern hero who should be given every chance to serve his country and win promotion unobstructed by domestic reaction. The establishment of a military base in South Georgia was an assertion of Argentine sovereignty in the South Atlantic which provided Astiz with the opportunity of doing just that.

Within days of Astiz's departure, Davidoff had returned to the British Embassy. On 23 February he informed British officials that a new expedition was planning to set sail for South Georgia on the naval transport *Bahía Buen Suceso*. Although he himself was not going, Davidoff assumed responsibility for the new venture and apparently tried to make amends for the past by offering to transport supplies to the British Antarctic Survey station on the island. Even at this late stage in the Falklands story, Davidoff seems to have been less a leading protagonist than an innocent pawn of the secret military plan. The Franks Report says of Davidoff's meeting at the Embassy, 'He was anxious not to create difficulties and had asked for full instructions on how to proceed.'[4] It was at this point that naïvety seems to have taken over British diplomacy. In spite of the incident involving Trombetta, in spite of the suspicions of Captain Barker (shared by the Governor of the Falkland Islands, Sir Rex Hunt), in spite of the uncooperative reactions of the Argentine government to Mr Williams's two protests, Davidoff enterprises was given a further chance to redeem itself.

On 11 March, the British Embassy decided that there was no reason to try and prevent the *Bahía Buen Suceso* from sailing as 'this in itself was not illegal'.[5] On that day it had received a telephone call from a man called Oliva, who in the past had claimed that he was a lawyer acting for Davidoff. Oliva confirmed that the *Bahía Buen Suceso* was about to set sail; he was in turn reminded that the ship would have to first report to the British authorities on South Georgia before starting any work.

Whether Oliva was a *bona fide* lawyer or simply a front for the navy, we have not been able to establish with any certainty. Subsequent events suggest, however, that he might have been the latter. The message from the Embassy was never conveyed to the forty-one 'workmen' whose list was in the Embassy's possession. Nor did Davidoff himself receive any clarification as to why, the night before the *Bahía Buen Suceso* sailed for South Georgia, his workforce had been joined by a small contingent of navy personnel, bearing crates filled with military equipment and a large piece of blue and white cloth with a sun painted in the middle – the Argentine navy's equivalent of the blue ensign.

Subsequently Captain Briatore, the Captain of the *Bahía Buen Suceso*, behaved almost exactly as Captain Trombetta had done on the previous visit to South Georgia. He sailed to the island with his radio transmitter silent. This was an apparent attempt not to attract the attention of Captain Barker on HMS *Endurance*, which at the time was anchored near South Georgia and about to set sail for Port Stanley. By the time the *Bahía Buen Suceso* arrived, Captain Barker had left, but what followed did not go undetected by the British. On 19 March 1982 a four-man party from the local British Antarctic base observed about fifty men on shore, including military personnel. They also spotted an Argentine national flag flying atop a disused generator station. Operation Alpha had begun.

5
BEHIND THE EUPHORIA

Even those commentators most used to the volatile and unpredictable nature of Argentine politics were amazed by the dramatic change in atmosphere that occurred within twenty-four hours of the invasion of the Falkland Islands on 2 April. The most poignant symbol of the change undoubtedly lay in the scenes of euphoria that pervaded the streets of Buenos Aires in response to the communiqué broadcast on national radio and TV by the junta:

> The military junta as the Supreme Organ of State communicates to the people of the Argentine nation . . . that the Republic through the mediation of the armed forces . . . has recovered the Malvinas islands . . . Let the nation understand the profound and ineluctable national sentiment of this decision so that the collective sense of responsibility and effort can accompany this task and allow, with the help of God, that the legitimate rights of the Argentine people, postponed prudently and patiently for 150 years become a reality.

In the eyes of many Argentines President Leopoldo Galtieri had indeed become the hero of a historic moment in which the country's armed forces had recovered their *raison d'être*. Only three days previously thousands of Argentines had converged on the presidential palace in the first major demonstration against a military government since the 1976 coup. Galtieri had ordered that the rally should be repressed and the riot police had acted on his orders with a vengeance. Hundreds of demonstrators and innocent bystanders had been brutally attacked with sabres, gas canisters, long truncheons and even live bullets. Many hundreds more were thrown into prison. I remember watching one old woman, shopping bag in one hand and walking stick in the other, being surrounded by a group of heavily armed police and beaten to the ground. The incident seemed to encapsulate the desperation of a regime that felt itself on the defensive.

And yet after the invasion many of the same Argentines linked arms with the same security forces who had previously beaten them down, joyously waving Argentine flags and bringing Galtieri on to the balcony to rapturous applause. It was the World Cup final all over again. Small wonder that Galtieri in his first post-invasion speech vowed that the military would remain in the Falklands and would go to battle if and when a British Task Force arrived.

By invading the Falklands the Argentine military had solved in a matter of hours what no amount of policy directives over the previous six years had achieved: the unification of the nation behind them.

Behind the effervescent nationalism and self-congratulatory jingoism, however, there was little real patriotism. Behind the euphoria lay the first symptoms of a society collectively disintegrating. As the flags were waved around the city and the rhetoric reached fever pitch, ordinary citizens queued inside banks and finance houses and withdrew their deposits. On the first full banking day following the invasion, a large dollar demand by panicking small investors and wily speculators combined, with the enthusiasm of the unofficial money changers, to send the price of dollars soaring on the black market to 14,500 pesos, a gap of 26 per cent with the official quotation of 11,500. As a result the latest in the country's long line of Economy Ministers, Roberto Alemann, was forced to take the kind of measures that undermined the very principles on which his economic programme had always stood.

A few days before an invasion he had never been consulted on, Alemann had completed a tough Budget proposal and a tentative list of economic sectors he believed should be opened up to private hands. Alemann was aiming not just for a few minor readjustments to the economy but for substantial change, namely the eradication of inflation, considered to be Argentina's national disease. Equally important was what appeared to be the first serious attempt to grasp the country's public sector nettle against which successive Argentine Economy Ministers had struggled in vain, mainly because of military resistance.

Alemann had succeeded in trimming his Budget deficit estimate for the year to a record low of 2 per cent of GDP through sweeping cuts in the spending plans of most State enterprises and government departments. The measures had been far from popular but, like Mrs Thatcher, he had suggested that along with strong control on money supply and careful handling of the country's exchange rate, such austerity could bring the country's inflation down well below 100 per cent from its 1981 world record of 131 per cent. His privatisation plans had been equally ambitious, nowhere more so than in his apparent handling of Fabricaciones Militares, the largest militarily controlled industrial complex in Latin America. When the invasion took place, negotiations on transferring the group's steel and petrochemical interests to private civilian hands were at an advanced stage. Alemann had also made much progress in drafting a proposal for the opening up of the oil industry – a key sector of the economy and a source of national pride – to foreign investment.

On 2 April, however, Alemann's plans were shattered. Faced with an imminent liquidity crisis, this champion of the free market suspended all foreign exchange transactions except for payments on imports, opened up emergency rediscount lines within the banking system and regulated domestic interest rates. Faced with the imminence of conflict, the man who had boasted of his ability to demilitarise the economy found himself forced to impose emergency taxes and loosen up on spending targets so as to meet the armed forces' requirements for defending the islands. Initial estimates of the cost of the occupation of the islands alone suggested the need for an immediate five hundred million dollars in new funds.

At the outset of the war, most political analysts predicted that international isolation would bring the Argentine economy to its knees within weeks if not days, forcing an early peace agreement. Argentine was still heavily dependent on Western credit lines for balance-of-payments support, and foreign banks like the Bank of London and South America (Lloyd's), the First National Bank of Boston and Citibank had strong profiles domestically. Western countries such as West Germany were not only important suppliers but also participants in key sectors of local industry like cars and energy. Europe, in particular Britain, remained an important outlet for meat – one of Argentina's main agricultural exports.

However, Alemann, for all his difficulties at home, was remarkably successful in diluting the effect of financial and trade sanctions, playing on the wider interests both of the international banking community and of European governments, who saw little point in tying their future to an issue of political principle. Following in the steps of his predecessor Martínez de Hoz, the Economy Minister went on a tour of Europe's financial centres, and was able to convince bankers that they had a mutual interest in not rocking the boat. Argentina might be taking on militarily a NATO and EEC member, Alemann argued, but what mattered was its ability to pay back its debt.

By mutual consent creditor and debtor agreed to suspend negotiations on new loans until 'after the conflict was over', but payments falling due were automatically rolled over. When some of the smaller, less-experienced North American regional banks started getting itchy feet, leading US, Japanese and European financial institutions stepped in to reassure them that Alemann was a man of his word and that Argentina would never formally renege on her obligations.

The US Treasury, for instance, was one such institution. It was instrumental in calming the fears of investors even after the State Department and the Pentagon allied themselves to the British military effort.

In Britain a conflict between the military determination to defend the sovereignty of the Falklands and the need to take into consideration much wider interests, particularly financial ones, with sophisticated diplomacy[1] involved the government and the Bank of England. When the invasion took place, Mrs Thatcher insisted on freezing Argentine assets in London worth 1·4 billion dollars and cutting back on new loans. But the Bank, forever jealously guarding its theoretical independence and fearful that tough action against the enemy might jeopardise the City's reputation as a safe offshore island, subsequently displayed discreet flexibility in financial transactions involving Argentines and allowed Alemann to open an escrow account in New York, into which interest due to British banks could be paid.

Officially all EEC members joined in a collective embargo on trade with Argentina on 16 April. The measure did not formally extend to any contracts previously signed. This proved an important loophole, allowing traders to backdate new transactions and, with the exception of arms, maintaining a regular flow of products such as meat and fruit. Within Europe, Italy was eventually to re-establish its trade links with Argentina, judging that it was better served by looking after the interests of the strong Italian community in Latin America than in indefinitely backing Mrs Thatcher's Churchillian enterprise. A similar attitude was adopted by the Spanish and Irish, both of whom also had significant historical and cultural ties with Argentina and large local communities there.

The most subtle approach was adopted by the Japanese. They declared that they would not formally impose sanctions against Argentina but would hold back from trading in products which the Europeans themselves were unable to sell because of the war. It thus became party to the loopholes, maintaining regular contacts with the Argentine authorities, rolling over payments due to its banks and energetically pursuing its bid for a construction project on Argentine soil.

Although exports of meat and grain suffered initially, the slack was soon taken up by the Soviet Union, as had occurred annually since the 1976 coup and in particular during the Carter grains embargo. The Soviets were careful to keep out of military involvement in the conflict, but they saw no reason why trade should not continue as usual with their leading Latin American commercial partner. Iran also signed several contracts with Argentina during the war. On an average annual export potential of twenty-two million tonnes in cereals and meat products, during the three months of the war Argentina secured contracts for over seven million tonnes. Following the war, in the only detailed account of the economic aspects of the Falklands conflict, Alemann declared unhesitatingly, 'At no moment during the conflict did the embargo or other economic and financial sanctions modify in any way the decision of the Argentine authorities to defend the sovereignty of the islands.'[2]

Ironically Argentina's main difficulties in securing useful allies during the war occurred within the United Nations and most significantly in Latin America. One of the diplomatic calculations which lay behind the invasion of the islands was that most Third World major powers like the Soviet Union and China, and some European countries like Spain would vote against any British-led resolution. But the Soviet Union, China and Spain abstained within the Security Council, and many Third World countries fell short of offering the unqualified support for Argentina's 'liberation from colonial rule' that the junta had hoped for.

Panama's argument at the United Nations that any military counter-attack by Britain would inevitably line up Latin American armies behind the Argentines consciously echoed the nineteenth-century regional projection of the great liberator, General San Martín. Peru and Venezuela offered a limited amount of military and economic support. Among the Latin countries Peru was the most actively pro-Argentine during the Falklands War. Senior Peruvian military officers, including the army chief General Cisneros, had trained in Argentine military academies and maintained close professional and personal ties with their Argentine counterparts. In strategic terms, both Peru and Argentina shared a deep suspicion of Chile's military intentions and believed that General Pinochet might use the Falklands War to boost his territorial claims in both the Andean region and Patagonia. Peru sent ten Hercules transport planes to Argentina soon after the British Task Force had set sail in April 1982. From the outset the Peruvian military, particularly the air force, were in favour of sending more equipment and men but were initially restrained by their civilian President, Fernando Belaunde Terry. He believed strongly in pushing for a diplomatic solution to the conflict. Following the failure of his peace initiative (after the sinking of the *General Belgrano*) Belaunde's room for manoeuvre became limited. Although Peru remained active at the

United Nations, its support for Argentina became increasingly expressed in military terms once the Argentine air force began to suffer heavy losses. On 22 May, Peru sent ten Mirage fighter planes – part of a squadron normally stationed near the Ecuadorian frontier – to the southern Argentine air base of Comodoro Rivadavia. Peru also stepped up its supply of ground crew and munitions, including Exocet missiles.[3]

Brazil, one of Latin America's major military powers, supported Argentina's sovereignty claim but refused to condone the invasion. Behind the façade of solidarity expressed at forums like the Organisation of American States, Brazil conducted its own trade and financial business with Britain and Europe very much as usual, and even moved in to capture Argentina's lost trading outlets in products like corned beef. Equal duplicity was shown by Chile, which throughout the war offered constant logistical and military support to the Task Force, putting its own navy and troops on standby near the Argentine-Chilean border.

Chile had no doubt that the Argentine invasion of the Falklands formed part of the junta's territorial ambitions, and from the outset of the conflict worked on the assumption (based on its own intelligence assessments) that an Argentine victory over the British would be quickly followed up by an occupation of the Chilean-owned islands in the Beagle Channel – historically disputed by Argentina. Following the invasion the Chilean armed forces were put on full alert: the navy moved most of its surface ships to the south, and the army reinforced its presence at key points along the Andean border with Argentina. Under the terms of an agreement negotiated by the British Ambassador to Santiago, John Heath, and the Chilean military, Britain was allowed the use of Punta Arenas, an air base in southern Chile, for RAF planes disguised in Chilean markings. Punta Arenas is also believed to have been a point of departure for SAS special forces engaged in espionage activities against Argentine air force bases on the mainland.

Throughout the war Britain and Chile are believed to have exchanged intelligence including monitoring and code breaking of Argentine signals. The Argentine navy remains convinced that Chile was instrumental in helping the British Task Force to track down the *General Belgrano* and that this forms part of the information withheld from the British Parliament by Mrs Thatcher.[4]

The predominant consideration of Argentina's Latin American neighbours appears to have been the possible future direction of Argentine foreign policy. They feared that any vindication of Argentina's military exploits in the Falklands might tempt Buenos Aires to deal with its neighbours in a similar way, particularly as both Chile and Brazil had always been involved in territorial disputes of their own. Reinforcing this apprehension was the nature of Argentina's military regime, which over the previous years had shown little hesitation in crossing borders in pursuit of its objectives. There was also a more deep-rooted lack of trust in the self-conscious land of the gauchos which, for all its talk of San Martín and regional unity, had always looked towards the United States and Europe for inspiration.

The junta for its part had boasted of invincibility on the assumption that the invasion would not develop into a full-scale confrontation. Privately Argentine military strategists knew from the beginning that a full-scale war could risk the destruction of the Argentine navy and the bulk of the air force. Caught in the popular euphoria it had created at the outset, the junta was nevertheless unable to modify its strategy accordingly. For, just as the invasion had saved the regime, any admission of the prospect of defeat or a climb-down over the islands risked precipitating the collapse of military rule. Thus irrationality was to build on irrationality as the junta struggled to save itself, sacrificing its principles and a nation's sense of identity in the process.

Of the many diplomatic expressions of goodwill and solidarity that were delivered to the Foreign Ministry's Palacio de San Martín in the first forty-eight hours after the invasion, few were greeted with such a degree of initial caution by the junta than the short, passionate speech by Mohamed Khalifa Rhaiam, the Chargé d'Affaires of the People's Republic of Libya.

'We are ideological enemies of Great Britain because we have suffered British colonialism,' said Rhaiam. 'We believe in the relations between peoples and not between governments. That is why we want to express our full solidarity with the Argentine people's anti-imperialist struggle.'

Rhaiam's visit came soon after Britain's diplomatic victory at the United Nations Security Council and thus at a moment when Buenos Aires was anxiously looking around for new friends to bolster its flagging cause. The junta, however, was not totally converted – not yet at least. The Argentine military knew that Rhaiam did not accurately reflect his government's position. From the moment Argentine troops had set foot on Falklands soil, Tripoli had taken an uncharacteristically objective view of the conflict. With the exception of an occasional piece of inflammatory rhetoric, the local news-papers published reports on events from both the Argentine and British perspective, giving equal attention to both. Official government statements were few and far between and, when they were made, restricted to measured generalities.

The invasion had coincided with a boom in British–Libyan relations and there seemed to be little willingness on either side to upset this. The memory of the expropriation of British oil companies and of Libya's crusading price war with OPEC had faded with the advent of a growing interchange in research and development in areas ranging from aviation to sewage. In Tripoli there was a working population of close to 10,000 British expatriates spread through more than 100 representative and full company offices and factories.

A year before, the United States had broken off diplomatic relations with Libya over what it alleged was mounting evidence of Colonel Qadafi's support for international terrorism. This, however, did not dissuade Mrs Thatcher from sending to Tripoli a long line of officials and businessmen keen on cementing what one British diplomat described to me as a 'co-operative and warm relationship'. Co-operation and warmth flowed from one country to the other and back again. In Britain a 7,000-strong Libyan community was enjoying the kind of hospitality denied to Spaniards and Jamaicans. Over 2,000 Libyan students were studying at British universities and places of higher education, and at Gatwick and Oxford an élite group of 250 were being trained as aircraft technicians and pilots. Less visible but equally enthusiastic were the efforts of British arms manufacturers to carve themselves out a convenient niche in the Arab world, rivalling the Italians, the French and the Soviets. Arms contracts then already signed or in the process of negotiation included the supply to Libya of British-made electronic and com-munications equipment as well as 'non-killing parts for armoured cars' – a classification used before to excuse the delivery of arma-ments to such politically sensitive client states as Chile and El Salvador. All three countries shared their willingness to buy British, thus bypassing the evidence thrown up by Amnesty International of human rights violations.

By contrast Argentina's military regime's experience of Qadafi had not been an entirely happy one. Qadafi's support for international terrorism had in the mid-1970s spread to Latin America, aiding the very guerrilla movements which men like Galtieri had made their military careers fighting against. The Montoneros and the Ejercito Revolucionario del Pueblo (ERP), the two Argentine guerrilla organisations at the forefront of the opposition to the military, had turned to the Middle East for political, moral and logistical support once their leaders had been forced into exile. The Montonero leader Mario Firmenich had been photographed in Qadafi's desert tent, shaking hands and smiling broadly in apparent evidence of a newly forged alliance. Following the 1976 coup the relationship between the Argentine extreme left and the Socialist International deteriorated as leaders like Felipe González of Spain saw the spectre of terrorism looming over their own democratic horizons and the links of ETA, the Basque guerrilla organisation, with Libya. Qadafi filled the gap, offering to act as a willing conduit for false documentation, travel expenses and arms, not only for the Montoneros and the ERP but also for guerrilla movements in Central America, at a time when Argentine military officers were becoming increasingly involved as surrogates for the United States.

In spite of this recent background, the Argentine military was not entirely united in its attitude towards Libya on the day that Rhaiam came with his diplomatic greetings. Captain Benito Moya, a member of the presidential entourage and one of Galtieri's closest advisers, was only one of several officers who advised caution rather than outright rejection of the Libyan diplomat's approach.

'We'll pact with the devil if the pressure of events so determine,' Moya is alleged to have confessed to a journalist as the war entered its main phase in May.

During the repression, the military had consistently argued that the ends justified the means. So it was that when the Falklands War broke out men like Moya stressed that what was important was to consolidate the political achievement of getting back the islands – the manner in which this was done was secondary. Thus with the peculiar rewrite of history at which the Argentines were particularly adept, Moya's military sector happily ignored Libya's connection with left-wing terrorism and instead resurrected the figure of the late General Juan Perón.

During the last Perón government (1973–6) sectors of the military had secretly supported a complex web of business links with Libya, particularly in the arms and oil trade. There is at least circumstantial evidence suggesting that this alliance was forged under the aegis of Licio Gelli, the head of the outlawed Italian Masonic Lodge Propaganda-Due. Gelli was one of two Italians who accompanied Perón, his third wife Isabelita, and the future Minister for Social Welfare, José López Rega, on his triumphant return from exile in Madrid in June 1973. The other was Giancarlo Elia Valori, an entrepreneur with strong links with Libya. During the transatlantic journey, Valori was overheard in conversation with Perón, advising the President-to-be that one of his first acts should be the granting of Argentina's highest diplomatic honour, the Order of San Martín, to Gelli for 'services rendered to the nation'. Perón complied.[5]

Subsequently Perón made Argentina's relations with the Arab world, and in particular Libya, one of the priorities of his foreign policy. As he had when he first came to power in 1946, Perón publicly defended his 'third position'. Theoretically this signified a repudiation of the two imperialisms represented by the United States and the Soviet Union and its replacement by a dogged non-alignment. In practice this meant the exploitation of antagonisms between the two superpowers whenever these arose so as to allow Argentina to consolidate its aspirations to regional leadership in alliance with the Third World. To this extent Qadafi provided Perón, and any Argentine military officers who wished to imitate him, with a mirror image. Although Qadafi's 'bible', the 'Green Book', favours a people's democracy rather than a corporate State, it conveys a strong commitment to non-alignment and nationalism as a fundamental tool in dealings with the rest of the world. Moreover, while religion clearly could not unite the Catholic with the fanatic Muslim, military sentiment could: both Perón and Qadafi owed their rise to power to the uniform and to a plot organised by young officers. By the time of Perón's return from exile, little effort was required to translate mutual ideological respect into a more practical marriage of convenience.

Perón believed that oil was playing an increasingly crucial role in international relations. He calculated that this factor, taken together with the spread of Islam at the expense of Communism, had given Qadafi a strategic importance which far outstripped the size of his country. The reality in fact was rather different, since even at that early stage there was more bluff than power in Qadafi. Falling oil demand from the Western world due to zero growth and the greater availability of tankers had from 1974 onwards begun to make Libya's geographic position less important and to bring about a decline in the country's impact as the spearhead of a militant drive to raise oil prices. Moreover, Libya's good relations with Arab states, particularly Egypt, had begun to deteriorate from about the time of the Arab–Israeli war in October 1973. While in public Qadafi spoke boldly of a mighty Arab nation that would eclipse the West in power and purity, he was in fact failing to win over Arab governments to pan-Arabism and resorting instead behind the scenes to erratic 'cowboy' diplomacy, providing so-called 'liberation struggles' with bases, weapons, money and diplomatic cover.

Thus just as in 1946, when Perón convinced himself that the Third World would emerge supreme from an imminent holocaust involving the superpowers, 1973 found Argentina once again embarked on an exercise in diplomatic self-delusion. The newly forged Argentine–Libyan alliance made its public appearance in August 1973, two months after Perón's return from exile, in a meeting involving Ibrahim Ibijad, the Director General of Libya's information services. Emerging from the talks, Ibijad praised Perón's leadership of the Third World in extravagant terms. A few days later Perón returned the gesture during a rally organised by the main trade union federation, the General Confederation of Labour (CGT). The Argentine leader spoke enthusiastically about the Arab world's determination to use its control of the bulk of the world's oil reserves to confront the United States and warned that unless the Third World united, Latin American countries would run the risk of being invaded and 'plundered' by the West.

Perón's inauguration as President a month later brought about the formal establishment of diplomatic links between Argentina and Libya, and Argentina became one of only three Latin American countries, along with Cuba and Allende's Chile, to attend a conference of Heads of State of the non-aligned movement in Algiers. By the New Year, Argentine relations with Libya were reported in the local press as having never been better. The collected works of Perón, translated into Arabic, were being generously distributed by the Libyan Information Ministry in Tripoli, while the Argentine government gave its blessing to the sale of Qadafi's manifesto in the book stores and on the news stands of Buenos Aires. On the diplomatic circuit receptions held by Arab representatives including Libya became the most lavish and politically best attended, with an impressive array of media people, politicians, businessmen and Generals making an appearance.

On the more concrete level, the exact scope and scale of Argentina's Libyan connection was maintained a closely guarded secret, filtering only occasionally on to the pages of the local press. In January 1974, an Argentine mission, made up of businessmen and traders with close contacts with López Rega, returned from a three-month visit to Libya only to announce that progress had been made in forging links between the two countries. It took the Argentine press more than a year to pinpoint what most observers suspected of being only the tip of the iceberg in Argentina's Libyan connection: the sale of over three million tonnes of Libyan oil in exchange for agricultural products and various investments in agrobusiness in a trade transaction worth nearly a quarter of a billion dollars. Allegations at the time spoke of a web of intrigue and corruption, involving many more millions of dollars in triangular business deals, capital transfers, commissions and kickbacks of one kind or another. But the only trade transaction officially documented involved a 200-million-dollar wheat-for-oil deal towards the end of 1975. In one of the most publicised commercial scandals in Argentina for many years, it was disclosed that the Argentine wheat had arrived in Tripoli damp and rotting, while the bulk of the oil, classified as 'high quality crude', had turned up mixed with sea water.

By the time of the Falklands invasion, the memory of the Libyan connection had been anaesthetised from the collective conscience. But deeply entrenched vested interests remained ready to rekindle the relationship once the pressure of events and Qadafi's peculiar style of diplomacy permitted it. For most of the month of April, the junta reinforced the islands militarily, while at the same time gambling on a diplomatic breakthrough that would turn the British Task Force round and consolidate the Argentine presence on the islands. Following the outbreak of hostilities on 1 May – when British Vulcan bombers attacked Stanley airport – and the subsequent sinking of the *General Belgrano* – the junta changed its tack. Diplomacy wavered, logistical considerations became more important and the search for military allies took precedence over ideology.

Outside Argentina, there were predictable statements of protest from Latin American governments, caution in Washington and Moscow, and ambiguity in Europe – support for Britain in Spain, Italy and France weakened, while Ireland turned outright hostile. But the most dramatic change came in Libya, where Qadafi not only stepped up his anti-colonialist diatribes but decided to follow this with concrete action.

On 15 May 1982, six men sat down to lunch in the main restaurant at Madrid's Barajas airport before catching a Libyan airline flight to Tripoli. Dressed in impeccably tailor-made suits, and holding only attaché cases, the six looked indistinguishable from the numerous Spanish and European middle-aged executives on their way to various worldwide destinations. Apparently undetected by either

British or Spanish intelligence, the group formed part of a special mission sent by General Galtieri to negotiate a series of arms deals with Qadafi to help Argentina's increasingly desperate war effort. The group was composed of two army officers, an air force Brigadier, and the Rector of the Catholic University of Tucuman, a Jesuit priest called Anibal Fosberry, who before the 1976 coup had been a strong supporter of López Rega. The mission was led by Rear-Admiral Moya and Mohamed Khalifa Rhaiam.

When, a few hours later, the Libyan airline flight from Madrid touched down at Tripoli airport, Qadafi was temporarily absent from his country in secret talks with the Syrians related to the recent Israeli invasion of Lebanon. But the Libyan leader had left instructions that the Argentine delegation be given VIP treatment normally accorded to foreign Heads of State. The Argentines were received in the luxurious people's palace by Major Abdel Salam Jalloud, the country's Vice President, acting Prime Minister, member of the revolutionary junta and close aide of Qadafi, who in previous years had roamed the world securing alliances and arms contracts. In spite of the initial courtesies, the meeting very nearly came to an abrupt end. Having confirmed Libya's willingness to offer all the political and moral support that Argentina needed, Jalloud told the delegation that Argentina's military requirements would require further study before a final decision was taken. At this Moya interrupted and with an angry voice said, 'I haven't come all the way to Libya to deliver a list for "study". In my country soldiers are dying and this fact doesn't seem to move you.'

Within two days the delegation had left Tripoli, having being reassured that they would get most if not all of what they were asking for. The Argentine shopping list is believed to have included 120 SAM-7 shoulder-handled anti-aircraft missiles, twenty Magic Matra air-to-air missiles for use in Mirage fighter planes, and an assortment of light artillery, mortars, munitions and infra-red night-vision scopes for sniper rifles. These arms were considered by the Argentine army and air force as essential if they were to match with any success the increasing technological sophistication of the British Task Force, which had been brought about thanks to the Americans. But the most important addition to the list was a plea for as many Exocets as the Libyans could muster, either from their own stock or from the black market, where Libyan arms dealers had excellent contacts. The French-built missile had been used to devastating effect against the British Type 42 destroyer HMS *Sheffield* in retaliation for the sinking of the *General Belgrano* on 4 May. But the Argentine military's direct access to replacements had been stemmed by the French arms embargo. Moya and company now looked to Qadafi for perhaps the one piece of naval armoury that could dramatically alter the course of the war.

Between 20 May and the end of the Falklands War, six reconditioned Argentine Airlines Boeing 707s flew on a regular supply run between Buenos Aires and Tripoli. Although delivery of some of the equipment was held up for most of the war because of inadequate co-ordination in the transport between the mainland and the islands, the Libyan connection sustained the Argentine military effort against the British. And yet British diplomatic reaction to the Buenos Aires–Tripoli axis was cautious in the extreme. Drawing on US signals intelligence and its own network of spies among the European expatriate community in Tripoli, the British Embassy had detected the air bridge from the moment military and civilian personnel had started loading the first Argentine 707 with crates in the military section of Tripoli's international airport. The matter was raised discreetly by the British Ambassador in a meeting with a member of the Revolutionary Council. The Ambassador was told that the 707s were transporting crates of bananas and apples as part of a trade agreement between the two countries.

For the rest of the war, the British government made no attempt to draw public attention to what it had no doubt was the supply of arms by Libya to Argentina. At a diplomatic level, the issue was raised only once when one of the planes made a stop over in Morocco. Britain's main concern appears to have been to maintain its commercial relations with Libya and to prevent any move against Tripoli that would escalate the war with Argentina. In spite of the damage caused by Libyan arms to the British Task Force, the calculation in London was that any confrontation with Qadafi would only increase the potential for destruction. The one exception to this general policy of laissez-faire towards Libya concerned the Exocet. Active diplomatic work appears to have focused on convincing the French not to supply Libya with the missile and on preventing any other intermediaries in the arms trade from helping out Argentina.

The full history of Argentina's attempts to secure the Exocet may never be fully known. However, the scope and scale of the military's desperation to equip itself was hinted at in November 1984 when an Italian judge closed a four-year investigation into what was described as the biggest world arms and drugs trafficking organisation. A list of the thirty-seven men implicated included Italian politicians, businessmen and three Arabs. Among the Italians was the former head of the military intelligence service SISMI, Giuseppe Santovito, who was perhaps little more than a piece in a complex network involving his organisation in Libya and the attempted provision to Argentina of fifty-two Exocets.[6]

Two years later one of Santovito's colleagues declared in an interview with an Italian magazine that the Italian secret services had had as their highest priority in the Middle East the protection of Italy's substantial economic interests and thus had been more than willing to defend Qadafi from his enemies and provide him with arms. In addition, throughout the 1970s Qadafi was the recipient of virtually a constant supply of sophisticated weaponry from the Soviet Union. The resulting armoury made Libya by the early 1980s the Arab country with the highest ratio of military equipment to manpower in the Third World.

Argentina had first joined the list of clients for Libyan arms export in 1975, a year in which an increasingly militarised Argentine society was seeking to re-equip itself with an eye on its territorial claims to the Falklands and the Beagle Channel. Encouraged by reports from Buenos Aires indicating that Anglo–Argentine relations had reached a particularly low point over the Shackleton incident, Qadafi had sent a letter through a special emissary offering the then Perónist government two squadrons of Mirages recently purchased from France. The offer was never formally accepted by the Perón government, but it was kept in an archive by a close confidant of Perón and resurrected during the Falklands War as evidence of Qadafi's potential usefulness as an ally.

Following the sinking of the *General Belgrano*, the Libyan leader needed no further encouragement to tempt him into a more direct involvement in the Falklands conflict. Washington's decision to give logistical and military support to the Task Force put the conflict into a different strategic dimension, which the Libyan calculated – wrongly as it turned out – would inevitably involve the Soviet Union and the whole of the Third World. It was the kind of scenario Qadafi had always treasured. In many respects Libya's *rapprochement* with the Argentine military had striking parallels with Qadafi's earlier wooing of Dom Mintoff in Malta. If, as Churchill once said, Malta was the only unsinkable aircraft carrier in the Mediterranean, then Qadafi must have felt he had found its perfect equivalent in the South Atlantic.

As far as Argentina was concerned the history of the Libyan connection once again showed up the underlying continuity between Perón and subsequent military regimes. What to many statesmen would have been an unacceptable risk to world peace – involving Qadafi as an ally – to the junta became a necessary factor in its self-deluded quest for international recognition and territorial conquest. Libyan Exocets never made it to Argentina. Had British diplomacy and intelligence not been so successful in securing alliances and exposing intermediaries, the outcome of the Falklands War might have been different. The Libyan connection does, moreover, have an important postscript. Qadafi's involvement in the Falklands War, although tolerated initially by Whitehall, was to colour Mrs Thatcher's relations with Libya following the conflict. Evidence of arms supplies to the Galtieri junta, like the evidence of supplies to the IRA, strained Britain's pragmatism. Although it was never alluded to in public, it must have been at the back of Mrs Thatcher's mind when in April 1986, almost exactly four years after the outbreak of the Falklands War, she fell in four-square behind the unprecedented US bombing of Tripoli.

At the height of the Falklands War, once what had begun in South Georgia had developed into a major military clash involving the destruction of planes and ships and the death of soldiers, Britain is believed to have considered an attack on the Argentine mainland to neutralise the growing possibility that a leading NATO member might suffer irrevocable military humiliation at the hands of a Third World military power. The option, which would have involved several contingencies including a series of commando raids on military targets as well as a nuclear attack on the northern city of Cordóba – heart of one of Argentina's most productive industrial regions – was discounted in favour of a more contained operation in and around the islands. The most daring exploit on the Argentine mainland is understood to have involved a group of the SAS. At the time the British Ministry of Defence let out an official story that a British Sea King helicopter belonging to the Task Force had lost its way in bad weather and crash-landed near the Chilean port of Punta Arenas. The 'pilot and his crew' had subsequently handed themselves over to the Chilean authorities. There was nevertheless much press speculation that the helicopter had been on its way from landing an SAS 'aircraft watch' party near the Argentine air base of Rio Gallegos. This version was subsequently confirmed by Rear-Admiral Horacio Zaratieguí, the commander of the naval base of Ushuaia and in charge of reconnaissance in the area. Zaratieguí swore that the helicopter was tracked by Argentine radar, and that it landed momentarily in a private farm near Río Gallegos before taking off again in the direction of the Chilean border. The only undisputed facts about this bizarre episode were that the SAS were never found and no Argentine base was ever destroyed.

Thatcher is believed to have been convinced by Washington and some of her own officials that, as with Libya, there was a need not to do anything that would provoke an escalation of the conflict. The sinking of the *General Belgrano* altered the diplomatic balance, which until then had been unanimously in favour of Britain; to have bombed the Argentine mainland would have run the risk of tempting other Latin American governments to become more actively involved militarily, thus giving the conflict a continental dimension of unforeseeable consequences for Southern and Central America.

Argentina's military junta appears to have shared no such reservations. A regime that had sacrificed over 8,000 civilians – many of them innocent men, women and children – for the sake of its defence of 'Western civilisation' against the advance of international Marxism – showed itself quite willing as the war progressed to implicate the rest of the world in its heroic 'reconquest' of 'Las Malvinas'. The Libyan connection was one plank of this strategy; the other was a contingency plan to strike at British military targets in Europe. The latter, like the attempt to purchase additional Exocets, was successfully intercepted. But it is worth recording if only as a reminder of the extent of the junta's ideological confusion and how close it came to turning the Falklands débâcle into total war.

The sinking of the *General Belgrano* on 2 May by the British nuclear submarine, HMS *Conqueror*, forced Admiral Anaya, the Argentine navy chief, radically to alter his strategy. The surface fleet, which had been harassing the Task Force, was ordered back to port and kept there for the rest of the war. While navy front-line aircraft remained operational, less conventional methods of hitting back at the British were adopted by Anaya, who was now desperate for revenge. From early May onwards the navy's crack commando squadron – the *buzos tácticos* – was ordered to form special units capable of undertaking kamikaze-type suicide missions against selected targets on the European mainland. The exact composition of these units is still surrounded by considerable mystery, but according to several sources the *buzos* worked closely with former members of the Montoneros, the Perónist guerrilla organisation who were experts in sabotage.

This was not the first time the navy had shown itself willing to make an ally of a former sworn enemy. As recently investigated by one of Argentina's most prestigious journalists, Horacio Verbitsky, a number of Montonero prisoners collaborated with navy officers in formulating highly nationalistic, geopolitical considerations about the future of the Falklands in the late 1970s.[7] Among the ideas shared by captors and captives alike was that the military should aim to revive the spirit of San Martín and defend the nation's legitimate aspirations. Anaya's predecessor, Admiral Emilio Massera, is also believed to have held a secret meeting with Montonero exiled leaders in Paris, at which the junta member proposed the release of political prisoners. In return Massera asked for an end to the Montonero's terrorist offensive against the regime and a pledge of Perónist support for his future presidential candidacy. Subsequently a number of Montonero prisoners were released to act as informers.

At the outbreak of the Falklands War, a group of Montonero exiles volunteered to charter a plane in Paris and go and fight alongside Argentine conscripts on the Falklands. The offer was turned down by the Argentine Embassy, but the potential usefulness of these experts in terrorism was never forgotten by the navy.

On 31 May 1982, two Spanish detectives swooped on a car-hire agency office in the tourist capital of Málaga. Inside were two Argentine nationals who in the previous few days had been observed moving between office, apartment and shops spending lavishly in cash, mainly dollars. Their extravagance was brought to the notice of the Spanish police, who immediately suspected the pair of belonging to one of the many drug and robbery rings which dot Spain's 'Costa del Crime'. But the suspects turned out to be more extraordinary than that after an initial questioning: 'I am Naval Lieutenant Fernández of the Argentine navy and I have come to Spain on a special and secret mission for the intelligence services of my country. From this moment on I consider myself a prisoner of war and I am not going to say another word.'[8]

The detectives subsequently identified the two men's living quarters – a hotel in the nearby town of San Roque. There they found two more Argentines and four magnetic mines stashed in plastic bags. The Spanish police next located a car hired by the group, containing sophisticated sub-aqua equipment, torches, a small horse-powered engine and a rubber dinghy. Much to its embarrassment the Spanish government, in the course of further investigations by its own military intelligence, established that the four men belonged to a commando unit which had arrived in Spain from various capital cities on a special mission to blow up two British

Task Force ships temporarily stationed in the port of Gibraltar. The Spanish authorities have since drawn a veil over an incident that, had it not been discovered, would have seriously compromised Spain's position within the EEC and NATO. Three weeks before the arrest of the Argentines, one of Madrid's right-wing newspapers *El Alcázar* had run a front-page 'proclamation' in support of the junta. Elsewhere less extreme representatives of the Spanish media had conducted an unhesitatingly biased pro-Argentine campaign. Sabotage of the Task Force ships would have raised the suspicion in British eyes of military collusion between Spain and Argentina because of their common claims to Gibraltar and the 'Malvinas'.

Before their expulsion from Spanish soil, the three Argentines apart from Fernandez identified themselves to the local police as Sergeant Godoy, and soldiers Madana and González. These names, along with Fernández, seem to have been false however, perhaps with the deliberate intention not only of saving the unit for further raids, but also, for political reasons, of hiding the presence in the group of members of the Montonero organisation.[9] Significantly the contingency plan for Operation Gibraltar was a virtual carbon copy of one of the Montoneros' most notorious acts of sabotage against the military in 1974. In an operation meticulously planned by a unit which had studied in detail and then adapted the lessons drawn from the Second World War underwater attacks of British and Italian commandos, the Montoneros infiltrated the navy's main shipyard in Ensenada and blew up the 3,500-ton modern missile-carrying frigate, the *Santisima Trinidad*. Ironically a Montonero statement afterwards justified the bombing by urging the navy to abandon its ties with Britain and concentrate on the 'Malvinas' instead. The *Santisima Trinidad* had been built by the British at a time when Argentine navy officers still wore black stripes on their trouser legs in memory of Nelson's death.

6
THE REGIMENTED SOCIETY

In a democracy the actions of government, in time of war as much as in time of peace, come under constant scrutiny. In Thatcher's Britain, where an attempt was made to neutralise Parliament and the press behind a common patriotic cause, the voice of dissent was kept alive, forcing defence chiefs and troop commanders constantly to justify their actions. In Kennedy and Johnson's United States it was the images flashed on TV and the outspokenness of churchmen that helped to quicken the end of the Vietnam War.

The Argentina of the juntas which, for the sake of its patriotic cause, befriended Qadafi and exported the State terrorism of an earlier dirty war of military heroes and 'disappeared', had no such checks and balances. Military history and the politics of repression had regimented society to such an extent that no distinction was made between the cause and the means; war was celebrated with the fanaticism of a football match played in torrential rain. The obsession with victory blurred and distorted the identity of the main players.

Just as had occurred in the Perón years, during various stages in military government, and in particular following the 1976 coup, a key element in this process was the Catholic Church: the symbiosis between Church and State gave the soldiers a sense of moral crusade and the junta the certainty of political cohesion. This was apparent from the first day of the war, when the commanding officer of the invasion forces, Rear-Admiral Carlos Busser, agreed to rename Operation Azul with the legend Operation Rosario.[1] The feast of the Virgin of Rosario was established in 1573 by Pope Gregory XIII to commemorate the crushing defeat of the Turks by the troops led by Don John of Austria. Busser had no doubt that the infidel, personified by the kelpers and seventy-odd British marines, was about to suffer an equally Virgin-sent defeat.

The equation between Argentine sovereignty and holy conversion had its precedent, and is deeply engrained in the national consciousness. Argentine history books devote many pages to the first Spanish missionaries to the Falkland Islands and their Argentine successors; the priests are portrayed as picture-book saints laying their sacramental rock in the heathen land. What is perceived as a subsequent decline of civilised life on the islands is blamed on the spiritual emptiness of British colonialism.[2] Building on this tradition, the junta and its collaborators expanded the concept of the conversion so that the invasion and its aftermath was presented to the population and the outside world as a holy war where everything was permitted for the sake of the cause. Thus, just as Bishops and priests had lent their tacit blessing to the defence of 'Western Christian values' during the repression of political dissidence, they now established the theological validity of 'Las Malvinas'.

'The gaucho Virgin is Mother of all men, but is in a very special way the Mother of all Argentines, and has come to take possession of this land, which is also her land.'[3]

Thus did Monsignor Desiderio Elso Collino bless a statue of the Virgin of Lujan, along with eight crucifixes, some five Generals, party leaders, trade unionists, and an estimated 6,000 to 10,000 troops on 7 April, when Argentina's military Governor, General Mario Benjamín Menéndez, formally took charge of the Falkland Islands. The junta's propaganda machinery made a point of contrasting the venerable nature of the ceremony with the 'immoral' vestiges of British rule: newspapers had made much of the 'barbarism' of the British marine barracks. The media had reported, with a sense of moral outrage, that the barracks had been filled with pornographic magazines and videos.

For the rest of the war a succession of military chaplains, taking their cue from Monsignor Collino, ensured that the crusading spirit was kept alive in language reminiscent of the speeches delivered to Franco's forces during the Spanish Civil War. In the fight against the infidel no churchman was perhaps more fanatic than Fr Jorge Piccinalli, a young priest who arrived on the islands on 24 April to boost troop morale in the face of the growing awareness that the war might be for real. In an interview with the Argentine TV journalist Nicolas Kasanzew soon after his arrival, Piccinalli said that the time had come for Argentina to have some real heroes. 'No, I'm not talking about footballers, I mean heroism in the Greek sense of the word,' he told Kasanzew.'[4]

While other chaplains left either because of exhaustion or because they were not crusading enough, Piccinalli stayed until the bitter end, riding through the troop encampments on a motorcycle and sharing their trenches, comforting his heroes by blessing death. Of his many sermons one deserves to be quoted at length. There can be no better illustration of the uses to which religion can be put at a time of war:

We the Argentine people who are Catholic, Hispanic and Roman, have today ensured the reconquest of a piece of territory on behalf of the Nation. A Nation that has Christianity in its origins . . . It is a great honour to be here, an immeasurable honour. We have to see it as a war fought for the defence of our Nation and for Jesus Christ. We have to take in our hands the Holy Rosary and commend ourselves to the Holiest Virgin who is always going to be with us. Because this fatherland has been consecrated by the Virgin of Lujan. And the Virgin of Lujan and the Virgin of Rosario are going to protect us, you can be certain of that. And that rosary which you have round your necks and in your hands is a great instrument. It is a great defence because it is the defence of the spirit against matter . . . That is why we have to put our trust fully in God, totally in Christ, totally in the holiest Virgin, queen and lady of 'Las Malvinas', which is now Argentine territory . . .[5]

From that moment on pilots hung rosaries round their sights before shooting their missiles at the British Task Force, bits of Harrier jets were dedicated to the Virgin of Lujan, soldiers carried bibles to protect themselves from bullets, and military chaplains broadcast regularly to the Argentine mainland proclaiming their troops first as heroes and then as saints.[6] Their beatitude was invoked not so much because of the very real suffering most conscripts were going through but because of their alleged courage in taking on the atheistic hordes from the north. On the mainland the theme was taken up by *Esquiu*, the Catholic weekly, which throughout the war was sold aggressively inside and outside churches up and down the country. One cover story showed a picture of two human arms, one tattooed with the British flag, the other with the Argentine, wrestling over a map of the Falklands, and the caption 'More power to you, Argentina'. It was accompanied by a map of Argentina surrounded by a rosary and the slogan, 'We have a powerful weapon.' The centre page was taken up by an editorial entitled 'Our Advantage', written by Monsignor Manuel Menéndez, Bishop of San Martín.

'We Catholics fight for peace, but we also know that the Fourth Commandment tells us to love our country, and, if necessary, give up our lives for it. In the present circumstances, the commandment is quite clear: if they attack us, we have to defend ourselves,' the Bishop wrote, conveniently forgetting the fact of the invasion.[7]

A year earlier, sensing the winds of change, the traditionally conservative Bishops' Episcopal Conference had ended its acquiescence with the military regime and demanded a return to law and democracy. The Bishops' sharp criticism and their call for a 'new and moral order' ushered in a period of increased opposition to the regime from outlawed parties and the unions. Following the invasion of the Falklands, however, the conference diluted all criticism of the regime. The Bishops postponed a follow-up statement on Argentine politics and society, and concentrated instead on the 'Malvinas'. 'Argentina has recovered its sovereignty over the islands with the right that it has been demanding for 149 years,' the conference stated. In common with the bulk of politicians and the unions, the Church's view was that the Falklands was a national issue which was above domestic political considerations, even human rights. Bishops and priests showed themselves particularly adept in defending Argentina from charges that the military invasion on 2 April was a flagrant violation of the islanders' right to self-determination and property, and international rules of law, even though these were the views expressed by many non-Argentine Catholics. The Argentine Church, however, not only blessed the occupation, but refused to acknowledge that human rights were an issue. 'All Argentines, in church and out, believe our cause is just. I think that the good God is content with this faith of ours,' commented Fr Augustín Luchia Puig, editor of *Esquiu*.

The fact that the invasion was indeed carried out bloodlessly, and that subsequently the bulk of government propaganda concentrated on alleged 'atrocities' committed by the British Task Force, strengthened the Church's moral judgment in the public eye. The combination of a perceived historical justification and the spotless way in which the 2 April invasion was carried out, allowed the Argentine Church to rally the faithful around the Christian concept of a 'just defence' in its backing for the Argentine armed forces.

During Sunday Masses, priests dedicated their sermons to a call for generous contributions to the 'Patriotic Fund', which was collected by the military for their war effort although never publicly accounted for. In their only major joint statement during the war, the Bishops expressed their fear of a 'war of unforeseeable consequences', and referred to papal condemnation of military conflict. However, by their emphasis on defence of Argentina's sovereignty claims, the Bishops implicitly gave the green light to the junta to prolong its warmongering if it saw fit.

Significantly the few churchmen who refused to toe the official line were censored by the authorities and isolated just as they had been during the years of the repression. Bishops Novak and Nevares, both of whom had been outspoken critics of the junta's human rights record, wrote their own position papers prior to the Bishops'

Conference, recommending that the Church adopt a more explicitly pacifist line while at the same time maintaining its political distance from the regime. Novak warned that the moral, cultural and economic costs of the invasion could be irreparable. However courageous the action, he wrote, it lacked 'wisdom and prudence'. The papers were discarded by the hierarchy before they had even reached the conference table.

Adolfo Pérez Esquível, the 1980 winner of the Nobel prize for peace and a committed Catholic layman, was also ostracised by the authorities for taking a pacifist line. Somewhat ambiguous as to whether or not he felt human rights had been violated in the Falklands, Esquível was more openly critical about the way the invasion had been decided without any popular consultation. His opinions never reached the troops.[8]

Of somewhat greater influence on the islands was the local English Catholic Bishop, Monsignor Daniel Spraggon. From the moment the first Argentine marines set foot on the islands, he was a tower of strength among the kelpers, offering them encouragement and acting as a mediator with the Argentine authorities. His Sunday Masses, with the church doors always open to uniformed Argentines as much as to local civilians, were a symbol of Christian reconciliation. But the junta never forgave him for his outspoken condemnation of the invasion. For most of the war, Spraggon angered military chaplains and officers alike. With a few exceptions, most of the Argentines regarded Spraggon as a dangerous 'resistance' priest whom they would have preferred to have seen arrested and expelled from the islands.[9]

The Church's official position over the Falklands contrasted with the attitudes struck by the Bishops in Argentina's other outstanding territorial dispute – its challenge to Chile's claim over the Beagle Channel. In 1981 the Argentines joined Chilean Bishops in giving their full backing to a peace settlement in the dispute, and the Archbishop of Buenos Aires, Cardinal Aramburu, led a massive peace rally through the streets of the capital.

One of the main reasons for the Church's pacifism in the case of the Beagle Channel was that an influential sector of the military regime remained unconvinced of the convenience of fighting a war over it. Quite apart from the weak juridical arguments in favour of Argentina's claim, the Beagle was always seen as a naval preoccupation over which the army stood to gain little politically. On the contrary a war would destroy any chance of collaborating with President Pinochet in the fight against left-wing subversion. Another reason for the Bishops' attitude was that Vatican commitment to a mediation effort from 1978 onwards left them with few alternatives. The Vatican showed itself more ambivalent at the outset of the Falklands War. On the eve of the invasion, the papal nuncio in Buenos Aires, Monsignor Ubaldo Calabresi, failed to heed a desperate last-minute request from President Reagan to urge Galtieri to call off further military action. The nuncio was in bed when he received the call from Washington. He agreed to ring up the Foreign Minister Nicanor Costa Méndez. When he was told by the Minister's secretary that Costa Méndez was at a meeting and unavailable the nuncio went back to bed. Within hours Argentine troops had landed on the islands.

The Vatican subsequently found itself in a quandary over the Falklands which no amount of its characteristic diplomatic skill seemed for a time able to resolve. A historic visit to Britain by the Pope had been planned months previously, and the Vatican Curia had little wish to allow the war to undermine the prospect of progress towards ecumenicism that it implied. Even if it had wanted to offer its good offices for mediation, these would have almost certainly been rejected by Mrs Thatcher. Also the Vatican had to be careful to maintain its links with the junta for fear that any direct challenge to its policy would undermine the peace treaty over the Beagle.

If, as an American Senator pointed out more than half a century ago, truth is the first casualty of any war, there were many early victims in Argentina – and few of them soldiers. The media was as important as the Church in securing unquestioning support for the junta's campaign and, in the process, for prolonging the conflict. It was equally responsible for stimulating the extraordinary backlash against the regime that followed the surrender of Port Stanley. An obsession with winning was maintained throughout the conflict; but the media did nothing to prepare the nation for defeat. The shock was thus even greater.

The regimentation of Argentine society, as reflected in the media, was evident from the day Argentine troops invaded the islands. Newspapers, which forty-eight hours before had reported at some length on the brutal repression of a demonstration by trade unionists, instantly whitewashed any critical reference to the nature of the regime and joined in the mass euphoria. Political analysts who in previous weeks had diligently chronicled Galtieri's palace coup with veiled allusions to the symptoms of a regime in decline, now devoted themselves to a simple account of the military's 'glorious recovery' of the islands. History was instantly rewritten; memories of the junta's human rights record and economic problems suppressed and replaced with a carefully selected version of the run-up to the invasion and its aftermath. Anyone reading the local newspapers or watching the TV at the time would have been left in no doubt that the military occupation had been a last-minute defensive reaction to growing British hostility over the islands; no Argentine journalist attempted to investigate further back than the South Georgia incident and even those who in previous weeks 'predicted' the military consequences of the alleged diplomatic impasse now conveniently ignored the stringent last-minute efforts made by the United States and Britain to avert a military outcome. But perhaps most striking of all was the media's inability to place the invasion in a political context and to look beyond the euphoric early communiqués to a more realistic assessment of the international situation, particularly the reaction in Britain.

Such an omission set the tone for the rest of the campaign. In Britain there were Fleet Street newspapers like the *Daily Mirror* and the *Financial Times*, which, together with the British Broadcasting Corporation, adopted a balanced attitude towards the conflict – sometimes so 'balanced' as to attract accusations from their rivals and government officials of being too pro-Argentine. But in Argentina there was no such diversity of view. From beginning to end there was an eerie unison, in which the military was once again identified as the nation state. Typical of the double think was a front-page comment in the conservative *La Prensa* by the well-known journalist Jesús Iglesias Rouco.

> What we are talking about is no longer the survival of a specific military sector, or of a government, but the very integrity of the Nation and its short- and long-term future. The President could not have spoken to us at a more appropriate time, and his words have expressed points of view and feelings that are common to all us Argentines, and I include those who do not normally share his ideas, still less approve of his government or the regime he represents.[10]

Undoubtedly many Argentine journalists shared the sentiment expressed on the 'day of the journalist' – that every Argentine whatever his profession felt it his patriotic duty to support the recovery of the islands. But, just as there were ordinary Argentines who both at home and in exile were unable to separate their feelings over the war from their virulent disgust with the regime, there were also journalists who questioned the manner in which the invasion was carried out and predicted privately from the outset what they were certain would be a disastrous outcome. Unable or unwilling to express their views in their own newspapers or broadcasting channels, these 'dissidents' collaborated with the 'enemy' instead. As a result they earned more dollars in a week than they had previously done in a year acting as stringers, translators and general odd-jobmen for the visiting foreign journalists and international networks.

With a few notable exceptions the attitude of Argentine journalism was a mixture of unprofessionalism, cowardice and cynical opportunism.[11] Far from being an overnight response to a patriotic enterprise, the media reflected many years of conditioning in the context of Argentina's militarised political culture. During the Perón years, and following the 1976 coup, the media had been subjected to censorship and intimidation to such an extent as practically to eradicate the concept of a 'free press' in Argentina. The best journalists had either 'disappeared' or been forced into exile. There remained at least two generations of one-time writers who because of their willingness to compromise had lost all sense of objectivity: even during the worst period of human rights violations, truth became indistinguishable from official communiqués. The corollary of this was that any attempt to offer an alternative version of events was tantamount to treason, as subversive to the nation's well-being as the bomb placed under a General's car by a heavily armed guerrilla. This refusal to allow a free flow of information extended to a blanket dismissal of foreign press reports as anti-patriotic.[12]

The regime found little difficulty in transporting such a regimentation on to the Falklands stage. From the moment the British Task Force ventured forth, the Argentine Chiefs of Staff issued strict guidelines governing the media. For 'reasons of national security' journalists were advised to refrain from publishing any material that 'attacks national unity', 'provokes panic', 'helps the psychological objectives of the enemy', or 'gives information on military positions other than those officially confirmed'. It did not matter that at no stage during the Falklands War did official censors sit in on news desks; Argentine journalists, all experienced veterans of the politics of repression, were left with no doubt as to what the consequences for their physical well-being might be if they didn't play safe. As had occurred in the aftermath of the coup, the local English-language daily, the *Buenos Aires Herald*, proved an exception and a victim.

The *Herald* is not strictly a British newspaper. Sixty per cent of it is owned by the *Charleston Evening Post* of the United States and 40 per cent by an Argentine family. Its staff consists of a majority of local workers, who over the years have steered some of the pages away from a myopic interpretation of the British community and towards a more wide-ranging record of domestic and international affairs. And yet, so far as the military was concerned, the *Herald* on the eve of the Falklands invasion remained what it had been since its first issue in 1876: a mouthpiece for British maritime interests. Worse still it had a record of outspoken denunciation of human rights violations which had earned it a readership out of all proportion to its meagre resources.

On the day Argentine forces landed on the Falklands, the *Herald*'s editor, James Neilson, seemed nonplussed by the fact of becoming in that instant the junta's public enemy number one. As it had persisted in doing throughout the events prior to and during the South Georgia incident, the *Herald* published a well-balanced editorial. While emphasising the consequences of Britain's diplomatic foot-dragging, the newspaper condemned equally the junta's use of force. In the days that followed it not only kept up this editorial line but also went more out of its way than any other Argentine newspaper to dedicate several column inches to the British view of the war. Only a few months before, the military would have had no doubts about the methods to use in dealing with such a rebellion. But in the immediate aftermath of the war, it had to choose its strategy carefully. Part of its diplomatic offensive was focused on convincing international opinion that the junta that had invaded the islands was very different from the junta that had liquidated over 8,000 Argentines. If possible, human rights violations had to be kept to a minimum so as not to play into the hands of those who argued against the regime's ability to look after the 'interests of the islanders'.

Thus the junta looked for a way of controlling the *Herald* while avoiding being seen to repress an organ which the Anglo-Argentine community in Buenos Aires had always regarded as a reassuring reflection of their own lifestyle. Within days of the invasion the intelligence services had infiltrated the leadership of the newspaper's distributing union and assured itself of a national 'voluntary ban'. The unionists, many of them orthodox Perónists and extreme nationalists, needed little convincing about the antipatriotic activities of the 'English newspaper'. The adherence of the rank and file was assured by Mafia tactics of intimidation which had been tried and tested by labour hit squads both before and after the coup. The result was that the *Herald* was not banned but simply not available on the streets of Buenos Aires for ten crucial days of the war.

Then the threats began. An anonymous caller rang the newspaper's offices to announce that Operation Thunderbolt had been prepared: 'for every Argentine soldier that falls, three British will be killed'. The caller left it unclear whether he referred to soldiers or civilians or both, but the threat, coming as it did in the wake of the sinking of the *Belgrano*, caused alarm and fear not just in the *Herald* staff but throughout the 17,000 British-born community living in Argentina. Another call threatened Neilson with death for himself and his family. The editor had been subjected to similar intimidation ever since he had taken over in 1978, but he was sufficiently convinced of the seriousness of this threat to put himself and his family on the first plane out of Buenos Aires, thus joining the list of *Herald* journalists who had been forced into exile because of their outspoken views.

The ban – which cost the *Herald* sales revenue on top of the large-scale withdrawal of advertising by local companies including British subsidiaries fearing victimisation – combined with the departure of Neilson, was a succession of blows not easily absorbed by the newspaper's Argentine management. As Neilson's successor, Dan Newland, explained soon afterwards, 'In this war, anything can happen now ... there could be a public reaction and then we could be in trouble ... it's now a matter of survival. We're no good to anyone if they close us down.'[13] He had earlier pledged defiantly that the paper's editorials would continue to speak out in defence of truth as they had always done. Initially this proved no bluff. The day after the military issued its 'guidelines' for the press, the *Herald* with characteristic bravado carried an editorial entitled 'censorship' which criticised the straitjacket placed on local information. On the same day the mass-circulation daily *Clarín* carried an editorial about the ecological problems of 'historic Buenos Aires'. Soon, however, on Newland's desk and much to Neilson's chagrin, there was a growing pile of British and American agency reports of the latest military action which were kept out of the day's edition. Editorials were watered down and their comment became almost indistinguishable from the arguments of government officials. Finally, against the background of an increasingly intense military and diplomatic battle, the *Herald*'s usual dose of parish news seemed less defiant than self-consciously apolitical: its sports pages carried full coverage of the British soccer league and the MCC test trial against Nottinghamshire at Lord's. On page 7, its weekly column, 'Dog's

Life', had a picture of a handsome cocker spaniel followed by a long and anguished article about the fate of pets in the Falklands.

In a book published both in Britain and Argentina after the war, the London-based Latin American Newsletters reproduced the official communiqués issued throughout the conflict by both the Argentine junta and the British Ministry of Defence.[14] By their own admission in the introduction, the authors set out to destroy what they allege was one of the major myths of the war: that the British version of the conflict was more truthful than the Argentine. It is simply not true, they insist, that the 'Argentines gave a triumphalist version, inventing victories and hiding failures'. Such an assertion coming from such a usually reliable and respected source of comment on Latin American affairs needs to be carefully analysed as part of any serious retrospective on the war as it was lived and suffered in Argentina. Other books on the media and the Falklands, published in Britain, concentrate exclusively on the difficulties faced by Fleet Street and the BBC. Robert Harris, in a harsh attack on the British government, concludes that the Falklands conflict could well prove the last war in which the British armed forces are completely able to control the movements and communications of the journalists covering it.[15] Such a view had inspired many an Argentine commentator to declare that the junta in fact behaved more democratically than Margaret Thatcher. In his best-selling account of the war as seen from Argentina, the author Sergio Cerón states, 'British fair-play ... is a concept invented by the English so that the rest of the world can recognise in them qualities they simply do not have. While London boasted of its freedom of press, the fact is that within the Task Force there was much greater censorship than that imposed by the Argentine military junta.'[16]

Let us look again at the facts. It is certainly true that in the first stages of the war the junta was often quicker and more concise in publicly recording events as they happened than their counterpart, British spokesman Ian McDonald of the Ministry of Defence. The most striking example of this occurred at the start of the conflict. British correspondents like myself who were stationed in Buenos Aires at the time will never forget the anguished moments leading up to the invasion. Alerted to the imminence of the military operation in time for the final edition on 1 April, we found the British Embassy as reluctant as it had been for most of the preceding weeks to concede that something dramatically out of the ordinary was amiss. Meanwhile in London our night editors heard our versions with incredulity: surely, if an invasion was taking place, the Ministry of Defence, Number 10 or the Foreign Office would know about it, was the question that was thrown back at us. It was not until six o'clock in the evening British local time on 2 April, twenty-four hours after we had heard our first rumours and ten hours after Argentina knew that its troops had actually landed, that the British government finally confirmed that the islands had been seized. Subsequently, the junta was often first to confirm, usually with accuracy, a military incident, even if – as in the case of the sinking of the *General Belgrano* – it risked a public admission of a major strategic reversal.

Such concern for accuracy, however, proved short-lived. A closer look at the communiqués of the junta reveals that once hostilities officially broke out on 1 May, there was a conscious attempt both to exaggerate 'Argentine' successes and discredit Britain's military advance. Although such misinformation formed part of the British government's strategy throughout the war, the propaganda which emanated from Whitehall paled into insignificance compared to the distortions projected by the military regime. There was, after all, more at stake in Buenos Aires, where the country's history had been suppressed for the previous six years. Far from being a limited military action as perceived by certain sectors of British political opinion, Argentina's military society was left with no doubt that this was a total war in which the destiny of the nation faced a historic resolution. Privately some Argentine journalists I talked to were fully aware that it was the junta's war rather than Argentina's and thus defeat would mean the end of the regime;[17] this made the junta all the more desperate to nurture the morale of the civilian as much as the soldier by exaggerating the heroics of the officers whose professional careers had been moulded by political repression rather than conventional warfare.

It is perhaps not surprising that the earliest and most blatant example of misinformation by the junta involved the recapture of South Georgia by the British on 25 April. As described in a series of official communiqués to the Argentine nation, the defence of the islands by Argentine naval commandos was as heroic as General Martín's epic crossing of the Andes. It lasted several days, during which the Argentine contingent faced overwhelmingly superior forces in a determined effort to fight until it had 'exhausted its defensive capacity'. The end of Argentina's defence was never officially recognised. The last reference to military action on the island was that the commandos had broken up into smaller units and were resisting in the hinterland. On 26 April, amid reports from London and elsewhere that the commando contingent had surrendered the day before, the junta issued a formal denial and warned Argentines to beware of a British campaign to confuse public opinion.

Had the communiqué been issued five days before it would not have been so far from the truth, since on that day a group of the SAS were forced to abort a helicopter mission because of bad weather. The incident was kept from the junta and from the British people. But coming when it did, the junta's statement was little more than crudely managed propaganda of the kind that would eventually backfire politically. For the officer who in fact had not resisted until the bitter end in spite of having a garrison of 140 men – double the number of British landing troops – was none other than Lieutenant Alfredo Astiz, hero of the 'dirty war', who had been sent to the island assured of earning himself a clean medal. Much later, when the navy chief Admiral Anaya was eventually tried for his misconduct of the war, the navy chief told a military tribunal, 'Never did it cross my head that that young man would surrender; never.'

Official communiqués on the last stages of the war confirm the extent to which the junta grew to believe in its own propaganda, so that it lost sight of the political risks involved in not telling the truth. While swiftly confirming the landing of British troops in San Carlos Bay, the junta was equally quick to conjure up a vision of heroic counter-attack, insisting at one point that the 'invaders' were completely surrounded and on the point of humiliating retreat. The policy of not admitting publicly that the British had taken prisoners of war was first adopted in South Georgia, where the existence of Astiz was blotted from military records. It was pursued at Goose Green, where the reality of Argentina's crushing defeat at the hands of Colonel Jones's paratroop regiment went unrecorded in the local media.[18] Until the very end of the war the myth of a brave defence by General Menéndez was maintained, although it subsequently emerged that the Argentine military commander had virtually conceded defeat from the moment the British established a beach head on Falklands soil. In the history books 14 June 1982 went down as the day the Argentine nation experienced the full spectrum of emotion: from elation with the alleged heroic resistance to psychic breakdown at the realisation of humiliating surrender. Like a speeded-up film, the official communiqués came out one after the other, suggesting initially that the battle had only just begun and next that it was all over.

The communiqués, distorted as they were, were the civilised face of the government campaign to ensure that the nation remained committed to the military occupation of the islands. In a strategy exercised to near perfection during the 'dirty war' against left-wing guerrillas, individual officers linked to the intelligence services attached themselves to newspapers and 'leaked' their account of the war. Sometimes these minders simply made a point of ensuring that the communiqués were treated seriously; but most of the time they embellished here, invented there, bringing the propaganda war to a point of exaggeration rarely seen since Dr Goebbels. Nowhere did the work of these 'unofficial spokesmen' prove more effective than in the mass-circulation glossy weekly magazines like *Gente* and *Siete Días*, which with their provocative comment, slogan headlines and assumed patriotic fervour made even Britain's tabloids seem unimpressive by comparison. For the magazines did not present a limited number of pages filled with bold print about the war between the page 3 nude and the backpage football story. They published over sixty pages of detailed interviews, reports, illustrations and colour photographs which together aimed to convey an aura of respectable journalism. Illustrative of this formula for winning the hearts and minds of ordinary Argentines was the 6 May issue of *Gente*, insisting, complete with illustrations and eye-witness reports, that the Argentine commandos were still fighting it out in South Georgia, hiding in caves. The same issue contained a report about an Argentine airforce pilot's kamikaze attack on HMS *Hermes* with a Pucara ground-attack aircraft. Not only did such an attack never take place, but the pilot mentioned by name had in fact died five days before the report was published in a British bomb attack on a temporary landing strip near Darwin. The Pucara had been hit before the pilot had time to get it airborne.

Editorial Abril and Editorial Perfil, the two family-run publishing companies that exercise a monopoly on Argentina's glossy magazine market, have in common their lack of tradition and their desire to use newspapers simply as a way of making money. To look at past issues of *Gente* and *Siete Días* is to discover Argentina's political culture in all its flippancy, opportunism and ideological confusion. If during the Falklands War magazines like *Gente* and *Siete Días* supported the military effort, it was less out of genuine patriotic sentiment than as a way of increasing circulation. It also had a lot to do with keeping on the right side of the State, which, in the final analysis, had the power to dictate the scope and scale of profits. *Gente*, which in the early 1980s had waxed lyrical about Mrs Thatcher's radical revolution and the splendours of Prince Charles's wedding – increasing sales in the process – now unflinchingly changed its perspective, less to enlighten than exploit the national mood.[19]

The Ministry of Defence had twenty-six journalists attached to the Task Force constantly bombarding it with requests for clarification and protests about censorship. In Argentina the junta dictated that a select group of local journalists witness the invasion and the swearing in of General Menéndez as Governor. Subsequently even these trusted friends were sent back to the mainland. On the islands remained two correspondents of the official newsagency TELAM, Nicolas Kasanzew, a journalist on the State television channel ATC, and an officer working for BAI Press, a military run news agency of dubious professional status. The two TELAM reporters were expelled soon after the hostilities began for breaking with official directives. Kasanzew later reported that he was never allowed to accompany front-line troops and that of the material he sent back to Buenos Aires 'less than 10 per cent' was eventually shown on the TV screens. His colleague, ATC's main newscaster José Gómez Fuentes was rather luckier. A regular drinking partner of Galtieri, the man one satirical magazine lampooned as an alcoholic Dracula was given virtually free rein to commentate on the progress of the war and simultaneously Argentina's World Cup efforts. The same sense of collective jingoistic enthusiasm was applied to both events: 'If there is a war in my country, I will give information which unites the country and I will omit everything which does not. Now this is called disinformation. What's that? I don't understand.'[20]

While Gómez Fuentes stayed in the studio, Argentina's remaining 'war correspondents' were flown south, to join the troops who were preparing to go to the Falklands. 'Most of them have done their national service, but few have written a word before the war,' one editor told me privately. In Patagonia, the journalists were told that they would not be able to go to to the islands because there was no room in the Hercules transport planes. To compensate, the authorities treated them to two regular rituals. The first involved freshly groomed and uniformed conscripts staging a mock battle against an unseen enemy. The next day photographs of 'troops in combat in "Las Malvinas"' would appear in some of the newspapers and magazines; the fact that the photographs showed trees as well as men, even though the Falklands have no forest to speak of, seemed to go by unnoticed. The second ritual had Colonel Esteban Solis, the official press spokesman of the Fifth Army Corps, giving his regular briefings on the progress of the war. Rather than explaining military operations, the briefings concentrated on emphasising the moral degeneration of Britain. Journalists were treated to graphic descriptions of the British troops' alleged homosexuality and alcoholism with the intrepid Solis holding up empty bottles of beer, pornographic magazines and women's underwear. To many of the 'press men' present such a ritual was already well known. For during the fight against subversion following the coup, the military often dismissed political dissidence as a symptom of sexual degeneracy.

For the 500-odd foreign correspondents stationed in Buenos Aires, the experience was no less frustrating, although on balance more dangerous. Seldom in the history of modern journalism have so many hacks been under such pressure to report a war and yet been so far from the scene of battle. To the veterans of Vietnam and the fresh arrivals from El Salvador – and there were many – the Falklands became a war quite unlike any other, without a recognisable front line and yet with the certainty of local colour adding to a pervading sense of insanity. There was many an impassioned mass rally over a group of islands no one really wanted except a few hundred sheep shearers and a group of corrupt Generals. 'Las Malvinas son Argentinas,' everyone kept screaming, but what did it all mean?

The Argentine military minders tried their best to explain, adopting at the outset a virtually open-door policy with the two exceptions of trips to the islands, and public mention of the word Falklands.[21] Two fluent English-speaking and English-trained intelligence officers from the Joint Chiefs of Staff doubled up as press relations officers. They were constantly at hand in a special operations room set aside for foreign correspondents on the second floor of the Sheraton Hotel. On a top floor, and unknown to the press at the time, the security forces had set up their own bunker, from which they tapped phones and co-ordinated the shadowing of suspects. Unofficial sources were always lurking in the foyer, ready to plant the latest round of *carne podrida* (rotten meat), the local term for military and political misinformation.[22] Few of these officers had any love lost for the foreign press corps following the coup; international press reports about human rights violations were part of a Marxist conspiracy. And yet in the aftermath of the Falklands invasion, when the junta was caught up in the illusion of international sympathy with their cause, such memories were temporarily brushed to one side. The minders seemed to have no doubt that the foreign press corps could be made part of the military's propaganda machine as easily as their Argentine colleagues. Such confidence was reflected in the officially organised outings. To their amazement, correspondents were taken round the Museum of Subversion, a macabre testimony to the 'dirty war' consisting of waxwork guerrillas, photographs of terrorist outrages, and a library of banned books which most journalists recognised from their university reading lists.

Trained as they had been by the Americans, it was perhaps not surprising that the Argentine military at the beginning of the Falklands War should have emulated the early US experience in Vietnam. And just as happened to the Americans in Saigon, the junta found that its policy proved self-defeating. By making Argentina initially accessible to any correspondent who turned up in Buenos Aires, the junta also 'lost control of the situation'. The adrenalin was difficult to sustain in the Sheraton. While some journalists spent most of the war there, inventing stories with their non-existent Spanish, a great many more went out into the field to find out what was behind the military façade. And once that happened the military became truer to its political culture. On 13 April three British journalists, Simon Winchester of the *Sunday Times*, and Ian Mather and Tony Prime of the *Observer*, were arrested on spying charges and imprisoned in Tierra del Fuego for reporting on Argentina's military build-up in Patagonia. For the rest of the war, scarcely a week went by without a foreign correspondent being arrested. Several were expelled for suggesting that the war was not going entirely Argentina's way. Among the British, one TV crew was kidnapped, and a reporter, Andrew Graham-Yooll, the then correspondent for the *Guardian* and author of one of the most vivid accounts of the military's repression of press freedom,[23] was so badly beaten up that he had to return to England.

Officially the junta professed its innocence, blaming such intimidation on uncontrolled elements of the security forces. Similar arguments had been used to excuse the 'excesses' leading to the disappearance of over 8,000 Argentines. Now as then, the intimidation was part of the machinery of repression, not an exception to it. Evidence emerging since the end of the Falklands conflict suggests that the military had secret plans to step up their control of foreign journalists in the event of the war prolonging itself; these ranged from a mass expulsion order for all British journalists to the issuing of a 'death warrant' – to be carried out by the hit squads of the 'dirty war' – against selected correspondents including the author. A navy source subsequently confirmed that I was suspected throughout the war of being a British spy using an Argentine name as cover. The name 'Marañón', which I was using, was in fact not so much Argentine as Castilian Spanish, and is my mother's.

The net effect of the military's manipulation of information was that the rest of the world found out about Argentina's war long before the Argentines themselves. In Britain, Argentines were given freedom to express their views – pro and anti the junta – both in newspapers and television. Such debate was anathema in Buenos Aires. Meanwhile foreign correspondents who managed to identify misinformation often managed to convey a better sense of what was going on behind the Argentine lines than the so-called military correspondents. Newspaper journalists picked the brains of well-informed diplomats, relatives of soldiers and returning visitors from the Falklands to patch together a more or less accurate account of life in Port Stanley and the growing problems facing the junta.

In Britain and the United States the fact that the networks obtained more pictures from Argentine television than they did from their own organisations was celebrated as the first time in history that the media had been permitted to report freely the enemy's view of the war. But seen from Argentina such professional satisfaction missed a more crucial aspect of the war. Much of the film taken by Kasanzew of the State television network and by BAI Press, the military news agency, was never shown to domestic audiences. Instead it was sold for substantial sums and used to bolster the personal fortunes of individual officers. Similar corruption extended to the use of photographs. The famous shot of the *Belgrano* sinking, which was syndicated around the world, was originally taken by a young conscript sailor with his pocket camera. The sailor, on returning to the mainland, innocently handed it in to an officer, who in turn sold it internationally for a handsome profit.

Thus did the Falklands War illuminate another aspect of Argentina's military society. When it came to power in 1976 the junta had proclaimed that democracy and corruption were synonymous. But subsequently the military, like the Nazis in post-Weimar Germany, set about consolidating a State system beside which even the misinformation of the Task Force officers and Ian McDonald of the Ministry of Defence seems benevolent. Corruption became a principle of government – that many Argentines were unaware of this fact throughout the Falklands War showed the extent to which their society had been regimented.

7
THE PEOPLE'S WAR

Argentine authoritarianism cannot simply be described as a form of government; it is also a collective state of mind which is the heart of the nation's political culture.[1] During the Falklands conflict the mainland was never attacked, there was never any need for rationing; conscripts sent to the islands were drawn in their majority from isolated provinces rather than from the capital and never numbered more than 10,000; with the exception of towns near military bases in Patagonia, where limited civil defence precautions were taken such as black-outs, and the relatives and friends of the 1,000-odd victims of the war, the country as a whole was not touched physically. In Buenos Aires, the capital where the majority of the nation live, work and play, life went on more or less as usual. Offices, cinemas, night clubs and shops stayed open. And yet the regimentation of this society, so dominated by the military and yet so innocent of the meaning of international conflict and the experience of battle, ensured a collective sense of total war. This went much further in its political repercussions than the Falklands factor ever did in Britain.

Some of the early devices used by the junta to ensure collective solidarity with its war effort needed little instigation. A sense of militarised ritual was already deeply engrained in the political consciousness of this 'nation at arms'. A cycle of national days, commemorating events of military grandeur following independence, had for long been part of the national calendar; during the Falklands War they were revived, providing a point of reference for commentators and government officials alike. In schools, history lessons obliterated all reference to the military's human rights record and concentrated instead on a one-sided account of the history of the Falklands dispute. Schoolchildren had their lessons constantly interrupted for renderings of the national anthem; and at the start and end of the day there was the most popular ritual of them all: the gathering of pupils, teachers and parents to witness the raising and lowering of the flag.

As important in prising the adolescent away from his own imagination and critical sense and delivering him to a collective veneration was conscription. From the moment the junta announced its intention to defend the islands and to call up as many reservists as it deemed necessary (in a communiqué issued on 7 April), the nation was left with little option other than to feel militarily involved. Although the call-up applied initially for only one year, from the outset the junta appealed to collective involvement in its military enterprise, redeeming with a vengeance the concept of a nation at arms. The symbiosis between war and ordinary life expressed itself in diverse ways. Even in the cinema and at the opera where *porteños* of all social persuasions tend to seek their relaxation, there was a belligerent psychosis. *Chariots of Fire* was shown not because it demonstrated British grit and determination to win but because it exposed racial prejudice and the arrogance of empire. The military also temporarily relaxed censorship to allow the showing of *Nobody's Woman*, a previously banned film by the director María Luisa Bemberg about women, in one of the world's most 'macho' societies. First, however, the audience was subjected to a twenty-minute documentary showing a simulated tank battle between British and Argentine troops in which the Argentines won easily. It did not seem to matter that tanks had proved to be unusable in the soggy peat fields around Port Stanley. Meanwhile at the city's impressive Parisian-style Colon Theatre, a production of *Tosca* was interrupted by the orchestra playing the national anthem. Subsequently the Spanish international star, Plácido Domingo, was replaced by a local unknown for 'reasons of health', something which was warmly applauded by the usually selective audience. The applause erupted into an impassioned roar when, in a climactic aria, the tortured hero collapsed on the stage clutching his national flag.

Among the civilian population, emotional mobilisation was assured by the launching of the Patriotic Fund in support of the war effort. The success of this manipulation of popular feeling was vividly demonstrated in the course of a marathon 24-hour-long benefit performance broadcast live nationally on 9 May. Anchored by an Evita-lookalike called Lydia Stangnaro 'Pinky' and one of the most often used voice-overs for publicity shots, Jorge Fontana, the '24 Hours of the Malvinas' had a long procession of personalities including musicians, politicians, Bishops and journalists donating something to the Patriotic Fund. Gifts ranged from the accordion of the country's most famous tango composer, Astor Piazolla, to a chalice used by a priest in his first Mass. Politicians brought medals, and the widow of Captain Giacchino, a veteran with Astiz of the 'dirty war' and Argentina's first hero on the Falklands – killed while attacking the Governor's house in Port Stanley – handed over his knife and emblem.

Emotion, stirred up by Pinky and Fontana, most of the radio channels in the country, and priests at their Sunday masses, spilled out of the TV studios and into the streets. Huge bottlenecks of traffic were soon forming as ordinary citizens tried to make their own contribution to the Fund. The scenes were captured thus by the pro-government newspaper, *La Nación*, the next day.

> As from yesterday, it is now difficult to establish somebody's marital status by following the classical formula of observing the presence – or absence – of the wedding ring. So many wedding rings have been delivered to the TV studios that naked fingers no longer signify unmarried. There were some who took their rings off in front of the cameras. Others who brought, in addition to their own rings, those of their beloved deceased; there were children who brought the rings of their parents. It was a collective and spontaneous gesture which, it needs hardly be said, symbolised a tacit alliance ... and there were many who gave much more than they had originally planned; they came crying with the emotion of collaborating, and with the pain of abandoning something cherished. This was another alliance, that between the actor and the ordinary man who has applauded him, and the whole country. A union without exclusions, since the TV showed a number of well-known faces that do not usually appear on our screen.[2]

The nation's depersonalisation was completed by the inability of Argentina's intellectual class to analyse the war beneath its façade of assumed patriotism. Argentines are among the best-read and best-written people not just in Latin America but in the rest of the world, and yet no author or academic living in Buenos Aires at the time published a serious analysis of the political and social meaning of the war that ran contrary to the military's position. This was in striking contrast to the varied and often profound public debate about the war generated by their British counterparts and which was compiled in book form.[3] Ernesto Sábato, one of Argentina's leading novelists who strongly opposed Perón and after the coup took a public stand against the junta, was quite literally overwhelmed by the collective emotion during the Falklands conflict. Almost inaudible between muffled sobs, Sábato declared in an interview on Spanish radio:

> In Argentina it is not a military dictatorship that is fighting. It is the whole people, her women, her children, her old people, regardless of their political persuasion. Opponents to the regime

like myself are fighting for our dignity, fighting to extricate the last vestiges of colonialism. Don't be mistaken, Europe; it is not a dictatorship that is fighting for the 'Malvinas'; it is the whole Nation.[4]

Sábato, whose novels claim a profound insight into the psychology of alienated society, accurately reflected the collective euphoria but ignored the reality of the few individuals who refused to get trapped. Trade unionists, political leaders, Bishops, the Communist Party and the Perónist guerrilla organisation all supported the military occupation of the islands. The union of will was sanctified at the swearing in of General Menéndez as Governor of the 'Malvinas'. The officials present included Deolindo Bittel and Carlos Contín, the then leaders of the Perónist and Radical parties respectively, Saul Ubaldini, the head of the main trade union organisation, the CGT, and the nationalist Trotskyist, Jorge Abelardo Ramos. Although many of their supporters had been murdered by the junta, they stood beside a generous selection of Generals, including Galtieri and former President Videla.

Absent from the event was Raúl Alfonsín, Argentina's current President, who at the time formed part of a dissident group within the Radical party opposed to the war. Outside the parties the most intransigent position was taken by the 'Madres de Plaza de Mayo', the human rights activists who since 1977 had been campaigning on behalf of their 'disappeared' children in silent vigil before the presidential palace.

> They were forgotten by the political parties, the union bureaucracy and the Church hierarchy, cold-shouldered even by former comrades of their 'missing' children, and harassed by jingoistic currents feeding on the Junta's war. And yet their response remained crystal-clear throughout. Talks would come and go, bombs would fly between the two conflicting armies, but the Mothers continued the demonstrations they had held every Thursday for five years.[6]

During the Falklands War, intimidation of the Madres reached new levels: anonymous death threats and insults of *vende-patria* (that they were selling out the Fatherland). They pushed on, regardless, issuing a statement at the height of the war which aimed to remind their flippant countrymen of the importance of memory, 'The Malvinas are Argentine and so are the missing.' The Madres would no doubt have gone missing themselves had they not been so persistently protected by the foreign press.

From the safety of exile, there were other Argentines who spoke out against the war. They belonged to left-wing groups, mainly living in Caracas, Mexico City, Paris, Madrid, Stockholm and Rome, who in spite of their nationalist sympathies managed to arrive at a more objective analysis of the conflict through following the local media. Within these groups there were a few notable intellectuals who had been forced to flee Argentina because of the coup, such as Osvaldo Bayer, David Vinas, Osvaldo Soriano[7] and the internationally respected short-story writer Julio Cortázar.

As always, Jorge Luís Borges throughout the Falklands War remained beyond good or evil. The master of parody and parable, widely respected as a unique figure in world literature, was on a lecture tour in the United States when the invasion took place. He chose to stay away until the conflict was over, but, as he travelled, the blind poet learned of the war preparations and became increasingly critical, 'I thought the whole thing was meaningless, a military man took a decision overnight, no opinions asked,' he told me in an interview. But the war inspired him to write the only decent poetry to come out of the Anglo-Argentine conflict. In a poem entitled 'Juan López and John Ward', he reflects on the background of two soldiers killed in action. One – Argentine – was born 'near the river' (whether this is London or Buenos Aires Borges leaves up to the reader) and was brought up reading Conrad; the other – an Englishman – was born on the outskirts of a town 'where Father Brown walked' and learned Spanish in order to read *Don Quixote*. 'They could have been friends,' the poem goes on, 'but they only saw each other's faces once, on some islands that were far too famous, and each one was Cain, and each one was Abel. They buried them together. Snow and ashes know them. What I have just recounted belongs to an event we cannot understand.'

At one level the poem, like much of Borges's work, is a play with words and names, invoking, with an underlying sense of nostalgia the cultural symbiosis between Spanish and Anglo-Saxon literature he so skilfully masters in many of his short stories. It is a reaffirmation of personal identity, an acceptance that for Borges (Argentine but descended from Europeans like so many immigrants) the denial of Britishness signifies the denial of a part of himself. But the poem is perhaps more important for what it has to say about war; it illuminates its irrational, and ultimately tragic element, echoing perhaps subconsciously Robert Graves's 'The Leveller'. Its measured tones and the circumstances in which it was written make the poem a courageous statement by one of Argentina's few real personalities. That it was not emulated can largely be explained by the militarised nature of Argentine culture – which has tended to either confront or confuse intellectuals with the masses. This has made authors either inaccessible élitists, or equally uncompromising political vehicles.[8] To many ordinary Argentines, who do not read Chesterton or Conrad, the late Borges during the Falklands War remained in the former category.

Ostensibly, the Patriotic Fund – consciously parodying the International Fund, so hated and so widely blamed for the regime's economic failings – was launched to relieve the State budget and boost resources on the islands. The military, however, never published detailed accounts of the Fund. Independent evidence emerging after the war showed that at least part of it was collected under false pretences. Symptomatic of the extent to which corruption had become an organising principle of the regime was the discovery that some of the goods collected, far from going to relieve the genuine deprivation of the conscripts, were pocketed on the mainland by their non-combatant officers. The spontaneity, so heralded by *La Nación*, also was in some measure deceptive. Some local managers of foreign companies who were asked to contribute products to the armed forces were, for example, left in no doubt that their operations would be forcefully wound up if they didn't comply.

To the outside world the most visible expression of Argentina's soul-stirring during the Falklands conflict was the mass rallies in the Plaza de Mayo. But once again patriotism proved deceptive; the military exploited these manifestations for its own political ends. More important than diplomacy, more important even than logistics and strategy, these rallies were conveyed as the irreversible statement of a just cause and with all the conviction of ultimate victory. And yet to those who did not participate but simply observed, the rallies seemed to echo the restless, irrational emotionalism elicited by the rituals of the Third Reich and Mussolini's Ordine Nuovo. They were less a vindication of Argentina's right to the islands than the symptom of a political malaise. Before the Falklands War, there were the 1978 World Cup celebrations, and before that the demonstrations organised in support of Perón and Evita. The events shared in common the suppression of individuality and a negation of history and their replacement by an extreme nationalism verging on xenophobia. In political terms it signified the victory of totalitarianism over democracy, underlined by a curious continuity of slogans and symbols. During Argentina's World Cup final tie against Holland in 1978 the favourite chant of the crowd was 'El que no salta es un Holandés' ('If you don't jump you're a Dutchman'). Thousands of Argentines would then bob up and down, making anyone who chose to remain sitting or standing feel like a social leper. During the Falklands the ritual war dance was revived, changing the catch phrase to 'El que no salta es un Inglés'. Many foreign camera crews found themselves joining the mass aerobics for fear that not to do so would lead to their equipment being smashed.[9]

Of the several rallies that took place during the war one in particular seemed to bring ritual to a climax. On 10 April, Alexander Haig was preparing to make his way to the presidential palace to present his first serious peace proposal along the $1\frac{1}{2}$ kilometre route leading to it from the Foreign Ministry's Palacio de San Martín. As he came out on to the street and began motoring across the city he found that most of the route and the whole of the Plaza de Mayo was garlanded with loudspeakers. The sound being relayed was a mixture of martial music, slogans about unity and war, and an insistent rallying call to all Argentines of whatever political, social or religious background to demonstrate their patriotic spirit to Mr Haig. The square was packed – most news reports agreed that there were nearly 300,000 people, the 'biggest demonstration since the days of Perón'. British and American flags were burnt and their ashes merged in a sea of blue and white – the Argentine national colours. Inside the crowd some groups tentatively voiced their disrespect for the military regime, but for most of the time they were drowned by a collective chant of 'Argentina, Argentina, Argentina'. The suppression of individuality was matched in its intensity by the eradication of cultural identity. There could have been no better symbol of this than one poster held up by a Japanese immigrant, 'We have Japanese faces, but we have Argentine hearts.'

A similar surrender had been secured from the Anglo-Argentine community. For years these descendants of the first British pioneers had basked in the economic privileges gained through their influence on the railroads, trade and finance.[10] Even after Perón nationalised the railways, their privileges remained largely undisturbed; they lived in the best houses, farmed the best land, owned the biggest yachts. With one or two exceptions the majority had chosen to turn a blind eye to the realities of Argentine politics rather than risk losing their status. When the Falklands War came, the pattern remained the same. Those who had made such a show of being more English than the English themselves, hanging on to left-overs of empire such as polo, church fêtes and private education – their schools spread across Argentina had all the exclusivity of the English public schools – adopted a low profile. Never venturing to express their hidden sympathies for the imperial majesty of the Task Force in public, they dutifully suppressed language and customs for the sake of financial survival. Annual events like the Caledonian Ball and the dinner of the English Club were cancelled, and the older generation of Anglos, for the first time in their lives, took to talking Spanish as a first language. Some allowed their sons to go and fight as conscripts on the islands, although they themselves had fought alongside British forces in the Second World War. Others collaborated more directly, offering their services as translators and helping intercept messages from the Task Force, or, as in the case of the local Anglican Bishop Richard Cutts, travelling to the Falklands to try and impress on the kelpers the great benefits of living under military occupation. The few Anglos who found it impossible to resolve the inherent contradictions of existence suffered nervous breakdowns or left for England.

On 10 April the junta put its propaganda machinery into full operation. On the television networks, programmes were increasingly interrupted with spot propaganda emphasising unity and commitment to the cause above all other social considerations. Galtieri's catchphrase 'Todos juntos será mas fácil' ('United is easier') echoed Perón's manifesto, 'La unión de todos los Argentinos' ('The unity of all Argentines') and the opening lines of the Perónist march.[11] Newscasters invoked the collective 'us' rather than 'the government' to describe events. A song written about Argentina's determination to hang on to the islands with its chorus 'Todos juntos a cantar, Las Malvinas Argentinas' ('All together now, the Malvinas are Argentine'), was broadcast continually. Preceded by a bugle call and a roll of drums, the song's beat was indistinguishable from the martial music so beloved of barracks and *coups d'état*. Communal listening became obligatory; in the centre of town, where the bulk of administrative and commercial life takes place, large speakers extended along side streets and were tuned in permanently and at maximum volume to Radio Rivadavia, one of the country's most popular private stations, which for years had adapted itself to the politics of the regime in order to keep its franchise. On other occasions it had stirred popular enthusiasm for anything from a coup to a counterdemonstration; in 1979 it had urged football supporters to hurl abuse at human rights activists during a visit to Buenos Aires by an international commission. That evening thousands of factory

workers and unemployed were bussed free of charge from the provinces and the poor suburbs of Buenos Aires to express their 'patriotism'.

If the junta's motivation for the rally was to pressurise Haig at a
crucial stage in his mediation effort, the outcome proved very different. In his memoirs, the former US Secretary of State contrasts the
fanatical enthusiasm of the Foreign Minister Costa Méndez and
Galtieri with his own apprehension that history can repeat itself. 'I
was reminded of the newsreels filmed in Rome and Berlin in the
'30s,' Haig recalled.[12] But, more important than the negative effect
they had on diplomacy, the mass reunions proved a two-edged sword
in domestic political terms. When they saw those crowds, men like
Galtieri and Costa Méndez were convinced that there could be no
turning back. The momentum they themselves had created contained the seeds of the regime's self-destruction. For just as the
invasion, the prospect of war and military victory, stimulated a sense
of collective euphoria, so did defeat, surrender and peace bring in
their wake a sense of collective vertigo.

Although society's break with the junta was as sudden as the
surrender of Port Stanley, the process by which euphoria diminished
and the regime lost control of the society it had engendered was
gradual. Events not directly associated with the fighting on the
islands but nevertheless intimately linked to Argentina's political
culture became like the advanced stages of a collective shock therapy.
Just as had occurred in 1978, the World Cup had a crucial impact
on the relationship between people and government. Coinciding as
it did with the last days of the Falklands War, Argentina's fading
fortunes on the football pitch exteriorised the notion of defeat and
shattered the illusion of invincibility. This identification was made
all the more acute since the media covered the war with the same
comments and in the tone usually devoted to sport. Following the
invasion there seemed to be little distinction made between a battlefield and a football pitch; no attempt was made to convey a feeling
that the 'players' in the Falklands were not well fed and fit, but
starving and mutilated. Typical of this symbiosis between war and
sport as engrained in the popular consciousness was the commentary
by the TV journalist Nicolas Kasanzew on 1 May, the day the British
bombed Stanley airport. The occasion, representing as it did the first
outbreak of serious hostilities on the islands, involving numerous
casualties, should have been a cause for reflection. Instead, in a
commentary that was beamed around the world, Kasanzew
described the advance of the British planes and the response of the

Argentine artillery as if what was at stake was nothing more than a counter-attack from the mid-field by Maradona.

In fact Argentina's number one player was, at the time, destined for failure on the playing fields of Spain. In the run-up to the World Cup, local TV, as part of its official war propaganda, made a habit of replaying the crowning final minutes of Argentina's victory over Holland in 1978. But by early June 1982, enthusiasm with the past had given way to a growing despondency with the present. The media could lie about what was happening in the trenches, but there was little it could do about the football matches beamed live from Spain, short of blacking out the screens and risking a national riot. Glued to their boxes, millions of Argentines ignored the news that shells were falling on Port Stanley and that their troops were being forced to retreat. But they watched the national team go down 1-0 to Belgium and Maradona sent off – his blatant foul on an opposition defender was the humiliating climax to the worst performance of his international career. The next day a leading article on the game appeared in the pro-government *La Nación* under the heading, 'A formula for defeat: little conviction, and no direction'. The mass-circulation daily *Clarín* chose a split headline for its front page – beneath 'Bombardment of British Troops' came 'Failed Début in the World Cup'. For the first time in the war, the population sank into deep depression, Alfredo di Stéfano, the Argentine coach of Réal Madrid, had earlier demanded publicly that his compatriots boycott the World Cup in solidarity with the war effort; in a rare display of individuality permitted by the circumstances of his self-exile, di Stéfano clearly felt that the orgiastic exultation of sport should not be allowed to overshadow the reality of death and the pain of bereavement. For the junta, however, football was, as it had been in 1978, part of the war effort; the regime's only tragic flaw was in believing it could win a second time. As for the national team, which only a month before the outbreak of the Falklands War had distinguished itself by criticising the military's politics and striking over pay, the only thing that seemed to motivate its presence in Spain seemed to be less patriotic than commercial. As conscripts died in the fields around Port Stanley, Maradona signed a 7·7 million dollar deal with Barcelona football club. It was one of the largest sums in football transfer history. Paradoxically, the lucrative contract actually symbolised the moral bankruptcy of a nation.

The collective tension initiated by Maradona intensified thanks to the Vatican. By the start of the last week of the Falklands War a different kind of effervescence was pervading the streets of Buenos Aires. To some Argentines jubilation had been caused by the first positive news from the front – a surprise air force attack on Bluff Cove (described by the Argentine media with the enthusiasm usually reserved for a Maradona hat-trick) had killed fifty-four troops and two Chinese cooks. Others rejoiced at the weather – the sun had momentarily broken through the clouds, tempering the rain and the cold of the local winter. The expectations of the majority of the population, however, were focused on the imminent arrival of Pope John Paul II, fresh from a pastoral visit to Britain.

In my local stationery shop at the time I heard the following conversation. 'We are licking the British ... We may lose Puerto Argentino [Port Stanley] but we won't lose the war ... This country is not Communist, but we would rather have the Soviets come here than lose the Malvinas ... The Pope's not as welcome as he should be. He went to Britain first. But never mind, they're Protestants, we're Catholics. That's a point in our favour...' On the streets the flag- and trinket-vendors reflected a collective schizophrenia – in one hand they held the Vatican flag and pictures of the Pope, 'the pastor of peace'; in the other they held postcards of Thatcher, astride a broomstick, naked and with Dracula teeth, and posters declaring 'Las Malvinas' were Argentine and a total commitment to war. One poster surmounted the apparent contradiction by having a flag split between the Argentine and Vatican colours, and the slogan, 'The Holy Father is coming to pray for our soldiers.'

On the evening of 9 June, any prayers were trampled under foot in the Plaza de Mayo. It was the 'Malvinas' Sovereignty Day and some 10,000 Argentines gathered between the presidential palace and the metropolitan cathedral to watch President Galtieri pay homage to the national colours, which fly on a gigantic flagpole. The crowd was noticeably smaller than the demonstration that filled the square immediately after the 2 April invasion, and filled it again some days later at the time of Mr Haig's ill-fated mediation effort, but its collective features appeared the same. Perched like monkeys in a cluster of trees, the *barras bravas* were burning the American flag: on firmer ground elderly Argentines were holding up placards with the words 'British pirates', while chanting, 'El que no salta es un Inglés.' Everyone was jumping up and down.

Two days later, it was pouring with rain again when the Pope finally arrived. He was either slightly early or the Bishops were slightly late – whatever the reason, the TV public was treated to the spectacle of a group of anxious prelates running across the tarmac clutching their soutanes, like characters from a Fellini film. The TV editor was unable to censor the live performance. The Pope's official welcoming party consisted of men in uniform, President Galtieri, and more men in uniform. In addition there were a few bureaucrats in civilian clothes. The party was so big that even Pope John Paul II's large frame was swamped by it; when he was eventually allowed to surface, his kissing of Argentine soil had been witnessed only by officialdom. 'We cannot see it, but the Holy Father has just kissed the ground,' said the TV commentator rather unconvincingly. As the Pope made his way to the rostrum, President Galtieri stuck to him like a leech.

'At this moment, humanity should question itself once again about the absurd and always unjust phenomenon of war, on whose stage of death and pain still stands the negotiating table, which could and should have prevented it,' John Paul II told the Argentines in his first piece to camera. He stressed that his visit, like the one to Britain, had no political overtones, 'It is simply a meeting between the father of the faith and his suffering sons ... I shall pray that the governments of both sides and the international community will find ways of avoiding further damage, heal the wounds of war, and find the necessary solutions for peace.'

It was a clear message in this shortest yet arguably most delicate of papal pilgrimages, hastily arranged at the last minute to dampen Argentine anger at Pope John Paul II's visit to Britain and to counter suggestions of favouritism.[13] But it fell like a political bombshell, undermining the concept of total war with which the regime had mobilised the masses. The Pope looked drawn, tired and grave, as if reflecting the complexity of it all. He was taken down the long avenues of Buenos Aires, where thousands and thousands of people waved blue and white flags and yellow and white flags. They had been camping out all night, and they threw flowers and bits of yellow and white paper so that soon the avenues looked like cotton fields. This was spontaneity indeed, it seemed to those of us watching the event.

Only when the Pope reached Plaza de Mayo did the mood change a little. There were fewer people than the night before: and police cars with their grim sirens were circling menacingly as if wanting to remind everyone that the regime was still watching. But the crowd control was poor, and in the ensuing scramble into the cathedral by guests Cardinal Raúl Silva Henríquez of Santiago (the Chilean primate) had his sash ripped off by a police car. There seemed something sinister in the fact that it was this virulent opponent of

Pinochet and fervent supporter of peace in the Beagle Channel who was thus victimised. As if responding to a hidden signal anonymous hands in the crowd raised billboards with the slogans, 'Holy Father bless our just war'; 'Holy Father bless our soldiers'; 'May God defend our cause because we defend his'. But again the junta's strategy came to nothing. Inside the cathedral, just a few yards away from San Martín's mausoleum, the Pope spoke to a congregation of about 2,000 priests, nuns and Bishops of the Latin American Church. He talked about peace and reconciliation and about what should be the Church's contribution to it. 'Genuine love of your nation . . . may lead some of you to sacrifice, but at the same time it must take into account the patriotism of others, so that both can peaceably communicate with each other and enrich each other in a spirit of humanism and Catholicism.'

Surrounded by millions of Argentine flags, and listened to by churchmen who throughout the Falklands crisis had given unhesitating support to Argentina's war effort, the Pope's words were courageous, and seemed at the same time to be equally aimed at those across the Atlantic, touching a universal theme. To some of those present, the message came as fresh air to a closed room, light in a world that had turned dark, almost insane. His words boomed out across the cathedral and through the loudspeakers positioned around the Plaza, frightening the horses of the presidential household cavalry dressed in the uniforms of San Martín. With sabres and trumpets at the ready, they were waiting to accompany Pope John Paul II to a meeting with the junta.

Minutes later local television brought the nation live coverage from the presidential palace as General Leopoldo Galtieri, head of the Argentine army, Brigadier-General Basilio Lami Dozo, the head of the Argentine air force, and Admiral Jorge Anaya, the head of the Argentine navy, stood by the Pope in the 'white room' of the 'Pink Palace', basking in the reflected glory of the papal visit. The junta members each presented the Pontiff with a gift, like three kings. In a private conversation the junta tried to convince the Pope about the justice of their cause, but John Paul II stuck strictly to what he had said in his speeches, urging only that peace be extended to the Beagle Channel. Later the Pope acceded to popular demand and waved to the crowds from the balcony of the palace. What followed demonstrated the junta's determination to exploit the situation for political ends. The crowd could only see the Pope, and he was alone. But the State-run TV cameras, which recorded the occasion for the nation, filmed from inside looking out, deliberately distorting the perspective. The viewer saw a large enthusiastic crowd and three junta members standing behind the Pope.

Later that day the Pope was taken through the suburbs of the city to Luján. The basilica, which lies forty miles from the centre of Buenos Aires, is the Lourdes of Argentina. The TV commentators lost little time in underlining the poignancy of its symbolism. Our Lady of Luján was not only a miracle-worker; she was also credited with having helped the Argentine forces repel British troops when, twice in the early nineteenth century, they tried to seize Buenos Aires. The minute Virgin is also Captain-General of the Argentine armed forces. Throughout the Falklands War, Argentine air force pilots had offered her bits of Harrier jets in thanksgiving. Somehow, though, these references were momentarily lost on the crowd that day as John Paul II made his way by train, for the first time since his arrival in Argentina, to a public function without the junta; for the first time the war placards were lost in an ocean of song and prayer; for the first time since his arrival the Pope was smiling. There were no men in uniform, only pilgrims. 'How beautiful it is to watch . . . the messenger of peace come down from the mountain,' sang an estimated one million people. 'We want peace, we want peace,' they chanted.

The sky by then had been darkened by rain clouds again but, miraculously, the sun's rays had managed to filter through; the towers of the basilica were dappled by the evening light, like an El Greco painting, giving the kind of solemnity to the occasion which had been utterly lacking from the many rituals put on by the junta throughout the war. In Luján the Pope meditated on the cross, on the themes of love, sacrifice and suffering, and described himself as the 'messenger in troubled times'. The commentators were hard-pressed to know what to make of it all, but they recorded it faithfully, turning the collective imagination with them.

Finally, the next day, 12 June, as British troops on Tumbledown and Wireless Ridge prepared for their final assault on Port Stanley, two and a half million people gathered around an open-air altar in Buenos Aires's Palermo Park. It was the biggest crowd ever assembled in Argentina. Even the small groups of Perónist youths who were there with their placards raising the message of peace had to admit that what they saw made the rallies gathered by their late leader look like tea parties by comparison. The Pope came through the crowds in his pope-mobile looking rested, smiling and strong, a striking contrast with the haggard faces of his hosts. The men in uniform were again up there on the platform, as were their wives, rattling their jewellery and stroking their furs. There were also present Presidents and past Presidents – each having removed his predecessor in some military coup. They were now united in a special reserved compound. The scene has to be taken in its totality – and it felt as though Argentina by a miracle, for all its divisions and mutual hostility, had been momentarily united in a collective urge for peace. 'He talked with serenity from a position of serene authority to a people that had lost all sense of serenity,' commented Joaquín Morales Sola, the political commentator for the mass circulation *Clarín*.

In Palermo Park, John Paul II dedicated his sermon to the youth of Argentina. There were far fewer young men then than would have been usual for a warm day in the park. There was a generation languishing in trenches, or behind barbed wire or in graves. John Paul II reminded his audience that just a few days before Welsh boys in Cardiff had handed him a message of peace for their Argentine 'brothers'. And, as the TV channels interrupted his speech with news flashes of the final clashes between Argentine and British troops, the papal message pervaded the park, 'Do not let hope wither your generous energy, and your capacity for understanding.' In Argentina, at that moment in history, to understand meant inevitably the collapse of the regime.

8
A RELUCTANT TRANSITION

The fall of Maradona and the Pope's visit undermined Argentina's state of mind and quickened the process of political change. But even before the national team had been defeated both in Spain and the Falklands, the regime had begun to collapse internally. By the time General Menéndez agreed to the surrender terms proposed by General Moore, the government had the fragility of a house of cards. Emptied within, it needed only a small push to bring it crashing down.

Within the armed forces, the institution around which the destiny of the nation had revolved for so long, serious cracks had begun to appear two weeks before the Pope's arrival. From the men out in the field of battle, and from General Menéndez in particular, veiled but increasingly urgent warnings were being transmitted to Buenos Aires about the course the war was taking. For all his public statements of defiance General Menéndez was privately convinced that without more troops and increased supplies his men would be unable to put up a successful defence of the islands. Nearer to the seat of power, the seemingly relentless advance of the Task Force and the parallel impotence of Argentine diplomacy had upset a delicate balance of power within the military hierarchy.

In Argentina, power had traditionally resided in an all-powerful army, from which successive Presidents were drawn, a less powerful but nevertheless influential navy, and a small and politically insignificant air force. This equation has remained virtually unaltered since the Second World War. It was to change dramatically following the Argentine invasion of the Falklands on 2 April 1982, when the country's armed forces became involved in their first contemporary international war. As the Falklands War developed, the Argentine air force, thanks to the exploits of its pilots, earned itself a prominent place in public opinion. Even the British press, which all too readily lingered on the brutal human rights record of the army and the navy, was full of praise for the heroism of the squadrons that descended with such devastating effect on the fleet in San Carlos Bay. As a result, for the first time in its history, the Argentine air force began to make its voice heard politically.

In the last two weeks of the war, the most important political comment to come from the junta was issued by Brigadier Lami Dozo. In a statement widely quoted by the local press, the air force chief said that once the war was over the military would have to consider seriously a change of economic policy as well as a greater participation in decision-making by civilians. Indicative of the air force's growing self-confidence was the way it used its control of the Buenos Aires municipality to erect a monument to itself – the first dedicated to any branch of the armed forces since the outbreak of the war. The picturesque Plaza de Los Ingleses, site of the imitation Big Ben clocktower donated by the local British community in 1910, in commemoration of the first centenary of Argentina's independence from Spain, was renamed Plaza de la Fuerza Aerea.

The navy, however, showed itself reluctant to give up second place in the military pecking order. Less bombastic in public, navy officials used their contacts with the local and foreign media to insinuate their own heroic role in the war. They argued that it was their infantry which had first set foot on the 'Malvinas', their conscripts who had been sacrificed in the *General Belgrano* and their aircraft in the fleet air-arm which had first used the infamous Exocet missile.

More equivocal was the attitude of the army. The changes of policy provoked by the Falklands crisis had stirred old rivalries and confused priorities in an institution which had ideologically always been far from monolithic. The army hierarchy, which pulled off the 1976 coup, was essentially made up of 'liberal' officers – pro-Western in foreign policy and military alliances, virulently anti-Marxist in their domestic politics and defenders of the free market on the economic front. Such priorities, however, were put into the melting pot under pressure of events following the invasion of the Falklands. The ensuing contradictions precipitated the downfall of the regime.

Before the war, Argentine foreign policy had focused on forging renewed links with Washington following the awkward hiccup of the Carter years. General Leopoldo Galtieri found it easy to find common cause with President Reagan. Both saw a clear-cut division between Communist and Western influence and for the need to defend the latter in Latin America in particular. General Galtieri, on assuming power in December 1982, had passionately declared his pro-Western sympathies and subsequently offered full backing for President Reagan's policy in Central America. Argentine advisers, skilled in the art of torture and anti-guerrilla warfare, were sent to Honduras and El Salvador. In return the Reagan administration adopted a more generous attitude towards Argentina than that favoured by Jimmy Carter as part of his human rights policy. The fact that Argentina had been the only major grain producer to refuse to back the embargo following the Soviet invasion of Afghanistan, was diplomatically forgiven. Instead the Reagan administration went out of its way to concede that Argentina's human rights record had improved and that the junta deserved to be rewarded with a repeal of the Humphrey–Kennedy Amendment, which, by theoretically banning the sale of US arms to Argentina, remained a symbolic thorn in the side for the junta.

However illusory such benefits turned out to be, there is little doubt that by the time Buenos Aires decided to invade the Falklands, the military junta felt sufficiently secure in its ties with the United States to predict a lukewarm response from Washington. Equally, for that matter, Washington had convinced itself that it wielded sufficient influence with President Galtieri to dissuade the Argentine armed forces from embarking on an exercise that ran the risk of sapping the strength of NATO where it was most needed, and thus of playing into Soviet hands. Only when President Reagan telephoned General Galtieri on the night of April Fool's Day did both men probably realise for the first time the potential extent of their mutual self-deception. However, the illusion of friendship persisted throughout the subsequent efforts of Alexander Haig to mediate in the dispute, which Argentine officials believed would extract an agreement from Mrs Thatcher leading to British recognition of Argentine sovereignty over the Falklands.

By June 1982, a new cartoon was being brandished around Buenos Aires by sectors of the army state intelligence. It showed Mr Haig hiding under a heavy cloak, clutching a machine gun – a shady bodyguard behind a demonic Mrs Thatcher. Nationalist officers within the army claimed that the Haig initiative had really been a diplomatic trick aimed at playing for time and allowing the British Task Force to get near the islands. The subsequent intelligence and logistical and material support given by Washington to the British navy was in their eyes conclusive proof of Mr Reagan's treachery. The Argentine junta resisted breaking off diplomatic relations with Washington throughout the war. But towards the end of the conflict, Argentine foreign-policy makers began to act as if they had been severed. Costa Méndez's famous bear hug with Fidel Castro in Havana, General Galtieri's flirtations with the Soviet Union and Libya, and the sending of members of the Argentine Communist Party to Eastern Europe as unofficial emissaries of the 'Malvinas' cause, were all symptoms of the underlying ideological confusion within the regime.

Ideology was not particularly close to Galtieri's heart. He had emerged through the ranks of the armed forces, carefully side-stepping the politicking of his colleagues, and gaining a reputation instead for his toughness in the fight against guerrillas. When the presidency came within his grasp in the final months of 1981, it was a burning desire for power for its own sake rather than a dream of a national project that drove him on. Galtieri was a latter-day Perón without the *caudillo*'s intellect. It was his blindness to reality that led his country towards the final débâcle. Galtieri had conceived of the invasion of the Falklands less as a revindication of a sovereign right than as a politically expedient exercise which, if it proved successful, would secure him in the presidency for at least another ten years. And because his political fate was so closely linked to the outcome of the war with Britain, he resisted surrender obsessively to the bitter end.

On the morning of 15 June for the first time in three months the Argentine newspapers broke from the shackles of self-imposed censorship and admitted on their front pages that General Menéndez and his 11,000 troops had thrown in the sponge and were now prisoners of the British. During the early hours of that day a nation that had been duped into believing in victory reacted in a mood that ranged from stunned depression to vehement anger. The feelings of a demonstration in Plaza de Mayo that day were passionate in the extreme. Screaming 'Cowards' and 'Sons of bitches' men and women threw coins at journalists and tried to storm the presidential palace. For Galtieri, however, the Casa Rosada remained an ivory tower. Locked inside one of its inner rooms, he tried to contact by phone some of the country's leading politicians in the hope that they would send their party faithful in support of his presidency and a continuation of the war. Later that day, when his appeal had met with silence, Galtieri dropped his plan to make a rallying call from the palace balcony and brought in TV cameras instead. With Plaza de Mayo literally in flames, as demonstrators clashed with riot police and journalists ran for their lives, Galtieri doggedly persisted with his lunatic dream of self-perpetuation in power. 'The taking advantage of the current situation will be judged an insult to those who fought in the war, and any defeatism will be treason,'[1] he told his invisible audience in a muffled, somewhat contorted voice that hinted at too many whiskys. It would have been comic opera had it not been the final act of a real-life drama that was to leave a nation traumatised for many years to come. Two days later, in a bloodless palace coup, General Galtieri was removed from the presidency by the army high command. Right up to the last moment Galtieri had passionately argued that after the defeat in Port Stanley Argentina could still look forward to its 'Maipu' – a reference to the battle fought and won by Argentina's liberator General San Martín in the nineteenth century before he went on to secure the continent's independence from Spain. 'This is only a battle,' Galtieri had told his Generals, 'but the war is not over.'

The Generals didn't bite on the bullet, however. The 'Liberals' feared that the continuation of the war would make inevitable a strengthening of alliances with the Communist world. The ideological confusion was exacerbated by a growing professional awareness of the misconduct and mismanagement of the campaign which had made surrender irreversible. The nationalists, who had never really put much faith in Galtieri's ideological convictions, now saw only his professional misconduct of the war. Both sides agreed that a purge was the minimum step that could be taken if the regime was to avoid total chaos. On 16 June, General Galtieri collected his papers and clothes and left without calling out his 'loyal troops', thinking, as Perón before him had done in 1956, that by so doing he would avoid a civil war. For Galtieri, the war ended as it had begun – with the conviction that Argentina owed the junta a noble place in its history books.

'We have to stop asking ourselves what's wrong with us and do something about it.' Thus did General Reynaldo Bignone, Argentina's first post-war President and the man entrusted with orchestrating the transition to democracy, counsel his fellow countrymen on nationwide TV towards the end of June 1982. Bignone sat with a book of prayers visible on the table in front of him and uttered his concepts with a quiet moralising air which contrasted with the jingoistic, almost demented attitudes of his predecessor. But the performance smacked more of Molière's hypocrite Tartuffe than of restrained statesmanship. The crisis of the military regime detonated by the surrender of Port Stanley was far from resolved by Galtieri's overthrow. This was apparent in the tortuous manner by which the men in uniform decided on his succession. Those last days in June had indicated that however much the civilian population may have wished for a peaceful transition to democracy, the subsequent months were destined to be marred by political conflict of the kind that has held up Argentina's development as a nation for most of this century.

The aftermath of the Falklands War was a period of visible decline in a clear central authority. An awkward interregnum was established under General Cristino Nicolaides, the commander of the crack First Army Corps whose tanks ultimately decided whether a coup would succeed or not. Nicolaides, like Galtieri, had earned kudos inside the military institution for his 'professional' conduct during the 'dirty war', but had never shared in the former President's lust for power. In June he had taken charge by default rather than choice – every other senior General in activity had been directly involved in the war with Britain and was therefore under a less than generous microscope within and outside the armed forces. His innocence was in fact only relative. Although Nicolaides himself had not personally led troops on the islands, a part of the First Army Corps had fought the British. More important, his presence symbolised the army's attempt to maintain a privileged political status within the armed forces at a time when this had become severely questioned by the other two services.

Bignone was remarkable only to the extent to which the Argentine public knew so little about him. He had been an armchair as opposed to a field commander as a former head of the Military Academy, and had generally steered clear of past political controversies. His indirect involvement in the disappearance of a group of Communist militants was known to human rights groups but had not received a public airing. By pulling the soft-spoken and discreet Bignone out of retirement, Nicolaides was counting on a figurehead compromise President capable of cooling civilian political passions and of not interfering in the delicate problems of reshaping and resurrecting the army from the demoralised and divided state it found itself in after the surrender of Port Stanley.

The navy and the air force however remained unconvinced. The navy commander Admiral Anaya, and Brigadier Lami Dozo publicly withdrew from the junta and chose not to represent their services at Bignone's inauguration on 1 July. Popular reaction to the succession was no more generous. In the hours before General Bignone's accession, the police had put up crowd barriers around the presidential palace and the Congress building in expectation of an enthusiastic turn out. Instead, fewer than a hundred rather listless individuals witnessed the occasion. Compared to the huge crowds that had converged on the square during the war, Bignone's lacklustre inauguration as President turned into a poignant comment on the fragility of military power at the time. 'The Process of National Reorganisation is dead, buried under an incredible heap of tangles and controversies and choked by a chaos infinitely greater than that which usually precedes classic coups against constitutional governments. The military regime is dead,' proclaimed one local newspaper at the time.[2]

The military regime may have been dying but it was not yet dead. It was to limp along for another sixteen months, resurrecting the junta with the help of the new navy and air force chiefs and making every effort to paper over its internal differences. Such an extension of military rule proved a blessing as much as a curse for those civilian politicians who were thirsty for power. On the one hand it gave the parties time to organise themselves after over six years of semi-clandestinity. At the same time, however, the permanence of the military in power aggravated many of the tensions that had been bubbling below the surface before the outbreak of the Falklands War. It also made the resolution of these problems all the more difficult once a democratic government had been installed. Reaction and a call for vengeance became the inevitable legacy of military rule. Thus Argentina was robbed of the kind of political skills that initially secured the metamorphosis of Francoism in Spain and the subsequent transition of power to a democracy under the king.

While Bignone's early pledge was to 'pave the way to democracy', Nicolaides's was to 'professionalise and heal the wound of the armed forces'. The decision by the army chief to carry out an inquiry into the conduct of the Falklands War was made less out of conviction that the army should repent for its sins than out of sheer political expediency. It was a calculated risk aimed at defusing a public outcry that was fast showing signs of getting out of control. In defeat, returning prisoners of war – most of them young conscripts – were bundled off to barracks, where they were subjected to intense psychological debriefing sessions conducted by military intelligence. The trauma of these young men thrown into war with little military training went far deeper than the Generals had calculated. When they were eventually handed over to their families, they wasted little time in recounting their experiences. Their descriptions of their war experiences were eagerly snatched up by the local media, anxious to get their revenge on the authorities for months of misinformation. Popular magazines like *Gente* and *Siete Días*, which during the war had tended to reflect the official triumphalism, now printed stories of corruption and cruelty.

One report told of how chocolates wrapped up in special messages for the conscripts had left a charity centre in northern Argentina only to wind up in a food store. The implication was that the General in charge of supervising their transportation to the Falklands had chosen to keep the money instead. In another report, a conscript described how he had been stripped naked and tied to a stake for stealing food. The officer who had ordered the punishment had kept part of the regiment's rations for his own consumption. Finally, in a timely summary of the reality of the war, a young freelance journalist called Daniel Kon published a series of interviews with a group of war veterans. His *Los Chicos de la Guerra* became a runaway bestseller.[3]

In the wake of the Falklands War, many conscripts and non-commissioned officers were hastily discharged, but the bitterness persisted and filtered out through junior- and middle-ranking 'professional' officers. In heated meetings behind the scenes they demanded not only a purge of 'guilty' superiors but also a thorough reorganisation of the armed forces. It soon became evident that Galtieri was not a lasting scapegoat. General Menéndez and three other senior Generals who had fought in the Falklands – Daher, Joffre and Parada – were relieved of active duty pending the official investigation. They were followed by over 150 officers from the three services. The purge stirred the internal debate over the Falklands even further, bringing interservice rivalries to the verge of confrontation at periodic intervals and giving the impression of a dangerous power vacuum that made it impossible, even if he had sincerely wanted to, for Bignone to ensure an orderly transition.

Both Bignone and Nicolaides encountered early opposition from Brigadier Lami Dozo in a series of confused but highly controversial incidents which reached a climax when Lami Dozo was sacked as air force chief in August 1982. At the time, the army intelligence services made much of his alleged ambitions to set up a military-backed 'Officialist Party', with himself as President. In an emotional farewell speech, the Brigadier insisted that his aim had always been to help consolidate democracy and not obstruct it. Whatever the truth, it seems that the army had little difficulty in finding allies within the air force keen on removing this last remaining and somewhat embarrassing link with the Galtieri junta. The air force was to remain a thorn in the army government's side for months to come, however. The new leadership based around Brigadier-General Augusto Hughes reflected a brand of right-wing Catholic nationalism which had a traditionally strong influence in the service. One of its chief proponents, Jordan Bruno Genta, had been killed in 1974 by left-wing guerrilla groups. Genta's main legacy was a book called *Counter-revolutionary War*, in which he blamed the ills of the world on the French Revolution, liberal democracy and freemasonry.

Strong nationalistic attitudes were behind the air force's opposition to the government's debt strategy. This came to a head in September 1983 when a federal judge, working under the auspices of the air force, ordered the arrest of the central bank's Governor, Julio González del Solar, in the midst of crucial negotiations with Argentina's commercial bank creditors. Over the Falklands, the air force's most controversial reassertion of its own alleged superiority came on 24 November 1984, when it leaked its own investigation into the conduct of the war. The investigation, written by Brigadier Horacio Crespo while the war was still on, was a scathing critique of the lack of co-ordination between the three services and in particular the failings of the army and the navy. Referring to the army, Crespo claimed that the officers were 'excessively used to comfort and far too reluctant to undergo the sacrifices entailed in war'. The navy, Crespo claimed, for its part, bore the brunt of responsibility for conducting a campaign of misinformation to hide their own failings.[4]

The navy added its own particular ingredient to the political melting pot, showing that as far as it was concerned the Falklands War, far from being a focus of disgrace, continued to be its reserved watering ground. In August 1982 it moved quickly to exploit an incident involving Argentine fishing vessels and British warships off the Falklands, forcing the Argentine Foreign Ministry to issue a strong formal protest at a time when it was trying to pave the way for a reconciliation with Britain. The navy also appears to have been behind a series of death threats against a number of British diplomats and journalists, including the author, on the first anniversary of the Falklands invasion. But perhaps the most controversial occasion involving the navy occurred in September 1982, when the commander of the country's naval South Atlantic region, Admiral Zaratiegui, staged a rebellion against the authorities. Although Zaratiegui stressed that the move was strictly an institutional affair aimed at his own naval commander, Admiral Anaya, and not General Bignone, the 'rebellion' proved a further destabilising factor at a time when the government was already under pressure from deep divisions within the army.

The army had suffered the greatest blow to its self-esteem from the war. It had adopted the highest profile at the outset only to suffer the most humiliating defeats subsequently – the routs at Darwin and Goose Green, and the final surrender at Port Stanley. By moving quickly to isolate some of the culprits General Nicolaides hoped to deny the army's collective responsibility and re-establish its shattered public image. None the less his repeated assurances that the unity of the army remained intact flew in the face of reality.

In the second week of August, Iglesias Rouco, the Argentine columnist who had correctly forecast the invasion of the Falklands, published the draft of an alleged putsch plan written by a group of unnamed Colonels and five senior Generals. The document was never authenticated, but it had already become an open secret in diplomatic and well-informed journalistic circles that there were dozens of groups manœuvring within the armed forces. At the time it was thought that the most influential dissidents would probably back a plan similar to that leaked by Rouco, a radical economic populist programme, defaulting on the national debt and splitting with the United States. A second group was inclined to resurrect the liberal free-market policies that had been put on the back-burner as a result of the Falklands débâcle. Although it had allies among the landed groups and some business leaders, this military sector was always thought to be a minority and unlikely to succeed without resorting to excessive violence, since its views were not shared by most of the population.

What was clear even at this stage was that the Falklands débâcle alone could no longer explain the growing disquiet among army officers. Internal debate had begun to revolve around the subject of democracy and in particular the one major issue that could influence the manner and the timing of its dawning: human rights. For all the interservice rivalries stirred up by the Falklands, there was widespread fear that political liberalisation might increase demands for a Nuremberg-style judgment of military personnel, linked to an investigation into the disappearance of many thousands of Argentines, which ultimately tempered the democratic tendencies of most officers.

Just before Christmas 1982, the Argentine satirical magazine *Humor* carried a cartoon on its cover showing the country's military rulers shrouded in bandages from head to toe and barely able to support each other. It was a succinct statement on the crisis of the regime. Since the end of the Falklands War, Argentina had been showing signs of spinning out of control with a deepening crisis in central authority being intensified by the absence of any viable alternative.

Against the backdrop of the military's internal divisions over the Falklands *post mortem*, opposition to the government had been spreading through all sectors of society. It ranged from middle-class housewives banging empty pots to a large group of Falklands War veterans who called senior Generals 'sons of bitches' and staged an unprecedented sit-in during a ceremony to honour the fallen. In the space of only a few months, the country had witnessed bloody riots in the working-class suburbs of Buenos Aires because of increases in municipal taxes, and had faced virtual paralysis during a twenty-four-hour general strike. Bishops had warned of social and moral disintegration, and moderate politicians of imminent civil war. Bankers meanwhile remarked dryly that a combination of falling export prices, rising interest rates, inflation of over 300 per cent, the cost of the Falklands War and an oversized and inefficient public sector had left Argentina without any cash – a worrying prospect indeed for a country owing 39 billion dollars.

On 5 December, thousands of Argentines led by politicians, Bishops, trade unionists and such international figures as Adolfo Peréz Esquivel, the Nobel peace prize winner, had defied a government ban and staged a massive demonstration through the streets of Buenos Aires. The resounding chants of 'Liberty, Liberty', and 'Dictatorship is going to end', underlined the essentially political nature of the 'march for life' originally called in support of a thorough investigation into the 'disappeared'.

Until the final run-up to the Falklands War, human rights had been largely a taboo issue. Those who dared to protest publicly were numbered in hundreds rather than thousands and the political impact of their efforts was restricted because of the self-censorship imposed by the media. Many Argentines remained silent either because they feared reprisals or because they had accepted the government propaganda and tacitly collaborated in the repression of 'left-wing subversion'. Still more – and this was true of the wealthier middle and upper classes – were affected by an obsessive materialism which left little room for ethics.

For the 'dirty war' (at its most brutal in the years 1977–80) had coincided with *La Epoca de la Plata Dulce* (the time of sweet money) remembered even today by many Argentines, much as their English counterparts remember the swinging sixties, as the years, to quote Macmillan's favourite phrase, when 'they never had it so good'. On coming to power in 1976 the junta's Economy Minister José Martínez de Hoz had wasted little time in applying an orthodox monetarist recipe to the chaotic financial situation he had inherited from the government of Isabelita Perón. He curbed wages and trimmed government spending, against the background of an aggressive pursuit of foreign investment and deregulation both of the financial system and trade. The main victims were the workers – affected by a nearly 50 per cent drop in real salaries – and some Argentine businessmen who were unable – after years of protective tariff barriers and generous State subsidies – to deal with the competition from abroad.

The regimentation of the rest of society, however, was assured by a policy that could really be described as a free market guided from above. The great dividing line between the haves and the have-nots was drawn by the new banking reforms introduced in 1977. Up to then, interest paid and charged by banks had been frozen and lending capacity for years did not depend on a bank's deposits but on arbitrary allocation by the central bank. The reforms allowed banks to charge what interest rates they wished. At the same time the government introduced a crawling peg of mini-devaluations published and guaranteed in advance, which in practice ensured that the depreciation of the local currency always lagged behind domestic prices, however high they were. The result was a proliferation of banks and a speculative boom – the scope and scale of which had few precedents even in a society such as Argentina, where inflation had been traditionally high and the methods for dealing with it elaborate.

Investors were encouraged to bring in dollars from abroad, either in the form of bank loans or in straight transfers from the savings accounts many Argentines held in places like Miami, New York and Zurich; they would then buy pesos, temporarily put them into high interest-bearing accounts, much higher rates than anything offered abroad, before withdrawing from the market and reconverting to dollars, then to start the whole mechanism all over again. The speculation dubbed the *bicicleta* or bicycle because of its seemingly self-sustaining momentum meant that, for over a year, local and foreign investors stood to make a profit of 3 to 4 per cent a month on their capital in foreign currency. An increasingly overvalued peso also meant a flood of cheap imports. The result was that Argentines became as easily rich and spendthrift as the Arabs in the wake of the oil crisis. People would sell their flats in Buenos Aires and buy at little extra cost houses three times the size in Europe or the United States. Across the River Plate in neighbouring Uruguay, the coastal town of Punta del Este was transformed into a major luxury resort in the kind of property development most Mediterranean countries would take at least ten years to match. Usually, however, Argentine tourists went much farther afield, finding that with their monthly wage converted into dollars they could fill half a plane with anything they wanted from a small pocket calculator to a washing machine.

In Latin America and Spain, the Argentine came to be dubbed *el dame dos* (the give-me-two) because of the seemingly irrepressible consumerism Martínez de Hoz seemed to have unleashed.

By early 1980 a sense of euphoria floated above the hidden grave-yards. By then over 8,000 Argentines were estimated to have dis-appeared according to human rights organisations. Tales of torture, plunder and cold-blooded execution were well known in the research rooms of Amnesty International and the United Nations and written about by foreign journalists. On the surface, however, there was money, and a lot of it. As David Rock puts it, the blandness of his comment echoing accurately the underlying soullessness of Argentine society at the time:

> the country appeared to have undergone a dramatic change. With the guerrillas vanquished, discernible repression had waned: the troops had returned to barracks and the covert police squads, agents of the 'disappearances', were no longer active. Although wages and manufacturers' profits remained bitingly low, the press gagged, and the unions cowed, much of the population found solace in speculation, and the purchase of cheap imports.[5]

The sudden collapse in the same year of the Banco de Intercambio Regional, one of a number of new financial institutions which had mushroomed into the largest domestic private bank in terms of deposits, should have signalled that the dream was over. However, the regime proved a great deal more resilient than some people thought at the time, deliberately playing on the divisions within the civilian opposition and limiting the fall-out of the first discernible splits within the military hierarchy. In March 1981 Martínez de Hoz resigned and Videla was succeeded by Viola; Massera subsequently left the junta to form a 'social democratic party'; there was much talk of '*apertura*' – a gradual political liberalisation leading to elections sometime in the 1980s. But these were cosmetic changes designed to win time before a more ambitious project to consolidate the regime could be attempted.

The Falklands War had the same effect on Argentines as the *plata dulce*; it subverted the collective conscience and made society momentarily lose sight of its real past and real future. For the regime it proved less a solution than an interlude after which pending problems would re-emerge with a vengeance.

With the war with Britain over, the measures which had kept the human rights issue under control were imposed more harshly. The regime reimposed law number 20,840 which carried minimum sentences of three to eight years in gaol for anyone found guilty of writing anything detrimental to social peace and institutional order. The security forces carried out occasional but tactical intimidation, murdering left-wing militants and issuing death threats against out-spoken journalists and lawyers. In the ultimate travesty of military justice, the junta brought out what it hoped would be accepted as the last word on the 'dirty war': a lengthy document which whitewashed the military's responsibility and urged the nation to turn over a new leaf.

The regime's capacity to rule through selective terror and lies was undermined by the sequence of events set in motion by the Falklands defeat and the mounting economic crisis, which affected every Argentine increasingly. Underlying the opposition to the regime was a widespread feeling that the Falklands débâcle was not a lost battle, as Galtieri had argued, but the result of a far deeper national malaise, for which not just the military but most of the population was responsible. Hard as it was for the people to accept, Argentina owed the initial collapse of the military regime not to any efforts of their own but to the resolute approach of Mrs Thatcher.

9 ALFONSÍN:
THE ROAD TO POWER

Even the most charitable traveller will find it difficult to enthuse about the villages and towns that dot the huge expanse of Argentine prairie called the pampa. Dull geometric architecture, squat houses and straight streets, silent corner shops selling only the rudiments of daily living and an absence of visible social or cultural life far from indicating the energy of a frontier society smack of mediocrity and soullessness – a people without an identity.

At a glance the town of Chascomus, some 120 miles south-west of Buenos Aires, along the main highway to Patagonia, seems no exception. A kitsch statue of the Virgin Mary and a 'Welcome to Chascomus' sign are followed by an empty space of dull fields and huts. And yet the anonymity of the outskirts is deceptive. Follow the route heralded by the Virgin and you will eventually find a beautiful tree-lined natural lake where, in a festive atmosphere, the local inhabitants gather every day for boating or fishing or just for energetic conversation. In other towns in the pampa there is a feeling of desolation which has divided the population; but here the lake has become a symbol of community.

Chascomus is the birthplace of Raúl Alfonsín. The man who today rules Argentina has not lived many of his fifty-six years there, but he seems to have carried with him much of its spirit. In an important sense the town goes a long way towards explaining Alfonsín. He was born into a family of shopkeepers of mixed Spanish and English descent. The Alfonsín shop, selling everything from a small knife to directory in this town of 20,000 is filled too with French, Italian and Jewish names. It has one of the oldest churches in the country – a small wooden chapel built by the first and last of the country's slaves, and a 'cemeterio de los ingleses', the picturesque postcard image of an English village graveyard where the early pioneers who came to work on the railroads are buried. The railroad no longer begins and ends here as it once did, but the inhabitants still feel that within their boundaries lies the heart of Argentina.

Chascomus is the birthplace of Raúl Alfonsín. The man who today rules Argentina has not lived many of his fifty-six years there, but he seems to have carried with him much of its spirit. In an important sense the town goes a long way towards explaining Alfonsín. He was born into a family of shopkeepers of mixed Spanish and English descent. The Alfonsín shop, selling everything from a small knife to curtains, was a focal point, like the lake, of communal activity, where the family was able to gauge far more accurately than any barrack-room General the hopes and fears of ordinary people.

On his father's side, the Alfonsín family were originally Galician peasants who left an impoverished Spain to seek their fortunes in Argentina when this southern Latin American country was attracting more immigrants than Australia, Canada and New Zealand. Alfonsín's maternal grandfather was a Welshman called Foulkes. 'He was a medical student and when he came to Argentina he proved himself a great radical by fighting for Yrigoyen,' Alfonsín recalled many years later.[1] Yrigoyen was Argentina's first democratically elected President, whose second term in office was cut short by a military coup in 1930. In that year Raúl was just three, too young perhaps to absorb fully the traumatic effect on his family and their town of this first direct intrusion into Argentine politics by the country's armed forces. But in the 1930s he was to grow up under the influence of his father Serafín, an embittered and frustrated radical capable of occasional sparks of passion. Like most Argentines, Serafín had kept his head low when the military moved in. His political catharsis came when his republican sympathies revolted against news of Franco and the success of the Fascist cause in Spain.

At the age of thirteen Raúl was sent by his parents to military school. Serafín saw no inconsistency in this. He had not stopped disliking the military, nor did he nourish any hopes of his son becoming an officer; but, an astute Galician, he realised that a military education, like studying for the priesthood, was a cheap and easy way for a boy to get a reasonable private schooling. In fact the experience turned out to be much more useful than expected, giving the future President an early insight into the military mind. Although what he discovered was not much to his liking – his libertarian legacy rebelled against the myopic social and political vision of the barracks – some of his classmates were to prove useful political allies once they had been promoted to the rank of General.

Alfonsín quit the academy as soon as he had completed his secondary schooling and took law exams instead. Once he had graduated as a lawyer, he turned to politics. Local inhabitants of Chascomus recall that from an early stage in his career, Alfonsín's professional life left much to be desired. He was rarely at his desk and more often than not in debt – he had an amateurish sense of finances and a great love for food, dancing and women – although his early marriage to a local teacher María Lorenza Berreneche, of northern Spanish origins like himself, appears to have been a happy one. In the end it was politics which focused his energies.

It was hard not to be passionate about politics in the mid-1940s when Alfonsín was twenty. The period coincided with the rise of Perón – a moment in which Argentina seemed to be split between two irreconcilable camps. Alfonsín joined the anti-Perónist forces not because he had anything in common with the right-wing military sectors and the landed classes, but because like many Radicals, he feared the potential for a corporate authoritarian State based around the personality of Perón, and a nationalist and bigoted troika of military, unions and Church. The Perón years, with their suggestion of Fascism and corruption, proved fertile ground for the political evolution of the young Alfonsín. Ethics became of paramount importance to this President-to-be. The context was similar to the 1890s, when the authoritarianism and corruption of the country's conservative parties led to the birth of the Radical party under Leandro Alem. Drawing on the immigrant classes, which were then unrepresented by the conservative parties, Alem pledged in his first revolutionary manifesto to restore the purity of administrative morality and free suffrage in the face of the 'tyrants'.

Seventy years after Alem came on to the political scene, Alfonsín had a keen understanding of the Radical party's early roots and wished to return to them. Refusing to sink into the ranks of the embittered radicals, forever brooding about how they had been robbed of power in 1930, Alfonsín took to politics with almost messianic fervour and youth just as Alem had done. In the 1940s and early 1950s, Argentine party politics were plunged into a seemingly endless state of limbo, with Perónism exercising control over Congress and pervading almost every aspect of political and social life. The Radicals were relegated to an occasionally vociferous but ultimately ineffectual opposition. Sociologically they failed to make any inroads into Perón's main power base within the labour movement. At the same time they saw even some of their middle-class support shifting towards the governing party.

While the Perónists remained solidly controlled by the figure of the *caudillo*, the Radicals were hampered by faction fighting – as one historian put it, during this period 'it was virtually impossible to talk of the Radical position on any given issue'. The internal contradictions of the party intensified following the overthrow of Perón's first government in 1956. Rather than adopt an outright opposition to military government consistent with their founding principles, one sector of the Radicals under Arturo Frondizi jockeyed for political power on the military's terms. The party that at the turn of the century had made its demands for free elections and universal suffrage its key principle found itself agreeing to participate in elections in which the Perónists were proscribed. Frondizi campaigned on a nationalist, populist platform designed to gain votes clandestinely cast by Perónists, but he never recovered his political credibility. Moreover, once he had won the election he followed completely different policies, opening up the economy to foreign investment and allowing the military an increasing role in repressing opposition. This lack of strategy quickened his downfall.

In spite of his leanings to the right, Frondizi never managed to win the full confidence of the armed forces and was overturned in a military coup. But when elections were held three years later, the Radical leadership – this time under Arturo Illía – again allowed itself to gain power through the back door. The Perónists were excluded from the electoral process by the party of 'universal suffrage'. The Illía government, born under the illusion of democracy, was destined to fail from the outset. Excluded from the political system, the Perónist party pursued its own authoritarian paths to power, using the unions in tacit alliance with the military to make the country ungovernable. The 'tortoise', as Illía was dubbed by his opponents, earned a dubious distinction. He was hailed not for his policies but because he had very few. Had he provided a genuine alternative, the military coup that toppled him might never have occurred, and subsequent Argentine history might have turned out very differently. For Illía's government became the first Argentine administration to put its full political weight behind a negotiated settlement of the Falklands dispute. Taking advantage of Britain's looming crisis in Rhodesia and renewed efforts by Spain over Gibraltar, Argentina managed to secure a resolution at the United Nations inviting the 'Governments of Argentina and the United Kingdom to proceed without delay with negotiations with a view to finding a peaceful solution to the problem'. Peace was the key word for a Radical party that from its birth had pursued a strongly pacifist line, to the extent of not participating in the First World War when Yrigoyen was in power and opposing the sending of American marines to Santo Domingo. 'The Falkland Islands had been the most somnolent of sleeping dogs. The UN resolution meant this could no longer be.'[2] The return to military rule after Illía developed the militarisation of Argentine society and paved the way for war.

Although elected a congressman for the provincial capital of La Plata in 1958, Alfonsín never participated in the front line of either the Frondizi or Illía administrations. These were formative years for him, none the less. He watched with increasing despair as the Radical party leaders conducted their politics like alchemy, mixing the formulae that would best keep them in power rather than providing a genuine programme for the transformation of the nation. Argentine policies were reduced to the confusion and incoherence of an exiled Perón and the reaction and opportunism of a Radical party anxious for power for its own sake – not to mention the behind-the-scenes machinations of the fawning conservative landed classes and their allies in the military. These were years of decadence which cried out for a redeemer.

In 1972, Alfonsín formed Renovación y Cambio – Renewal and Change – a dissident faction within the Radical party, risking both his political career and his life in so doing. Argentina was on the threshold of civil war between the armed forces and left-wing guerrillas, in which words like renewal and change had become synonymous with Marxism and revolution. Like Alem's party, Renovación drew on young blood, mainly in the universities, and thus became for the military a sitting target. Alfonsín was neither a Marxist nor a revolutionary, but a social democrat firmly committed to moral renewal and the establishment of a full parliamentary system as the only political solution to Argentina's long-standing problems.

His decision the following year to represent legally the head of the guerrilla organisation ERP, Mario Santucho, was held up by the military as clear evidence of Alfonsín's Marxist leanings; but to his supporters the gesture was a principled stand by a man who believed that in a genuine democracy any man, whatever his political persuasion or activities, has the right to a fair trial. The defence of Santucho and of other political prisoners showed Alfonsín the lawyer and Alfonsín the politician had become one and the same person, committed to human rights as an issue around which Argentina's moral renewal would stand or fall.

Alfonsín was none the less the rebel in the conservative pack. His left of centre faction contrasted with the cautious politics of Ricardo Balbín, who succeeded Illía after his retirement. Balbín was a more forceful character than Illía had been. But he was small and plump, and his slit eyes earned him the disrespectful title of El Chino. His politics were woolly and his rhetoric outdated. 'Cautious critical opposition' was how Balbín liked to describe his attitude first towards the military government of President Lanusse and subsequently to the second Perónist government. It was an understatement about behind-the-scenes compromises which failed to provide a genuine way out of the deepening political crisis. When the coup of 1976 was being hatched, it was Balbín who gave the last passionate cry of alarm in a memorable speech to Congress. When the coup was launched, however, Balbín chose silence, tacitly accepting the intervention of the armed forces as a necessary means to an end – the restoration of stability after the chaos brought about by Perónist misrule.

Alfonsín's opposition to Balbín effectively cut off the aspiring candidate from Chascomus from the mainstream of politics. Balbín never gave him a party post and Alfonsín was not elected to parliament in the national elections of 1973. Occasionally, through the barriers first of party intransigence and afterwards of military censorship and intimidation, Renovación y Cambio would issue a statement that took a forceful stand on a particular issue. In April 1975, encouraged by the results of a provincial election in which Alfonsinistas had made strong gains on the local Perónist candidate, Renovación y Cambio brought out a document exhorting Balbín to oppose the government's 'totalitarian projects' and to take up the defence of freedom of education and the media. When the military began to criticise Isabelita Perón, he urged Congress to impeach the President on corruption charges as a gesture of its determination to retain the political initiative. Too few listened and the junta moved in.

In September the following year it was Renovación y Cambio that goaded the Radical party from its non-committal silence into open protest, following the kidnapping by security forces of two Radical Senators, Hipólito Yrigoyen – a nephew of the former President – and Mario Anaya. Anaya died under torture. A few days later two other Radicals, Sergio Karckachoff and Domingo Terrugi were shot by the security forces. Alfonsín was one of the few politicians to sign a public letter of protest, and to intervene to try to save the lives of the missing. It was his schooldays friendship with General Albano Harguindeguy, the junta's first Minister of the Interior, which saved Yrigoyen's life.[3]

Only once – on 17 June 1977 – did Balbín's Radical party allow itself to come out with a more general policy statement calling for a return to institutional normality and an end to repression. Throughout this period, however, Alfonsín was hard at work – more often behind the scenes than in public, but consistently gaining a reputation as a man of courage and conviction. These were years when the Argentines prepared to take a stand on human rights were few and far between and when the easiest way to power was to turn a blind eye. Alfonsín joined the General Assembly for Human Rights and interceded on behalf of the victims. One of his more memorable interventions involved Hector Gutiérrez Ruíz and Zelmer Michelini – two Uruguyan Senators. The two men were kidnapped by the Argentine security forces working in conjunction with their Uruguyan counterparts, on 18 May 1976, less than a month after the coup. Three days later they were found under a bridge on the road to Buenos Aires main airport, Ezeiza. Ruíz had one eye poked out, half his face crushed, burn marks on his front and back and his knuckles shattered. Michelini had simply a bullet through his head.[4]

Throughout the short period of their 'disappearance', Alfonsín agreed to act as personal friend and lawyer for their families, interceding on their behalf with the authorities and using what contacts he had among the military to try to secure their release. When they were found dead, most of the Senators' political colleagues were forced into clandestinity; but Alfonsín personally supervised their funeral, offering to pay even for the copper inscription on the dead men's coffins.

Alfonsín demonstrated a similar sense of political conviction in 1977 during a controversial visit by a team from Amnesty International in 1977. Most of the local media at the time condemned the visit as an inadmissible intrusion by a foreign entity into Argentine political life. Newspapers echoed the official propaganda that Amnesty, with other organisations such as the United Nations Commission on Human Rights, formed part of an international Marxist conspiracy at the service of left-wing subversion. The story succeeded in intimidating senior political figures and forced them to keep a low profile on the human rights issue. Alfonsín was one of the few who were unafraid to meet the Amnesty team.[5]

From the 1976 coup right up to the Falklands War, Alfonsín continued to be shunned as a black sheep by his party leadership and kept at a hostile distance by the authorities. But his continuing exile from the mainstream of political life was to prove an asset as most political establishment figures became discredited in the public eye as collaborators with the military regime.

Throughout this period, moreover, Renovación y Cambio was gaining experience which would greatly help Alfonsín once he came to power. Within Argentina a number of economic, political and scientific think-tanks were established discreetly to circumvent the ban on party political activity. In addition to providing militants with an opportunity to co-ordinate their strategy against the regime, these organisations analysed the country from a sociological perspective. Data on unemployment, family relations, the state of women and regional underdevelopment were processed, written about and circulated within Renovación y Cambio. None of these results were taken into account by the military authorities and very few of them managed to make their way into the still highly self-censored national media. However, they allowed Renovación y Cambio to build up important background material, which would prove crucial in formulating a party programme and an electoral campaign once Alfonsín became presidential candidate. Important information was also provided by Alfonsinista sympathisers, who left Argentina during this period to study in foreign universities as postgraduates. In countries such as Spain and France these exiles also laid the groundwork for Alfonsín's international relations with the European social democracies.

Equally important in forging the future administration was the willingness of Alfonsín and his closest aides to travel abroad and study political developments in countries such as Spain and Britain, both of which had experienced radical change under Suárez and Thatcher respectively. In addition to gaining them experience, these trips helped them to secure useful allies for the future. Towards the end of 1981, while the military were secretly plotting their invasion, Alfonsín travelled to London to make contact with human rights organisations and friends in the Social Democratic and Labour parties. Accompanied by Dante Caputo and Roque Carranza, his future Foreign and Defence Ministers respectively, Alfonsín travelled unpublicised and on a minimum budget. So minimum in fact that when the three individuals turned up to book a room at the Charing Cross Hotel, the receptionist took them for tramps and sent them away. In his humble aspect, the future President was already proving himself a very different kind of political animal from his predecessors. His ability to learn from the outside world was also a change from the provincial attitude of Balbín, who declared it his patriotic duty never to leave Argentine soil.

Alfonsín's personal prestige and the activities of what in effect was a 'shadow' government gave Renovación y Cambio a strategic advantage over other political groups once the opportunity to make a bid for power arose. The Perónist party, although traditionally the country's major political grouping, was divided, weakened and unsure of its own identity as a result of the vacuum left by Perón's death in 1974 and the military's brutal repression of the party's left-wing factions. In 1974 to have had active political experience in Argentina one had to be old enough to have been active during the first Perónist government. This meant that the surviving political leadership had an average age of sixty-five. During the intervening limbo years, between the first and second Perónist governments, no intermediate political generation emerged. Instead the initiative was to pass down to a much younger generation, separated by more than eighteen years from Perón's contemporaries, who came to the fore in the armed struggle against the military regime. There was thus an unbridgeable gap between the young revolutionaries and the more orthodox elder statesmen, arising from widely differing experiences and expectations.

A similar generation conflict did not exist within the Radical party. The university movement around which Renovación y Cambio was founded in 1972 never participated in armed action against the authorities. Instead it allied itself to the intermediate generation as represented by Alfonsín in order to survive physically and provide a genuine political alternative to the party elders.

In 1983 Ricardo Balbín 'El Chino' died and, although a brief internal power struggle ensued, the stakes were firmly weighted in Alfonsín's favour. His message and style had been relegated to the political doldrums for the previous ten years. Now it represented the aspirations of the majority of Argentines as they struggled towards the future following the Falklands War.

In his personal manifesto, Raúl Alfonsín devotes several pages to analysing the phenomenon of Perón's rise to power. Although adamant that Perón's eventual government smacked of authoritarian corporatism that often verged on fascism, Alfonsín pays tribute to Perón's historical contribution. Alfonsín recognises someone who, in the immediate aftermath of the Second World War, managed to identify the wishes of large sectors of the population which until then had been unrepresented by the political system. 'He knew how to convey to his people a message of hope in the language they understood,' he wrote.[6]

The assessment could well apply to Alfonsín's own emergence on the political stage following the surrender of Port Stanley. One of the first initiatives of General Bignone on becoming President was to lift the ban on political activity and to call on the parties to prepare themselves for internal elections. It was a tactical move aimed at forcing the main political groupings into an internal power struggle, thus diverting their attention away from a more direct assault on the military regime. To a large extent the tactic worked. Many political leaders chose tentatively to explore their potential support in cautious behind-the-scenes lobbying and it was not until December, five months after the war had ended, that the Multipartidaria, a loose *ad hoc* coalition formed by the main parties, managed to thrash out a minimum of consensus behind an anti-government demonstration calling on Bignone to speed up the transition to democratic rule. By contrast Renovación y Cambio wasted no time in pressing its advantage in the face of what it analysed as utterly discredited and demoralised armed forces which for the first time in their history had lost their capacity to resist change. Previous transitions from military to civilian rule had been essentially political compromises in which the Generals had always retained the minimum leverage necessary to dictate terms to the future government. However, Bignone's attempts to thrash out a common programme covering essential areas of policy from human rights to foreign debt were unanimously rejected by the major political groupings. As a result he was forced to bring forward the date for the elections to October 1983.

Alfonsín's first proposal was pressed on his main political rivals and senior military officers while British and Argentine troops were still fighting it out in the fields around Port Stanley. This was that the military should declare an immediate cessation of hostilities, and make way for a government of national salvation headed by former Radical President Arturo Illía.[7] The government, as planned by Alfonsín, was to pick its Ministers from all the major political groupings and have two immediate priority tasks: the negotiation of an honourable peace with Britain, and the immediate holding of elections. Alfonsín himself had been one of the few Argentine political figures to have been firmly against the 2 April invasion from the outset: not because he did not believe that the islands rightly belonged to Argentina, but because he was convinced that the invasion was logistically and diplomatically doomed, and was essentially the last irrational act of a military regime that had lost all domestic political support. While Bishops, trade unionists, academics, journalists and party political figures including Radicals, Perónists and Communists aired their support for the junta in public, attended the swearing in of General Menéndez as military Governor of the islands, and toured Europe and the United States as the government's ambassadors at large, Alfonsín stayed in Buenos Aires and kept a cautious distance from the public domain. Instead of lending a patriotic voice to the muzzled local media, he chose instead to keep in close and constant contact with the news from abroad as transmitted by friends and foreign correspondents based in Buenos Aires. It was a two-way relationship, allowing Alfonsín to ventilate his dissident views to a more comprehending audience and to keep in close touch with reality.

His support for the Illía option seems to have had two principal motives. Firstly he believed that a peace treaty negotiated by civilians would help a more permanent settlement of the dispute in the future. He believed that not only would it commit Argentine parties to a common position by which the future government would be bound, but it would also make it easier for Mrs Thatcher to be magnanimous in victory. Secondly, Alfonsín believed that a transition supervised by civilians rather than the junta provided greater guarantees of stability and manageable concessions on controversial issues like human rights. It was, as far as Alfonsín was concerned, a classic example of 'united we stand, divided we fall'. The proposals failed to gain sufficient support however. The acting Perónist leader, Deolindo Bittel, produced his own rival plan for the post-war period, also while the fighting was still on. The plan involved the election of a civilian Prime Minister by an *ad hoc* committee of Generals and politicians. The junta was to be allowed to continue as a collegiate executive branch with powers of veto over the composition of the Cabinet and entrusted with guiding Argentina through a minimum transition period of two years. Implicit in the plan was the replacement of Galtieri by a more manageable populist figure drawn from the ranks of the armed forces, and subsequent military dominated reforms along the model tried and tested in Brazil in the 1960s and 1970s. The acceptance by the Perónist leadership of what amounted to a new civilian military alliance was traditionally rooted in the party philosophy – the party's founder, Juan Perón, was first and foremost a General who courted civilian support. But the plan failed to materialise because of the basic misconception that it was possible to find a Perón-type figure at a time when the then current batch of aspiring populist military figures were held closely responsible for the Falklands débâcle and thus lacked either sufficient military support or the assured backing of the civilian population.

At the time one former Radical Congress leader, Antonio Trocolli, dismissed the proposals of both Alfonsín and Bittel as 'alchemy' – an unrealistic attempt to forge the divided political groupings around a figure without political clout. It is arguable, however, that Argentina's democratic experience would have turned out to be less turbulent had there been a negotiated cushion of transition, as occurred in Spain following the death of Franco.

The rejection of the Illía option convinced Alfonsín that he would have to take the bull by the horns unilaterally and force an early withdrawal from power by the military. While the Falklands War had opened up a Pandora's box of vested interests within the political establishment, exposing deep apprehension amongst the military and most civilians about the scope and scale of future change, Alfonsín had no similar doubts. The public rally held by Renovación y Cambio in a leading sports stadium in the suburbs of Buenos Aires a few days after the Falklands War was the first test of the regime's lifting of the ban on political activity. Alfonsín's supporters did not quite fill the stadium, but the turn-out was still impressive given the circumstances; for to be political even then in Argentina could be a matter of life or death. Six months later, just before Christmas, Alfonsín repeated the performance. This time the event clearly demonstrated the extent to which his popular support had grown. An audience of over 30,000 people made the rally the biggest gathering to be staged by a single political organisation since the 1976 coup.

In contrast to the somewhat orthodox first rally, this second one at the Luna Park, just around the corner from the presidential palace, had all the razzmatazz normally associated with a US primary – balloons, pretty women, folk and rock singers, poets, were all there to declare their allegiance to the new white hope of Argentine politics. And in a sense it *was* a primary. A few weeks before the rally, an attempt by Renovación y Cambio to wrench control of the party leadership from the conservative Carlos Contín had failed to get through the party bureaucracy in a complex internal election. But this second show of strength was sufficient to convince Contín that his position had been irreversibly eroded and that he could not afford to stand as a future presidential candidate. It took Alfonsín another seven months, however, before he had finally secured the withdrawal of his main rivals, Antonio Trocolli, and the former Senator Fernando de la Rúa – both of whom belonged to the right wing of the Radical party. By then early opinion polls showed that although the Radical party trailed well behind the Perónists Alfonsín had himself emerged as the country's most popular figure. Within the Radical party it was unanimously decided that only 'Raulito' had any real chance of breaking the Perónist hold on Argentine politics. At Luna Park, Alfonsín had told his audience, 'We must fight to make sure that the armed forces not only leave government but that they never return.' For a majority of Argentines, this post-war message seemed to go to the heart of the matter.

By September 1983, the majority of Argentines appeared to be gripped by feelings ranging from euphoria to high anxiety. For many, the very fact that the election campaign seemed at last to have got under way indicated that the preceding months of political confusion were now over and that the military regime was really resigned to the inevitable advent of democracy. Doubts lingered, however, and were reflected in the schizophrenic attitudes of the local media – reports on massive rallies shared pages uncomfortably with daily rumours of assassination plots and disruptive activities by *agents provocateurs*. The intensity of feelings underlined a collective sense that Argentina had reached a crossroads in her history, like the advent of Yrigoyen, the military coup of 1930 and Perón's rise to power after the Second World War. Whatever their political feelings, the majority of Argentines seemed to have a common conviction that after 2 April 1982 nothing was ever going to be the same again. The regime that was then withdrawing from the political scene had only been in government since 1976 – a mere interregnum compared to say Franco's Spain or Salazar's Portugal. And yet the legacy could not be measured in years. The previous six years had put the average Argentine through the kind of experience most countries in the world have shared only over many generations: a guerrilla war involving thousands of deaths, which had a profound impact on the framework of society; an economic crisis which had swung between the extremes of speculative bounty and abject recession, quadrupling the country's foreign debt to over 39 billion dollars in less than six years; and last, but by no means least, the country's first experience of international conflict which had brought military prestige to its lowest level ever.

If the nature of the outgoing regime had no precedent, the same could be said for its proposed replacement. The preparations for the elections of 1983 found most Argentines poised between the devil and the deep blue sea. The Perónist party, the grouping with the largest number of members and the only one with a relatively recent experience of government, had tried hard to resurrect the figure of their late leader towards the end of the Falklands War. This was the first election his party had fought without him since its foundation in 1946. The Radical party was also treading unknown territory. Raúl Alfonsín was a maverick without an official, political past. He had moved into the limelight only recently, and he ran the risk of being considered the product of circumstances rather than design. Nevertheless, this was the first election Argentina had ever had in which political patronage and conspiracy mattered less at the outset of the campaign than the party programme and the candidate himself. There appeared to be a genuine choice. This was never properly understood by the Perónists and it cost them dearly on voting day.

Nine years had elapsed since Perón had died, impotent and semi-senile at the age of seventy-nine, and yet the resurrection of the Perónist mystique became one of the main themes of an increasingly emotional campaign. In rallies the length and breadth of Argentina, his name and recordings of his favourite speeches reverberated through strategically placed loudspeakers. 'Perón, Perón, que grande sos' ('Perón, Perón, what a great man you are') chanted thousands in ecstatic approval, repeating over and over again the main lines of the General's hymn to machismo, as if it was the national anthem. In the streets, men shrouded themselves in the blue and white of the national flag and held posters showing Perón resplendent on his favourite horse – the macho *par excellence*. Chocolate portraits of Evita Perón, his second wife, dead for thirty-one years, were busily snatched up. Perón had had her body embalmed after she died, riddled with cancer of the uterus. A Spanish doctor had subsequently filled her with strange liquids and made her face up. In 1983 she remained no less enshrined, her face beautiful and passionate, begging to be eaten in reverential sacrifice. For those of us covering the election campaign, such scenes seemed to offer a glimpse of Argentina, but quite what sort of Argentina it was hard to fathom. I had asked one of the Perónist campaign managers what it all meant, and he had simply answered, 'By remembering the old man, it helps us to forget the chaos of what we are.'

Perón returned from exile in 1973 to rule for one year before his death. But it was his first government (1946–55) that was remembered as the golden period by the Perónist party machinery, emphasising particularly its record on social justice and anti-imperialism. Potential voters in 1983 were reminded that in the years following the Second World War, Argentina's urban working class and emerging lower middle class had found a new sense of dignity. Perón's innovations had included generous welfare schemes, a reinforced central trade union organisation, greater popular access to education and culture, women's suffrage, and a substantial increase in wage earners' incomes against those of other sectors. The redistribution of income

had been brought about largely thanks to Perón's ability to national-
ise the economy and build up a manufacturing sector at the expense
of the landed classes and their foreign, particularly British, partners.
Railroads, power plants and telephones, all once wholly owned by
the British, had become wholly 'Argentine'. Anti-imperialism had
been consolidated in Perón's foreign policy, strongly committed to
a non-aligned 'third position' between the two empires emerging
from the Second World War, the United States and the Soviet
Union.

Superficially, in 1983 the time appeared just right for the Perón
mythology to be resurrected. The previous seven years of military
rule had seen a steady erosion of wage levels, particularly among the
lower classes; health, education and housing had suffered major cut-
backs and were well behind defence in the priority of military
government; and last but by no means least the Falklands War
showed that Britain's imperialist ambitions had been far from
quelled. Seven months earlier President Bignone had asserted at the
non-aligned summit in New Delhi that his country did not 'accept
a world view that reduces everything to a permanent ideological and
military conflict between East and West'. Diplomats viewed it as a
worrying U-turn for a military regime nourished on anti-Com-
munism and high-level contacts with US Generals. But the Perónists
claimed it in their election campaign as a belated return to the golden
days of Argentine neutralism under their late leader.

While it may be true, as Ernesto Sábato himself has asserted, that
in every Argentine there is and always will be a small part of Perón,
it is no less true that many Argentines had a very different memory
of his government. For them, far from being golden, the eight years
of Perón's first administration had been a nightmare. Their view
was that instead of bringing prosperity to the nation, Perón had
ensured its decline and ruin. He had squandered the foreign
exchange reserves built up as a result of Argentina's neutralism
during the Second World War, wasting them on inefficient prestige
projects; unemployment had been disguised by the creation of
useless jobs in an illusory non-productive State sector; while his
high spending, including the housing programme, was a major factor
in the stagnation of agriculture and industry and the fuelling of
inflation. By the end of his administration, a poor reaction to fluct-
uating commodity prices on the international market and exclusion
from the US-backed Marshall plan had combined to leave the coffers
of the Argentine central bank without a dollar to its name. Thus the
country's sovereignty had been undermined rather than enhanced.

From a political perspective, there were members of at least two generations in Argentina who remembered Perón as an unscrupulous dictator who, like Mussolini and Hitler, had simply exploited the resentments of a poor and socially excluded class of *descamisados* or shirtless ones for his own ends. In the process he had made violence and corruption the linchpins of the State, repressing culture, imprisoning and torturing political opponents, and manipulating a submissive troika of Church, labour bosses and armed forces to stifle meaningful parliamentary life and democratic trade unionism. The seeds of authoritarian rule in Argentina were firmly planted in the post-war years and were revived on Perón's return, when right-wing death squads and left-wing Perónist guerrilla organisations contributed to the biggest genocide in the country's history.

The major tactical blunder made by the Perónists in the election campaign of 1983 was to assume not so much that their version of history was necessarily more correct than their opponents' but that history had stood still. Mrs Thatcher may well have succeeded in getting her own countrymen emotionally involved in the Falklands campaign by resurrecting the old imperialist lion; but the reality of Britain's relationship with Argentina in the early 1980s was very different to what it had been in the 1930s and 1940s. The so-called British influence, manifested in the use of the English language, fashion and customs by a sector of Argentine society, bore no relation to the real extent of Britain's economic presence in Argentina – almost non-existent in the infrastructure and with a greatly reduced profile in overall investment and trade.

It was true that Argentina was a sadder place than it had been under Perón. People were poorer, more people had died. But in the aftermath of the Falklands War, the majority of Argentines found themselves involved in a more complex collective self-analysis than that which had reduced politics to a simple division between Perónists and anti-Perónists in the past. The military who had come to power in 1976 had thrown unprecedented ingredients into Argentina's social and political structure. The politics of repression, combined with the Falklands War, had brought about a disruption of established attitudes towards the Church, the military and even Perón – for he might have been elected to government, but he was first and foremost a Colonel who came to power in the wake of a coup. By contrast, the country that prepared itself to vote on 30 October 1983 was above all a nation demoralised by death and defeat, and in a mood desperate for a change. The emotional circumstances were similar to those that had existed in 1946 when a majority of

Argentines had longed to be delivered by a saviour. The problem for the Perónists of course was that General Perón was dead and short of saddling his bones on a horse like a latter-day El Cid, no amount of propaganda could alter this. Thus, as the campaign developed, the inevitable happened: voters began to look beyond the mystique into what they perceived as the real world. There they found a party racked by internal rivalries and incapable of providing a cohesive electoral response to issues like human rights, the economy and foreign policy, around which Argentina's political future to a large extent revolved.

In spite of having been given an essentially symbolic role as party Chairman, General Perón's surviving third wife, Isabelita, remained mute, fuelling negative speculation from the media about her precise intentions while exiled in Madrid. One of the few political figures she talked to just before the campaign was Admiral Emilio Massera. The former junta member is believed to have obtained Isabelita's formal blessing for a populist–militarist party. The project foundered, however, when Massera became the subject of a celebrated court case linking him to the murder of his mistress's husband. Massera was also identified in Italy as an alleged member of the outlawed P-2 Masonic Lodge chaired by Licio Gelli. The confusion surrounding Argentina's last civilian President had therefore contributed in the weeks before the election to a hectic jockeying for positions within the party hierarchy.

Overshadowed by a ghost, the Perónist candidate Italo Luder could do little else than go through the motions. He allowed himself to be rivalled on his right flank by Herminio Iglesias, the party's candidate for the key political post of Governor of Buenos Aires. Iglesias's alleged past arrest in connection with a robbery and his rumoured links with right-wing death squads, the military and a police protection racket involving drugs and prostitution were repulsive to the party's intellectuals and those on the left. However, this did not stop the official Perónist campaign propaganda from proclaiming the leather-jacketed and open-shirted Iglesias as a 'man of the people', the protector and interpreter of the 'forgotten ones' in the shanty towns and many of the industrial suburbs surrounding Buenos Aires. If there was a macho reincarnation of Perón, it was Iglesias, supporters claimed. By contrast Luder proved a lacklustre candidate, mechanical in his gestures, uninspired in his rhetoric. A former head of the capital's penitentiary system, he always looked awkward in public rallies, as if he had been only recently ejected from his lawyer's office and thrown against his will before the unruly mass of drum-beating *descamisados* (shirtless ones). On one occasion, Iglesias publicly referred to the presidential candidate as a 'powdered woman who doesn't know how to embrace the ordinary man'. The statement showed the extent to which Perónist party discipline had broken down. In all some thirteen national parties and three dozen provincial groupings entered the campaign. From the outset it shaped into a two-horse race between the country's two traditional parties – the Perónists and the Radicals – in which Iglesias failed dismally to rekindle the spirit of Perón.

The legacy of Perón, not as the symbol of authoritarianism and corruption, but as the charismatic leader of the majority, passed to the Radicals. Even before the campaign had officially started Alfonsín had shown himself as the politician with the greatest capacity for communication with the ordinary public Argentina had seen in decades. A good public orator, a 'natural' before the TV cameras – both were gifts that helped Alfonsín. The image needed skilful management for it to succeed outright. In March 1983, Alfonsín had held what was arguably one of the key meetings of his political career with David Ratto, a member of the Radical party and head of one of the country's leading advertising agencies. At the meeting Alfonsín showed Ratto the findings of the latest opinion polls, which confirmed the Radical candidate as the most popular political figure, although most people would vote for the Perónist party. 'With the help of your publicity we can win by at least 42 per cent to 38 per cent,' Alfonsín told Ratto.

The importance of image had been brought home to Alfonsín in his contacts with European political parties and in particular the Spanish socialist party of Felipé González. His publicist, brought up like the bulk of Argentine advertising men under the influence of the United States, needed no convincing about the power of communication in the world of contemporary politics. Ratto was later to recall that it was never his intention to 'manufacture' a presidential candidate but rather to allow Alfonsín to communicate his message rapidly and efficiently. Whether this was genuinely his intention or not, the fact was that Ratto found his work made easier by the coincidence between the politically opportune and Alfonsín's beliefs. This was indeed a 'selling of a President', but there was more Kennedy than Nixon in Alfonsín, as a subsequent cover of *Time* magazine recognised. Nowhere was this better demonstrated than in one of the main symbols of the Alfonsín campaign – the two arms held high and together to one side in an anonymous embrace. The gesture was made by Alfonsín quite spontaneously during his second public rally in December 1983 before he had been officially declared presidential candidate and before Ratto had been brought into the party's inner political team. The *abrazo* was subsequently picked out by Ratto, edited and incorporated as a central plank of his attempts to portray Alfonsín as the President of 'all Argentines'. It proved the most popular symbol Argentines had had since the 'V' sign of the Perón days.

The Radical campaign devised by Ratto and Alfonsín's two closest advisers, Dante Caputo and German López, concentrated on two basic lines of communication which drew on Alfonsín's personality and political convictions and on the circumstances in which the election was being fought. After carefully researching political feelings through opinion polls and more detailed field studies, the Radical team was convinced that the election would be won with a mixture of new and old ideas projected mainly through the figure of Alfonsín. Ideas on morality, justice and democracy clearly conveyed a refreshing start after the human rights violations and corruption of the Perón years and the military regime. It was a bridge between the Radicals, conscious of their roots, and those disaffected Perónists on the left who saw little difference between the orthodox thugs who were then trying to monopolise Luder's campaign and the death squads who had driven their friends underground both before and after the 1976 coup. No campaign, however, could ignore Argentina's latent nationalism and the important role a strong leader has historically played in regional politics. These sentiments were judged to be psychologically a key reaction to the humiliation of the Falklands War when a General had been beaten by a woman. Hence such campaign slogans as: 'Raúl Alfonsín: El Hombre que hace falta' (The man we need) and the initials 'R.A.' used by the Alfonsín camp to confuse their candidate with the initials of the Argentine Republic.

Ratto's publicity did for Alfonsín what Saatchi & Saatchi did for Mrs Thatcher in the 1979 British general election. Out of the scepticism that had been deeply engrained in the body politic, the publicity created the certainty of change and innovation. The Perónists concentrated, as they had always done, on posters and mass rallies. Ratto insisted that Alfonsín should be filmed not just in front of a huge rally but also close to camera, alone, talking to the audience in a soft but reassuring voice as if he had just walked into his or her room. Thus the man came across as much as the candidate.

On the surface there was little to separate the electoral platforms of the Perónists and Radicals. Both parties invoked human rights and social justice without detailing what this would mean in terms of future government action. The difference lay in emphasis and style. In one memorable election slot put together by Ratto for television, a film began with a black screen against the background of police sirens, door slammings and tortured cries; the blackness then gradually opened in the middle, like a door in the wall through which bright light began to shine, then the caption, 'Not just an electoral way-out but an entrance into life. Vote for Alfonsín.' For a country that had experienced death in the torture chambers as well as in the fields around Port Stanley, it was a pithy message of hope which could not easily be ignored. An equally frontal approach to a previously taboo issue was demonstrated by Alfonsín himself in a dramatic press conference towards the end of the campaign, in which he publicly denounced a military–union plot against democracy involving metal workers' boss Lorenzo Miguel and senior military figures.

The election results, in which the Radicals were swept to victory, showed the extent to which Alfonsín had managed to bridge the enormous emotional distance which had traditionally separated his party from the working class and the landed and business élites. In the shanty towns and poor industrial suburbs, previously the undisputed fiefdoms of the Perónists, the majority of votes went to the Radicals. Nevertheless the Radicals failed to gain a majority in the Upper House or Senate and lost some of the regional Governorships to the opposition. Moreover, the same elements which contributed to Alfonsín's election victory were to prove a two-edged sword. The obsessive focus on the figure of Alfonsín ill-prepared his future Ministers and Congressmen to act truly responsively to the needs of the country. At the same time the Radicals' election programme did not adequately convey the seriousness of the economic situation and the sacrifices in the early stages of democracy this would entail. False expectations were thus created, making the task of future policy implementation that much more difficult.

The bold promises made about the economy sprang from a mixture of electoral opportunism and genuine conviction. To the extent that the latter was true, the blame must fall on the government of General Bignone for not having adequately prepared for the transition. Even in the last months before the election, neither the central bank nor the Ministry of the Economy made any attempt to allow the politicians into decision-making or into the sharing of statistics. Instead the military government embarked on a last-minute round of wage increases, arms purchases and commitments to its creditors, which it knew a future government would be unable to match.

10
CULTURE'S REBIRTH

On the night Raúl Alfonsín was sworn in as his country's democratically elected President, the people of Buenos Aires had themselves a party. In parks and avenues across the city there were poetry
recitals, dancing and free concerts, as artists who had for so long
been blacklisted by the military joined people off the streets to
celebrate the newly won freedom. There could not have been a more
striking image of the cultural rebirth of a nation that counts among
its inhabitants some of the most gifted artists in the world. This
renaissance has played a vital role in the early stages of Argentina's
transition to democracy. At one level it has helped Argentines forge
for themselves a new identity, more critical of the past and more open
to change. At another level, culture has become the government's
unofficial roving ambassador at large, ensuring that after the
'disappeared' and the Falklands débâcle the new Argentina be
reaccepted as part of the human race.

Nowhere has this process been more pronounced than in the
cinema. Argentina was one of the first countries in the world to
import the pioneering silent movies from France at the end of the
nineteenth century.[1] One of the first short films shown in Buenos
Aires's Odeon cinema in 1896 was treated with the attention usually
accorded to visiting Heads of State; so engrossed were the front
stalls with the shot of an advancing train that several people fell off
their seats, believing the sequence to be real. Since then the cinema
has grown to be intellectually respectable in Argentina, although art
has not always been allowed to imitate life. Argentina has more
cinema-goers *per capita* than any other Third World country, and
Buenos Aires now has more cine theatres than a small European
capital. The passion for the medium felt particularly by the large
and influential middle class far outstrips interest in any other art
form such as literature and the theatre.

Small wonder that successive regimes have felt themselves compelled to make the cinema the focus of their cultural policy, while
the opposition has turned to films to express its alternative vision of
society and the future. In the past this politicisation tended to
provoke a mix of censorship and propaganda. During the first Perón
government, the Subsecretariat for Information and the Press
became a form of Propaganda Ministry, using the same monitoring
system for the cinema as it did for the press and the radio. In 1968,

thirteen years after Perón's removal from power, his supporters took to making films as the radical expression of their opposition to military rule. Perhaps the most famous film of the time was *La Hora de los Hornos* ('The Hour of the Furnaces'). This mammoth four-hour documentary, made by Fernando Solanas, Octavio Getino and Gerardo Vallejo, recommended 'revolution' – expressed through Perónism – as the only deliverance from the 'neocolonialism' and backwardness Argentine society allegedly found itself in.

The film was banned by the then government of General Juan Carlos Onganía on the grounds that it was subversive and immoral. As a result, *La Hora de los Hornos* was at first less a commercial film than a cult movie shared out by the intellectual community of Buenos Aires in clandestine showings. With the brief cultural revival which occurred in the last Perónist government (1973–6), the film went commercial and became a box-office hit – even though Solanas agreed to tone down the original revolutionary fervour in honour of the older, more reactionary Perón who returned from exile. 'Soon after, the two film makers were forced to go into exile for political reasons. Censorship and self-censorship again.'[2]

Under the juntas, no alternative vision was permitted; politically suspect actors and directors were put on a 'black list' and banned from television or making major films; many went into exile rather than risk joining the ranks of the 'disappeared'.[3] Imported foreign films had controversial scenes expurgated from them or were simply banned outright.[4] The closest the Argentine cinema came to reflecting the social reality of the time was to bring out detective films whose gratuitously violent action could be interpreted as a vague allegory of repression and its results. Generally though, 'production dropped and inoffensive comedies and musicals became the norm',[5] anaesthetising society as a result. In 1980 the Argentine director Hector Olivera commented, 'Censorship in Argentina has become the most reactionary, incoherent and castrating in the Western world'.[6] Only after the Falklands, and during the troubled interregnum of President Bignone, was there some relaxation. Foreign films previously regarded as politically sensitive, such as *The Deer Hunter* (because of its anti-draft viewpoint), were released, while a limited number of 'serious' Argentine productions had their first airing. Each of them showed the limitations of self-censorship. Thus *Señora de Nadie* by María Luisa Bemberg looked at the problems of being a woman in a macho-dominated society, without attacking the Church or the military; *Plata Dulce* 'exposed' financial corruption during the regime, putting the blame on civilian speculators.

Easily the bravest of this stable of immediate post-Falklands films was Olivera's own *No Habrá Mas Penas ni Olvido* ('A Funny, Dirty Little War'). Released a month before the elections, when some opinion polls were still predicting a defeat for Alfonsín, the film is a biting satire of the irrational and violent in-fighting in the Perónist party.

This trickle of socially and politically sensitive films became an avalanche thanks to the restructuring of the film industry almost as soon as Alfonsín took power. One of the first acts of Parliament, introduced by the ruling Radical party, was the abolition of the infamous Ente de Calificación Cinematográfica (the Cinema Classification Board). Superficially similar to the Board of Censors operating in some democratic European countries, the Ente under the military had become a latter-day cultural inquisition. Made up mainly of military officers determined to use whatever means they could to stamp out 'subversion' and with the blessing of Bishops and the conservative Catholic lay organisation Opus Dei, the junta's Ente had assumed the responsibility for the nation's 'moral education', censoring films with sharp scissors or simply with a blanket ban. Beneath this cultural overlord, the Instituto Cinematográfico, the National Film Institute, which in the past had subsidised such internationally respected Argentine film directors as Torre Nilsson, became little more than a rubber-stamp institution. Quality in film making was not considered as a factor in the allocation of government funds.[7]

The abolition of the Ente was accompanied by a revamping of the National Film Institute, which although officially under a restructured Secretariat of Culture, immediately assumed a considerable degree of political and financial autonomy under the skilful guidance of Manuel Antín, a member of the country's generation of banned film directors. One of Antín's first measures was to guarantee 10 per cent of the box office earnings to the film industry, thus reducing his own dependence on the central government budget. These measures had been adopted by the first Perón government, but Antín did not fall into the trap of excessive protectionism; as the first batch of films from the new Argentine cinema demonstrated, he showed that it was possible to make good films with modest budgets, while maintaining a regular inflow of internationally successful foreign films to stimulate competition.[8] Antín was criticised for not following the Perónists in imposing a quota on foreign films; and yet the traditional preference of exhibitors for North American distribution companies and their products has become less of a drawback as a result of the growing international recognition won by the new Argentine cinema. María Luisa Bemberg's third feature film, *Camila,* outstripped the popularity of Spielberg's *E.T.* after being nominated for an Oscar as the best foreign film of 1985. One year later, the Cannes film festival award for the best foreign actress went to Norma Aleandro, the leading lady in Luis Puenzo's *Historia Oficial* ('Official Version'). The film subsequently won the Oscar for the best foreign film. Released over an eight-month period the film became an enormous box-office hit in spite of an influx of successful foreign productions ranging from *Rambo* to *The Killing Fields.*

Aleandro at the age of forty-nine became a symbol of the changing face of Argentina. Interviewers expecting to find a latter-day 'sex queen' discovered that here was a woman who lived not in a mansion but in a small flat filled with good paintings and old books; with no bodyguards or 'walkers' for her one Alsatian dog; and, most important, with neither a particularly pretty face nor a corpulent body. During previous regimes, this fact, along with her larger than life nose and outspoken political views, had forced Aleandro out of the cinema and into the less popular or visible theatre and radio. Following the military coup, even theatre became a risky business. One night in June 1976, as she took the stage for a one-woman recital of classical verse, an extreme right-wing group acting under government orders invaded the theatre and threw gas canisters into the stalls. A few hours later she was sleeping in her flat with her husband and young son when a bomb exploded in the hall of the building, shattering the ground floor and seriously injuring the occupants of the room nearest the explosion. 'We didn't want to kill you with the first two, but the third time you won't be so lucky,' an anonymous telephone caller told her soon afterwards. 'You've got twenty-four hours to get out of the country.' She did.

After leading a nomadic existence, first in Uruguay and then in Spain and Venezuela, Aleandro took the risk of returning to Argentina in the summer of 1981. Exile, she later told me, had become 'like a slow death'. She preferred to risk the limited cultural liberation of the military regime. A standing ovation greeted her first night in a play in Buenos Aires by the Peruvian novelist Mario Vargas Llosa. The theatre was ringed by bomb-disposal units and police, because she had received an avalanche of death threats – but the show went on, and this time survived as a box-office hit for two years. In between came the invasion of the Falklands, which Aleandro recalls as the last demented act of a regime under pressure. 'We have a just claim to the islands, but we should have got them by negotiating. I remember the day of the invasion ... it seemed as if the world had gone mad and I cried my heart out.'[9]

Given her background, it is perhaps hardly surprising that Aleandro's first film made under democracy was a strong critique of the former military regime. The film is set in the Bignone period and identifies Argentina's defeat at the hand of the British as a crucial turning point for the country's social and political development. Aleandro plays the role of Alicia, a secondary-school teacher, trying to make sense of history in a society that has been forced either to rewrite or forget it. One of the early scenes has the professionally orthodox and apolitical teacher facing a rebellion by her pupils, who refuse to accept any longer the versions of events described in the textbooks. At first Alicia reacts angrily, expelling the culprits from the classroom; but gradually, under the influence of a left-wing colleague, she accepts and collaborates with their point of view. These developments in the classroom become a mirror image of Alicia's own personal discovery that her adopted daughter may be the abandoned child of one of the 'disappeared', who has been forcefully taken from her natural family by her husband, a close collaborator with the military. Again, Alicia's initial reaction is one of rejection, resisting the advice first of a close friend recently returned from exile, and afterwards of a member of the Madres de Mayo human rights group who claims to be the child's real grandmother; but the film's denouement has Alicia helping the grandmother trace the child's records in open defiance of her husband.

'When the film starts up, Alicia is not a heroine, but she ends by committing an heroic act: sacrificing the husband and daughter she loves, paradise in other words, for the sake of truth ...' Aleandro commented.[10] In Cannes the French critics told her that Alicia's story reminded them of the Jews and the Second World War; in Los Angeles and New York, the Americans recalled children taken from the highways and exploited by the porn movie industry. Both Aleandro and the director, Luis Puenzo, were showered with offers from international film producers and US distributors. In Argentina *La Historia Oficial* became the most popular film of the decade, quickening the real-life investigations into the children of the disappeared,[11] and elevating Aleandro to the status of most popular actress. The television networks which, during the Falklands War, had urged patriotic support for the military, organised showbiz extravaganzas in her honour. In Argentina *La Historia Oficial* was regarded less as an instrument of revolution like much of the country's Liberation Cinema in the late 1960s and 1970s but more as a 'reflection on society's ills and conflicts'.[12]

The majority of quality films which have emerged since 1983 have contributed, like *La Historia Oficial,* to the post-war collective catharsis, touching on themes like exile, torture, women's liberation and corruption which were previously taboo, and forcing traditionally untouchable institutions of State like the military and the Church to justify themselves within the new democratic reality. The process has perhaps been most ambitiously encompassed in *Camila* and *Tangos,* which have also collected their share of international prizes and become money spinners both at home and abroad. In *Camila,* Bemberg applies her feminist cutting edge to the legendary love affair between a rich Argentine Irish girl, Camila O'Gorman, and a young Spanish priest Ladislao Gutiérrez. Set in the nineteenth century, the film is a full-blooded costume melodrama and often threatens to exude 'nothing more than surface art-house allure'.[13] But *Camila*'s strength lies in depicting the young couple's struggle against the outraged reaction of family, State and Church as an allegory of the prejudice and violence of contemporary Argentine society. In *Tangos* Fernando Solanas uses Argentina's quintessentially popular dance and song form as an image of his country's capacity to develop new cultural forms and conscience levels. At the same time many old tango lyrics are revived to evoke nostalgia for Buenos Aires, family and friends – the tragedy of exile in other words. In the portrait of the young troop of dancers who act out the tango in its various stages of evolution, Solanas also focuses on the hopes and dreams of an emerging generation that survived the military regime and hopes to inspire a brighter future. Although himself formerly a militant Perónist, Solanas returned from exile following Alfonsín's inauguration as President. His film, less dogmatic and violent than his earlier *Hours of the Furnace,* shows the extent to which the Argentine cinema industry has managed to evolve in its search for alternative ways of depicting reality.

It says much for the new Argentina's capacity for analysis and self-criticism that the first feature film to deal directly with the Falklands War, *Los Chicos de la Guerra,* points an accusing finger at the empty rhetoric of patriotism as used by the repressive regime of the juntas. Rather than focus on the war itself, the director Bebe Kamín and co-scriptwriter Daniel Kon – place the conflict with Britain within the wider historical context of a generation that moved from adolescence to conscription under the military. Based on Kon's best-selling book of interviews with returning war veterans, *Los Chicos* recounts the lives of three young draftees from the day they have to sing their first national anthem at school to the day they suffer hunger, mutilation and death as part of the final battle for Port Stanley. 'The war was the final suicidal act of a generation of Argentines. The conscripts who went to the islands were only just coming out of childhood when the 1976 coup took place. From that moment on, they never experienced anything but social and political repression,' Kon told me.[14] When it was shown at the London Film Festival in 1984, *Los Chicos* disappointed some critics for not showing more of the Falklands War. But others recognised in Kamin and Kon the traumatic political and social effect the conflict had had on Argentina, and suggested that the tragedy of the three main characters stood its ground as a reflection of the more universal alienation of the Punk generation.

As yet not internationally recognised but as influential in raising the political conscience of contemporary Argentines through the depiction of the past are *La Rosales* and *Asesinato en el Senado de la Nación*, directed by one of the country's most prestigious film makers Juan José Jusid. *La Rosales* recounts a true incident in 1892 when a group of naval officers abandoned their crew during a shipwreck in order to save their own lives. This act of cowardice was kept from the public eye for many years with the surviving officers claiming that they had heroically done all in their power to save the others. Only in a subsequent trial did the truth emerge. In *Asesinato,* Jusid again takes up a true story, that of the Radical Senator Lisandro de la Torre, who in 1935 risked his life and those of his closest collaborators to conduct a parliamentary inquiry to expose high-level corruption involving senior politicians, policemen and a British meat-packing company. At one level Jusid adopts a nationalist revision of history to remind his audience of Argentina's colonialist status under the British empire. But by contrasting the methods of the police – a somewhat unnecessarily long torture sequence is shown – with the legalistic and impassioned methods of de la Torre, the film is a direct allegory of present-day Argentina. As with Solanas, the previously militant Jusid ends on a basically optimistic note, even though Lisandro committed suicide, the company he was investigating was fined. *Asesinato* can thus be interpreted as an allegory and both as a warning and a statement of hope by bearing a direct correlation to the new democracy and the ethics of Alfonsinismo.

Generally speaking the emerging Argentine film industry had

tended to accompany rather than lead change in the post-Falklands era. Technically even the more talented directors like Bemberg and Puenzo are behind their European counterparts. What they lack in style, however, they make up for in passion. And although it would be an exaggeration to talk of a new innovative cinema similar to the French 'nouvelle vague' of the 1960s, in the context of Argentine history there is a renaissance, which has certainly helped to shape people's attitudes.

In May 1984, seven months after Alfonsín's inauguration, Buenos Aires's main cultural complex and Argentina's answer to the Kennedy Center, the Centro Cultural San Martín, was virtually under siege as riot police half-heartedly 'fought off' an attack on it by extreme right-wing groups wielding sticks and chains. Youths in leather jackets, who only minutes previously had been seen fraternising with plain-clothes policemen shouted a selection of slogans such as 'Beware of God', 'We're going to get rid of Alfonsín's synagogues' (an apparent reference to the Jews in the new Cabinet) and 'Englishmen and Communists, you are one and the same.' The Communist in question was Dario Fo, the Italian playwright whose satire on the life of Pope Boniface VIII was being shown that week in one of the San Martín's main auditoria. In Italy, the play had had a stormy reception from the Bishops when it was first shown on TV, but survived censorship after being examined by a special parliamentary commission. In Argentina, the fortunes of Fo's play were even more indicative of social change. The hecklers and the half-hearted resistance put up by the police, with the resurgence of death threats against actors and playwrights, was a throwback to the cultural repression that existed under the military regime. But the fact that the audience fought back, expelling the hecklers, and endorsing Fo's decision to carry on as normal, was perhaps more significant. It showed that the climate of fear so essential for ensuring self-censorship was no longer as effective as it once had been and that the men in leather belonged to a nostalgic minority.

Although cinema has been the most dynamic sector of Argentina's cultural revival, theatre, as in the case of Fo's production, music and literature have also come into their own under Alfonsín. The Centro Cultural built originally by Perón to popularise culture, between 1983 and 1986 became a more genuine symbol of culture accessible to a wide cross-section of society. With an annual audience put at over 1·5 million people, San Martín's eleven auditoria competed for the attention of practically every taste and generation. On a good day the Centre presented the visitor with a virtual 'magical mystery tour' – everything from a live debate on Buddhism and Zen to a popular adult circus. In between there was a wealth of translations by American and European dramatists and experimental theatre put on by flourishing theatre groups such as the Teatro Abierto ('Open Theatre') most of whose members had only recently returned from exile.

Political theatre in Argentina, as in most industrialised countries, traditionally has been an intellectual art form rather than a popular one. It was because the theatre audiences were limited in their social scale that successive military governments had reacted to it with a level of tolerance absent from official attitudes towards the cinema or TV. Teatro Abierto was launched in 1981, a year before the Falklands, in an attempt to test the limits of official tolerance. A group of playwrights, directors and actors, many of whom had fled the country following the 1976 coup, were determined to demonstrate that theatre could become a living art in Argentina in spite of censorship and physical repression. 'We reckoned that if we all appeared together, they couldn't possibly silence the whole thing,' one of the founding group commented. The original idea had been to put on twenty-one short plays at the rate of three a day over a week, with repetitions of the plays over a month. But the group didn't get beyond the first few days. The theatre staging the plays was broken into by right-wing extremists (almost certainly under the orders of the government) and gutted with phosphorus bombs.

Of another play in the series put on by Teatro Abierto, the playwright Eduardo Pavlovsky has left a vivid testimony, 'In my play *Telarañas* ('Cobwebs') there is a scene in which two gas board officials force their way into a home. In fact, they are not from the gas board at all, but are torturers ... I received a letter from the Secretary of Culture in the City of Buenos Aires asking me to withdraw it. Possibly because I wasn't fully aware of the kind of situation we were really in, I took no formal notice, and forced them to issue a formal banning decree. Three months later, two "gas board officials" came to my place asking for me. Luckily my secretary realised what was going on, and phoned me upstairs. By this time, another eight "gasmen" had appeared. If I'm here to tell the story, it's because by then I had climbed out of my window and escaped across the roofs.'[15]

One of the most interesting of an early post-Falklands stable of hard-hitting political plays was *Knepp*, by the Argentine dramatist Jorge Goldenburg. In it one of María Luisa Bemberg's protegées, the actress Lusiana Brando, gave a moving performance as the young wife whose only form of communication with her husband – one of the estimated 8,000 disappeared – was through a periodical phone call arranged by anonymous torturers. A glimmer of hope that the couple may one day be physically reunited is presented by Dr Knepp, a sinister 'scientist' who barges into Brando's room in the opening scene claiming to be conducting an investigation into the psychological reactions of victims of the State. The plot twists and turns in on itself like a Borges short story. Only in the end does it resolve itself in tragedy when Knepp reveals himself as a government agent bent on forcing his latest victim to accept the 'disappearance' of her husband as irrevocable and justified. The fact that one is never quite sure where symbolism ends and real people begin makes *Knepp* all the more disconcerting as an allegory of political repression.

One of the first administrative innovations of the Alfonsín government was the setting up within the Foreign Ministry of a department specially entrusted with the promotion of culture. Backed by a team of attachés in Latin American capitals and in friendly social democratic countries such as Spain and France, the idea was not only to attract artists from abroad but also to develop a native culture capable of being accepted not just domestically but internationally also. While the Ministry has been active in taking the new Argentine cinema to international festivals as a key diplomatic function, it has also poured some of its energies into trying to ensure a balance between Western and indigenous influences to forge a sense of national identity under democracy.

'Culturally speaking, Argentina is a headless chicken scurrying about in a quixotic search for an identifiable future.'[16] This statement by Edward Shaw, a leading local art critic, was an accurate comment on the cultural diversity brought about in Argentina's transition to democracy. Half-way through Alfonsín's presidential term, punks and poncho-clad Indians vied for attention along Buenos Aires's fashionable Calle Florida. The Foreign Ministry created the Municipal Centre for Artisan Crafts with stock, quality controls and production controls for would-be wholesale buyers of flutes, guitars and drums from the Andean north. But more popular among the youth were the Calvin Klein and Levi jeans made under local licence and the pop records of the new mega stores. A symbiosis of cultures has been emerging, however. Leon Gieco, whose voice and guitar-playing style resemble early Dylan and whose personal contribution to the Falklands War was a moving protest song called 'Solo le Pido a Dios' ('All I ask from God'), toured the poor regions of Argentina in search of new cultural influences. Mercedes Sousa, a member of the Communist Party whose return from exile during the Bignone government helped set the pace for the subsequent cultural rebirth, has gradually merged her Andean rhythms with blues and jazz; a similar process has affected the tango composer Piazolla, who wrote the award-winning soundtrack for Solanas's film *Tangos*. A form of national rock has also come into its own; more often than not imitative, but with occasional sparks of inspiration. The extrovert singer Charly García – a homespun cross between Elton John and Frank Zappa – has tried his hand at several musical styles including Punk and cabaret and has made acting 'gay' almost respectable among a younger generation whose parents have been strictly macho-orientated. His 'No bombardeen Buenos Aires' ('Don't bomb Buenos Aires'), released as the military bowed out, mixed rock's traditional obsessions with sex and drugs with the paranoia of modern warfare. It was as an acute comment on a generation's experience of the conflict with Britain as *Los Chicos de la Guerra*. Against the recording of one of the junta's official communiqués proclaiming that Argentina is winning the war, García screams, 'I don't want the world of Cinzano, I mustn't lose my faith ... I want to make love to you but nothing happens, I can't even eat a steak and feel well. I'm hungry, I'm scared ... the Gurkhas are advancing, the old cats are still on TV, the parents of the boys are drinking whisky with the rich while the workers are holding a mass demonstration in the square like that other time ... If you want to, you can listen to the BBC, but please don't bomb Buenos Aires.'

As a mixture of sheer entertainment and measured political statement, García's only female rival is Nacha Guevara. During the growing pre-coup terrorism in 1975, Guevara took a premature final curtain when a bomb exploded in the hall of the theatre where she was singing, killing two people and injuring several others. Guevara, who although no relation, was always accused by the military of being a follower of Ché, fled the country with her husband, the actor Norman Brinski, and for the next nine years roamed the world scratching a living. She returned in triumph soon after Alfonsín's election victory to give a sell-out performance of her one-woman show, *Aqui estoy*. This was a breathtaking combination of cabaret, music hall, jazz, rock and tango, but two scenes in particular drew an ecstatic roar from the audience. The first was when she walked across the stage in total silence, turned on an old 1920s gramophone and sang in perfect harmony to a recording of Argentina's most famous pre-war tangoist, Carlos Gardel; the second when she marched to the front of the stage and sang the title song, 'I've lived better times, bad times ... watched winters pass, seen dictators die ... only God knows what I've been through ... and yet here I am.' Her repertoire seemed to encapsulate the broken dreams, suffering, and lingering hopes which characterised Argentina's transition to democracy.

Before the Falklands War it used to be a tradition in Argentina that every change of regime be ceremoniously celebrated by the incoming officialdom and its supporters by a public burning of books. In 1955, when the first regime of Perón was toppled in a military coup, the anti-Perónists gathered the available literature on the works of El General and Evita and set them aflame. Following the 1976 coup, it was not just the military that tested Fahrenheit 451. As a clandestine opponent of the junta told me later in a conversation, 'One day the troops surrounded the block of flats I was living in and switched on the search lights. It meant there was going to be a raid and I thought they were coming for us. So I took every book I could find into the kitchen and one by one, as quickly as I could, burnt them over the sink.'

When Raul Alfonsín was inaugurated as President the only book that was burnt was a registry of some of the 'disappeared' kept in an army barracks. According to human rights groups at the time, sectors of the armed forces were bent on destroying any evidence that could be used against them as quickly as possible. Elsewhere literature was resurrected from dark cupboards and foreign publishing houses in a further dimension to Argentina's cultural revival. Its most poignant symbol was the effervescence of the annual book fair in April 1984. Its two predecessors had already taken advantage of the post-war confusion of the Bignone government to display some previously banned books. But the first fair under democracy was expansive rather than condescending. There was no military overseer left to dictate what could and could not be read. There was an element of defiance in the thousands of civilians who poured into the fair. Just a few hundred yards away from where it was being held was the site of the National Library – or at least what should have been the National Library. The building and restoration work was never completed under the military, because the junta judged that battleships, nuclear reactors and colour TV (developed at enormous cost to coincide with the 1978 World Cup) were more important than books, even though a previous director of the National Library had been Borges.

In democracy's first book fair each stand was like a chapter of a history book – it too forming part of the collective catharsis. Among the publishers few perhaps attracted as much attention as Daniel Divinsky, whose popular house Editorial de la Flor had been closed down by the military in 1977. In that year Divinsky was arrested, after being accused of being 'an ideological instigator of subversion in children'. His crime had been to publish a children's book which tells the story of a battle between two personalised hands. When the book had first been taken off the shelves, Divinsky had appealed to a military judge, claiming that it was a simple story about hands 'one of which is united, the other isn't. The one that is disunited gets it together and beats the other one.' Divinsky, along with his wife, was subsequently imprisoned. The publisher had had books banned by previous military governments, but this was the first time he had been made to feel close to death. He was separated from his wife and held virtually incommunicado for two months – it was a time when Argentines were 'disappearing at a rate of hundreds a week'. One day a military officer came into Divinsky's cell with a file stashed with letters. 'Your relatives must be very famous,' he commented cynically. In fact Divinsky had become a *cause célèbre* not just in his family but in the international publishing world. Friends and colleagues – among them Andrew Graham-Yooll, the Anglo-Argentine historian and journalist whose witty book of poems, *Spanglis,* Editorial de la Flor had published some years before – had mounted a worldwide campaign on his behalf. Divinsky was finally released and put on a plane to exile when General Videla received a very official-looking letter from the organisers of the Frankfurt Book Fair. Although the fair began in October and it was only March, the letter said that Divinsky's presence in West Germany was required immediately and that it was imperative that he catch the first plane out of Buenos Aires.[17]

Divinsky returned to Argentina soon after the Falklands War to help organise Alfonsín's election campaign. Drawing inspiration from some of his more humorous banned books, he circulated many of the stories picturing the Perónist party in its less attractive light, exposing such characters as Herminio Iglesias, the candidate for the governorship of Buenos Aires, as a sinister if politically incompetent crook. For his efforts, Divinsky was rewarded once Alfonsín came to power with the Chairmanship of Radio Belgrano – one of the capital's most popular radio stations. It would have been tempting to fill the top journalist jobs with militant members of the ruling Radical party. But Divinsky was under a specific order from Alfonsín not to turn Belgrano into an officialist station, and so he drew on professional people of varying political currents.

Radio has traditionally enjoyed looser censorship and the advantages of competition between State and private stations in Argentina. Under the military, however, all channels were put under military control and several journalists purged. Following Alfonsín's inauguration, Radio Belgrano put its full weight behind the new democracy and as a result picked up a new generation of listeners. Its phone-in programmes, satire and news programmes attracted many thousands of Argentines starved of good comment and analysis. It also attracted the wrath of the extreme right, who provided Radio Belgrano with a constant stream of death threats.

TV and newspapers proved less dynamic. The Alfonsín government treated the three state-controlled TV channels 7, 11 and 13, with extreme caution. Journalists who had worked for the military regime were allowed to go on working, and some were even promoted to heads of news departments. There was, however, a change of content – members of the armed forces were given much less time to air their views, the human rights trial of the juntas was reported on a regular basis (although not recorded live as the prosecution had wished) and new programming developed around other previous taboo subjects such as sex education, women's rights and conscription. Some of the programmes conducted by journalists who had been banned by the junta had a genuine sense of commitment; some of their colleagues appeared to be motivated less by political conviction than by a sense of opportunism. The other weakness was the inexperience of many of the new faces – writer journalists picked because of their allegiance to the Radical party who proved professionally inept in front of the cameras. The only major privately controlled station, Channel 9 emerged less as a genuine alternative than a blatant attempt to reproduce the junta's perception of society under a different guise. It absorbed many of the journalists considered too anti-democratic by the government and excelled in a mixture of cheap sensationalism and superficial comment, appealing both to the apolitical masses and right-wing sectors of the political establishment.

In 1986 Alfonsín is reported to have confessed to one of his close aides his disappointment with the inability of the Argentine press to accompany the process of democratic change. Government officials found it difficult to accept that journalists whom they regarded as friends during the military regime were critical of the policies of the new democratic government. But the greatest danger emerged not so much from a greater pluralism of views and comment but from the continuation of many of the attitudes moulded by years of repression and self-censorship. Jacobo Timerman, the former publisher and editor of *La Opinión* (see *Prisoner Without a Name, Cell Without a Number* for an account of his arrest and torture by the military) returned to Argentina in 1984 hoping to revamp the daily newspaper *La Razón* into the democracy's first 'genuine newspaper'. But far from acting as a catalyst for change, *La Razón* exposed the inherent weaknesses of Argentine newspaper journalists. Timerman resigned in 1985 in the midst of sharply declining sales. His critics blamed him for turning *La Razón* into a pro-government propaganda sheet. Timerman himself blamed his failure on his inability to find journalists capable of digging beneath the surface and providing enlightened comment.

There were exceptions, however. The new weekly *El Periodista,* although often dogmatically left wing, managed to investigate the corruption of the former regime. Its political commentary also provided the Alfonsín government with some refreshing insights into some of its failings.

On the de la Flor stands at the book fair were the titles – children's and otherwise – that had been banned in the past. Among the stable of new books, easily the most original was *Los Pichy-Cyegos* by Rodolfo Enrique Fogwill. Subtitled 'Visions of a Subterranean Battle', the book was a funny and extremely original satire on the Falklands War told through the conversations of a family of voles. On other stands, as Andrew Graham-Yooll has noted, 'the literature of exiles, their bravado protected by distance ... found their way back to the Buenos Aires bookshelves'. Osvaldo Soriano whose 'Funny Dirty Little War' was so despised by military and Perónists alike was there, as was Eduardo Galeano, whose Marxist epic history of the continent, *The Open Veins of Latin America,* had provided fuel for more than one pyre. Then there were those authors who were familiar to international readers but who also had at some time or another been considered subversive by the junta: books by Gabriel García Márquez and Mario Vargas Llosa at the fair also proved that times were changing.

There were some tombstones. Books by Rodolfo Walsh, the journalist, and Haroldo Conti, poet and novelist, both of whom had 'disappeared' never to be seen again.[18] It was the memory of committed artists such as these that gave the fair a distinctly political thrust. Arguably much of what was on display was less high literature than retrospective journalism but it was a refreshing attempt none the less to look at the past with the kind of equanimity that was largely unknown in Argentina. Pablo Guissani's *Montoneros: La Soberbia Armada* and Miguel Bossano's *Recuerdos de la Muerte,* for example, rather than toe a party line, took a critical look at the roots of political violence in contemporary Argentina as expressed both by the military and the guerrilla groups. The perfect complement to their analysis was provided by the more profound intellectual musings of journalists like Rudolfo Terragno, whose *Memories of the Present* and *Argentina in the 21st Century* became instant best-sellers thanks to their ability to break free from the immediacy and provincialism characteristic of much of Argentine writing and to present a more generous universal vision of the future.

In July 1986 Divinsky himself was forced to admit the limitations of the cultural renaissance. 'There is as yet hardly any first class fiction that deals directly with the events during the *proceso* [the military regime],' he confessed in an interview. 'Nobody like a Grass or Solzhenitsyn has appeared . . . the events are still too close. Reality is too hard.'[19] Powerful political fiction there has been, however. *La Novela de Perón* ('The Novel of Perón') by Eloy Martínez demonstrates both extraordinary imagination and keen journalistic exposure. It is an account of the irrational and the complex in the Perón years, which so stamped contemporary Argentina. Although written as fiction, it is more real than history, as Borges used to say about so much of his own work. Its account of the corruption and pervasive violence of the Perónist regime exposes the darker side of Argentina's political culture with devastating effect.

Less ambitious but worthy of note are the short novels of Jorge Asís, one of Argentina's more controversial journalists who had spent much of his adult life in hiding, accused locally of being a left-wing subversive and abroad of being a fascist. Asis was one of the first authors to re-emerge in the months following the Falklands War, signing copies of his instantly best-selling novels: true-to-life texts which looked back with a mixture of cynicism and nostalgia to the 'lost generation' of the 1970s caught up in the confused ideology of the guerrilla war. Andrew Graham-Yooll has noted:

> Asís will go down in Latin American literature as the author of feuilletons – but he helped to bring about the torrent of political texts that shoe-horned Argentina into the electoral campaign and into the constitutional transition. It is no mean achievement of

the country's writers and journalists: by May 1983, with the help of the writing community which had created a political awareness, the parties which planned to contest the October elections recorded the highest ever levels of affiliation. The people, having read about their recent past, registered their protest by signing a party card.[20]

Argentina's cultural revival under Alfonsín did not take place in a vacuum, but in the context of a changing institutional framework capable of absorbing the new intellectual outpourings and channelling them back into society. Educational reform was one of the key points of Alfonsín's electoral programme. It was an ambitious project which threatened to clash with the deeply entrenched influence of the Catholic Church on private education and the distortions of the national budget. In recent years the Treasury had pushed education well down the list of priorities to make way for issues considered of more immediate importance such as military spending.[21]

Of all the policy issues revived in the post-Falklands era, education was the one that came most naturally to the Radical party. Argentina's first Radical President Hipólito Yrigoyen is best remembered as the man who gave substantial support to La Reforma, the early twentieth-century Argentine university reform movement which aimed to break the conservative and élitist mould of higher education and make it more accessible to the emerging middle classes. The reforms implemented by Yrigoyen included an end to nepotism in the appointment of university staff, a less restrictive and cheaper entrance procedure, and greater administrative autonomy, including the involvement of students in university government. The universities of Córdoba, La Plata and Buenos Aires were given more liberal charters and two new universities were created in the provinces of Santa Fé and Tucuman, bringing higher education for the first time to the poorer regions of Argentina.

The shifting fortunes of Argentine education following the military coup of 1930 mirrored the quagmire into which national politics sank before the Falklands War. Under the first government of Perón, much of university life became synonymous in official eyes with reaction as Radical students spearheaded an offensive against what they considered was an emerging fascist state. The Perónist movement, with its roots in the working class and strongly influenced by the military and the Catholic Church, remained deeply suspicious of Yrigoyen's reforms, which it considered essentially a continuation of élitism under a different guise. In the 1960s a different kind of Perónist infiltrated the universities – inspired by Guevarism and the writings of Europe's radical left, he turned education into the manifesto of revolution. A familiar pattern developed – anarchy followed by repression followed by anarchy followed by repression again. No one really gained. Instead education, which one of Argentina's most eminent nineteenth-century thinkers, Juan Batiste Alberdi, had prophesied would help deliver his country from 'barbarism' to civilisation, came to epitomise Argentina's inability to organise itself as a modern nation. Seemingly irreconcilable extremes first emerged with a vengeance at the beginning of the government of General Juan Carlos Onganía (1966–70). In what was dubbed the 'night of the long sticks' the security forces stormed the University of Buenos Aires and forced lecturers and professors to run the gauntlet of baton-wielding police. The intervention was followed by the banning of student organisations and the repeal of the university's autonomous status.

This was followed in May 1969 in an eruption of student-worker protest in the northern city of Córdoba. The 'cordobazo' developed into two days of pitched battles between protesters and police reminiscent of the Paris riots of May 1968. The event engrained itself in the conscience of military and revolutionaries alike as a watershed in contemporary Argentine history which marked the future direction of the 'dirty war'. Within the universities the influence of students linked to the Montoneros and other guerrilla groups increased in the early 1970s to the extent that lectures were invariably turned into political meetings and professors were 'vetted' by gun-wielding extremists before they could start their classes. Such extremes produced an unprecedented repression against the whole education system after the 1976 military coup. Universities and schools were purged of 'subversives'; students, teachers and professors joined the ranks of the 'disappeared' or else went into exile, contributing to the brain drain that had begun under Onganía.[22] Those forced to work abroad by the junta included César Milstein, the Nobel prize winner for medicine, and many of the country's best scientists and doctors. The attitude of the military regime was epitomised by decree law 538 issued in May 1978. The decree made a pamphlet called *Know Your Enemy* obligatory reading among all teachers and administrative staff. The book was intended to make clear to the reader the methods used by 'Marxism' to distort the minds of young Argentines. 'It is in education', the pamphlet insisted, 'where you have to act with firmness to destroy the roots of subversion by showing your students the falsehood of doctrines and conceptions that were forced on them for so many years.'[23] Thus did the military depoliticise a whole new generation of Argentines – the generation that as adolescents lived through the coup and as young men went to die in the Falklands.

One of the most positive aspects of the post-Falklands period was the way this same generation, far from allowing itself to be further exploited by the forces of fascism, reacted against the passivity of their parents and joined in the political creativity of Alfonsinismo. Rejecting violence either of the left or right, they paved the way for an invigorated university reform movement as crucial to the emerging State as the previous movement had been under Yrigoyen. One of the major achievements of the Alfonsín government in the years 1983–6 was to manage, against considerable political and financial odds, to secure a more or less orderly transition from the autocratic, anaesthetised educational system of the juntas to an autonomous democratic one. There have been problems: a law reducing university fees and deregulating entrance procedures caused chaos in some faculties in the first months of democratic government. In a country which already had one of the highest *per capita* ratios of university students in the world, the new influx of young men and women, mainly from the provinces, crowded out lecture halls, disrupted programmes and forced even some of the more liberal teachers to long for the days of military orderliness. It would have been surprising though if, after all the years of extreme reaction, there hadn't been a measure of benign chaos once the universities and schools were unchained. There was also the problem of finding the available resources to subsidise the twenty-seven state universities without infringing too obviously on the deeply entrenched interests involved in private education or digging too deep into meagre Treasury resources.

On balance educational reform post-Falklands had played a fundamental role in directing the emerging generations towards the acceptance of democracy not just as a passing fad but as something crucial to their future. At all levels of education a new concept of living in the community began to be taught to a people that had traditionally excused their lack of collective responsibility as a commendable individualism. New books entitled *Know Your Community* replaced *Know Your Enemy*. Instructions on subversion were replaced by discussions on human rights, conservation and women's rights. Dialogue was taught to be a far more civilised form of growing up than the use of force, evolution more effective than revolution.

History was not so much rewritten as recovered. During the trial of the juntas, secondary school students would organise themselves into groups and discuss the day's evidence. No one came out of the classroom with a machine gun in his or her hands, but as a teacher told me at the time, 'the more my pupils learn about the trial, the more they grow to respect human rights, and the less likelihood of a coup re-occurring in the future'.

One of the first laws approved by the Alfonsín government reinstated the autonomous status of universities, giving students and teachers equal representation at administrative level; but rather than ordering the immediate expulsion of Rectors appointed by the military regime, the reform gave the new bodies the option to incorporate part of the old administration if they so wished. A transition period of one year was decreed, during which the universities were expected to elect their new authorities. Traditionally the educational system had been split between victors and vanquished. But the elections produced unprecedented scenes of reconciliation. In the university of Buenos Aires, the government-backed candidate for Rector, Oscar Shuberoff, was elected after a bitterly fought contest had forced three successive polls. No sooner had Shuberoff secured his post than he called in his rival candidates – some of whom were of very different political persuasions – to invite them to join in his administrative staff.

Ultimately, however, no member of the Alfonsín Cabinet better personified the changing face of Argentine culture than Alfredo Bravo. One-time general secretary of the teacher's union CTERA, during the regime of the juntas he had been abducted by the police while giving a lecture in an institute of higher education. His only crime appears to have been his refusal to abide by the instruction *Know Your Enemy* and for that he 'was tortured as badly as anyone who has survived to tell the tale. His teeth were broken by hammers, he was half drowned several times in bath water, he was tortured with an electrical cattle prod by other prisoners ... finally he was crucified upside down'.[24] Bravo, however, was resurrected from the dead. Within days of Raúl Alfonsín's inauguration as President he was appointed Under-Secretary for Education. As a senior civil servant he was made responsible for bringing a sense of ethics, philosophy and scientific discovery back into Argentine life.

11 HUMAN RIGHTS AND THE MILITARY

Argentina's cultural rebirth formed part of the collective catharsis provoked by the Falklands War. Such a renaissance was made possible by President Alfonsín's conscious decision to bring the nation face to face with its recent past. The presidential decree issued almost as soon as he took office, ordering a full-scale inquiry into human rights violations committed by the previous regime and the trial of those responsible, is a unique feature of Argentina's transition to democracy. The notion of military accountability is unprecedented in the Third World, where the armed forces have traditionally held a firm grip on politics both inside and outside government. Elsewhere in the world it is rare enough. Nuremberg was not organised by the Germans but by the Allies. In Greece, where the Colonels who seized power in 1967 were put on trial in 1975, the armed forces do not have a long record of political intervention. The risks involved were thus much smaller.

The military junta which staged a coup in 1976 was convinced that Argentina would never go the same way as Chile. The world would not glimpse torture and executions on the very public football pitches; political dissidents would be liquidated secretly, and exiles capable of telling the true story be kept to a minimum. The passing of time would ensure that the majority of Argentines would either never know the truth or at the very least would accept the military's version of events at face value. The self-censorship of the press, the collaboration of the judiciary, and the silence of Bishops and politicians, became part of an elaborate whitewash of history. It was not until the end of 1979 that the junta agreed to a detailed international inspection of its human rights record by the Organisation of American States' Inter-American Commission on Human Rights. By then the 'war against subversion' was officially over and the junta had moved quickly to cover its dirty tracks. Clandestine concentration camps where prisoners had been held after being kidnapped were walled up, turned to rubble, or converted into new wings in police and army barracks. Houses and new roads were built over mass graves where some of the 'disappeared' had been dumped. Some officers who had exposed their true identities during the 'dirty war' were granted temporary leave of absence or sent abroad as military attachés. An attempt was made to ensure the complicity of the relatives of the 'disappeared' through the announcement of special decree laws granting them extra family allowances. Finally, in the most publicised move of all, timed to coincide with the presence of the Commission in Buenos Aires, the junta released the newspaper editor Jacobo Timerman from prison and put him on a plane bound for the United States. The junta of General Videla subsequently gave considerable publicity to an alleged attempted coup by the commander of the Second Army Corps, General Luciano Menéndez, contrasting his extremist attitudes with its own self-proclaimed moderation and respect for legality.

There can be no better illustration of the military regime's self-assurance with regard to its human rights record than a statement made in April 1979 by General Roberto Viola. The then army chief said that the only explanation the armed forces had to give about the past was 'We have done our duty'. He then went on to say, 'Don't look for explanations where there aren't any. I trust that the rest of the world will also understand us. The army is sure that this country which suffered the war [against subversion] has understood and absorbed it.'[1]

One year later the Commission brought out its conclusions. It claimed that between 1975 and 1980 numerous and grave violations of fundamental human rights had been committed, including widespread use of torture, illegal detentions and execution without trial. The Commission assumed that thousands of Argentines reported missing were in fact dead, and urged that the regime immediately start legal proceedings against those responsible. It also demanded a thorough investigation into the methods used by the security forces, places of detention and the current whereabouts of the alleged victims. The report was widely covered by the international press and recorded in abridged form in the local media, prompting the first full-length statement on the subject since the coup by the opposition Perónist party. But the junta remained unmoved. The Organisation of American States, which had originally instigated the report under pressure from the United States, was no longer what it once had been – Carter appeared to be more concerned with preventing the Russians taking advantage of the Iranian Revolution than with hitting out at Argentina. Domestically the repercussions remained limited, although the junta felt compelled to bring out a new statement reiterating its position in no uncertain terms. Taking over from Viola as army chief, General Galtieri said that the methods used were a justified means to a noble end: the preservation of a nation's integrity. 'Don't ask us for explanations because you won't get any.'[2]

However, the lengthy timescale which this implied was under-mined by the military defeat at the hands of the British. A regime which would have almost certainly survived with only cosmetic changes to its structure, now found itself unable to resist the forces of change. Thus months before Alfonsín came to power, human rights had become *the* issue in Argentine politics. The military had taken pride in the professional competence of their campaign against the urban and rural guerrillas; but the misconduct during the Falk-lands War brought the armed forces under the microscope. They were faced with a growing number of people determined to prove the defeat was a consequence of the military's involvement in politics and its alienation of society. No sooner had it suffered humiliation on the battlefield around Port Stanley than the military regime found itself abandoned by the three pillars instrumental in ensuring the conspiracy of silence: the Church, the media and the judiciary. While individual Bishops urged some explanation for the recent past 'in a spirit of reconciliation', newspapers began to be more generous in their coverage of human rights, providing graphic descriptions of kidnappings by military personnel in addition to exposés of cor-ruption involving military officers – significantly one case involved an Admiral alleged to have misused public funds during the previously celebrated paradigm of national glory, the 1978 World Cup. A similar turn-around affected numerous judges. They either initiated proceedings against military officers or resigned in an apparent 'crisis of conscience'.

By September 1982 the junta was facing such a barrage of criti-cism, that it was forced to issue a decree prohibiting State-controlled television and radio stations from broadcasting further reports on cases of human rights violations. The ban was extended to newspaper editors, who were informed that they could face sentences of three to eight years if found guilty of writing material detrimental to 'social peace and institutional order'. Included in the decree was any unauthorised coverage of human rights violations, the Falklands War and alleged corruption. In the following months the junta was to follow up its threats with closure of newspapers and death threats against journalists and judges, as well as a permanent campaign of intimidation against human rights activists. Six political prisoners were reported to have 'committed suicide' – relatives assumed they had died while being tortured. In a conscious attempt to revive memories of the post-coup repression and restore a climate of fear, members of the security forces, officially described as 'uncontrolled elements', kidnapped, tortured and killed seven individuals for no other apparent reason than that as members of grass-roots labour organisations and opposition parties they were symbols of political change. In the case of two members of a Marxist faction of the Perónist party, the Buenos Aires police chief General Verplaetsen personally assumed responsibility, knowing full well that his act of murder would be excused by his military peers: 'Faced with subversion, there can be no dialogue, no armistice, no laying down of weapons, no resignation, no ceasefire, no gentlemen's agreement, no raising of the white flag.'[3] The military had surrendered to the British, Verplaetsen seemed to be saying, but it would never surrender to its own people.

In May 1983 his thoughts and those of most military officers were included in an extensive document published by the junta which explained the military's actions both before and after the coup. The document was delivered on nationwide TV in a sonorous disembodied voice which bore a striking similarity to the official press communiqués issued by the junta throughout the Falklands War. For forty-five minutes it was accompanied by an elaborately made collage of the military's version of history. Argentine terrorists were either pictured with Castro and Ché Guevara or else shown blowing up official cars. The military looked very conventional, making orderly arrests in broad daylight and parading the flag. The message was a repeat performance of every official statement issued since the coup: the armed forces had intervened to save the nation from self-destruction and to resurrect its ethical values. There had been some excesses but these were excusable, given the nature of the opposition. The junta admitted that those who had gone missing were almost certainly dead, but qualified this by saying that most of the victims were guerrillas killed in open combat with the armed forces. Throughout the 'dirty war' junior officers had acted in the 'line of duty' carrying out orders imparted by their military superiors. The document, like previous military statements, was as notable for what it said as for what it left unsaid. Thus the junta admitted the word *desaparecido* but refused to detail its methods or the whereabouts of its victims. 'In Argentina there are no secret detention camps, nor are there political prisoners being detained secretly. It is therefore perfectly clear that those reported missing . . . are in legal and administrative terms dead . . . let them receive God's pardon.' The claim of a few excesses and of thousands killed in combat ignored the fact that international agencies like the Organisation of American States had found evidence of widespread crimes being committed against individuals who had never carried a sub-machine-gun in their lives.

Finally, while claiming that some officers had been tried for their excesses, it excluded any mention of the many who were still in active service and who, like Astiz, had committed some of the most bloody crimes of all.

Just before it abandoned power, the junta brought out its final word on the human rights issue – an amnesty for all officers involved in the 'dirty war' which was aimed at giving them immunity from future trials. As with the document that preceded it, the law touched off some ripples of disagreement within the military hierarchy; there were some officers who argued that the junta had no need to justify itself further and viewed the self-amnesty law as an implicit admission of guilt; there were others who thought that a good carrot to feed the opposition with might be the publication of those names of the 'disappeared' which had been kept by certain sectors of the armed forces. But these were mere nuances of strategy which did not affect essentials. Evidence that the military remained moulded in *esprit de corps* on the human rights issue was borne out towards the end of the Bignone transition when some barracks and police offices began to destroy their records. No one from within the institution raised a public objection.

However, if the military government thought that it could bury the past once and for all by continuing to dictate its own terms, it could not have been proved more wrong. Each line of defence set up by the junta was simply answered by a new offensive in the run-up to the country's first democratic elections at the end of 1983. Although new censorship laws and intimidation muffled some sectors of the media, it had little effect on the majority of newspapers and magazines. Those who persisted in their offensive included a small handful of publications motivated ideologically; such was the case of the left-wing *La Voz* and the pro-Alfonsín satirical magazine *Humor*. Others such as the glossy weeklies adopted an anti-military stance because it was an issue that seemed to sell. Then there was a third group, headed by a new publication *Quorum*, which by writing deliberately obscure conspiracy tales, appeared to be driven less by a genuine desire for democracy than by the wish to promote complex military interests. Whatever the motives, the final result was that by the end of the military regime human rights were a source of public debate in Argentina which could no longer be ignored.

Thus only a few days after the junta had issued its instructions to the media, considerable coverage was given to a news conference given by Dr Emilio Mignone, the director of the Centre for Legal Studies, one of the country's most important human rights groups.

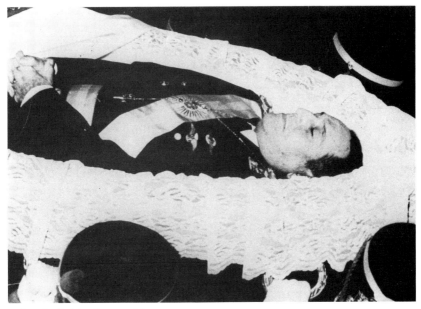

1 Juan Perón lying in state, July 1974

2 The Process of National Reorganisation: the junta reviews its troops. (*From left*) Admiral
Emilio Massera, General Jorge Videla and Air Force General Orlando Agosti

3 The victorious Argentine team line up for the World Cup final in 1978

4 Diego Maradona is sent off during the 1982 World Cup

5 The special War Cabinet meets. (*From left*) President Leopoldo Galtieri, Joint Chief of Staff and head of propaganda, Rear-Admiral Leopoldo Suarez Del Cerro, Navy Commander-in-Chief Admiral Jorge Anaya, Foreign Minister Nicandor Costa Méndez and Air Force Commander-in-Chief Brigadier-General Basilio Lami Dozo

6 The massed crowds in Plaza de Mayo (*left*) during Alexander Haig's visit, 10 April 1982

7 General Mario Menéndez takes the oath as the Argentine military Governor of the
Malvinas, 7 April 1982

8 Argentine TV personality Lydia Stangnaro (Pinky) urges support for the patriotic fund on
nationwide television in the telethon

9　A *chico de la guerra*

10　The Church blesses the holy crusade, April 1982

11 The propaganda war: photographs claim imminent victory after an Exocet hits HMS *Invincible*

12 The Argentine press's view of Mrs Thatcher

13 Argentine soldiers surrender their guns in Port Stanley

14 Nobel peace prizewinner, Adolfo Peréz   15 Leopoldo Galtieri
Esquivel

16 The Madres de la Plaza de Mayo – human rights campaigners demand information about
the disappeared

17 Lieutenant Alfredo Astiz signs the surrender of South Georgia, watched by Captain Nicholas Barker of HMS *Endurance* (*second from right*)

18 Raul Alfonsin casts his vote in Chascomus in the first democratic elections in Argentina for ten years, 30 October 1983

Dr Mignone, whose courageous investigation into cases of missing persons had been consistently ignored by many of his fellow countrymen before the Falklands War, was listened to attentively as he disclosed that a federal judge had been asked to order the exhumation and identification of unmarked graves near a major army base. The judge subsequently asked to be removed from the case, after it was alleged that security forces might have been involved in the clandestine burial of hundreds of victims of repression, a charge that ran directly counter to the regime's repeated denials that it had no knowledge of missing persons' whereabouts.

In that same month, October 1982, the weekly vigil of the Madres de Mayo outside the presidential palace – so small and vulnerable both before and during the Falklands War – received the support of seven other human rights organisations, political leaders, Bishops, trade union officials, students and journalists, turning it into a massive demonstration against the government. Predictably, many of the demonstrators were students and relatives of the 'disappeared'; but public concern over the 'disappeared' was already much greater than it had been at any stage since the coup. A few days before the demonstration Juan Alemann, a former Treasury Secretary of the regime and brother of Galtieri's Economy Minister, Roberto Alemann, told the local media that sectors of the military had been connected with the disappearance of two senior Argentine diplomats in the late 1970s, Elena Holmberg and Hector Hidalgo Sola. He singled out Admiral Massera, whom he also accused of being a member of the Italian Masonic Lodge, Propaganda-Due. Although local journalists had known about the cases for at least two years they had never written about them. With Alemann breaking his silence they no longer felt so constrained, and used his statements to air publicly a subject that had been virtually taboo since 1976. The revelations about Holmberg and Sola shocked sectors of the middle and upper classes. Until then these privileged sectors of Argentine society had been satisfied that the military's offensive had been conducted only against terrorists and Marxists. But here were members of their own Establishment being liquidated, according to Alemann, for no other reason than that they had fallen out of grace with one military faction. Outrage increased a few days later, when Marcelo Dupont, an advertising executive and brother of a prime witness in the Holmberg and Sola cases, was kidnapped and subsequently murdered in the kind of operation developed to a fine art by the military during the 'dirty war'.

When the junta brought out its official document on the 'dirty war', Italy's President, Sandro Pertini, sent a telegram to the Argentine authorities describing it as 'blood-chilling and beyond human civility'. Juan Aguirre Lanari, Costa Méndez's successor as Foreign Minister under Bignone, dismissed the telegram and the ensuing barrage of worldwide expressions of outrage as all part of an international conspiracy aimed at discrediting Argentina. But this ignored the domestic reaction to the document, which in its scope and scale had few precedents. All the major political parties and labour leaders were openly critical; even the conservative Bishops had to abandon their plans for a Mass of reconciliation after the Vatican issued its own statement of repudiation.

Once they had secured a guarantee from the junta that there would be elections, some political figures, particularly within the conservative UCD and the right wing of the Perónist and Radical parties, privately expressed their view that an amnesty for the military was an adequate compromise which would smooth the transition to democracy and also resolve their own rather ambiguous involvement in the 'dirty war'. The Bishops also shared in this view; for there were military officers who had publicly claimed that their actions had been endorsed by members of the political parties and blessed by certain churchmen – not an inaccurate statement on the collective complicity which gripped Argentine society both before and after the 1976 coup. It soon became clear, however, with the persistence of human rights demonstrations and the slogans most popularly shared during political rallies, that the junta's final word could not satisfy many thousands of Argentines who had lost a friend or relative, been outraged about what they heard, or simply wanted to express their sense of patriotic frustration because of the outcome of the Falklands War. Some of these Argentines were stirred solely by motives of personal vengeance; but perhaps the majority shared in a more profound political logic. They argued that unless they were told the truth and those guilty were brought to trial there could be no guarantee against the past reoccurring. The military persisted in a diametrically opposed view; warning again and again that the only guarantee for the future of democracy was to recognise that the nation owed them a debt or, at the very least, to forgive and forget. For, as the official junta document on the 'disappeared' pointed out, the military was prepared to act in exactly the same way in the future if it felt the integrity of the nation was being undermined.

The airing of the human rights issue during the Bignone period gave an appearance of political tension that often verged on the edge of civil war. But the period proved crucial in identifying the parameters within which the debate could be conducted under a future democratic government. For, as surely as human rights could not be ignored, no less certain were the seemingly irreconcilable positions between the two extremes of the political spectrum. To govern and to survive would require some political fine-tuning: a sense of ethics but also a good dose of pragmatism. Argentina's transition to democracy was destined to be as tricky as a walk on thin wire.

Raúl Alfonsín's determination to walk the political tightrope was apparent from the first day of his presidency. He was inaugurated on a wave of euphoria, with thousands of Argentines celebrating the 'end of the dictatorship' and demanding swift retribution against the guilty ones. In the preceding weeks the majority of political groupings, including the majority Radicals and Perónists, sensing mounting outrage against the military, had been forced to absorb the human rights issue as a key element in their election manifesto. Alfonsín himself had fully exploited his past record of commitment to the subject and won over those voters who doubted the sincerity of the Perónists. When it came to polling day, 75,000 people put human rights before even party loyalties. They split their ballots, voting for Alfonsín as President but rejecting the candidates for Congress of any of the established parties in favour of Augusto Comte, a member of the minuscule Christian Democrat party. A father of a 'disappeared' Comte had consciously campaigned as a one-issue candidate, promising in his manifesto 'to bring human rights to Parliament'. And yet in spite of the popular pressures for sweeping and immediate action, Alfonsín moved cautiously in an attempt to dampen expectations of a revolution.

His first initiative on the human rights issue, almost as soon as he had been sworn in, was the announcement that the nine members of the juntas that had ruled Argentina between the coup of 1976 and the Falklands War would face trial for homicide, torture and 'any other crimes against them that might be proven'. But this was accompanied by orders for the arrest on similar charges of seven members of left-wing guerrilla organisations, including the exiled leader of the Montoneros, Mario Firmeních. During his campaign, one of Alfonsín's favourite phrases was 'We cannot go forward into the future pretending that nothing has happened here'. This first presidential decree underlined his wish to overcome the temptation to capitalise on the euphoria surrounding his electoral win and retain a sense of political proportion. The lesson in history should not be one-track, but evenly balanced so as to redress wrongs and expose

myths. There seemed to be no doubt in Alfonsín's mind that the
juntas carried the major responsibility for conducting large-scale
political repression, much of it against men, women and children
who had no links with guerrilla organisations. He was equally sensitive to the divisive nature of Argentina's political violence and
the existence of terror as much as counter-terror. Many of the
'disapppeared' had belonged to organisations committed to violence
as a means to an end. And although their ideology may have been
different to the military's their methodology was arguably equally
morally reprehensible. For not only had the Montoneros and ERP
killed selected 'political targets' in cold blood, but a whole generation
had followed their culture of violence. Of the two sides, though, it
was the latter that the majority of Argentines knew best. For six
years under a military regime they had been the passive recipients
of government propaganda including a full-length illustrated book
called *El Terrorismo en Argentina* ('Terrorism in Argentina') in
which the bloody acts of the guerrillas were described and condemned in minute detail. The other side of the coin was only now
beginning to be shown.

Alfonsín's initial selection of the nine Generals for 'exemplary'
justice and his exclusion of the fourth junta implicitly recognised
Bignone as a transitional President who had avoided some of the
worst excesses of his predecessors. It was also a concession to the
military as an institution. In their document on the 'disappeared'
the junta had declared that the military chiefs assumed full responsibility for what had happened and that junior- and middle-ranking
officers were simply carrying out orders. A similar determination to
walk the middle ground lay behind Alfonsín's announcement two
weeks after he came to power that he was setting up the National
Commission on the Disappeared (CONANEP) to investigate the fate
of those alleged to have gone missing following the coup. On the one
hand the setting up of the CONANEP underlined Alfonsín's electoral
pledge not to go forward without first analysing the past. On the
other the Commission was an alternative to the more drastic proposal
demanded by Comte, human rights organisations and left-wing
groups: that all officers charged with human rights violations should
be immediately subject to a political trial conducted by Parliament.
Alfonsín felt that he should avert the prospect of a direct confrontation between the military and civilian worlds at all costs, now
that the armed forces had withdrawn from power.

If equanimity was what Alfonsín was striving for, the message
failed to get through to the military, who regarded the mere fact that

the juntas had been put in the same boat as Firmenich as an insult
to their institution. For they still saw the 'dirty war' as a crusade
which had saved the nation rather than as a struggle between two
sides who believed that right was their own exclusive preserve. In
their view, moreover, the setting up of CONANEP was a political act
which they were convinced had no guarantee of impartiality; the
Commission was made up of authors, lawyers and Bishops who had
made their views in defence of human rights public in the past. To
add insult to injury it was headed by Ernesto Sábato – a man officers
saw as a Marxist and a turncoat. Military suspicions were aggravated
even further by the increasingly belligerent tone of the media. After
the years of silence, newspapers continued to fill their pages with
more and more graphic descriptions of torture and murder, using
not just the statements of victims and relatives but also of the alleged
perpetrators of the crimes.

The military's residual distrust of democracy was an irritating but
concealed thorn in the side of the incoming government as soon as
Alfonsín had won the election. It became an open wound less than
a month after his inauguration as President. In January the newly
appointed commander of the Fifth Army Corps, General Aguado
Benítez, publicly expressed his opposition to the trial of the juntas
and warned of growing unrest in the ranks of the military as a result
of what was perceived as a personal vendetta out against them
by the press. General Luciano Menéndez elaborated on this,
claiming that it was all part of a conspiracy 'perfectly planned by subversives' – it was the kind of language which in 1979 had led General
Menéndez to attempt a palace coup during the government of General
Videla.

There was as yet, however, no real threat of a conspiracy. Hardline
sectors of the military were simply testing the waters. Once again
they found a government bent on consolidating democracy but
nevertheless sufficiently wary of the power of the armed forces to
treat them with kid gloves. Benítez was called in by the Minister of
Defence, Raúl Borras, and reminded that senior officers in active
service were prohibited from making political statements. But he
was allowed to keep his job. Menéndez was hauled up before a
special parliamentary commission and told to apologise. He refused.
Within five months, the government was again facing a military
offensive against its human rights policy. This time Borras's reaction
was less compromising. He sacked the army Chief of Staff, General
Arguindeguy, the commander of the Third Army Corps, General
Pedro Mansilla, and two Generals of the industrial complex Fabrica-

ciones Militares – although a carrot was held out by Alfonsín during
the annual dinner given for 300 graduating officers at the Military
Academy. He told them,

> I'd be a hypocrite if I didn't tell you here and now that in all
> honesty I believe our men of arms have committed grave errors.
> But I would also be insensitive to reality and I'd be hiding part
> of the truth if I didn't also say that civilian society's performance
> hasn't been up to the required standards in Argentina.[4]

On this occasion, the government does not seem to have considered a coup to be a serious possibility. It was only in April 1985,
half-way through Alfonsín's presidential term, when military officers
began to share their opinions with sectors of the civilian population,
that the government chose to go public and denounce the threat of
destabilisation. 'The enemies of democracy have always conspired,
but never has the Argentine nation been so under attack ... I
denounce before the Argentine people an attempt to weaken the
government by those forecasting anarchy and chaos,' Alfonsín told
the nation on television.[5] Dramatic as his words sounded at the time,
the threat of conspiracy even at this stage seemed to be more apparent
than real. The focus was on General Juan Carlos Onganía, President
from 1966 to 1971, who in an address to conservative politicians had
lashed out at the government's 'socialising leadership' and what he
claimed was a 'ferocious attack' against the prestige of the armed
forces. Among the civilians singled out as potential plotters was
former President Arturo Frondizi, who in a newspaper interview
had suggested that the government was undermining the 'social
fabric of the nation'. Onganía was a retired officer who, although
well known for his political ambitions, did not command the loyalty
of any active units. Frondizi's party had obtained less than 3 per
cent of the vote in the elections. A former member of the Radical
party and himself the victim of a military coup in 1962, Frondizi
was less an extreme right-winger than a political has-been like
Onganía, who was always anxious for press coverage. Both men seem
to have been picked out by the government as convenient whipping
boys to underline its determination to keep the political initiative,
and to present the waverers within the military establishment with
a clear sign of what might be the consequences if any of them was
tempted to step seriously out of line. The ruse was timed to coincide
with the start of the historic trial of the juntas, which the government
always assumed would test its relations with the armed forces to a
greater degree than any other policy decision. As a result of Alfon-

sín's speech, the majority of political parties closed ranks behind the government and a demonstration 'in defence of democracy' drew more than 250,000 to the Plaza de Mayo. Such a mobilisation over the perceived threat of a coup (Argentine public opinion at the time did not speculate on the possibility of a ruse) contrasted with the lethargy which had historically surrounded successful *coups d'état* against civilian governments. It was thus a welcome signal for the government that, even if military attitudes were not yet in the process of changing, those of the rest of society were. This was a view that was to be confirmed by the trial of the juntas.

Argentina's 'trial of the century', officially described as a court martial by civilians, lasted from 22 April to 10 December 1985. The fact that civilian judges presided over the proceedings and that the defence dismissed the whole occasion as a show trial lacking any legal basis, underlined the limited extent to which the military as an institution had been incorporated into the democratic process. Alfonsín's original plan had been that the military should judge themselves and make a public act of contrition. However, the Supreme Council of the Armed Forces, initially charged with prosecuting the juntas, had dragged its feet. When it was urged to reach a verdict, it simply brought out a statement claiming that it saw nothing legally reprehensible in the methods used by the juntas during the war against subversion. By contrast the CONANEP acted with remarkable speed; its enthusiasm for discovering the truth was such that it went beyond its initial brief, further aggravating tension between the government and the military. As Sábato himself recognises in the prologue to the Commission's final report, the CONANEP was set up by Alfonsín not to sit in judgment, because that is the task of the constitutionally appointed judges, but to investigate the fate of the people who disappeared. And yet so moved were the members of the Commission by the thousands of statements and the testimony they received that they found themselves unable to give a dispassionate account of their discoveries. Thus, although the cases are described factually and without comment, the prologue states the Commission's conviction that

the recent military dictatorship brought about the greatest and most savage tragedy in the history of Argentina ... This went far beyond what might be considered criminal offences, and takes us into the shadowy realm of crimes against humanity. Through the technique of disappearance and its consequences, all the ethical principles which the great religions and the noblest philosophies have evolved through centuries of suffering and calamity have been trampled underfoot, barbarously ignored.

By turning the juntas over to the civilian courts, Alfonsín contributed to Argentina's essential lesson in history. Ordinary citizens were allowed into the public galleries; the press filled their pages with daily reports; the television had a daily summary in its news bulletins; on the bookstands media coverage was supplemented with a newspaper specially printed for the course of the trial and filled with detailed testimonies and background interviews. In all, nearly 1,000 people gave evidence concerning some 700 cases, which were chosen to illustrate the allegations against the accused: they were charged with a variety of crimes including murder, torture, unlawful detention, house-breaking and falsification of public documents. The prosecution concentrated on proving what the official CONANEP report had already established: that the pattern of terror embarked upon following the 1976 coup was so organised and consistent that those in government at the time must have known or endorsed it. The juntas were thus in the dock not so much for carrying out the crimes directly but for bearing the brunt of responsibility for them.

Julio Strassera, the State prosecutor said in his emotional summing up: 'The trial has meant, for those of us who have had the painful privilege of following it closely, a descent into the most terrible depths of the human soul, where misery, degradation and horror have been registered with such intensity that it could scarcely have been imagined or understood.' On the days I attended the trial, each case seemed to be more horrific than its predecessor. Even those of us who had read about Argentina's human rights violations in the script of international reports were traumatised by the immediacy of the horror. One of the first women to take the witness stand described how she had been forced to have her child in the back of a police car as she was being driven relentlessly to her next torture chamber; there was an old couple, the wife blind, the husband with an artificial leg, who had each been subjected to the *picana* (the electric prod torment). They were subsequently released when the officer in charge had realised that with their physical disability the couple were unlikely to be in a condition to carry arms. A similar 'mistaken identity' involved members of the FAP (Federation of Argentine Psychiatrists) whom the military believed were members of the PAF (Perónist Armed Forces). Another case described the disappearance of fourteen secondary-school boys and girls in what came to be known as the 'Night of the Pencils'. The only survivor described in court and later that evening on television how at the age of sixteen he had been kidnapped from his home by security forces. He was taken to a clandestine detention centre. In a voice that often seemed on the point of cracking and surrounded by muffled weeping in the courtroom, Pablo recalled conditions in the camp. 'They burnt my lips, my genitals, my gums; there was a smell of burnt flesh. I don't know how long I was there ... They asked for names. "Give us a name and we'll let you go. Tell us another, another ..."' Only five days later was Pablo told the reason for his detention: the fourteen had been accused of subversion for participating in a campaign for reduced student-rate bus fares.

An account of the trial subsequently recalled:

> As these stories emerged, not only did the defence begin to crumble, but old myths fomented by the military government were revealed as lies. When people disappeared, people used to say 'Por algo será' ['He must have done something to deserve it']. The defence tried to reinforce that idea during cross-questioning, by trying to insinuate the prosecutor's witnesses had been implicated in the subversion. Testimonies like Pablo's served to show people this was not so.[6]

Like Nunca Más, the trial demonstrated how the repression, from being a means to an end, came to be an end in itself; torture and murder corrupted the perpetrators to such an extent that the uncontrolled subjection of the weak and innocent became a way of life.

Thus testimony delivered at the trial became the climax of an experience set in motion immediately after the Falklands War and which had extended itself both in scope and scale after Alfonsín's inauguration as President. A society that had only recently turned a blind eye to reality either by omission or complicity was thus sucked into the tapestry of horror. But as important as the testimony was the trial itself. Although some of the evidence produced by the prosecution collapsed in court – usually when it turned out that a witness had given false testimony to the CONANEP or that an alleged victim was in fact a terrorist who had died in combat – the defence's argument that the whole trial lacked legal validity was laughed out of court. The trial was in fact the very image of fair justice, and was interpreted as such by the bulk of Argentines and the outside world.

While the public was allowed into the court, the judges honoured the defence's request that their clients be saved from the public humiliation of attending the court until the very end of the trial. The six judges applied the strictest standards of evidence and procedure, only occasionally letting their frustration at the time-wasting nit-picking of the defence get the better of them. The Madres de Mayo were banned from using their symbols of protest, white bandanas, in court on the grounds that this might intimidate witnesses. Rather more leniency was shown towards members of the armed forces, some of whose members were allowed to turn up in their uniforms. Towards the end of the trial, the presiding judge ordered the court be cleared at once when the public gallery erupted in unanimous applause for Strassera's summing up. More important, however, was the way the trial respected an important jurisprudential distinction. Unlike Nuremberg, the trial of the juntas did not have a conquering army creating 'crimes against humanity' as a retroactive piece of universal legislation applicable to the Nazi regime. In Argentina no new legislation was needed, since the crimes with which the juntas were accused were illegal under the laws existing between 1976 and 1982. The junta had never enacted special laws permitting murder, torture and falsification of public documents. Their last line of defence – the amnesty for military officers approved by Bignone – had been repealed by Parliament and the Supreme Court had held this repeal valid.

Where Alfonsín was exposed in legal terms was the form of the trial. At the time the alleged crimes were committed, the former commanders would have been entitled both constitutionally and juridically to judgment by their natural peers. However, under a law approved by the Argentine Congress in January 1984, cases of human rights violations which had not been resolved within a limited timescale by military judges passed automatically to civilian courts reconstituted as court martial boards. Defence lawyers argued all along that this was retroactive justice orchestrated by the civilian authorities to serve their own political purposes.

There is an important sense in which the trial of the juntas was a show trial, but not in the way the defence saw it. As *The Economist* remarked at the time:

> It shows that however important a man may seem to be when he is in power, however much his word may be law and his misdeed applauded by his cronies and overlooked by his peers abroad, there can be a time of reckoning. Such a come-uppance is unprecedented in Latin America. Dictators have been assassinated, but never before in the region has a democratically elected civilian government dared to put yesterday's military rulers in the dock ... from now on jackboot rule may be a little less assured.[7]

Like the court martial of General Milans del Bosch and Lieutenant-Colonel Tejero in post-Franco Spain – accused of plotting a coup to topple the government of Adolfo Suárez – the trial of the juntas highlighted two completely different concepts of society. For the upholders of democracy, by allowing their officers to rob, rape and murder, the juntas had behaved no better than common criminals and should be punished accordingly. For the military establishment and a very small section of civilian society, the war against subversion was a necessary means to an end: the salvation of the nation. In their view this act of patriotism was equivalent to San Martín's crossing of the Andes and the loss of life in the fields around Port Stanley. Two versions of history thus confronted each other across the courtroom, as much as two Argentinas: the old Argentina, militarised and regimented and resistant to change; and the new Argentina, represented by Alfonsín, committed to modernisation and as respectful of human life as any Western democracy.

12
DEMOCRACY AT WORK

The Armed Forces: 'The Sabres Still Rattle'

It says much for the military's persistent presence and influence in Argentine politics that an occasion as momentous as the condemnation of long prison sentences of the main protagonists of the 'dirty war' had by the end of 1986 not resulted in the permanent banishment of the armed forces to barracks. President Alfonsín himself forced General Bignone out of the back door of the Casa Rosada rather than have him present at his inauguration celebration; he subsequently greeted his new Chiefs of Staff in a donkey jacket. Such initial gestures of defiance – the outward expressions of the radicalised rhetoric pursued during the election campaign – were subsequently modified, however. Early in his administration Alfonsín came round to the belief that if the armed forces were to be incorporated into the democratic system, they had to be treated with deference. Subsequently he provided the military with the opportunity to clean up its own house without interference from the civilians. He selected the Supreme Council of the Armed Forces to judge the juntas and other officers accused by the relatives of the 'disappeared'. When the CONANEP report was issued, he banned the publication of a list of over 1,000 officers which the Commission had compiled as a result of its inquiries into human rights violations. He then modified legislation to incorporate the concept of 'obedience to orders' as a factor which could mitigate the alleged guilt of the junior- and middle-ranking officers who had physically carried out the instructions handed out by the juntas.

Such escape clauses provoked the wrath of human rights groups, and stirred the first signs of a major break between Alfonsín and the broad left which supported his election in October 1983. The concept of a *punto final* or final curtain on the human rights issue – a cut-off point at which the government can say 'enough of the past, let's get on with the future' – remained repugnant to those who argued that only by bringing those responsible to trial and clarifying totally the past can there be any guarantee against tyranny in the future. Human rights groups were extremely critical of the way the Argentine Senate, the organ ultimately responsible for ratifying military promotions, allowed alleged torturers to remain in positions of authority. Far from reinforcing democracy, they argued, such continuity could only weaken it.

What was certainly true was that the trial of the juntas was not in itself conclusive. It broke some crucially important new political and moral ground and was fundamental in restoring Argentina's presence in the community of nations. Democracy in any form would have not been possible without it. And yet, as has been pointed out in a penetrating analysis by Ronald Dworkin, Professor of Jurisprudence at Oxford University, the historic condemnation of yesterday's military rulers was 'legally much easier, morally less perplexing, and politically less dangerous'[1] than the further trial of some 500 other members of the military lower down the command structure, who towards the middle of 1986 began to be brought before the same civilian courts which had convicted the juntas. There had been few problems of evidence in securing a verdict against the former commanders. The fiscal prosecutor did not have to prove that General Videla and Admiral Massera, the main conspirators in the 1976 coup, had pulled the trigger or pressed the electric button. He only had to collect cases, covering the length and breadth of Argentina and in every sector of society, which established, beyond doubt, that innocent people had suffered not just the excesses common to any war, but a systematised form of State terror.[2] The 1,700-odd prosecutions against the lower orders in the military hierarchy were much more difficult to prove.

There was the first level of officers – among them the 'Butcher of Buenos Aires', General Ramón Camps – whose outspoken boastfulness about their part in political repression made their early condemnation a foregone conclusion.[3] Beyond this, however, the memories of witnesses had to be jolted and the whole concept of military training turned on its head for any judge – let alone a military judge – to reach a verdict against a more junior-ranking officer. The difficulties were made only too apparent in the case of the failed 'hero' of South Georgia, Lieutenant Astiz, whose case bounced backwards and forwards between military and civilian courts without a final verdict throughout the first four years of the Alfonsín government. Towards the end of 1986 it had become only too apparent to senior government officials that the longer the human rights trials were extended the more the risk would be that Argentina's traditionally most tribal institution would become irrevocably alienated from the nascent democracy. In April an army prosecutor, Brigadier-General Hector Canale, had warned, 'The growing number of prosecutions is harming the morale of the ranks, and generating the possibility of projecting an image of collective trial against members of the armed forces.'[4] And yet not even the prospect of a general amnesty seemed to pacify some military sabres. In a courageous interview with a self-confessed torturer conducted by the Anglo-Argentine journalist Andrew Graham-Yooll,[5] the officer points to the basic dilemma at the heart of the democratic government's relationship with the armed forces, which perhaps only time can solve.

> How do you negotiate the end of a civil war when there is no supreme victor? We beat them; but we cannot claim victory. There are political considerations. And if we have to negotiate the end of the past, we have to know with whom. We must know if the negotiators are strong enough. The talk of amnesty is the babble of imbeciles at the Interior Ministry; or maybe the command is flying a balloon. An amnesty does not end the shooting, nor stop the mad men who want to take revenge. You need to make a deal with political figures who can control the mad guys, the *loquitos*.

To what extent has Argentina's democratic government been able to control the *loquitos*?

Alfonsín's human rights policy was one of the two most bitter pills that the armed forces had to swallow with the advent of democracy. The other was the sweeping cuts in defence spending which in their scope and scale have been without precedent in Argentina. During the first year of democratic government the military share of the national budget fell officially from 6 per cent of GDP to just over 3 per cent. Traditionally arms spending, military schools and hospitals and other items of almost exclusive interest to the armed forces had been purposely obscured in the national accounts. Apart from defence the military drew their funds from such items as education and social security, to the detriment of the vast majority of the population. Such anomalies were eradicated almost immediately by the Alfonsín government so that the true extent of reduced spending on the military was perhaps even greater than was officially admitted.

Initially the curbs affected mostly the standard of living of individual officers rather than their technical expertise, since for the first time in many years military salaries have lagged behind inflation. Much of the equipment destroyed during the Falklands War was replaced during the Bignone period, so Alfonsín's bold electoral promise that not another peso would be spent on a weapon as long as the country's poverty was not eradicated was not as significant as it seemed at the time.[6] Where the radicals broke new ground was in imposing tighter controls on arms exports – traditionally a source of dangerous parallel diplomacies and financial corruption in the form of hefty commissions – and on the country's ambitious nuclear programme, which in recent years had been converted into a virtual fiefdom of the navy. One of the final acts of defiance by the head of the National Nuclear Commission, Admiral Carlos Castro Madero, was to announce just a few days before Alfonsín's inauguration that Argentina had completed its nuclear cycle and thus had the technical capacity to produce a bomb. Subsequently Madero was replaced by a civilian, and the work of the Commission subjected to much tighter scrutiny by the Foreign Ministry. The Alfonsín government also rejected publicly the notion of developing a nuclear warhead. Nevertheless, the new democracy's attitude to nuclear power remained tinged with nationalist pride at having the most developed technology in Latin America, and in international eyes a question mark still hangs over Argentina's real ambitions. Alfonsín was a leading member of the group of six nations publicly committed to multilateral disarmament; but he refused to sign or ratify the Nuclear Non-Proliferation Treaty (NPT) and the Treaty of Tlatelolco governing the spread of nuclear weapons in the region. He claimed, as Castro Madero had before him, that these treaties· reinforce the nuclear *status quo* and prevent the Third World from benefiting from the transfer of technology. Similar ambiguities surrounded the development of Latin America's first nuclear-powered submarine. In September 1986, the navy chief, Admiral Ramón Arosa, announced that a prototype would be ready within the next two years.

The strategic advantages of possessing one or more nuclear-powered submarines patrolling Argentina's disputed territorial waters in the South Atlantic had been the subject of discussion within the Argentine navy for several years. But the approval for researching and developing the project – transforming conventional submarines bought from West Germany and their Argentine-made blue-print – was a direct consequence of the Falklands War. The virtual paralysis of the Argentine navy following the sinking of the *General Belgrano* by the British nuclear submarine HMS *Conqueror* in May 1982 left high-ranking officers (Castro Madero's son was among the *Belgrano* survivors) poignantly aware of their vulnerability and utterly committed to restoring the balance.

While the navy claimed a partial success in retaining some key aspects of the country's nuclear programme, the army was more victimised by military reform. Early efforts were made by the Alfonsín government to remove army men from the top management of the Dirección Nacional de Fabricaciones Militares (DNFM), the huge military–industrial complex. The transfer of the military's shareholdings in non-military concerns like the steel giant Somisa and the petrochemicals groups Petroquímica Bahía Blanca and Mosconi to the civilian sphere formed part of the government's ambitious privatisation programme announced in early 1986.

The main thrust of the early military reform was focused on organisation. During the former regime, Argentina had developed a top-heavy command structure. At the head was the all-powerful junta of service chiefs, with a supporting cast of over 100 Generals, Admirals and Brigadiers and over 1,000 retired and middle-ranking officers who had manœuvred their way into every area of society, often earning triple salaries. At the bottom were 90,000 conscripts and 70,000 professionals, making the Argentine armed forces proportionally one of the largest in the Third World. Of the two groups, the former was in particular a source of inefficiency and corruption; as the Falklands War proved only too well, conscription had long since ceased to be the fount of national union. It had become instead the expression of the nation's political and moral degeneracy. Under the juntas eighteen-year-old conscripts found that of the twelve months officially dubbed as national service, usually less than three were actually devoted to military drill. Training was a form of political repression, with students-to-be brutalised both ideologically and physically by their superiors. The rest of the year was spent carrying out menial tasks – national service came to mean anything and everything, from transporting black market petrol from barrack to barrack to driving an officer's wife to her favourite shop.

Alfonsín scrapped the junta and the concept of service heads and invoked his constitutional right to be the sole commander of the armed forces. Beneath him in the military hierarchy was a reinforced civilian Ministry of Defence with powers of control over promotions, sackings, troop deployment and military budgets. Following the example of post-Franco Spain, the Alfonsín government replaced the former military high command of the junta with the Joint Chiefs of Staff, who were to serve as the main liaison between the lower levels of command and the government and to advise as opposed to order specific policies related to the modernisation of the armed forces. An early reform of considerable symbolic and practical implications was the gradual demilitarisation of Buenos Aires. During the military years the presence of a regiment of infantry near the popular downtown Palermo Park and of several artillery units on the outskirts had proved an ever-present curb on basic freedoms with constant rumours of troops movements to dissuade anyone from stepping out of line. To a dictatorship, such a stranglehold on the capital where the majority of the country's population live and work made every sense politically, but it was bound to lose all justification once a democratic government was installed. Quite apart from wanting to shift the nation's political energy away from the jackboot towards the polling booth, the Alfonsín government saw little sense in maintaining its crack fighting troops hundreds of miles away from the historical military powder kegs such as the South Atlantic, the Brazilian border and the Andes. Under Alfonsín, the command of the country's First Army Corps ceased to be based in the capital, being transferred to the Fifth Army Corps based in Patagonia, although the removal of troops has been subject to administrative delays.

Since coming to power, Argentina's democratic President has ordered a number of shake-outs of the military high command, but the most notorious occurred in March 1985 when Alfonsín 'retired' ten Generals, four Rear-Admirals, and two air force Brigadiers, bringing to over sixty the number of high-ranking officers sacked since the end of junta rule. Among the most significant changes was the appointment of an air force officer, Brigadier-General Teodoro Waldner to head the Joint Chiefs of Staff. In a military structure traditionally dominated by the army such a move was unprecedented. Waldner became the first air force officer in Argentine military history to command the operations of all three services.

For all its apparent boldness, however, the Radical government's military reforms had by the end of 1986 brought about changes of form rather than substance. The government's apparent alliance with the new air force leadership, also demonstrated in the tactical transfer of several squadrons from the interior to Buenos Aires and official promotion given to research and development of the country's aerospace industry, appeared to be a policy of divide and rule designed to weaken the latent power of the military as an institution. But the policy of exacerbating deeply entrenched rivalries between the three services at a time of scarce financial resources seems to have been applied with little regard for the consequences in the longer term. Waldner's appointment did not itself solve the traditional power rivalry between the three services. Each service continued to defend its political autonomy, with its own buildings, training schemes and sense of history on crucial issues like the Falklands. On the subject of professionalisation Waldner found it impossible to formulate a common programme. The air force, which believes the Falklands War could have gone more Argentina's way had this service been given more room for manœuvre by the army- and navy-dominated junta, was seeking exclusive responsibility for all aerial operations and commitment from the government to a re-equipment programme based on radars, air-to-air missiles and supersonic front-line aircraft. Such recommendations were anathema to both the army and the navy, which continued to resist surrendering control of aerial transport and the Fleet Air Arm.

Nor did Waldner's appointment and the purge of the high command solve the issue of the conscript army. Although both the number of conscripts and the time spent in conscription were cut by 30 per cent and three months respectively, the Radical government did not follow through its electoral pledge to abolish national service. Faced with a reduced labour market because of recession, the government was torn between its commitment to military reform and the need not to inflate the ranks of the unemployed with school-leavers.

During the former military regime, the secret services of the three services as well as the special branch attached to the presidency had developed into a virtual State within the State. Thousands of agents had powers of control and repression and independent as well as official sources of income, including private 'detective' services offered at huge cost to civilian businesses. The Radicals came to power expecting to purge quickly the worst culprits and restructure the secret services around a centralised intelligence service answerable only to the President, but the plan faced innumerable obstacles from the outset. Antonio Pena, the first civilian to be appointed to head the presidential intelligence service (SIDE) in years, discovered that many agents were employed under false names; those who could be identified felt little allegiance to the new democracy; and their immediate replacement was a practical impossibility since no reliable cadres within the Radical party had any training in intelligence. The difficulties faced by the government in its last-resort plan of reforming the intelligence service from within was illustrated by the case of Raúl Guglialmetti, a retired army Major with alleged links to Contra rebels fighting the Nicaraguan government. Guglialmetti was one agent inherited from the military by the Radical government. Alfonsín followed the advice of Dante Giadone, an old friend and legal partner whom he had made Under-Secretary of the presidency. He agreed to make Guglialmetti the head of the presidential security staff with the specific task of tipping off the government about any military plots. Having manœuvred himself into presidential confidence, Guglialmetti secretly continued to carry out the kind of dirty work he had always done under the military. In June 1985, he was identified as a member of an extreme right-wing terrorist group which had carried out a series of kidnappings and which was plotting to destabilise the new democratic government. By then Giadone had resigned, after discovering, to his acute embarrassment and Alfonsín's political misfortune, that the two young naval officers who had recommended Guglialmetti were themselves working for a parallel intelligence outfit. One of the officers, Lieutenant Luis Cagliari, had carried out his basic training doubling up as military press officer responsible to the foreign press during the Falklands War.

Another deeply embarrassing *cause célèbre*, which led to the resignation of Alfonsín's third Minister of Defence, Germán López (he was preceded by Raúl Borras and Roque Carranza, both of whom died in mid-office), was the Sivak case, which was exposed in May 1986. Osvaldo Sivak was a businessman who was kidnapped in 1985 and held for a ransom of half a million dollars. The Ministry of the Interior initially put the police on the trail of the kidnappers but, when this failed to resolve anything, formed a special intelligence group to liaise with the family and try to locate the criminals. The group was formed by a former police officer, Mario Aguilar, Ruben Barrionuevo of army intelligence, and Pedro Salvia of navy intelligence. They were under the direct orders of the army's Lieutenant-Colonel Juan Carlos Sacco. In early 1986 the then Minister of Defence contacted Sivak's wife and told her to put her full trust in Sacco's team. Subsequently a man calling himself 'Mr Johnson' called the Sivak family claiming that he was one of the kidnappers and demanding payment. The caller was picked up by a police tap and eventually identified as the same voice which had been in touch with Lieutenant-Colonel Sacco (even the phones of the presidential household appeared to have been tapped). 'Mr Johnson' was none other than Pedro Salvia. In a blaze of publicity, Salvia, Aguilar and Barrionuevo were charged with kidnapping and extortion, although Sacco, trusted by the government as an innocent pawn, was initially allowed to keep his post as aide to the Minister of Defence.

The Radicals came to power with an electoral programme which promised 'armed forces formed by able professionals with a democratic formation'. Soon after Alfonsín came to power a group of about fifty retired officers, most of whom had served under previous civilian governments, formed CEMIDA, an *ad hoc* society which declared itself dedicated to the democratisation of the armed forces. CEMIDA maintained that the armed forces under the junta had corrupted the military's popular roots – independence from Spain fought for by militias and the enlightened San Martín – and served selfish interests rather than those of the people. Although some of the proposals for reform made by CEMIDA were followed by Alfonsín, the group itself failed to infiltrate the military's command structure. On the contrary, the fact that CEMIDA members were considered to be pseudo-Marxists and traitors to the *esprit de corps* of the armed forces by the bulk of serving officers underlined the deep ideological divide which still separated the military from the Alfonsín government. In their public statements military chiefs made some allowances to the new authorities, in trying to justify recent history less as a holy crusade than as an essential means towards the eventual consolidation of democracy. But there was still an almost blind conviction that the nation owed the armed forces a favour, and that the reality of the 'disappeared' and the Falklands did not deserve consideration in the public accounts. Argentines are often accused of being unable to accept their own history, but it was the armed forces which often seemed to be most at fault.

Between 1983 and 1986, the Alfonsín government publicly denounced a series of plots in which military officers were said to be involved. In such an atmosphere, and given Argentina's past history of coups, opinion makers understandably tended to emphasise the continuing power of the military and to credit them with unnecessary influence. Sectors of the Argentine media did not integrate themselves into the democratic process as well as they might have done and still allowed themselves to be passive recipients of *chismes* – the Buenos Aires rumour mill which the military intelligence services conducted with such effectiveness during the repression and the Falklands War. Even the left-wing weekly magazine *El Periodista* in 1986 agreed to take up half an issue with a five-page interview with the air force chief, Brigadier Crespo, in which this nationalist officer was allowed to sound off like a professor of constitutional matters about the meaning of democracy and republicanism. Parliament, the trade unions and the Church also spent much of their time consulting military officers, thereby adding to their sense of self-importance.

The military remain too discredited in the popular mind by the experience of the last ten years, and too uncertain about what they would present as an alternative government, to pose a real political threat. A move by some lunatic fringe similar to that carried out by Lieutenant-Colonel Tejero in Spain cannot be discounted, however. Moreover the biggest danger facing Alfonsín's relations with the military is a lack of clear government strategy.

Alfonsín's onslaught on the military immediately after the war, his subsequent boldness in tackling the junta trials, his defence cuts and the occasional denunciation of plots, appeared to respond to the kind of toughness which only the men in uniform can understand and respect. To have been more conciliatory on these issues might have been interpreted as a sign of weakness by hardline extremists bent on destabilisation. There was also another issue of political expediency: out of the ashes of national humiliation on the battlefield, Argentines were insisting on some kind of retribution on the human rights front. It was Alfonsín's sensitivity to the nation's wounded pride which won him the election.

We have described Alfonsín as a man of moral convictions and not a simple political opportunist, but he failed singularly to project this image to the armed forces. From 1985 onwards the President dropped his donkey jacket in favour of more sombre grey suits and regular visits to barracks, which aimed to convey the impression of symbiosis between the civilian and military powers in the newly established democracy. But such operatic gestures were over-shadowed by the government's inability to define a strategic and political context in which to quicken the military's return to barracks. Unlike post-Franco Spain, where membership of the EEC and NATO acted as an important stimulant of professionalisation and depoli-ticisation, the Argentine military still move in the ideological and strategic doldrums. The Falklands War was a shattering experience for armed forces indoctrinated with a hotchpotch of nationalism and commitment to defending the West. The policies subsequently pursued by Alfonsín's dynamic Foreign Minister, Dante Caputo, only added to the confusion. Officially the Alfonsín administration was committed to world justice and peace, but in practical terms it said all things to all men. It flirted with the non-aligned movement, nuclear disarmament, regional co-operation in debt, better relations with the United States, Europe and the Soviet Union. It signed co-operation agreements with practically every Latin American country, including its arch military rival, Brazil. It has accepted peace terms over the Beagle Channel, and persistently declared its commitment to a non-military solution to the Falklands.

A new law of national defence approved by Parliament in October

1986 defines the military's role as simply the defence of the nation, but specifies that this does not include any justification of internal military intervention *in extremis*. Only the democratically elected President is empowered to call on the support of the security forces and only once he has Parliament's consent. In August 1986, while the law was first being debated in the Senate, several senior officers rattled their sabres and declared that they were still the final arbiters in the country's politics. Air force chief Brigadier Ernesto Crespo, for instance, announced that his colleagues considered it their duty to intervene against terrorism, drug trafficking and 'ideological subversion'. He even went as far as to quote a remark from Pope John Paul II to the effect that armies 'should participate in the preservation of each country's domestic peace, as an instrument of the common good'.

The objections were overruled. Nevertheless no one either inside or outside Parliament stated the obvious: that if Argentina is committed to another hundred years of democracy, as Alfonsín insisted when he was elected, and peace reigns in the South Atlantic and in Latin America, the concept of a large military machine as a key factor in the nation's political culture should be redundant.

The Church: 'The Devil in Freedom'

In July 1986, Argentina's most venerated symbol of the Catholic faith, the Virgin of Luján, was hoisted on to a lorry and driven along the forty miles of highway and back streets that lead from the shrine to the presidential palace. It was only the second time in the Virgin's 350-year history that she had been so treated. In 1536, shortly after the introduction of Christianity in Latin America, the diminutive statue was shipwrecked on the shores of the River Plate, not far from the site of the present capital. It was then transported by ox cart across the wild plains of the pampa. When the ox cart stuck in the mud, the faithful took it as an omen from God and founded the site of the present twin-spired Gothic cathedral. In 1536, the Virgin was converted into the symbol of conquest of the heathen Indian by civilised man. In 1986 the image was called upon to play a no less providential role. Held high before the doors of the offices of President Alfonsín, a demonstration by 50,000 Catholic conservatives chanted and shouted against the government's plans to introduce divorce.

The Church historically has not been immune from the process by which almost every sector of Argentine society has at some time or another been in open or tacit alliance with the men in uniform. The symbiosis between religion and politics has tended to be at its most fluid whenever a General has been in charge and coups, including the invasion of the Falklands, have been carried out with all the passion of a crusade. Probably the fairest judgment one can make about the Argentine Church and its role in society since the return of democratic rule is that it has steered clear of any direct attempt to topple the elected authorities. Nevertheless the majority of Bishops have done so without any really profound reappraisal of the past, and have maintained a generally ambiguous attitude towards the pluralist society. In practice this has meant the Church has reserved its power to influence events politically behind the scenes, particularly whenever it has seemed that the new democracy could threaten its privileged role in society.

When Pope John Paul II came to Argentina in the closing stages of the Falklands War in June 1982, there was little doubting the enthusiasm and fervour with which he was greeted. The open-air Masses held in Palermo Park and at the shrine of the Virgin of Luján drew massive crowds in the biggest public gatherings in living memory. The popular reaction, with Argentines of every creed and political persuasion chanting in unison the phrase *Queremos la Paz* ('We want peace'), was, however, rooted in a moment of history: the vast majority of the population had woken up at last to the tragedy of the war and wished only that it be brought to an end. With the Pope thus taking centre-stage the Falklands War ended much the same as it had started – as an act of faith by a predominantly Catholic country. The success of the papal visit left the local Church with a new chance to close up the widening gap between the militarised Church and the laity in general as a result of the close collaboration between many Bishops and priests and the armed forces during the repression.

In the months following the dramatic demise of the Galtieri junta, the Church tried its best to recover moral ground and its former political standing, although its proclaimed attempt to bring about a 'just' transmission to democracy proved half-hearted. The Bishops' Pastoral commission, led by Bishop Justo Laguna of Morón, had in the early stages of the military regime acted as a largely ineffectual liaison between political groups and the junta, conveying privately its worries about human rights. When the military government of General Renaldo Bignone took power, the commission was revived in an attempt to secure the support of politicians and trade union leaders for a phased and largely controlled hand-over of power.

Bishop Laguna's skills as a negotiator undoubtedly helped to calm the mood that was provoked among the people by the Falklands débâcle, and the military were able to hold off the dreaded election day for seventeen months.

With the advent of democracy, the Church voluntarily stepped back from the centre of the stage. This self-limitation was most pronounced during the election campaign, when the Bishops' Conference cautiously avoided supporting any single political party. It also refused to make any statement attaching a confessional label to the small Christian Democrat party. Political activists of widely differing allegiances regularly took up strategic positions on church steps, canvassing voters as they came out of Sunday Masses. However, about the furthest the Bishops moved in trying to influence the election results was in issuing a thinly-veiled condemnation of Marxism, a clear attempt to undercut the Communist party's attempts to seduce the Christian electorate.

The neutrality of the Bishops was the product of a tacit compromise reached with the main political parties. The two major contenders for the presidency, the Perónist candidate Italo Luder, and Raul Afonsín, carefully avoided including anything in their electoral manifestos that smacked of anti-clericalism. Thorny issues like divorce and abortion were ignored in their respective campaigns, and both candidates made a point of presenting themselves as respectable family men in striking contrast to previous military leaders like Perón and Galtieri, whose extramarital affairs had been an open secret. Luder and Alfonsín thus complied to the letter with the constitutional stipulation that the President of Argentina has to be a Catholic.

While the Church's attitude undoubtedly contributed to making the October 1983 elections the fairest in Argentine history, some individual Bishops and priests found it difficult to hide their political sympathies. Bishop Antonio Plaza of la Plata openly declared his support for the Perónist candidate and went on record a few days before polling day as saying he had no doubt that Luder would emerge triumphant. Many other Bishops found it difficult to hide their sympathies for the Perónist cause. Such partisan attitudes were not new. Following the Second World War General Juan Perón had established a relationship with the Church which imitated the national Catholicism of General Franco in Spain. By contrast the largely conservative Argentine Bishops historically have viewed the Radicals as the party of Freemasons, Catholic liberals and Jews. The previous Radical government of Arturo Illía (1963–6) coincided with the progressive council Vatican II of Pope John XXIII and had tried to invoke the directives of Rome to bring about a modest if short-lived reappraisal of the highly privileged status of the Church and its role as an inseparable part of the establishment.

In his first year in government President Alfonsín pursued a deliberate policy of not antagonising the Church. Contrary to the wishes of some sectors in his own party, he restrained the government and Parliament from taking any initiative aimed at legalising divorce or at liberalising the current legislation on abortion. The Argentine penal code inherited from the military by the Radical government allows for abortion only in the cases of rape, danger to the mother's life or malformation of the foetus. Nor did Alfonsín mount a direct challenge to the traditional concept enshrined in the constitution that the State has an obligation to subsidise the Church because of its social and moral function.[7] Only one financial privilege was scrapped early on by Alfonsín's Ministry of Defence: the extraordinary perk by which certain dioceses where the local virgin had been adopted as patron by the armed forces drew the salary of a general.

Even with the demise of the military, the majority of private educational establishments remained Catholic. In a nation of just over 30 million people, the Church continued to run 1,384 primary schools, 964 secondary schools and 10 universities, including the important Catholic University of Buenos Aires. It had a widely circulated news service, Agencia de Informaciones Católicas (AICA) and 8 publishing houses. The news-stands offered three mass-circulation Catholic newspapers, and two Catholic intellectual magazines, and the State-run television and radio stations gave regular access to religious programmes and publicity at no charge.[8]

The initial deference to the Church shown by Alfonsín was in striking contrast to the experience of democratic Spain. There, the socialist government of Felipe González was much bolder in its early parliamentary legislation particularly in moving to make the Church self-financing. In one particular respect the Radical government was motivated politically from the start. One priority area in its foreign policy was an early agreement with Chile over the Beagle Channel. It was the Bishops who helped to avert a war when nationalist naval and army officers urged an occupation of the disputed islands in 1978 and the claims and counter-claims remained subject to papal mediation when Alfonsín took over. The Radicals eventually looked to the continuing allegiance of the Church in securing popular backing for a peace treaty with Chile in a national referendum. It has been unable to do the same with the Falklands. On this issue the Argentine Catholic Church has been reluctant to follow the example of the small Protestant sects in seeking a reconciliation with Britain through the common bond of Christianity.

On balance the honeymoon period between the Alfonsín government and the Church proved short-lived. From early 1984, the government's reconciliatory moves were overshadowed by a new source of tension on the cultural front, where Bishops and priests publicly alleged that the country was being submerged in a wave of pornography and 'Marxism'. One of the characteristics of the new democracy was the greater emphasis on regional autonomy. Largely for this reason from the outset the most outspoken statements were made at diocesan level. In the provinces individual Bishops have eagerly supported the campaigns of conservative lay groups with names like the 'League of Decency' and 'Fatherland, Family and Tradition' which laid siege to local cinemas and assaulted newsstands. During a Lenten sermon in 1985 Bishop Arsenio Casado of Jujuy went as far as to put the Christianity of the government in doubt. 'We declare ourselves to be faithful to a Western and Christian civilisation ... but in practice liberalism and Marxism are collaborating with each other in suffocating Christianity and in undermining morality, which in turn threatens to destroy our national identity.'[9]

Other anti-government statements soon followed. At the annual celebration of Corpus Christi in Plaza de Mayo – just a few yards away from the presidential palace – the Vicar-General of the archdiocese of Buenos Aires attacked the State-run media for 'distorting and degrading love, sex and the family', and for what he claimed was a widespread campaign against the Church. A similar theme was pursued by AICA. The Catholic news service syndicated a report which drew attention to the growing concern of Bishops in the face of the apparent 'infiltration by Marxist and other leftist groups' of the country's cultural and educational life. As for the Bishops, one of the first pastoral letters issued following the end of military rule was entitled 'Decency: the Defence of Human Privacy'. The official Church alleged that democratic Argentina was experiencing a 'profound moral crisis', and demanded an examination of conscience by the authorities.

The government did not ignore such criticism. The Ministry of the Interior led by Antonio Trocolli, one of the few Cabinet appointees belonging to the right wing of the Radical party, instructed police to impose tighter controls on massage parlours and street prostitution, although the democratic authorities found it difficult to break the protection rackets in which individual officers were involved. The authorities also curbed excessive nudity on television and imposed selective bans on controversial films like Truffaut's *Je t'aime, Marie*, which shows a contemporary Virgin Mary in a nude scene. Nevertheless, Alfonsín was careful to avoid re-establishing the full-scale censorship which existed under the military regime and which tended to lump together pornography and anything that remotely smacked of political and social dissidence. Judging by the numerous outbursts of the Bishops, the Church has not on the whole accepted this important distinction. On the contrary, religious prejudice led to a distorted sense of reality, as in the case of universities. Allegations that education was being steadily secularised by 'Marxists' was an inaccurate assessment of the democratisation of higher education after its severe mauling by the former military authorities.

The Church was equally blinkered in its attitude towards women's rights and marriage. One of the first initiatives of the new Parliament to provoke a hostile reaction from the Bishops was the discussion of a key Family Bill. The new legislation aimed to repeal the law of *patria potestad*, perhaps the most acute expression for many years of the male dominance of society and the subjugation of women. The *patria* gave exclusive rights to the father over a child's education, travel and finances, effectively separating the wife from any control over her own life and that of her family. The new Bill, which also granted illegitimate and legitimate children equal rights to inheritance, was subject to considerable filibustering by both Perónists and Radicals linked to conservative sectors of the Church, who for several weeks lent a willing ear to the counsels of their Bishops, but was nevertheless finally endorsed by both the House of Deputies and the Senate to the rapturous applause of women's groups, who had kept a persistent vigil in the public galleries.

The debate on the *patria potestad* with the government's arguments about the need to modernise society through greater social equality being countered by much heavy-handed theology about the indissolubility of marriage and man as the inheritor of Christ proved an important test case of public opinion. Generally Argentines reacted as citizens of a democratic State rather than as religious fanatics and there were no mass demonstrations against the Bill. The government emerged from the debate greatly reassured, the Church much less so.

After overturning the *patria potestad*, it seemed a natural next step to many parliamentarians to tackle the issue of divorce, for here too archaic legislation had put woman at a distinct disadvantage *vis-à-vis* man. Separation already existed under civil law, and was recognised by the Church, but nullification of the marriage and remarriage were prohibited. Resistance to divorce has its roots in Argentina's belated immigration and the obsession at the turn of the century with ensuring the unity of the nation through institutions like national service and marriage. At the beginning of 1986 Argentina was one of only a handful of countries in the world where divorce did not exist.[10] But the new authorities saw its parliamentary approval as an essential part of their efforts to modernise the country's economic and political institutions. In the absence of legal channels for divorce, the single woman–ex wife was a personality a great deal more discriminated against by traditional Argentine society than the single man–ex husband showing off a succession of mistresses as if they were his best suits. What the law aimed to do was to regularise a hypocritical situation faced by over one million Argentines who described themselves as separated. At the same time it aimed to reinforce the Family Bill by rescuing the status of an estimated half a million Argentine children born to 'unmarried parents', many of whom had left their original spouses but were unable to remarry because of the existing law.

Alfonsín's decision not to go for a referendum but to push the divorce law through parliament instead was an intelligent political move. A referendum would have forced a bitter public battle over the issue with unforeseeable consequences. Members of the armed forces and trade unionists were among those who had threatened to support the Church's stand – there were disturbing echoes of 1955 when General Perón was toppled in a coup after breaking off his alliance with the Church and allowing his supporters to burn religious buildings. The parliamentary debate, which lasted several months, defused rhetoric, allowed for nuances of opinion and blurred differences. In one esoteric speech, for instance María Julia Alsogaray, the female deputy of the conservative Union del Centro Democratico (UCD) – traditionally linked to the official Church – claimed that the Constitution was anachronistic for insisting that the President should be Catholic. She then went on to support the pro-divorce lobby.

The absence of a referendum did not eradicate the threat of an impassioned extra-parliamentary debate. *Esquiu*, the Catholic weekly which has been so vociferous in supporting the 'crusade' of the Falklands invasion, returned to the battlefield with a near apocalyptic vision of the future under democracy. 'Just as has occurred in Europe,' it editorialised after the Divorce Bill had been approved by the House of Deputies in August 1986, 'after divorce we can expect ... the legalisation of abortion, drugs, euthanasia and homosexuality.' A similar point of view was taken up by Monsignor Emilio Ognenovich, a Bishop of the Buenos Aires province and the man appointed by the Episcopal Conference to formulate policy towards divorce. He declared on the eve of the parliamentary debate, 'The divorce bill is a generalised attack on the family, which is supported by groups linked to foreign ideologies and drug traffickers.'

As with the trial of the juntas, the absence of more widespread public outrage to the parliamentary approval of the Divorce Bill showed a process of change in Argentine society. While the Church has by no means resigned its right to behave in society as a moral arbitrator, its moral authority and, in consequence, its ability to remain a powerful force in national life, have to some extent been eroded by its inability to come to terms with the issue of human rights, let alone keep up with social progress. The Bishops' Conference has yet to accept publicly that the Argentine Church, either through omission or outright collaboration, had a share of responsibility for the crimes committed by the former military regime. Nor, for that matter, has there been any attempt publicly to examine the moral implications of the alliance of certain sectors of the priesthood with terrorist groups like the Montoneros, which bear their share of responsibility for the abductions, violations of property, and murder of 'political targets' both before and after the military coup.

In 1984, the Bishops' Conference led by Archbishop Juan Carlos Aramburu reacted strongly to a report in the local left-wing magazine *El Periodista* suggesting that the former papal nuncio to Argentina, Archbishop Pio Laghi, had turned a blind eye to torture and executions when he visited a military detention camp. The occasion could have been used by the Argentine hierarchy to instigate a wider and more profound debate on its own attitude to human rights, but it was not. A similar failure emerged from the trial of the juntas. Although several priests and Bishops were called to the witness stand, not one of them made any attempt to admit their own guilt. Outside the courtroom a few Bishops have proved an exception, such as Bishop Jorge Novak of Quilmes and Bishop Jaime Nevares of Neuquén, who have been consistent in demanding that the judgment of the juntas should be extended to the Church as well. The Divorce Bill shows that to a large extent it has been.

The Unions: Inflation and the Fifth Estate

Ever since General Juan Perón transformed the Argentine labour movement into one of the main pillars of the State, no President, civilian or military, has been able to manage for long without the support of the unions. Alfonsín's pledge that he would democratise Argentine labour by breaking the Perónist monopoly of the General Confederation of Labour (CGT) became one of the key planks of his campaign. But once in government the bold promise proved hard to deliver.

Argentina's highly organised and politicised labour movement had its roots in the early twentieth century when anarchist, socialist and Communist ideologies were imported by successive waves of immigrants and spread first in the rural sectors and later, when Argentina experienced industrialisation, in urban areas. The early revolutionary days were short lived, however. The most militant of the trade unionists were imprisoned or killed. The CGT was created by left-wing groups in 1930, but until the outbreak of the Second World War most working-class Argentines found themselves exploited economically and unrepresented politically. The Radical party during the government of Yrigoyen in the 1920s improved some social services, but its efforts to achieve a more broadly based political support beyond the small farmer and the urban middle class never materialised. From around 1936 onwards import substitution saw the spread of unionism in manufacturing and construction and by 1941 membership of the CGT had risen to over 447,000. Such numbers could not for long be ignored by those bent on power. In 1943 a group of officers staged a military coup and immediately set about enlisting civilian support. At the forefront of these efforts was a hitherto little-known Colonel called Juan Perón, who had spent much of his short military career touring Fascist Europe, absorbing ideas about the corporate State. Perón used his post as Secretary for Labour and Social Affairs – a sort of super Labour Ministry – to establish a mass constituency, handing out generous social security schemes, pay increases and new labour laws. The benefits were handed out selectively. Perón actively encouraged divisions within the old CGT, often using military force to suppress the Communists, while gradually building up a corps of compliant trade union leaders loyal enough to ensure the co-operation of the rank and file. Railway workers were the first to dub this faithful disciple of Mussolini 'Argentina's Number One Worker'. By 1945 a reaction had set in. A marriage of convenience between employers worried at the growing politicisation of the workers, liberal political sectors influenced by the Allied cause and weary of what they alleged was a Fascist demagogue in their midst, and military sectors jealous of the young Colonel's ambitions, combined to oust Perón. By then, however, the social process which had been gestated was hurtling irrevocably towards its delivery.

The opposition which had united to oust Perón quickly divided once he had been removed from office. By contrast labour leaders, spurred to action by Perón's dynamic young mistress Evita, were quick to mobilise the working class in support of their leader's regeneration. On 17 October 1945 Argentine history stood at the crossroads. Thousands of workers crossed the bridge separating the meat-packing plants and their poor neighbourhoods from the affluent mainly residential centre of Buenos Aires and staged a mass demonstration calling for Perón's reinstatement. Within four months Perón had been voted President of Argentina.

That Perón was spurred on less by a genuine concern for workers' rights than his own lust for power was evident in his treatment of the Partido Laborista. This party was formed by a group of autonomous trade unionists in 1945 in support of his candidacy. Drawing their inspiration from the British Labour party, the Laboristas saw their alliance with Perón simply as a way of winning Congressional seats and thus gaining greater representation for organised labour within the political parameters of a liberal democratic system. They saw Perón as their candidate not as their leader, a *primus inter pares* much as a British Labour Prime Minister used to be regarded by the TUC. For Perón, however, such a concept of power-sharing was anathema, and no sooner had he been made President-elect than he set about purging the Laboristas from the CGT.

Once in government, Perón intensified his restructuring of the CGT, replacing plant-based organisations with industrial blocs. Controlled by a hierarchical and bureaucratic system of secretaries and branch committees, and supported by compulsory dues from the rank and file, the CGT was transformed into a monolithic giant fully conscious of its existence in Argentine society but seemingly unaware of the extent to which it had become a tool of the corporate society rather than its master. There is no denying that the main thrust in the history of organised labour in Argentina began with Perón. During the period of his first government (1946–55) the membership of the reorganised CGT grew from 520,000 to 2·3 million. Although some individual unions continued to rebel against Perón's authoritarianism, the bulk of union members willingly sacrificed their political independence for the sake of material advancement. For most of his term of office, Perón was able to maintain the workers' allegiance through substantially increasing wage-earners' incomes, and improving still further social benefits for the poor. Most of the working class remained unperturbed by such facts as Perón's purge of the universities, use of torture, and press censorship. What mattered was that they had enough bread to eat.

Perón was toppled in a military coup in 1955, but by then the political identity of Argentina's trade union movement was finely tuned. During the early post-war years the CGT had become accustomed to the benevolent patronage of the State expressed in high income levels (far higher than elsewhere in Latin America), and full if somewhat artificial employment (thanks to Perón's expansion of the State sector and his highly protectionist trade policy). More importantly, the Argentine trade union movement had become enmeshed in the political system. This involvement spread out through all areas of the State from the Church to the armed forces. Within Congress, the alliance between the CGT and the Partido Justicialista, the Perónist party, became much like that between Labour and the TUC, 'like Siamese twins, indissolubly linked to each other'.[11] Even during the long years when Perón was in exile, the CGT carried his stamp; the ideological struggles which developed between left- and right-wing factions were contained within the movement. When Perón returned from exile in 1973 he used CGT hit squads to squash the revolutionary tendencies of the rank and file. Perón died a year later, leaving government in the hands of his wife, Isabelita; but the military who took power in 1976 forged new alliances with some of the old CGT leaders and carried on the repression of the left. The right to strike, to better working conditions, and to a living wage became synonymous with 'subversion' and rank-and-file trade unionists topped the list of the 'disappeared'.

In February 1984, two months after Alfonsín had been inaugurated as President, a parliamentary session in the main chamber of Buenos Aires's imposing *fin de siècle* Congress building was stormed by a group of bare-chested workers banging drums and screaming 'Viva Perón'. The occasion smacked of comic opera. To the assembled deputies of the ruling Radical party, the incident was an unnerving reminder of the fragility of the nascent democracy. In the sweltering heat of the local summer, the deputies in their suits seemed as startled by this expression of political violence as those well-dressed *porteños* who had stood on the sidewalks of the city centre on 17 October 1945 and gaped at the invasion of the 'dark-haired, dark-skinned marchers' – the legendary *descamisados* who had transported Perón to power.[12]

In a session broadcast live on national TV and radio, the deputies had met to debate a crucial trade union reform Bill which aimed to break the forty-year-old dominance of organised labour by the Perónist party. The Bill proposed a system of direct elections to break the hierarchical structure of the CGT. At the same time, in a direct challenge to the long-established bureaucracy, minorities were to be given proportional representation at branch level and union ballots were to be supervised by government officials and judges. The controversial legislation formed part of an ongoing battle which had been officially launched by Alfonsín in the midst of his election campaign. In an extraordinary press conference, the Radical presidential candidate had accused Lorenzo Miguel, leader of the metallurgical union – dubbed the 'metallurgical fatherland' because of its past influence on government and national policy – of plotting with members of the armed forces. The accusation was followed up by repeated diatribes against trade union corruption and collaboration.

A secret survey undertaken by Alfonsín's chief campaign publicist David Ratto immediately after the Lorenzo Miguel press conference showed that a majority of Argentine workers did not share the same dissatisfaction with Miguel as the Radical party.[13] In fact the majority seemed to object strongly to what they perceived was an unwarranted intrusion into union affairs. The results of the poll, never aired publicly, were a revealing comment about the nature of Argentine trade unionism. It showed the majority of unionists were motivated by sectional self-interest rather than by concern for the wider democratic community. The lesson, however, was either ignored or misunderstood by the majority of Radical party officials. This in turn led to a misinterpretation of the results of the presidential and congressional elections that took place at the end of October 1983.

For the first time ever, the vote in the Perónist strongholds of the industrial belts and poor neighbourhoods swung to the Radicals. Officially Radical party strategists came to the conclusion that this swing had been a direct result of Alfonsín's political assault on the trade union bureaucracy. Alfonsín could thus look forward to a new alliance with a democratised CGT. While, there was undoubtedly no love lost between left-wing groups both inside and outside the

Perónist party and the likes of Lorenzo Miguel, subsequent events were to show that the main factor determining the working-class vote had not been political but economic. It was not the allegation of corruption that had tempted the working-class vote but the expectations of economic recovery, full employment and increased social benefits generated by much high-flung rhetoric emanating from the Radical camp. This miscalculation cost the Alfonsín government dearly in political terms in its first months in office.

In its early beginnings the Alfonsín administration showed itself ill-prepared to come to grips with the economy. To be fair to the government, Alfonsín and his Ministers inherited an extremely difficult situation from the military: a foreign debt of over 39 billion dollars, a bankrupt industry, a budget deficit equivalent to nearly 20 per cent of GDP and an inflation rate of over 300 per cent. And yet the kind of technical expertise which the Radicals had undoubtedly built during the previous military regime – and which could have been immediately used to alleviate its effects – was made largely inoperable by the President's initial lack of strategy. His priority was human rights and he somewhat naïvely believed that democracy alone would solve the country's economic problems. Meanwhile his first Economy Minister Bernardo Grinspún's policy was flawed by technical incompetence and political lack of tact.

The government's failure to provide the economic context for parliamentary activity to flourish doomed the Labour Reform Bill. The coming of democracy unleashed wage demands which had been repressed during most of the previous military regime. Officials argued at the time that the very fragmentation of the Perónist party following the election made it impossible to establish whom to negotiate with, and that it was thus impossible to resist handing out wage increases in a somewhat haphazard fashion. And yet, arguably, the very confusion of the Perónist party should have inspired the government from the outset to enforce a coherent prices and incomes policy underpinned by more wide-ranging structural reforms of taxation, the financial system and the public sector. The reforms were sadly lacking.

Instead, in the first quarter of 1984, inflation rose in leaps and bounds. Against this background trade union officials and their allies in the Perónist parliamentary group were able to launch a spirited rearguard action against the government's Labour Reform Bill. The reforms were carried by the Radical majority in the lower House of Deputies, but after a great deal of filibustering and dubious underhand dealings were defeated in the Senate by the combined votes of the Perónists and members of a small provincial party. The result proved much more than a mathematical accident. It was a shattering psychological blow for the government in its attempts to make substance of the new democracy as well as form.

In the preceding weeks some unions had pre-empted the Bill by staging their own free elections. In the majority of them young candidates had defeated the old bureaucrats. In one branch office in Villa Constución, previously dominated by a faction loyal to Lorenzo Miguel, an independent metal worker called Alberto Piccinini had come out on top in spite of being virtually ostracised by the official CGT after he had been released from military jail. The defeat of the Labour Reform Bill led to a period of retrenchment, with the old CGT leadership exploiting their parliamentary success and recovering positions. In September 1984, only eight months after Alfonsín's inauguration, the CGT staged a general strike against the government. The normal functioning of banks and other elements of commercial life in the centre of Buenos Aires, the running of some privately owned bus services and metro lines, and the lack of solidarity for the strike in many of the provinces, were all held up as evidence of Alfonsín's continuing support among the middle class and sectors of labour; but it was difficult to ignore the mass walk-outs by workers in the majority of factories in Buenos Aires and the industrial city of Córdoba. Railways and ports also came to a halt. In that same month the consumer price index rose by a dramatic 27·5 per cent, the highest figure recorded since April 1976 (the first month of military government) bringing the annual inflation figure to 688 per cent.

For all its electoral talk of 'social justice', Argentine democracy in its first months under Alfonsín was unable to bring much material comfort to the most needy. A political decision was taken to transfer budgetary allocations away from defence towards health, housing and education. However, government spending became distorted and neutralised by inflation. Perhaps the most controversial of the early initiatives to be attempted on the social front was the emergency National Food Plan (PAN). The programme was launched in June 1984 in a Buenos Aires industrial suburb, in an ageing primary school ironically named Villa Diamante (Diamond House). At the school a registry compiled by local authorities including the parish priest had classified a long queue of badly-dressed, tired-looking people pouring in from the surrounding streets as 'families in need' – the motley crowd of hundreds was led by the wives of the unemployed or low-wage earners who lived in the unseen world of sophisticated Buenos Aires: shanty huts without running water or electricity, where children were suffering from severe malnutrition. According to estimates by the Ministry of Social Affairs, some 2·8 million Argentines or 10 per cent of the population were living well below the breadline in Buenos Aires and the northern provinces which border Chile and Brazil. Such statistics, so common in Latin America, were a startling reminder of Argentina's social decline in the previous fifty years. This country rich in natural resources, with no problems of over-population, and thousands of miles of food-producing prairies, was facing the 1980s unable to feed its own.

The PAN was spearheaded initially by a central corps of 1,800 social workers, backed by local government officials and volunteers. Under the scheme each recipient family was entitled to 40 kilos of free food per month. The ration consisted of basic items like powdered milk, sugar, rice, beans, cooking oil, tinned beef and flour. Government officials estimated that this ration, which could be increased proportionally with the size of the family, was equivalent to half the minimum monthly wage. The opposition Perónist party and the CGT initially supported the PAN only subsequently to rebel against it, claiming that it was being used politically by the government. Trade unionists in particular drew negative comparisons between the PAN and the emergency welfare work headed by Evita Perón's social aid foundation in the late 1940s. Putting to the back of their minds the memory of the corruption which surrounded much of Evita's work, the CGT claimed that the foundation's work had proved more effective because it was inspired by the Perónist party's grass roots. They alleged that the PAN reflected the essentially middle- and upper-class paternalism of the ruling Radical party.

Fernando Alfonsín, the President's younger brother, was put in charge of the PAN. The appointment drew immediate accusations of nepotism, although government supporters insisted that Fernando's family status allowed him direct access to an honest President, cutting out middlemen and avoiding corruption. Fernando was certainly zealous in his work. He published quarterly balance sheets showing a breakdown of exactly how much had been spent and on whom, and the transparency of the operation was underlined by his frankness towards the press. 'We are convinced that if we carry out this plan well it is going to be an example to the world, but if we do it badly it will be used by the opposition as an excuse to bring us down,' he said in an early interview with the author.

In the first year of democracy, however, it was not so much politics as the government's mismanagement of the economy which undermined the effectiveness of the PAN. With triple-figure inflation, the PAN not only failed to attack the root cause of poverty, it also came close to failing as a palliative to the poor. Inflation deepened the social rift in Argentine society, threatening to cancel out such early political achievements as the arrest and trial of the juntas. Announcing a lurch in the consumer price index of 20 percentage points for March 1984, the Economy Minister, Grinspún, had suggested that the main upward pressure on prices had been generous wage settlements. The unions strongly resisted the suggestion that they were the main cause of the economic collapse. They claimed that wage increases in excess of increases in productivity were the result of inflation rather than its cause. Neither side seemed to want to see the wood for the trees: inflation in Argentina had become virtually endemic.

'The majority of survival techniques are devious and speculative and nothing to be proud of. It takes a shrewd, foxy and imaginative mind to keep afloat,' commented one businessman, once the euphoria of the Alfonsin election victory had given way to a crude perception of economic reality. Among the middle classes and above, the survival kit ranged from credit cards – timing shopping sprees carefully so the bill would not have to be paid for at least a month – to use of cash – either buying up dollars in your local travel agency or investing in index-linked deposit accounts and stocks and shares. Within the business community survival meant under-invoicing or over-invoicing combined with the dextrous manipulation of the black market exchange rate (which on an average week showed a 20 per cent difference from the official rate) and inter-company lending within a clandestine banking system which bypassed official bank rates.

Exchange controls and heavily regulated interest rates meant that on the surface at least the opportunities for speculation were not as great as during the days of *plata dulce*, the free-market policies pursued by the former military regime, which are estimated to have led to a capital flight of about 28 billion dollars in less than ten years. Clearly, though, fortunes were being made in the first months of democracy in spite of, and because of, inflation. Little of that 28 billion dollars was repatriated permanently. The Argentines who still held a share of this sum continued to prefer bank accounts in Switzerland, the United States and Uruguay, and to live royally on the interest on their deposits and the rents on their properties rather than put their savings towards productive investment. Within Argentina itself the initial attempts by the authorities to clamp down on the black market and create a healthier, more moral climate for the economy proved piecemeal. Police officers would make a swoop on an exchange dealer on one day and be quite openly collaborating with him on another. Along the Avenida Corrientes between San Martín Street and Reconquista, the fifteen square blocks that make up Buenos Aires's financial 'city' the *faroles* (lanterns) as the street-exchange dealers are called still cried 'Cambio, Cambio, Cambio' with the immunity of pimps offering whores in a red-light district. On television, the lifting of censorship brought better plays, singers who were previously banned, but the prime-time news programme still devoted half its time to financial comment, listing the parallel exchange rate – an officially endorsed synonym for the black economy – and advising viewers where to put their money.

To those Argentines lower down the social scale, such advice produced about the same degree of frustration as advertisements showing their fellow countrymen drinking Cinzano on a tropical beach or smoking a cigarette on the streets of New York. While wage settlements had been on an upward curve since the end of the Falklands War, they had not recovered the ground lost following the 1976 coup when incomes were savagely slashed. The Alfonsín government began by allowing wages to keep pace with inflation but only retroactively. Thus, with prices tending to outstrip government forecasts by dramatic margins, most low-income earners experienced several weeks in which their salaries decreased substantially in real terms. There was anyway a growing degree of popular scepticism regarding the validity of official inflation figures – the generalised view in trade-union circles was that they seriously understated the economic crisis. The consumer price index taken to measure the monthly inflation figures by the National Institute of Statistics did not accurately reflect the many distortions created by the Argentine way of doing business. Price controls became virtually unenforceable against an army of middlemen and small-scale retail outlets. Restrictions on imports to save foreign exchange encouraged scarcity and brought in the black marketeers.

Lack of public faith in the government's ability to cope in such an environment itself fuelled rises in the inflation rate. Products were snapped up by people who wanted to beat the next price rise, which in turn clogged up the distribution system and caused speculation on scarcity. From the moment he took office Grinspún consistently announced that the State would play its part in the fight against inflation by cutting back the budget deficit, but he failed to produce a coherent economic programme to back this. The nearest the government came in those first crucial months to calming troubled social waters was to try to establish a national consensus with the unions on fighting inflation. But against the background of the government's economic mismanagement and the belligerent nature of the CGT such an initiative was bound to fail. Political posturing developed when what was needed was a series of balanced trade-offs involving social security, tax benefits, selective credit policy and employment capable of mitigating the conflictive claims of different social sectors.

The posturing was nowhere more apparent than in the decision by Alfonsín in May 1984 – following the parliamentary defeat of the Labour Reform Bill – to recall Perón's widow Isabelita from her exile home in Madrid. The move was an attempt to build a bridge with the CGT following the replacement of the anti-Perónist Labour Minister, Antonio Mucci, by Juan Manuel Casella, a young Radical lawyer with a reputation as a conciliator.

'Now, if you don't behave yourselves I'm going to give each one of you a good spanking,' were among the first words Maria Estela 'Isabelita' Perón spoke to a group of trade unionists as soon as she touched down at Buenos Aires's international airport of Ezeiza.[14] She was dressed in an impeccable leather coat topped with a generous fur scarf. Her jewels, scent, fashionable hairstyle and studied Castilian accent completed the image of a rich lady from Madrid's Calle Serrano. Around her thousands of Perónists were doing everything but behaving themselves. Like an unruly football crowd, they jostled and screamed between occasional stampedes. The airport seemed to tremble visibly as passengers in transit huddled together in corners like a flock of frightened sheep expecting the worst. Eleven years before, the return of Isabelita's late husband from exile erupted into a pitched battle between right-wing trade unionists and Montoneros. Hundreds had been killed in the ensuing riot, many of the victims being hung, drawn and quartered in the forest near Ezeiza.[15]

There was no repeat performance, however. Instead the Perónists beat an orderly retreat from the airport and followed La Señora to her five-star hotel in the centre of town, a block away from where Borges lived. Not for the first time, the scene read like a Borges short story; caught in a time warp the blind writer, a self-confessed anti-Perónist, was nearly lynched one day outside Isabelita's window as he stumbled home from a very English tea. Isabelita spent her days closeted in her suite, holding court to a long line of seemingly repentant Perónist Congressmen and trade union leaders, most of whom had spent the post-election period criticising her lack of direction. She gave no interviews, but appeared in a great number of newspaper photographs. The evening vigil of the 'paparazzi' was usually rewarded as the five-foot woman in high heels flashed a feline smile and purred, 'Make sure I come out pretty.' When she wasn't dressing down CGT officials, Isabelita seemed to spend most of her time with Miguel Angel, a Spanish homosexual who doubled as personal hairdresser and confidant. Miguel Angel informed the local press that La Señora's hair was the kind that needed close attention or else she ran the risk of it collapsing like a bad soufflé. 'I've given her hair a honey-toned highlight at the front – exactly how she wants it,' crooned Miguel Angel in one lengthy interview.[16]

There seemed to be an element of *déjà vu* in the comic opera of Argentine politics, but clearly Isabelita had come a long way since she first enchanted the late General Juan Perón by wearing a skimpy dress of ostrich feathers in the Happy Land nightclub in Panama City back in the 1950s. Her smiles betrayed none of the strain which accompanied her in the years 1974–6 when, after her husband's death, she briefly took over the presidency of Argentina and plunged her country into political and financial chaos. After being toppled by the Videla junta she was put under house arrest before being whisked off to exile. Since 1981 she had been living in Spain; exile, so she told close friends, had 'transformed her spiritually'. Daily Mass was interspersed with shopping sprees, fleeting romances and holidays on the Costa del Sol. On her return to Buenos Aires she invoked the protection of the Virgin Mary.

She had agreed to return after the Argentine Congress had exonerated her from any future judicial proceedings against her based on allegations of misappropriation of public funds while she was in office. Isabelita was thus able to continue to enjoy thousands of dollars in unearned income, which were allegedly deposited in Swiss and Spanish bank accounts. Her physical assets included a house and flat in Madrid and three residences in Argentina, in addition to some gold bars which the Nazis were supposed to have given Perón for safe keeping soon after the Second World War.

The return of Isabelita in such circumstances appeared to signal a change of strategy by the government. Publicly, it was the first time since the election that the ruling Radical party had put political expediency before ethics. Contradicting the stand they had taken during the election campaign – when the Radical machinery had gone out of its way to destroy the Perónist myth – officials now stressed Isabelita's positive role as the fount of the Perónist mystique and only surviving heir of General Perón. Alfonsín himself treated her with the kind of deference usually reserved for visiting Heads of State, and the national accord which they agreed to was signed with the pomp and circumstance of a historic peace treaty. It turned out to be little more than a dead letter. After signing the accord Isabelita declared that she was prepared to give her full support to the democratic government and urged union leaders and her parliamentary party to offer only 'constructive' opposition. However, she subsequently showed neither the necessary political acumen nor the strength of will to sustain the loyalty of her party. She surrounded herself with a clique of orthodox right-wing 'advisers', alienating the new currents within the Perónist party, which had been consolidating their positions as a result of the election débâcle. She eventually returned to Madrid leaving disgruntled Perónists with the distinct feeling that she had been brought by Alfonsín not to govern by consensus but to divide and rule. The Perónist party split between the orthodox trade unionists and their allies in Parliament and a new 'renewal faction', making it even more difficult for the government to find someone to negotiate with.

By the beginning of 1985, Alfonsín could no longer afford political theatricals. Inflation was fast approaching an unprecedented annual rate of 1,000 per cent. The unions were once more on the warpath and for the first time since the elections seemed to convey a more generalised social exasperation with the government: there were protests from employers, bankers, farmers, renewed rumblings within the military, angry sermons from the pulpit by priests and Bishops predicting social disintegration. The government's labour relations no longer seemed to be the issue; there was a collective sense that democracy itself was disintegrating. It was a situation in which a politician less experienced than Alfonsín would have lost his nerve. Instead the President led from the front. In March he sacked his personal friend Grinspún, whom opinion polls showed had become the most unpopular public figure in Argentina, and replaced him with the younger Under-Secretary for Planning, Juan Sourrouille. The appointment turned out to be much more than a simple substitution. Sourrouille was a political independent. During the military regime he had worked closely with the numerous think-tanks developed inside the civilian opposition, which had concentrated on formulating alternative economic policies. During the first months of democratic government these ideas had never progressed much beyond the drawing-board.

When Sourrouille took over, the domestic situation presented a strikingly different picture to that which existed in the first months of 1984. Gone were the bold commitments to increase real salaries, economic growth and the servicing of the country's foreign debt, which had by then climbed to 48 billion dollars. Instead the country found itself immersed in an unprecedented stagflation and technically in default, having not paid interest on debt since the previous November. Putting behind him the public outbursts of Grinspún, Sourrouille argued with moderation both at home and abroad that neither trade surpluses nor budgetary or monetary restraint made sense any more, in a situation in which inflation had both built upon itself and destroyed all the known methods for controlling it. What was needed was a clean sweep of the system, as sweeping perhaps as that applied in a similar situation in post-war Germany – only then could Argentina resume growth. Sourrouille took two months to prepare his strategy and convince Alfonsín that the President had to fall in foursquare behind the government's economic policy.

Not since the military government of Galtieri announced that it had invaded the Falkland Islands had such a sense of profound change gripped the Argentine people as on 14 June 1985.[17] There was an element of dramatic irony in the fact that the third anniversary of the military surrender had been picked for what Alfonsín himself described as a new 'battle plan', similar to those adopted by nations whose economies had been shattered by the Second World War. It was a Friday evening, but the usual bustle of the weekend was replaced by deserted streets as the local population chose to stay at home to listen to the President's national broadcast, surrounded by the eerie mist of the local winter outside. Alfonsín's rhetorical powers had already been proven in a successful election campaign, a public condemnation of the former military regime and a national plebiscite on the Beagle Channel; but on that day it was the substance rather than the style which caught the audience's imagination. Alfonsín announced an overhaul of the economy on a scale unprecedented in Argentina's recent history. It involved a new national currency (the 'austral'), a prices and wages freeze, and a fiscal and monetary policy of such immediate severity as to make the adjustment programmes of other Latin American debtor nations look like a picnic by comparison.

The government needed a three-day bank holiday before conjuring up enough courage to test the reactions of the local financial markets to the new currency. The fear persisted that a run on deposits and a major slide of the austral against the dollar on the local black market would signal a pre-emptive death knell for Sourrouille's shock prescription for hyperinflation. What happened however, went beyond even the government's wildest expectations. Argentines put in more money than they took out: more than 80 per cent of deposits in the banking system were renewed. The exchange dealers were forced to declare an unofficial day of mourning as the austral firmed up, closing the gap between the 'black' and official rate to 1 per cent.

The government's propaganda campaign echoed the regimentation of the past – 'This is a war economy,' declared one poster loudly, 'he who speculates is a deserter.' The war did not get off to an entirely happy start. The ten emergency telephone lines set up by the Secretariat of Internal Commerce to record price violations reported by consumers proved utterly inadequate on the first day as an efficient checking mechanism on the 350,000 small shops and thousands more supermarkets which exist in the capital. Many people's initial sense of a collective contribution to the 'battle plan' was thus frustrated at a moment when it most needed to be encouraged. Not all the phone calls that did get through were well intentioned. When inspectors checked them out, they sometimes found that the accused were simply victims of personal vendettas or retailers with a seemingly genuine alibi for their price hikes: they were simply reflecting the price lists passed down to them by wholesalers.

Only when the price inspectors began to move against the big fish did popular reaction slowly turn from one of suspicion to cooperation with a government which was genuinely perceived to be doing justice. Raids extended themselves to one of the capital's largest wholesalers as well as a 'black' parallel food market which had been operating thanks to the protection of sectors of the police force.

When price controls had previously been enforced on a massive scale during the government of General Perón in 1974, police officers carried out the inspections so that bribery and outright repression became widespread. From the outset the Alfonsín government was careful in its selection of inspectors: some were drawn from the universities; others had survived the long succession of government changes without apparent corruption. Both groups seemed to be determined to prove their democratic credentials while having an in-built interest in seeing the price controls work. As one young inspector – a graduate in business law – put it to me at the time, 'If we allow inflation to go on the way it is, it is not just our wages that are going to suffer but democracy too. If this doesn't work we might as well pack our bags, turn off the lights, and leave the country.'[18]

Within three months of the 'battle plan' being announced, local opinion polls showed that Alfonsín's popularity had recovered and reached its highest peak since he took power in December 1983. The reason seemed to be the government's initial success in reducing inflation: prices which had increased by 30 per cent in the month before the measures were announced had been brought down to 4 per cent in August, the lowest monthly figure since May 1982. 'The atmosphere in Buenos Aires is a bit like the beginning of a Lenten fast from which everyone, and the country, will emerge chastened and hungry, but with renewed vigour,' commented the *Financial Times*.[19]

Faced with such initial popular support for the plan, the CGT had little option but to declare a *de facto* truce; but the peace proved short-lived. Towards the end of September it announced another general strike against the government. As before, the motives behind the CGT's decision were both political and economic. With mid-term elections looming that November, the CGT had no wish passively to surrender the political stage to the government by being seen to endorse its policies. At the same time militancy was being generated among the rank and file by the way the 'austral plan' had compounded the problems of the country's lower wage-earners in its initial stages. Lower inflation had allowed some companies to strengthen their capital base; inflation survival techniques were replaced by medium-term thinking on marketing and improving product range; some new jobs were created. Nevertheless, by September 1985, the government had yet to reach the ambitious target of zero inflation. With wages frozen, real salaries had fallen by 10 per cent since the previous June. Tighter credit had also meant that the 'austral plan' had started off by shedding more jobs than it created. Unemployment, which that May had stood officially at 6·3 per cent (the highest official figure in eleven years), had risen by another 270,000 according to trade union officials.

The general strike at the end of September again proved only partially successful. The normal functioning for most of the day of banks and other elements of commercial life, the virtually normal running of the transport sector, and the lack of solidarity with the strike call in some provinces, were all held up by some government officials as proof of Alfonsín's continuing support among the middle classes and sectors of labour, the combination that won him the election in 1983. There were, however, mass walk-outs by workers in most factories in Buenos Aires and the industrial city of Córdoba. But of more political significance than the strike was a mass rally called in Buenos Aires, which drew a crowd estimated at between 200,000 and 250,000. One of the early speakers conceded that the working class was no longer the majority in Argentina, but the main speaker, Saul Ubaldini, the brewery workers' leader and the most publicly active of the then four leaders of the CGT, indicated that he was not all that worried about votes. In a speech that was enthusiastically applauded, Ubaldini claimed that democracy had become an 'exhausted word' which sounded like 'authoritarianism'. He told the crowd that they and not the government would triumph, 'but our triumph is not electoral ... All we are looking for is the triumph of the people.' He concluded with what seemed to be a return to the old Perónist tendency to exclude all others, 'We are the Fatherland, the others can think what they like.'[20]

The results of the mid-term elections two months later appeared to confirm that a large majority of Argentines were finally resolved to treat democracy as more than just a transitory experience. Historically mid-term elections marked the beginning of the end for democratic governments in Argentina. In 1963 the Radical government of Arturo Illía failed the two-year test of his popularity and was subsequently toppled in a military coup. Now, however, the Radicals increased their parliamentary majority at the expense of the Perónists, underlining the shift in the balance of party political power. One of the most notable features of the election was the strong showing made within the Perónist party by the dissident 'renewal' faction. The campaign of the *renovadores*, with its commitment to a moderate economic programme and its social democratic approach to politics, was almost indistinguishable from that of the Radicals. The new Perónists expurgated the figure of General Perón and concentrated instead on projecting new youthful figures like Carlos Grosso, who had far fewer links with the past. The *renovadores* criticised the recession provoked by the recent 'austral plan' but privately admitted that by drastically reducing the rate of inflation the government had prepared the ground for a more viable prices and incomes policy.

The expectations generated by the results were dashed once the CGT relaunched its offensive against the government.

Between December 1983 and April 1986, the CGT staged seven general strikes against the government. With each one the unions showed that they had the power collectively to paralyse large sectors of the economy; throughout this period they also demonstrated a cohesion of action lacking in the majority of the political parties. As the defeat of the Labour Reform Bill showed, this was the case particularly when it came to the defence of their autonomy from interference by a government viewed as contrary to their interests as a social sector.

By contrast the ruling Radical government was unable to generate popular support for a more resolute approach, aimed at curbing the powers of the unions, similar to the strategy pursued by Mrs Thatcher after the 1979 election in Britain. Government officials consistently tried to convey their struggle with the unions as essentially a battle for the survival of the democratic State. And yet public attitudes towards the CGT remained ambivalent, rarely matching the open hostility expressed by the government. Statements by trade union officials were given as much space by the local media as those by Congressmen and military officers; impending strikes were reported with the coverage usually reserved for a national election; the self-importance of trade union officials remains inflated by the willingness of Bishops, Generals and members of the Cabinet and Congress to court them openly and submissively. A survey conducted by the Argentine pollsters SOCMERC showed that, in October 1985, 36 per cent of the population favoured general strikes while 68 per cent supported the 'austral plan'. In April 1986 those favouring strikes had risen to 46 per cent, while supporters of the 'austral plan' had fallen to 52 per cent. Questioned about their attitudes to unions in general, in December 1984 66 per cent said they favoured them. In April 1986 the figure had only dropped slightly to 62 per cent. Perhaps most significantly, successive polls throughout this period showed Alfonsín as the most popular figure in Argentina but Saul Ubaldini, elected General Secretary of the CGT in 1985, as his closest rival.

Dubbed the Lech Walesa of the River Plate because of his fondness for being photographed with images of the Blessed Virgin, Ubaldini's rise to power was enigmatic.[21] Although a member of the Perónist party almost from birth, until 1986 he never formed part of the party machinery officially. On the contrary he doggedly resisted being made a candidate for Congress both in the 1983 elections and the 1985 mid-term elections. Like Alfonsín his political advancement was favoured by default as much as design. His exclusion from the main stream of politics – the brewery union never headed any of the big industrial blocs created by Perón – ensured his survival at a time when more public figures than he were risking their credibility. He emerged from the sidelines in the late 1970s – a compromise candidate, vaguely acceptable as much to the collaborators of the military regime as to the rank and file, whose more militant leadership were either imprisoned or in the lists of the 'disappeared'. Ubaldini timed his own militancy to coincide with the demise of the military regime. His test of fire was the march on the presidential palace which he organised on 30 March 1982 and which was brutally repressed by Galtieri. Less than a week later Ubaldini was among the labour leaders who were present at the official inauguration of General Menéndez as military governor of 'Las Malvinas'.

Ubaldini personified the obscurantism of Argentine politics. His political leanings were described as those of a left-leaning Christian Democrat rather than a socialist; but he never entirely severed his links with the military sectors or reactionary Bishops, and his rallies were charged with the kind of political extremism, including anti-Semitism and nationalism, which earned Perón the title of neo-fascist. Perhaps it was his tendency to say all things to all men, combined with his undoubted ability to rally the masses, which made him such a formidable political proposition. For in many ways he became much more than just a trade union leader, he was *de facto* head of the opposition. Not only did the parliamentary Perónist party fail to produce a leader capable of healing its internal divisions, but the CGT managed increasingly to forge an identity of its own. Argentina's trade union organisation was also split between factions, but it showed that it was still far from undergoing the same degree of social and political disintegration as that suffered by organised labour in the industrialised nations.

A combination of recession and political repression has depleted CGT ranks in recent years. The wealth of the unions has also been greatly diminished because of their much reduced role in collecting social security contributions, which up to the mid-1970s were a major source of additional revenue. In the traditionally large industrial blocs the change has been dramatic. Between 1974 and 1986 textiles, mechanical engineering and construction lost 38 per cent, 55 per cent and 42 per cent of their members respectively. The metallurgical union has no centralised figures, but its membership is believed to have dropped by more than a third. The days when the big union barons like Lorenzo Miguel could accelerate the downfall of a government as he did in 1975–6 were clearly over by 1986. Nevertheless, Argentina's overall trade union density (55–60 per cent of the country's workers belong to the CGT) was still high compared to West Germany, Britain, France and Japan (under 40 per cent) and a great deal higher than the United States (19 per cent).[22] Trade union affiliations continued to be concentrated in Buenos Aires, hub of the country's political life and in Córdoba, the country's second largest town, which has always had a dynamic political life of its own. Regionalisation of the economy has been far more limited than in say Brazil, so trade union power has become less diffuse. Since the Second World War, the Argentine economy has undergone several transformations; the public sector has grown, as has the presence of more technologically innovative companies either directly foreign-owned or linked to multi-nationals at the expense of private Argentine manufacturing concerns. There has also been a growth in the service sectors such as tourism, banking and restaurants, and in teaching and the health service. Generally the unions have followed the jobs, although the power of the CGT would be much greater if it were not for the increase in the number of self-employed (an estimated two million out of an economically active population of nine million), and the political phenomenon of Alfonsinismo.

Union elections held in the course of 1985 and 1986 showed that organised labour was still dominated by the Perónist-controlled sectors of the CGT.[23] The Radicals had made important inroads into the trade union movement especially among the growing white-collar sector of bank workers, teachers, health workers and State employees.

Nevertheless the sharp drop in real salaries brought about by the 'austral plan' in the State sector, and the government's announced plans to streamline the country's inflated and inefficient banking system, pushed many white-collar workers behind the Ubaldini offensive against the government. In industry Perónist officials meanwhile found themselves coming increasingly under pressure from a more militant rank and file influenced by the Communist party and Trotskyite political groupings.

By surviving seven general strikes between 1983 and 1986 while maintaining its democratic credentials more or less intact, the Alfonsín government effectively broke the accepted wisdom in Argentine politics that no government could survive for long without repressing the unions or actively seeking their blessing. Nevertheless, the opposition of the trade unions remains a stumbling block in the way of the country's modernisation. Towards the end of 1986 the Alfonsín government was reported to be preparing new decree laws which would bypass parliament and outlaw illegal strikes. But that seemed to be an attempt to tackle the effect of trade union obstructionism rather than its cause. The political power of the Argentine unions was likely to continue to be largely negative as long as the government held back from going beyond the limitations of the 'austral plan' towards a more coherent medium-term economic strategy. At the same time the ease with which rabble-rousing trade union bosses with a penchant for anti-Semitic slogans could transform themselves into leaders of the opposition was due in part to the difficulties faced by the government in resolving the debt problem on a more equitable basis and the fragility of the institutions traditionally associated with a democracy.

Debt and democracy

In October 1986 President Alfonsín went to Strasbourg to be given the European Human Rights prize from the twenty-one-nation Council of Europe. It should have been an occasion for self-congratulation by this Latin American leader who had managed, against all the odds, to put the powerful military in the criminal dock. And yet, instead of making the speech that was expected of him, Alfonsín emphasised that the 'unshakeable commitment of the Argentine people and government to continue to serve with honesty and determination the cause of human rights' was in large measure dependent on the implementation of a more 'authentic universal justice'. This authenticity, Alfonsín argued, had to be based on a more equitable world economic order, for without it developing democracies such as Argentina would be doomed to failure.[24]

The connection between debt and democracy was a constant theme of the Alfonsín government in the years 1983–6, and one that Argentina made considerable efforts to project throughout Latin America and the international banking community. During this period debt influenced the pace and scope of economic change within Argentina – and the nature of political reaction to it – and to a large extent overshadowed the country's relations with the outside world, particularly the United States and Europe. Government officials saw the debt burden as a lead weight tied to their feet; the opposition, led by the trade unions, saw the debt issue as a convenient whip not only to hit out with at the alleged incompetence of the Economy Ministry, but also at the 'usury' of the international banking system and the 'economic imperialism of the United States'.[25] Western governments meanwhile, under the influence of their central bank governors and those commercial banks which stood most exposed by their past lending to Latin America, regarded debt as one of the main issues by which to measure Argentina's post-war credibility – or lack of it.

The debt problem was not initially of Alfonsín's making: it was the international banking community's and the military's. The 1976 coup saw the installation of the most repressive regime ever to rule Argentina: civil liberties were quashed; there was State-funded crime and torture on a nationwide scale; the inhumanity of Belsen and Auschwitz was reproduced in the clandestine prison camps of the junta; more than 8,000 people disappeared. And yet the early years of military government coincided with a period of intensive lending to Argentina by commercial banks. During the 1970s US, Japanese and European (particularly British) banks fell over themselves and each other trying to lend in Latin America. The Argentine military and the private and public sectors which they dominated became favourite clients with banks often offering to lend money even before they had been asked.

Banking in Argentina, as elsewhere in Latin America, had traditionally been a risky business: a combination of shifting international terms of trade, political instability, and economic mismanagement had produced a history of boom and bust. Debt crises in Latin America had followed an almost perfect fifty-year cycle since the 1880s, when Baring Brothers of London failed to attract subscribers for a loan it had underwritten to reorganise the water supply in Buenos Aires, triggering off financial panic and lurching the government towards default on its foreign debt.[26] By the time of the 1976 coup, however, bankers had every reason to put on the back burner whatever sense of history they might have once had. The oil crisis, provoked by OPEC's quadrupling of prices in 1973, found Western banks awash with deposits from Arab states but few Western countries to lend to. The ensuing recession in Europe and the United States had meant a fall-off in demand from the banks' traditional corporate customers. So the banks turned to Latin America. As one economist has put it, 'The developing countries of the Third World saved the bankers from the curse of idle money: it was love at first sight.'[27]

It is in the nature of an authoritarian regime, characterised by its concentration of political power and its lack of genuine debate over economic policy, for 'prestige' infrastructure as opposed to industrial projects to be given special priority status. Corruption is also endemic. In the case of the Argentina of the juntas, prestige projects towards which banks lent considerable sums of money included the expansion of the State airline's fleet of jumbo jets, the development of the nuclear industry and the building of motorways linking Buenos Aires to its airport. The projects entrusted to military officers, with a propensity for thinking 'big' inside and outside the barracks, made little economic let alone social sense. Jumbo jets were bought at a time when the forecast for international flight traffic was uncertain and when large areas of Argentina were not linked by train or internal flights; nuclear energy was promoted when the country's considerable oil and natural gas reserves remained largely untapped and when the State oil company Yacimientos Petrolíferos Fiscales was allowed to syphon off large amounts of dollar funds it received from abroad for purely speculative, non-productive ends; the motorways, the subject of dubious construction contracts surrounded by allegations of hefty under-the-table commissions, were built when the majority of the population living in the poor suburbs of Buenos Aires were still urgently in need of efficient underground and bus systems to get them to work in the centre, as well as hospitals for their sick.[28]

Loose lending by banks and speculative borrowing increased Argentina's overall foreign debt between the 1976 coup and the end of military rule from just over seven billion dollars to nearly forty billion dollars. Unlike Mexico and Brazil, the Argentina of the juntas experienced very little growth as a result of the inflow of foreign funds. By 1983, the per capita income was 15 per cent less than it had been in 1975 (between 1975 and 1983 per capita income grew by 60 per cent and 30 per cent in Brazil and Mexico respectively). Real salaries over the same period had fallen by 30 per cent, and unemployment based on official statistics and additional figures prepared by independent economists, taking into account non-unionised labour, was calculated at 15 per cent, an all-time record.[29] To make matters worse, the willingness of banks to go on lending to Latin America came to an abrupt end just as Alfonsín was beginning to make his bid for the presidency. The slowdown of available funds thus contributed to the economic instability of the incoming democratic government. International banks were only just beginning to get over the serious hiccups of the Falklands War when Mexico's President López Portillo announced on 23 August 1982 that his country was unable to pay interest payments on its ninety billion dollar foreign debt. Loans to Argentina subsequently dried up and bankers adopted a much tougher stance on rescheduling overdue payments.

By the end of 1983, when Alfonsín was inaugurated as President, Argentina's debt problem was massive. On a foreign debt of nearly forty billion dollars it was facing arrears on principal and interest of over twenty billion dollars with an annual trade surplus potential of between only three and four billion dollars. Interest payments alone were equivalent to over 50 per cent of Argentina's total export revenue, in striking contrast to the period 1970–4 when they had been the equivalent of only 12 per cent. The situation was further aggravated by international recession, which forced industrialised nations to erect trade barriers against exports from the Third World to keep inflation down. The USA was also forced to set high interest rates. Given that over 70 per cent of its exports were from the agrarian sector, the vulnerability of Argentina to the movements of the international market place had become extreme. Calculated on . the basis of commodity prices existing at the beginning of 1984 – Alfonsín's first year in power – just 1 percentage point increase in US interest rates added 300 million dollars to Argentina's debt bill: this extra cost was equivalent to two million tonnes of wheat and 60 per cent of Argentina's total meat exports measured in value terms.[30]

This background is necessary to understand why the debt issue was politically so highly charged in Argentina once the Falklands War paved the way for democracy. To many Argentines the world of City and Wall Street bankers was synonymous with dictatorship. To the new generation of young economists who joined the Alfonsín government, the debt problem meant they faced the stark choice of repaying the principal and interest debt a corrupt military government had incurred or defaulting. As perceived by the Alfonsín government at the time, each option carried with it serious political risks. To go on paying would limit the country's capacity for growth and the government's ability to push through its electoral pledge of social justice based on a fairer redistribution of wealth and improvements to health, education and housing. This would provoke the trade unions, which would in turn tempt the military to make a bid for power. To default risked undermining the reputation of Argentina as a reliable member of the international community which Alfonsín and his Foreign Minister, Dante Caputo, were so bent on securing after the loss of trust over the Falklands War. Default would also bring in its wake punitive measures restricting Argentina's commercial and financial links with the outside world and stimulating the extreme nationalists within the country to press for the kind of statist 'closed' economy they had always defended. It was a prospect that few Argentine officials relished since they doubted whether they could politically keep control of events once such an economic programme was applied.[31]

In an attempt to avoid the dilemma, the Alfonsín government initially opted for what it perceived as a compromise. It insisted that it favoured dialogue not confrontation with the banks but asked for a grace period in which to put its accounts in order. Argentina's debt strategy – to the extent that any strategy existed in the first confused months of democracy – was undermined by three factors. Firstly, it was clear that Alfonsín saw human rights and his dealings with the military as a priority of his government.[32] This was the result in part of the President's firm conviction that Argentine politics needed an ethical dimension if democratic government was to be accepted by the population as a genuine alternative to military rule; and was in part due to Alfonsín's lack of a firm grounding in economics. The second factor was the personality of Alfonsín's first Economy Minister, Bernardo Grinspún. The Minister was a personal friend of Alfonsín and a long-serving member of the Radical party who was best remembered for his street brawls with Perónists during his university days.[33] Close aides recalled the passion with which he had manned barricades against the Perónist police in the 1950s. Such credentials counted for little in the Argentina of the 1980s. Grinspún lacked both the intellectual sophistication and the diplomatic tact to deal with the complexities of international finance. His early debt negotiations in New York and Washington were tortuous affairs in which bankers found themselves confronted by what they considered to be a mixture of technical naïvety and bad manners. For Grinspún proved himself slow not only in gathering the statistics with which to argue his case but also extremely short-tempered. The third factor, which might not have proved so important, had Alfonsín picked a more skilful Economy Minister, was the nature of orthodox banking. It was profits not politics that had traditionally driven bankers, and their initial welcome of Argentine democracy was conditional on Grinspún paying as soon as possible the money they were owed.

Within weeks of Alfonsín coming to power, the honeymoon between Argentina and the banking community appeared to be over. Grinspún publicly described his first meetings with his foreign creditors as cordial and co-operative, but senior bankers painted a very different picture. 'We expected to get facts and figures, a detailed picture of the country's medium- to long-term economic plans. All we got were some platitudes about Argentina's new democracy,' I was told by a member of the steering committee which was then in charge of negotiating on Argentina's debt.[34]

In the first six months of democratic government, Argentina built up its reserves to over one billion dollars, thanks to the cash inflow from its grain exports and its deferment of debt payments; but its ability to use these reserves to hold out against and wring better

concessions from the banks and the International Monetary Fund
was undermined by Grinspún's mishandling of inflation. As prices
increased throughout 1984, the government lost its room for
manoeuvre both at home and abroad. During a time when banks were
neither lending nor being paid, the Argentine economic situation was
becoming worse than it had ever been under the military. Backed
by his President, Grinspún tried his best to focus public opinion on
not accepting IMF induced recession as the price for international
aid. But the fact was that his government had few alternatives. This
was brought home to Alfonsín on his first major tour abroad as
President in June 1984 by the French and Spanish governments.
Alfonsín had gone seeking both moral and political support from his
old allies in the Socialist International. Instead he was greeted with
a severe warning from French and Spanish officials that Argentina's
failure to play along with the IMF's requirements for financial orthodoxy was casting the country again in the role of international
pariah.[35]

Even after Grinspún's departure in March 1985 and his replacement by Juan Sourrouille, Argentina's relations with the banking
world remained tense. However, initial fears within the banking
community that a string of defaults in the Third World would give
way to a world financial crisis were replaced in some circles by more
cool-headed assessments of the outcome of the debt crisis. Anatole
Kaletsky, a senior commentator on Third World debt for the *Financial Times*, wrote in 1986 that, although bankers and politicians were
aware of the financial chaos and economic depression which still
prevailed in Latin America, this was gradually coming to be accepted
as an inevitable fact of life.

> Far from endangering social stability, the process of economic
> adjustment has been accompanied by political consolidation in
> Latin America and has strengthened ties between the debtor
> countries and the Western world. Internationally the debt crisis
> has radically altered the role of the banking system but has not
> apparently threatened the political or economic underpinnings of
> diplomatic alliances and world trade.[36]

The Argentine debt crisis of 1984 focused on President Alfonsín's
decision in June to confront the International Monetary Fund – and
following close on the heels of Mexico's moratorium – forced a
reappraisal of the whole Third World debt issue. As a catalyst for
change it was the economic equivalent of the Falklands War. The
early confrontations between the Alfonsín government and the inter-

national banking community did not resolve the immediate problem of Argentina's unpaid debt, but they did take Latin America as a whole towards a much greater degree of co-ordination in their policies *vis-à-vis* creditors than ever before. This in turn prompted industrialised nations, commercial bankers and international financial institutions such as the World Bank and the IMF to become more flexible in their approach to the Third World debt issue and to look for more imaginative and longer-term solutions than the orthodox formulae of the past.

The first major co-ordinated move on debt involving Latin American countries surfaced in June 1984 soon after Argentina's débâcle with the IMF. Largely as a result of intensive lobbying by Grinspún, the Argentine Foreign Minister Dante Caputo, and Alfonsín himself, the Finance and Foreign Ministers of eleven Latin American countries met for the first time in Cartagena, Colombia, to express their growing dissatisfaction with the trade barriers put up by the industrialised nations, the high level of international interest rates and the dwindling funds made available to correct the transfer of capital from debtors to creditors. Three months later the self-dubbed Cartagena group took their first declaration of principles a significant step further. In a meeting hosted by Alfonsín and his Ministers at the Argentine coastal resort of Mar del Plata, the eleven called for an urgent summit with Western governments and international financial institutions to secure a lasting solution to the 350-billion-dollar debt burden afflicting the region. A ten-point document reaffirmed dialogue instead of confrontation and made no mention of the feared formation of a debtors' cartel capable of threatening the West much as OPEC had done in the 1970s. However, Ministers strongly criticised industrialised countries for 'their loss of a sense of urgency' on the debt problem. They warned that, unless urgent steps were taken to reverse the crisis which had been provoked by high interest rates and trade barriers, there was a danger of a 'major international crisis of unforeseeable consequences'.[37] The final document was widely viewed as a diplomatic victory for Argentina. During four days of intense behind-the-scenes talks, the Argentines had struggled to reconcile divergent views of moderates and hard liners. They succeeded in producing a document that did not allow the banking community to issue a sigh of relief that Latin America had fallen back on its traditional regional and racial divisions. On the contrary, Latin American governments, spearheaded by Argentina, deliberately tried to find common ground with those members of the international banking community that had already begun to distance themselves from the orthodoxy of some of their colleagues.

Typical of the move towards a more flexible, less orthodox approach to the Latin American debt issue from within the banking community were the public attitudes struck by Pedro Pablo Kuczynski, a managing director of the First Boston Corporation. In a widely debated article published in *Foreign Affairs* in autumn 1983, Kuczynski had challenged the Reaganite belief in the capacity of market forces to deal with the problems of individual debtor countries as they arose. 'It is not clear whether such [market] mechanisms can continue to be effective by themselves,' he wrote,[38] and then went on to list the measures that could be taken to provide a longer-lasting solution to the regional debt problem.

Debtors and creditors should begin by accepting the principle of co-responsibility for the debt problem, correcting the one-way flow of capital from the developing to the industrialised world, even if this meant banks cutting into their profits by temporarily reducing their interest rates. Capital flows to the region would be further bolstered by a resumption of commercial lending by banks, greater private investment, the lifting of obstacles to export growth and an increase in the quotas available from such financial institutions as the International Monetary Fund. Kuczynski emphasised that none of these aims could be achieved unless the debt issue became largely politicised: industrialised governments had to be involved, with the US administration taking the lead.

Towards the end of 1984, Argentina was forced by the increasingly critical state of its internal finances to put on one side temporarily its radical rhetoric on the debt issue and sign an orthodox agreement with the IMF involving sharp reductions in public spending and strong curbs on monetary expansion. The Alfonsín government, however, subsequently broke the targets laid out in the agreement. Under Grinspún's successor, Juan Sourrouille, it then managed to defy the IMF's orthodox remedies and win through with the anti-inflation 'austral plan'. At one level the austerity implied by the 'austral plan' was more drastic than anything that the IMF might have dreamed up. But the government managed to sell the 'austral plan' to its own, highly nationalist, domestic audience. It explained that the plan was not an IMF prescription but the government's own medicine for the very Argentine disease of inflation which had by the first quarter of 1985 been diagnosed collectively as the biggest single threat to democracy.

The IMF had traditionally advocated a gradualist approach to decreasing inflation and solving the debt problem through the mechanisms of the free market. Its measures usually included ending government controls and using trade surpluses to pay off the debt. Sourrouille – a far less brusque and unpredictable personality than his predecessor – argued that all IMF agreements had done in Argentina's case had been to sink the country deeper into recession, provoke more inflation and make it increasingly difficult to pay off due interest without falling even deeper into the red.

In the Minister's early dealings with his country's creditors, the trade-off focused on the government's commitment to repay its debt and to balance its budget. In return the IMF reluctantly accepted price controls and a fixed exchange rate for the new currency as part of Sourrouille's conviction that the only way to deal with inflation, in a country where inflation had become endemic, was to freeze the economy in its tracks.

The manner in which Argentina came round to dealing with the problem of its debt was a reflection of President Alfonsín's development from inexperienced provincial lawyer and leader of an unofficial opposition to a modern-style statesman. When he started out bankers had been fond of suggesting somewhat cynically that as an economist Alfonsín was a politician – a recipe for disaster in other words. The first months of his administration, resonant with politically popular but economically conflicting targets such as economic growth of 5 per cent, increases in real salaries of between 6 and 8 per cent, and single-figure inflation, appeared to confirm the bankers' scepticism. In 1985, however, Alfonsín's determined backing for the 'austral plan' and his sacking of Grinspún in the face of growing popular disillusion with democracy showed what had formerly been considered a weakness being turned into a pillar of strength. 'As the country lost heart, the politician in Mr Alfonsín made him realise his biggest political problem was the economy.'[39]

The initial success of the 'austral plan' turned Argentina in the eyes of the industrialised nations almost overnight from pariah to the good boy among Latin American nations. It was regarded as an inspired example of a compromise between Third World economics and Western orthodoxy which other debtor countries were encouraged to emulate. The US administration became eager advocates that international financial institutions and commercial banks should reward what was perceived as Alfonsín's display of economic responsibility. The IMF and World Bank annual meeting in Seoul in October 1985 provided the international financial community with the opportunity to do just that. For at the meeting James Baker, the

US Treasury Secretary, launched a new initiative for dealing with Third World debt which appeared to go a considerable way towards satisfying the demands of bankers like Kuczynski and the more moderate members of the Cartagena group. Essentially the so-called Baker plan accepted that many debtor nations had suffered in recent years not simply because of economic mismanagement but because the bulk of their resources had gone into interest payments rather than into financing economic growth. There was thus a need, Baker conceded, for a solution based on stability through growth in which debtors and creditors had a shared responsibility. The Baker plan focused on a package of new funds spearheaded by the IMF, the Interamerican Development Bank, the World Bank and commercial banks. Debtors for their part were expected to take measures to restructure their economies, such as reducing the State sector and supporting privatisation.

Just before Christmas 1985, within weeks of the Baker plan being announced, the Alfonsín government found itself being visited by a growing list of senior international economists, led by US Federal Reserve Chairman Paul Volcker, Assistant US Treasury Secretary David Mulford and Franco Modigliani, the Nobel-laureate economist at the Massachusetts Institute of Technology. 'Argentina's economic programme is showing an impressive performance and deserves our support ... It is now one of the small number of countries that is in a position to take advantage of the [Baker] strategy,' Mr Mulford told a meeting attended by bankers and businessmen in Buenos Aires. He also claimed that he had recently emerged from a private meeting with President Alfonsín, at which the Argentine leader had expressed his 'delight' at the prospect of being considered a 'test case' for the Baker plan.[40]

Argentine officials, then facing the latest offensive from the trade unions, were weary of being publicly classified as clients of the United States and were quick to play down the significance of Mulford's words. Moreover, two months after Mulford's visit to Buenos Aires, Argentina used its newly earned bill of economic good health to help spearhead the Cartagena group into raising the stakes. Holding back from an all-out confrontation, the group meeting in the Uruguayan capital of Montevideo praised the Baker plan as a step in the right direction but claimed that it was insufficient to solve the debt problem. The debtor nations came out with their own package of proposals including a call for a separation between 'new' and 'old' debt in future negotiations. Quite what this should mean in practice was not spelled out at the time, but it seemed fairly evident that debtors, including Argentina, wanted the banks to write off part of the old debt and reduce their margins on the new one. The Cartagena group also called for an end to conditionality on multilateral lending. In the past the IMF and the World Bank had conditioned new loans on client governments following specific programmes determined by the banks. The idea was that this process should now be scrapped to give Latin American governments far greater control over their own future.

Successive meetings of the Cartagena group generated a feeling among sectors of the international banking community that there was really little to fear from such rhetorical shadow boxing. And yet events in 1986 showed that the banks could ill afford to be complacent. Initially it seemed possible to isolate Peru, with its radical defiance of the IMF and its determination to use up only a limited percentage of its export revenue on the payment of the debt, as the attitude of a black sheep in an otherwise unhappy but compliant flock. President Alfonsín's own determination not to be drawn into an all-out confrontation against the international financial system, during a much publicised and politically controversial trip to Buenos Aires by the charismatic and outspoken Peruvian leader Alan García at the beginning of 1986, appeared to confirm this view. And yet there were still potential storm clouds over the debt horizon. Latin America's two major debtors, Brazil and Mexico, faced with growing domestic economic problems, both pressed for new radical ways of renegotiating their debts in bilateral dealings with their creditors. Following their lead, Argentina made it clear, in a further round of negotiations with the IMF in the first months of 1986, that its sense of responsibility should not be interpreted as submission. As a result the banks and institutions overseeing them were forced to be more flexible. In September 1986 they agreed to roll over some 7·5 billion dollars' worth of principal payments on Argentina's 50-billion-dollar debt for a six-month period and extended short-term credits. By so doing the banks seemed to have realised once again that the only alternative was a dramatic debt write-off which ran the risk of sending their shares plummeting.[41]

Towards the end of 1986 there seemed to be a growing realisation, moreover, among debtors and creditors that the annual round of painfully protracted IMF-backed debt negotiations granted only a stay of execution not a lasting solution. Argentina's proposals that creditor banks link the level of debt-service payments and new lending to the price of the country's main exports, cereals and beef, bringing down interest rates whenever the international price of commodities fell, seemed to be part of an ongoing effort to alter radically the whole basis on which the debt issue could be tackled.

As Kaletsky has pointed out, Latin American history suggests that major defaults occur only when the economies of debtor countries are clearly on the mend. He argues that in the 1980s a government will be most likely to consider default as a serious option after three conditions are satisfied: first, it will need to have consolidated its domestic political standing and assured itself of strong popular support, including a willingness to accept further sacrifices in the unlikely event that default is followed by damaging sanctions; second, it will need to have built up adequate foreign exchange reserves and shifted most of the country's trade to a cash and barter basis to survive any temporary withdrawal of short-term credits; third, it will need to have performed some of the painful adjustments which would have been necessary anyway to put the domestic economy on a sounder footing.[42]

Arguably Alfonsín was closer to meeting some of these conditions in this fifth year of government than he was in his first, particularly since default seemed no longer to imply an outright repudiation of the debt. The attitudes emerging from Cartagena reflected growing support within the region not so much for a 'debtors' club' as 'some form of conciliatory default by one or more borrowers, acting independently in a formal sense, though doubtless with some co-ordination behind the scenes'.[43] This co-ordination has been greatly facilitated by the common denominator of democracy running through all the major debtor countries and the structural changes which have been forced on them by the debt crisis.

The most coherent economic explanation of Argentina's decline as a nation in the course of the twentieth century is that, for all its surface sophistication, the country remains a classically colonial society. Dr David Rock has described the most obvious colonial features:

> The country has always imported the bulk of its manufactured goods, and for long periods much of its capital; and economic progress in Argentina has largely stemmed from stable and comp-lementary commercial and investment partnerships ... Buenos Aires, as the leading port city and *entrepôt*, has constantly domi-nated an inescapably fettered hinterland. By and large 'col-laborating élites' with outside great powers have exercised stable enduring political leadership. Argentina's middle class is more

the *comprador* or 'clientistic' type than a classical capitalist bour-
geoisie ... Argentina is also colonial in that once an established
system of complementary external linkages lies shattered – as a
result of war abroad and changes in the international order –
Argentine society has invariably failed to revolutionise itself in
a self-sustaining independent direction. Instead, following such
ruptures, society has turned in on itself in fierce competition to
monopolise static or diminishing resources.[44]

After the Falklands, Argentina faced an economic situation as
extreme and as challenging as that which faced West Germany after
the Second World War.[45] Argentine cities did not lie in ruins and
the demography of the country had not been altered by the deaths
of over 1,200 members of the armed forces.[46] And yet beneath the
apparent physical normality lay a country whose main points of
reference had been shattered. The political collapse of the military
regime coincided with an international recession, characterised by
growing protectionism and a transfer of resources from the Third
World to the industrialised nations. External pressure combined
with economic mismanagement aggravated rather than resolved the
structural weaknesses of the Argentine economy in the first year
of Argentine democracy. The introduction of the 'austral plan',
however, showed the Alfonsín government was prepared for the first
time to break out of the limitations of a colonial society and devise
an autonomous path to development which could take Argentina out
of the Third World and into the twenty-first century.[47]

In subsequent months the first signs of a clear industrial strategy
capable of building a modern export economy, rather than one
dependent on grain and beef, began to emerge from the Alfonsín
government. The new Trade and Industry Minister, Roberto
Lavagna, outlined a policy based on export-orientated industrial
growth, the development of a regional common market with Brazil
and technological modernisation. Lavagna was a member of the
Perónist party's 'renewal faction' who had served in the government
of Isabelita Perón. That he publicly recognised that an economic
model based exclusively on import substitution and the domestic
market could no longer guarantee either the conditions for growth
or more adequate distribution of income showed the extent to which
economic thinking had progressed in Argentina. In practice Lavagna's policy focused on fundamental changes in fiscal policy aimed at
correcting the price distortions of Argentine industrial products
brought about by protectionism. In the past this protectionism had

both fuelled inflation and produced generation after generation of businessmen skilled in financial speculation, export of capital, and the manipulation of political alliances within the State, but either unable or unwilling to invest in a more competitive environment. Customs duties on 11,000 categories of imports began to be eliminated and efforts were made to streamline government decisions and remove the labyrinthine bureaucracy which had made doing business in Argentina so frustrating. Exchange rate policy towards the end of 1986 focused on a series of steady mini-devaluations of the austral. This appeared to be aimed at a gradual realignment of prices relative to the international market, while minimising the social pressures and shock on the local financial markets which would result from a maxi-devaluation.[48]

Traditionally Latin American governments have had a poor record in translating rhetoric into action, and nowhere has this been more the case than on the subject of regional solidarity expressed through economic and political integration. Ever since they took separate paths under Spanish and Portuguese colonial rule, Argentina and Brazil respectively have proved stark examples of this. Regional neighbours, these giants of Latin America have often seemed as far apart in practical terms as the United States and the Soviet Union. A combination of military rivalry and cultural differences have aggravated the contrasts between the two countries in terms of regional diversification and population size so that by the early 1980s less than 5 per cent of their combined exports was channelled towards each other and their respective industries remained competitive rather than complementary.[49]

The debt issue, the end of the Falklands War, and the restoration of democracy helped Argentina to reinforce its diplomatic links with the United States and Western Europe;[50] but the reluctance of industrialised nations substantially to ease trade barriers led Argentine foreign and economic policy to emphasise greater self-help and integration within the region. Under Alfonsín an early example of this was the behind-the-scenes co-operation that took place between Argentine and Brazilian economists on the 'austral' and 'cruzado plans'[51] within the Cartagena group of debtor nations, and in the aerospace industry, where both countries announced their intention to exchange research and development on Latin America's first jointly developed civilian aircraft. In July 1986, the basis for a future common market was laid when President Alfonsín and President Sarney of Brazil signed a twelve-point protocol agreement, focused on the elimination of all barriers to bilateral trade in capital goods.

Other points included mutual financial support between the countries' central banks for adjustments to trade imbalances, the creation of a special joint investment fund to expand production, increased trade in food products to eliminate trade imbalances and co-operation in energy. The emphasis on capital goods and food co-operation showed that Argentina was apparently determined to make better use of technology and to find alternative outlets for its agricultural products.[52]

Deregulation of trade was one area in which the Alfonsín government found a meeting point between its own development needs and the kind of reforms which creditors under the umbrella of the Baker initiative were looking for, as part of the shared responsibility for a longer-term solution to the debt problem. The other was the rules and regulations governing foreign investment. A clear signal that Alfonsín was prepared to adopt a more pragmatic approach to one of the most controversial issues traditionally dogging Argentine economic policy came in May 1985, anticipating the Baker initiative by five months. During a visit to Houston in the United States, Alfonsín made an impassioned appeal to executives of major oil companies to play a central part in the exploration of his country's oil reserves.

At the time his speech was widely seen as a watershed in the turbulent history of the Argentine oil industry, in particular the nationalist policies previously defended by the ruling Radical party.[53] The move stemmed from Alfonsín's apparent conviction that Argentina's oil interests could best be served by attending to the ends rather than the means. For while the radical rank and file remained suspicious of foreign involvement in the country's economy, the government had reluctantly accepted that without foreign investment in crucial areas like energy, the Argentine economy would weaken, further undermining the country's aspirations to be a regional leader. On the surface Argentina presented a glowing picture of energy self-sufficiency compared with the early 1960s, when 60 per cent of domestic oil consumption was provided by imports. This overview however concealed a dangerous stagnation in the country's oil resources because of the inefficiency of the State-owned oil company, Yacimientos Petrolíferos Fiscales – which exercised a virtual monopoly on the sector – and the absence of a coherent energy policy. Since 1970 Argentina's oil reserves had remained at 390 million cubic metres, and in subsequent years production had only been able to meet domestic needs because of a sharp drop in consumption brought about by recession.

The national energy plan, on which the Houston plan was based, envisaged a doubling of gas production for industry and a 30 per cent increase in oil production. To achieve these targets, the plan proposed the drilling of 3,000 exploratory wells, full production in a further 18,000 'development' wells, and the measurement of 50,000 miles of seismic lines, totalling an investment of twenty-five billion dollars in the years 1986–2000.[54] The government believed that the new oil policy would more than pay for itself by bringing in additional foreign exchange through oil exports and by acting as a catalyst to an economic upsurge. The upsurge, however, was slow in coming with foreign oil companies riding the 1986 oil price recession in the hope of obtaining better exploration terms. Nevertheless, the Houston initiative had an important psychological impact. The relatively subdued nature of domestic opposition to it convinced the government that public opinion was prepared to tolerate a more flexible approach to the economy than had been permitted in the past. The State was no longer a sacred cow, but was seen by many to be both a symptom and a cause of the country's economic decline, which had to be corrected if Argentina was to free itself from its colonial past and enter the modern age. Translated into practical terms, the first step in the reform of the energy sector came in the restructuring of the finances of Yacimientos Petrolíferos Fiscales. The source of much military corruption under the juntas, it had become the only major oil company in the world to lose more money than it made. By 1986 it had an accumulated foreign debt of five billion dollars, one-tenth of the national total. The government slashed the company's exploration budget and forced it to make administrative economies. Such a move would have been unthinkable in the days of General Suárez Masón, but it underlined the government's determination to renovate.[55]

'Entre lo dicho y lo hecho hay un gran trecho' – between what is said and what is done there is a huge gap – goes a favourite Spanish phrase. Perón himself is believed to have once said that the best way not to get anything done in Argentina is to form a commission. Bureaucracy, in other words, has traditionally ruled the roost in Argentina.

The need to implement far-reaching administrative reform, to give Argentine democracy substance as well as form and thus accompany the economic modernisation of this 'colonial society', was grasped somewhat belatedly in 1986 by the Alfonsín government. By then numerous initiatives had been caught up in the spider's web of regulations and political alliances which have historically concentrated the pulse of the nation in Buenos Aires.[56] Alfonsín's determination to stop this sense of drift and pick on a symbol capable of drawing together the positive aspects of his administration led to his announcement in April 1986 that he proposed to move the nation's capital from the 'uncontrolled megalopolis' of Buenos Aires to the small Patagonian town called Viedma. The President defended his announcement by contrasting the isolation and underdevelopment of the nation's regions with the concentration of population and resources in Buenos Aires and the surrounding temperate plain – the 'pampa'. The move, rather than a mere shifting of personnel was meant to 'herald a national rebirth, what Mr Alfonsín had dubbed the "second republic".'[57]

Opposition leaders initially greeted the initiative with scepticism, but, given the importance of the federal ideal and the sensitivity of provincial feelings, they were subsequently more subdued in their criticism. In political terms, Alfonsín appeared to have once again taken a calculated risk and won. The economic aspects of the new capital, however, presented a greater challenge. The government planned to complete the first phase of construction in time for the 1989 presidential elections: a 'modest capital of low-level buildings set in open spaces under Patagonia's broad blue sky, resembling Bonn more than Brasilia in ambition'.[58] Total projected costs were estimated at over two billion dollars for the transformation of this farming community of 400,000 into the administrative centrepiece of Alfonsín's New Argentina. In pitching its hopes on funds from international financial institutions like the World Bank and on foreign investment, the government once again focused attention on the link between debt and democracy and the need for co-responsibility involving creditors and their war-torn client.

13 FALKLANDS OR MALVINAS: TOWARDS THE FUTURE

Contemporary history provides more than one example of war acting as a catalyst for change: France after Algeria and Portugal after Southern Africa are only two of the countries where an experience of external conflict led to political changes at home. Argentina both before, during and after the Falklands War, in a period of less than ten years, went through the kind of institutional changes that most more advanced societies have had over a century to deal with. War – the internal war waged against political opponents and the second, less dirty war fought against the British – telescoped change to such a degree that the nation was forced to search for a new identity virtually overnight.

Argentina's wars, measured in deaths and days, were small affairs by comparison with other conflicts. Many more people died in Nazi Germany, Franco's Spain and the Middle East than did in the clandestine torture chambers of the junta and the fields around Port Stanley, but in contemporary history Argentina has few rivals as an example of collective social and political trauma. For proportionate to their years of existence there can be few countries in the world that have had their institutions so militarised, their attitudes so regimented. The armed forces did not develop as an autonomous sector within society, responsive to the dictates of Presidents, but became society. It was the military who dictated how Argentines treated each other and how they perceived their place in the world. This militarisation of the collective psyche gestated during the early nineteenth century and reached its delivery in the regime of the juntas. It was because the armed forces were inseparable from the nation State that their defeat during the Falklands War transformed itself domestically not into a confrontation between victors and vanquished but into a collective catharsis.

Mrs Thatcher's role in Argentine history is more complex than either her supporters or detractors make out. I hope to have established that her reaction to the threat of an invasion of the Falklands could and should have been much sooner, given the extent to which successive Argentine governments had militarised the 'Malvinas' issue and the detailed planning of the final invasion that took place from the end of 1981 onwards. Once the invasion had taken place, Thatcher's determination to win the war and her victory should, however, be seen in a more benevolent light. The nature of Argentine military preparations for the invasion, and the way the junta was subsequently trapped by the nationalistic euphoria it had initially exploited, should leave the reader with no doubt as to what might have been the outcome in Argentina – and what might have happened to the kelpers – had Thatcher not proved so resolute. As Galtieri himself recognised after the war, even with the Argentine flag flying jointly with the British – as opposed to a total Argentine victory – the military regime would have moved to perpetuate itself in power or at the very least to organise an arranged democracy suited to the military's survival. A British defeat would have also almost certainly inflated the Argentine military's self-image of regional superiority and led to other territorial disputes in Latin America being resolved by arms. This 'domino effect' would also have ended up threatening the way of life of the islanders. Much has been made of the militarisation of the South Atlantic as a result of Fortress Falklands, yet its political impact on South America is minimal compared to the democratisation of Latin America for which the Falklands War also acted as a catalyst. (Bolivia, Brazil, Uruguay, all moved away from military regimes towards democratic government.)

Publicly even today Argentines boast that the end of the military regime was assured by the courageous offensive of the people. Privately the more honest among them – and on this subject there have not been many – admit that they owe the early demise of General Galtieri to Mrs Thatcher. In this paradox lies Argentina's trauma – a defeated nation that somewhere along the line lost control of even its own destiny. Nevertheless the same paradox sheds light on a particular aspect of the Falklands War which since 1982 has generated much debate in Britain: the sinking of the battle-cruiser *General Belgrano*. Argentine naval officers interviewed for this book have no doubt that in military terms the sinking was totally justified. From the third day of the invasion the commander of the Argentine fleet, Rear-Admiral Walter Allara, had been given strict instructions not to attack the British Task Force unless Argentine forces were themselves attacked, and had been ordered back to port to await diplomatic developments.

On 23 April 1982 through the mediation of the Swiss, the British government handed the Argentine junta a note warning that as from that day any Argentine warship was likely to be attacked if it threatened the safety of the Task Force, even if the offensive action took place outside the 200-mile exclusion zone around the islands. Far from dissuading the junta, the statement appears to have tempted Admiral Anaya to meet the challenge. Four days later he ordered

Rear-Admiral Allara to sally forth from the major mainland base of Puerto Belgrano and start patrolling outside the exclusion zone. When the British attacked Stanley airport on 1 May, Allara and the Argentine air force were ordered to go on the offensive. The commander of combined operations, Admiral Lombardo, believed that the bombing was the prelude to an all-out military landing by British troops and was insistent that his navy should conduct an immediate search and destroy mission of British Task Force ships believed to be approaching the islands.

Essentially the plan focused on a pincer movement by two groups of Argentine battleships: one composed of three frigates, the other of the aircraft carrier *Veinticinco de Mayo* and two destroyers. The *General Belgrano*, accompanied by two escorts, was at that time in a southern position off the coast of Tierra del Fuego, keeping an eye on the Chilean navy, and on any British ship that might sail from Australia or New Zealand round Cape Horn. She was also offering protection to the main air force bases in Patagonia. On 1 May she was brought into Allara's attack plan. She was ordered to act as a decoy, drawing as many British surface ships as possible away from the main group and, if the opportunity presented itself, to use the Exocets then being carried by her escorts to sink them. Her course on that day was south-east, outside the exclusion zone but moving steadily towards a piece of shallow ocean called the Burdwood Bank, which could offer her protection from submarines.

Early that evening an Argentine reconnaissance plane picked up a British aircraft carrier and six medium-sized ships about 150 miles north-east of the islands and about 250 miles from the latest position of the *Veinticinco de Mayo*. Only a freak of nature appears to have prevented Allara's Task Force from sinking at least one British ship. A plan to launch an attack had to be postponed when a squadron of Skyhawks were unable to take off from the *Veinticinco de Mayo* because of an insufficient headwind. During the ensuing delay the bombing of the islands temporarily ceased, and Lombardo assumed that the British had postponed their invasion. On the morning of 2 May Lombardo ordered Allara to withdraw, although the *General Belgrano* appears at that point to have abruptly changed to a zigzag course still outside the exclusion zone.[1] That afternoon the *General Belgrano* was sunk with the loss of 368 lives. Interviewed after the war, one high-ranking Argentine naval officer said:

> I try not to be sentimental about the sinking of the cruiser. It was sunk because I think it was a threat. And there's nothing more to

it ... It was consistent with the rules established by the British when they set up their exclusion zone. They said they would attack any Argentine unit inside the zone or in any other part where it posed a threat. As a military man I cannot see the decision to sink the *General Belgrano* in sentimental terms.[2]

Following the *General Belgrano* sinking, the Argentine surface fleet returned to port, never to emerge again in what was left of the war.[3] To say, as some British officials have insisted, that the sinking was thus fully justified in military terms is not entirely borne out by the subsequent facts. As we have seen in Chapter 5, the action considerably raised the stakes. It forced the Argentine navy to internationalise the conflict, sending its sabotage teams to Gibraltar and securing a military alliance with Libya.

This argument, it should be noted however, is a personal one based on evidence which has been kept secret from the Argentines. Beyond the initial outrage generated by what was perceived by most of the population as a cold-blooded act of war the *General Belgrano* affair was given none of the persistent political or emotional mileage in Argentina that it was given in Britain. Even after the junta's demise had given way to less professional and more political considerations of the war, there seemed to be a deliberate policy by the newly elected democratic authorities not to turn the affair into a diplomatic issue. If anything there was concern lest it be exploited by Argentine military sectors bent on redeeming their image in the Falklands War.[4] The Argentine government also suspected – not entirely without justification – that those in Britain who were loudest in beating the *General Belgrano* drum were motivated less by a desire to see an early solution to the whole Falklands issue than by an obsessive desire to see the Labour party in power. There was no love lost between the Argentines and Mrs Thatcher, but they would have preferred the British Parliament to use the energies it expended on the *General Belgrano* affair on a more profound debate about the meaning of Argentine democracy and the future of the 'Malvinas'.

In purely historical terms the argument that the sinking of the *Belgrano* was in itself sufficient to destroy irrevocably any chance of peace does not stand up to investigation. Mrs Thatcher's detractors failed between 1982 and 1986 to provide conclusive evidence that the sinking was a deliberate decision to scupper the Peruvian peace initiative. In a sense, whether Mrs Thatcher and her government were informed about the Belaunde proposals before or after the sinking is largely irrelevant. As has been pointed out in the most detailed account of the *General Belgrano* affair, 'The indications suggest that Argentina was to be taught a lesson by the sternest military means, and the *General Belgrano* happened unfortunately to be the first target. To scupper the proposals, the British only needed to say "No", and to pick on some point of real or imagined Argentine intransigence.'[5]

Moreover, as Argentina's official investigation into the Falklands War admitted, the junta is ultimately to blame for having subsequently been offered peace on fairly beneficial terms and rejected it. 'The most rational and productive course would have been to accept the proposal in spite of the sinking of the *General Belgrano*,' the report states.[6] And yet the nature of Argentina's military regime was neither rational nor productive. That is why the junta started the war and also ended by losing the islands.

Argentina survived the immediate post-war period without disintegrating as a society; the old regimented society was not totally destroyed but reformed as the first step towards more fundamental change. Much of the credit for reversing the nihilism which has plagued Argentines for much of their history must go to Raúl Alfonsín. He emerged from the political doldrums partly because his political credentials were worthier than those of the majority of politicians. He defended human rights long before the 'disappeared' became an electoral issue, and saw the madness in the invasion of the Falklands at a time when Argentine society broadly supported it. The fact that he had demonstrated an ethical dimension in a country used to corrupt, opportunistic governments allowed him to emerge after the Falklands War to sow some genuine seeds of hope. At a time when most Argentines were disorientated and deeply depressed, Alfonsín talked about democracy as an essential right. He went on to launch himself into a presidential campaign before the military had officially declared it open. He challenged the forty-year-old political hegemony of the Perónist party by exposing its necrophilia – the Perónists insisted that the late General Perón was alive and well and living in Buenos Aires, but Alfonsín suggested that he was well and truly buried. The election result was thus in a sense a victory of life over death.

In the first weeks after the Falklands defeat, the military resisted the intense pressure it came under to give an honest account of the country's 'wars'. This did not prevent the media seeking exoneration from their past complicity and 'exposing' the reality that had hidden behind the official communiqués. Argentines literally dug into their past. They found unmarked graves filled with bullet-ridden skulls, clandestine torture chambers and eye-witness accounts of such horror that some Argentine Jews were reminded of Hitler. For a few months Argentina was back on its traditional pendulum-swing from one extreme to the other, replacing one intolerance with another. And yet the majority of the cries for retribution had a hollow ring about them: the politicians and trade unionists who demanded explanations had attended the swearing in of General Menéndez as military Governor of the Falkland Islands and turned a blind eye to the 'disappeared'; the Bishops who urged moral renewal had themselves tacitly blessed torture and the holy crusade against the British; the newspapers which pursued with such intensity the 'truth' had themselves consistently muzzled it for the past ten years. As a local observer put it at the time, 'This was a disaster that belonged to all Argentina. And so to rage at the military's economic failings and human rights abuses, to despair over the chances of a return to democracy and to mount the insanity of the Falklands campaign was in a sense to avoid once again the hardest realities.'[7]

It is against this background that Alfonsín has already earned himself a place in the history books as an entirely new phenomenon in Argentine politics. In the years 1982–6 no politician or military figure was able to match his charisma, yet he did not turn his resulting popularity into demagoguery. On the contrary he seemed to realise that the excessive dependence of democracy on his person ran the risk of turning into a two-edged sword, and made every effort to reform and consolidate the supporting institutions of the democratic state. A lawyer by training and with a family upbringing committed to the democratic ethos, he resisted the demands for vengeance and insisted on justice. This was epitomised by his Solomon-like handling of the human rights issue.[8] By condemning the worst culprits and acquitting the less guilty Alfonsín disappointed the human rights activists and still angered sectors of the military who have never thought of themselves as guilty of any crimes; but it restored a sense of balance and forced Argentines to confront a truer version of their own history. The trial of the juntas was important in reincorporating Argentina into the community of civilised nations, making amends for much of the distrust provoked by the invasion of the Falklands. In October 1986 the Council of Europe, for whom Argentina had once been synonymous with political violence and totalitarian rule, awarded Alfonsín the European Prize for Human Rights. The trial was also important in demonstrating that the concept of military accountability in the Third World is politically feasible. Argentina set out the parameters within which other Latin American governments such as Uruguay and Brazil could tackle the human rights issue.

Old taboos die hard, however. In a country where history has been dominated by strong-arm military Presidents backed by a deeply entrenched corporate structure of armed forces, unions and a conservative Church, the Alfonsín phenomenon proved difficult to digest. The most widely held view within the armed forces was that the nation owed them a favour rather than a reprimand. They were slow in adapting to the demands made on their professionalism by the incoming democratic government and continued to have an inflated sense of their duty to influence policy. The trade unions were partly motivated by a genuine economic grievance as a result of the government's failure to control inflation and the debt issue, but CGT officials acted with more virulence against a democratically elected government than they ever had against the military regime. So did the Church. In October 1986 Bishops instructed priests to deny communion and confession to Catholic Congressmen who had voted in favour of legalisation for divorce. The same Bishops only months earlier had failed to make their own public act of contrition for moral surrender during the military regime, when they had offered blessings and communion to torturers and sanctified the Falklands War.

The miracle is that Argentina survived the initial stages of its transition from military rule to democracy with perhaps no greater degree of political violence or social upheaval than that experienced by many countries in the industrialised world. It suggested that in spite of the survival among many Argentines of a relentless kind of fatalism, they had subconsciously absorbed to a much greater degree than would have seemed possible only a few years before the trauma of their history and the prospect of change. Argentine democracy proved imperfect and resilient at the same time. Argentines, who traditionally had shown a remarkable capacity to forget their own history, were forced by the pressure of events to remind themselves of the regime of the juntas before despairing of Alfonsín. The government's enlarged parliamentary majority following the mid-term elections in 1985 showed that for a majority of Argentines however bad the Radical government was it was certainly better than the juntas. Such negative thinking provided a breathing space for the government rather than a life insurance. By the end of 1986 the disillusion with democracy appeared to have increased.

Raymond Carr, writing about modern Spain, used the phrase,

'the psychology of great expectations falsified'.[9] Argentina clearly faces even greater difficulties than those faced by the Spanish after Franco. Argentines still dwell on what they perceive as their own distinctive reality – they are often called Europeans in Latin America and Latin Americans in Europe. They are moved by feelings of *grandeza*, not so much of being great as feeling great. Euphoria easily grips the masses whether on a football pitch or in a political rally. There is a sense in which the euphoria which surrounded Alfonsín's victory was the same as that which surrounded Perón's assumption of power in 1945, the World Cup victory in 1978 and the Falklands invasion. On each occasion Argentines expected that the event alone would be sufficient to solve all their problems. Alfonsín's chief failure lies in not having instilled in his fellow countrymen a sufficient sense of realism about the need for collective sacrifice from the outset of his government. The appointment of Bernardo Grinspún as the new democracy's Economy Minister was a political blunder which came very close to destroying the noble achievements on the human rights front. When the anti-inflation 'battle plan' was introduced in June 1985 there was a feeling among the sectors most hostile to the government that the measures were too much, too late.

Historically institutional change in Argentina has been brought about by the jackboot not through the ballot box. But the military not only lost its basis of social support, it also appeared unable to provide a cohesive alternative model for society. For although individual officers in their majority remained angry with the practicalities of democracy, the institution of the armed forces was unable to overcome its internal ideological contradictions and provide a viable alternative political programme. Argentina moreover cannot be seen in isolation from the context of the wider world in which she moves. The trend in Latin America, with the blessing of the United States, is away from military rule towards democracy and the three southern democracies – Argentina, Uruguay and Brazil – seemed to draw their inherent strength from the apparently shared realisation that united they can stand but divided they will certainly fall.

When I interviewed Alfonsín on the eve of his inauguration as President, he seemed utterly convinced that now democracy was installed in Argentina Mrs Thatcher had lost her main argument against negotiation about the future of the islands.[10] It proved a false hope. Between 1983 and 1986 Britain and Argentina embarked on confidence-building measures: commercial and financial relations were partially re-established, visa restrictions were relaxed and a number of cultural and sports events were arranged. Academics and parliamentarians from both countries meanwhile developed a two-track diplomacy aimed at getting round the absence of formal diplomatic ties by making unofficial contacts with each other. Nevertheless the issue of sovereignty remained like a seemingly immovable boulder in the way of a more genuine and more wide-ranging reconciliation between the two countries, undermining progress towards co-operation on such pressing issues as fishing conservation in the South Atlantic. Towards the end of 1986 it was tempting to conclude that both sides were back to square one and that the war had effectively changed nothing other than increasing the potential for intransigence.

A central theme of this book is that the main protagonists of Argentine history have been the military, and that it was the armed forces which played the leading role in the Falklands War by planning an invasion and exploiting the conflict for political ends. Recognition that Argentines for the first time in their history were making a genuine if as yet incomplete attempt to turn their backs on authoritarianism should fundamentally alter the parameters of future debate over the Falklands. As argued in an early background paper prepared by Dr Peter Gold, Alfonsín 'not only merited different treatment from that of General Galtieri because of his democratic credentials but also needed to be seen to be treated differently if he was to retain his legitimacy.'[11]

The survival of Argentine democracy clearly does not rest solely on the Falklands issue nor are British governments in the habit of formulating their foreign policy simply on the basis of reassuring democracy throughout the world. And yet there is a point at which democracy should be seen to serve the interests of Argentina and the islanders better. If Argentina were to continue to be treated by Britain no differently than it was under the military, the 'Malvinas' will provide the armed forces in the future with the opportunity to bring the civilians to account and rehabilitate themselves in a war of revenge in which the political, economic and human costs for both sides would certainly be much greater than in the last one.

Alfonsín's inauguration led to an exchange of telegrams between both countries expressing a desire for dialogue based on their common democratic credentials, without prejudice to their respective sovereignty claims. 'Where there is a will there is a way,' said the Argentine message. We have noted that Alfonsín's ability to make a fundamental contribution to Argentina's regeneration as a nation was enhanced by his separateness from the main current of militarised history. And yet in the initial months following his inauguration he and his Foreign Minister, Dante Caputo, increasingly favoured a myopic vision of the Falklands problem based on a perceived political need to uphold constantly the country's historic right to the islands. In a sense they played the junta's game, playing to the gallery – turning to the abstract, external 'Malvinas' cause to boost domestic support at a time of growing difficulties on the economic front. Extreme nationalists accused the democratic government of trying to eradicate the memory of the war, coining the phrase 'de-Malvinise'. And yet there was no real attempt to alter the collective conscience on the 'Malvinas' question. Alfonsín continued to pay frequent homage to the war dead; 'Malvinas' day was revived in the calendar; and there was a growing number of plazas, streets and stamps commemorating the war. School curricula meanwhile had history lessons on the 'Malvinas' still weighted firmly in Argentina's favour; there was no attempt to give an alternative perspective.[12]

The Alfonsín government has also shown itself less than honest in its reactions to the military aspects of British foreign policy. In May 1985 Caputo made much of the new Falklands airfield's offensive capability in respect to Argentina and the rest of Latin America, and its transformation into a possible scenario for East–West conflict. He conveniently ignored the fact that the building of the airport was essentially a political decision taken by Thatcher in the heat of the conflict, which was aimed principally at satisfying island opinion. There was no evidence initially that any wider strategic uses had been worked out or that NATO had overnight extended its field of action to include the South Atlantic simply to assuage Britain's sovereignty claims over a group of islands.

A similar distortion of reality was reflected in the way that the Alfonsín government consistently emphasised Britain's intransigence on the sovereignty issue, to the exclusion of the efforts made by London to mend its bridges with Buenos Aires through an improvement in bilateral relations. From the end of the Falklands War Britain took the initiative first in restoring links and subsequently in bringing about a commercial and diplomatic *rapprochement*. These measures were responded to only belatedly by the Argentine government and even then only half-heartedly. British initiatives, however, were deliberately either ignored or underplayed in the Argentine media.[13] By contrast the British press were consistently more generous in their coverage of Alfonsín's democratic achievements and in emphasising as positive Argentina's growing support within British opposition circles and the international community.

There have been instances when the distortion has reached such extremes as to echo the kind of double-think so beloved of the juntas. Such was the case in Argentina's official reaction to reports of British arms sales to Chile. The reports in the *New Statesman* focused mainly on the military co-operation between Chile and Britain during the Falklands War. And yet official reaction in Buenos Aires entered the realms of fantasy. One theory was that Britain and Chile were co-operating in preparation for an attack against Argentina; another was that the *New Statesman* article had been written by the Ministry of Defence with the deliberate intention of undermining the peace treaty between Argentina and Chile over the Beagle Channel. It is as if the British press had taken to interpreting a meeting between Argentina and Brazil to discuss debt as a veiled operation to attack the islands. Argentine journalists seemed genuinely surprised at the time when informed by British correspondents that the *New Statesman* was in fact a left-wing magazine with no working arrangement with the British establishment.

Thatcher proved no less myopic. Personally she was a great deal more involved in the war than Alfonsín, so her intransigence has often seemed not so much calculating as instinctive. In a sense the Falklands War allowed her to think and act just as she had always wanted, as a contemporary Churchill stirring the patriotic feelings of the island race. Her resolute approach was vindicated in political and military terms; she won a war, and through it consolidated her position in the government and the country. Although the last opinion poll taken before the Argentine invasion showed that the Conservative party was recovering its popularity from the low point it had reached the previous December, Mrs Thatcher's handling of the Falklands War improved her standing even more. According to surveys by Market and Opinion Research International the Conservative rating rose from 34 per cent in March 1982 to a peak of 48 per cent when the war ended in June. As Peter Riddell points out in his assessment of the Thatcher years, 'The Falklands factor may not have directly changed attitudes on the shop floor, but it did serve to underpin Mrs Thatcher's general style of forceful leadership and single-mindedness in pursuit of her goals, despite the many tactical shifts. This clearly paid off in electoral terms in June 1983.'[14]

It seems evident that Britain's conciliatory attitude towards Alfonsín's Argentina has been all along a Foreign Office initiative extracted with great difficulty from Number 10. Thatcher's emotional attachment to the war was symbolised by her visit to the islands at Christmas 1983 and by her habit of writing personal letters of support and condolence to the islanders and relatives of the war dead.[15] Her distaste for anything smacking of appeasement was demonstrated in her stormy political divorce from Francis Pym, her 'wet' Foreign Secretary, and her public outburst against Archbishop Runcie, who prayed for the dead of both sides during a remembrance service in St Paul's soon after the war. She has found it very difficult to separate Alfonsín from the past enemy – her telegram of congratulation to him came only after a great deal of haggling through official channels by David Joy, the head of the British Interest Section, acting under the protection of the Swiss Embassy. In subsequent months her coldness towards the Argentine President was stimulated by what she perceived as the essentially fragile and militaristic nature of the new government; its outspokenness on sovereignty; and in particular its attempts deliberately to split British public opinion by holding parallel diplomatic contacts with the leaders of the British opposition. The contempt she felt for what Argentine officials described as their 'search for a negotiated settlement to the Malvinas dispute' was reflected in her reaction to the United Nations General Assembly's overwhelming approval of an Argentine-backed motion calling for 'negotiations on all aspects of the future of the islands'. Speaking to the House of Commons on 28 November 1985, she declared, 'Anyone who thinks that a motion that contains the phrase "negotiations on all aspects of the future of the Falklands" does not contain sovereignty must be absolutely bonkers,' before going on to emphasise that sovereignty was of course not negotiable.

Such an emphatic rejection not only flew in the face of international opinion – only Oman, Belize and the Solomon Islands voted with Britain, 107 other countries including the USA, France, Italy, Greece and Spain approved the motion – but also conveniently ignored precedent. Such a formula had been used by Lord Carrington in the Lisbon agreement of 1980 to surmount the initial stumbling block in the way of talks with democratic Spain over Gibraltar. Thatcher moreover had also agreed to talk to the Irish government personally about Ulster, while firmly denying that she was giving away anything on sovereignty.

Thus the years 1982–6 saw rival and seemingly irreconcilable perceptions in which the two governments appeared to be talking past each other rather than to each other, just as had occurred before the Falklands War. In a sense the *impasse* seemed greater than it had ever been under the military. The Alfonsín administration, which

began rejoicing in its democracy and a generally 'open-ended' attitude towards the Falklands issue, giving some credence to the step-
by-step approach and finding other foreign policy questions like the
Beagle Channel of more pressing concern, gradually took a more
obsessive line on sovereignty both because of its own domestic
difficulties and Britain's intransigence. The referendum on the
Beagle Channel in November 1984 was campaigned by the ruling
Radical party on the basis that Chile was a Latin American brother
and that Britain was the only real enemy. The implication was that
the Foreign Ministry no longer wanted to be tied up in litigation
where Argentine rights had rarely been recognised internationally
and instead wanted to concentrate on the 'Malvinas' issue on which
it counted on considerable international sympathy. The national
accord signed with Isabelita Perón in May 1984 was vague about
economic and political issues, but on the 'Malvinas' it was specific:
the Argentine government agreed not to enter any negotiations with
Britain which did not specifically relate to the sovereignty issue. Its
aggressive fisheries policy – the so-called Neptune plan, based on a
stricter patrolling of its Exclusive Economic Zone, and controversial
bilateral agreements with countries such as the Soviet Union – was
formulated with the specific purpose less of conserving stocks than
of bringing sovereignty to the front of the Falklands debate.

Britain not only refused to talk about sovereignty but actually took
steps to reinforce its rights to the islands. It granted kelpers full
British nationality, formulated a new constitution for the islands,
and in October 1986 declared its rights to a 200-mile fishing zone,
declaring in the interim a conservation and management area within
the 150-mile military protection zone already in place. It also turned
the Falklands into the most sophisticated military base in the South
Atlantic. Its central feature was the all-weather airport at Mount
Pleasant, capable of catering for wide-bodied civilian jets as well as
RAF fighter, transport and reconnaissance planes (including nine
phantoms, and about a dozen Chinooks and Hercules) – all backed up
by anti-aircraft artillery and missiles, and early-warning intelligence
systems capable of detecting Argentine aircraft as soon as they
scramble from Patagonian bases, and providing raw evidence on
enemy troop movements and naval exercises. Spread out across the
Falklands and its dependencies with the bulk concentrated around
Mount Pleasant were some 3,000 troops. The army garrison consisted of a 'strong infantry battalion group, Royal Artillery
(6 × 105 mm light guns), Royal Engineers (now greatly reduced in
numbers), an armed reconnaissance squadron (Scorpions), an Army

Air Corps Squadron, nine Scout and Gazelle helicopters, Blow Pipe signal units and a logistics battalion'.[16] The troops by 1986 were no longer billeted in Port Stanley, as they were for at least a year after the war. But the islands' jagged coastlines were protected by isolated detachments of troops, two escorts (frigates or destroyers), three patrol vessels, a nuclear- or diesel-powered submarine and a detachment of Sea King helicopters. Supporting the airport and the troops was a new £22 million floating dock. With monthly imports of over 5,000 tonnes and exports of 2,500 tonnes, the flexiport's annual trade flow was estimated at about £30 million. Some 900 square yards of warehouse facilities ensure that the troops on the islands are permanently supplied with ammunition, petrol and almost every product imaginable from bars of soap to souvenir penguins.

Officially Fortress Falklands was justified throughout the years 1982–6 as purely reactive to the perceived Argentine threat. While Alfonsín has repeatedly declared his non-belligerence, the British government persistently referred to Argentina's refusal to declare formally a cessation to hostilities, the re-equipment which had taken place under the General Bignone transition, and the fragility of Argentina's new political system as reasons why Britain had to remain doubly sure of not being vulnerable again to unprovoked aggression. Whatever the military motives, however, the large presence (proportionate to the population) of British armed forces on the islands had a crucial political effect. Along the waterfront of Port Stanley, the Falkland Islands' only two major monuments in remembrance of the two World Wars was joined by a third. The Liberation Statue, paid for by the islanders as tribute to the British Task Force, became the most striking symbol of kelper feelings and the most poignant local reminder of those three months in 1982 that shook the world.

Islanders like to use the phrase 'Falkland heritage' to describe the symbiosis between the British military and local civilian population produced by history. For a community that has always lacked a deeply entrenched 'local culture' – as Anthony Barnett puts it rather cruelly, 'much of the actual kelper population consists of retired people who, after a lifetime of labour in the "camp" [the local term for the countryside, from the Spanish camp], invest their savings in a clapboard'[17] – war brought in its wake a wealth of experience, legend and folklore capable of binding this small civilian population together in a sense of common identity.

When I visited the islands in August 1984, I arrived fully briefed by my Argentine friends and their British sympathisers about the

essentially undemocratic features of 'kelper' society: the economic
political and social weight of the Falkland Island Company, the
élitist and somewhat corrupt nature of the 'elected councillors', the
lack of real communication with what the Argentines were thinking.
So I made a point of travelling as widely as possible, talking to as
many people as possible, and trying to establish whether below the
surface of officialdom there was a change of mood. Having already
lived in Buenos Aires since the beginning of 1982, I never felt as far
away from Argentina – with all its surface sophistication – as during
a ten-day stay among people who dressed badly, rarely worried
about inflation, and who could hardly put two words of Spanish
together.

In Buenos Aires Argentine military officers had made a point of
insisting on their humanity towards the kelpers and the essential
honesty and efficiency of General Menéndez's brief spell as local
Governor. I found it difficult to find an islander who did not have
his or her own story to tell about the disruption caused by the
Argentine occupation. There was neither rape nor widespread
looting and the only three islanders who died during the conflict
were accidentally shelled by the British, not by the Argentines.
Before the Argentine landing, the Falkland Islands Police Force
consisted of one chief police officer, one inspector, one sergeant and
four constables (all unarmed). Offences against local ordinances such
as licensing laws and road traffic regulations were the highest and
most crime could be traced to over-indulgence in drink. Serious
crime in the islands was practically unknown.

Barnett is only partly correct in asserting, 'Snobbish to the end, the
junta had treated the inhabitants with the velvet glove traditionally
applied to its country's privileged European settlements, rather than
the brutal knuckleduster applied to the workers of Córdoba or the
Indians in Tucuman province.' There was an invasion and there
was a war and for the majority of islanders the peace was shattered
on 2 April, and this was unforgivable. Some islanders suffered less
than others: one family for instance told me how their dog had had
its front teeth knocked out by falling masonry. Some islands hardly
suffered at all: one family who lived in an isolated farm off West
Falkland didn't even see an Argentine. And yet there were many
who had a very bad time of it indeed: sheep – their life support –
were shelled, fences were torn down, some houses ended in ruins,
the rough grass and the gorse turned black and crumpled in the
destruction of battle. One farmer had his horses and pigs hacked to
death. In Stanley the islanders watched incredulously as if, against

their will, they had become characters in some demented Wonderland like Alice. Public buildings had heavily armed sentries placed around them, as if Stanley Post Office was Palermo barracks. In the first days after the invasion they were made to drive on the right-hand side of the road when they had driven all their lives on the left. The authorities initially ordered the right-hand drive because they believed that their own personnel would run the risk of crashing into each other. Only when General Menéndez arrived was the order reversed for 'humanitarian reasons'.

Throughout the occupation, Argentine officers appear to have been divided between hawks and doves – the hawks acted the way they did from a mixture of motives – extreme nationalism, a wish to maintain a conduct that had been tried and tested during the 'dirty war' (the important thing to do is to survive politically, whatever the means) and sheer sadism. The doves acted in part from a snobbish attitude towards all things English; partly from genuine humanity; but their behaviour was guided in particular by a realisation that the junta's human rights record was being fully exploited on the diplomatic front and that they needed to be seen to be winning over the sympathy of the local population. The doves seemed to have taken as their guiding light the 1971 Communications agreement between Britain and the military government of General Alejandro Lanusse with which both governments had agreed to embark on a 'hearts and minds' campaign with the essential aim of bringing the kelpers closer to the Argentines and facilitating a transfer of sovereignty.

The agreement had got off to a more or less happy start. Argentine tourists began to arrive in planes and boats, striking up a fruitful if somewhat mercenary relationship with local shopkeepers; limited trade began, mainly in wood, fruit, sheep and cattle, between southern Argentina, particularly Tierra del Fuego, and the islands. Some kelpers sent their children on scholarships to schools on the Argentine mainland and their sick to Argentine hospitals; the Argentine State airline, LADE, opened offices in Port Stanley, as did Yacimientos Petrolíferos Fiscales, the state oil concern, which built a fuel depot and won an exclusive contract to supply fuel oil to the islands. All these moves are remembered by most kelpers as having brought a measure of material improvement to the islands. What the doves seemed to have forgotten or ignored was that the measures did not succeed in getting the island community any nearer to Argentina culturally, let alone to accepting the concept of Argentine administration.

One of the first initiatives promoted by the doves during the war was a visit to the islands by a group of Anglo-Argentines. The 'very English' visitors from Buenos Aires had agreed to do their best to convince the local population of the wonders of living under Argentine military rule. The Anglo-Argentines met with total resistance; one later recalled that she had never felt so insulted in her life, with the word traitor being used on at least one occasion. Had the doves considered their history more carefully, they and the Anglo-Argentines would have been saved the humiliation. For the tragic flaw of the Communications agreement had been based on just this assumption – that it was possible to assimilate the kelpers into the Anglo-Argentine community. Yet, as Max Hastings and Simon Jenkins rightly point out in their book on the Falklands War:

> The mainland community could hardly have less in common with the 'kelpers'. The Anglo-Argentines of Buenos Aires have their roots in the middle-class commercial life in the capital. The descendants of Scots and Welsh settlers in adjacent Patagonia might superficially seem to possess similar characteristics to the Falklanders. Yet even the Welsh of Puerto Madryn are fully fledged Argentinians and proud of it. Their lingua franca is Spanish (or Welsh), not English. The Falklanders, as one of them proudly said, have not an 'ounce of Latin America in them'.[18]

It was significant that the number of kelper children going to Anglo-Argentine schools tapered off not so much because the education was poor but because they objected to having to sing the national anthem and being taught history lessons containing references to 'Las Malvinas'. This aversion to Argentina's political culture was aggravated in the mid-1970s by the clearly deteriorating situation under military or semi-military administrations. Tuned in to the reports of the BBC correspondent in Buenos Aires, and summaries of 'What the Papers Say', the kelpers could draw striking contrasts between their own 'bobby on the beat' and the death squads of the Triple A.

On my visit to the islands I found a surprising number of islanders prepared to state openly their appreciation for the courteousness of General Menéndez and his senior team of advisers. The late Monsignor Spraggon, whom one can hardly consider an appeaser, fondly remembered the tact and patience with which two officers in particular, Captain Hussey and Brigadier Bloomer Reeve, had treated the inhabitants in an attempt to honour their 'interests'. Both officers were fluent English speakers and actively socialised with the

Anglo-Argentine community in Buenos Aires. The kelpers were not so naïve as to ignore the fact that even the most benevolent officers were probably on an intelligence-gathering mission, so even the best contacts had been cordial rather than effusive.

The hawks in the Argentine occupation forces were one of the main disciplinary problems faced by General Menéndez in the first weeks of the war. To tell a junior officer that his professional duty was to act with moderation and consideration for the civilian population was clearly a tall order for a military machine finely tuned in the art of repression. Major Patricio Dowling of army intelligence was one of the first to break ranks; put in charge of controlling the most anti-Argentine elements in the Falklands community known to the military before the war, Dowling very nearly started the 'dirty war' all over again. Soon after the invasion he ordered the deportation of several kelpers, including a local farmer and his wife, Bill and Pat Luxton, on the grounds that they were a threat to internal security. The couple were surrounded by machine-gun-wielding conscripts, shouted at by Dowling and then bundled into a helicopter. As they flew across the stretch of water that separates West from East Falkland, the Luxtons were subjected to something akin to psychological torture. 'At the time I didn't know what was going to happen to us. I just thought of the "disappeared", and I was terrified,' Bill recalled.[19]

Dowling and a number of the more hawkish officers were ordered back to the mainland by Menéndez. Nevertheless, the military's attitude towards the kelpers seems to have hardened generally once serious hostilities between Britain and Argentina got under way in May 1982. Troops were instructed to increase their controls and to report any suspicious activities. Menéndez also transformed his original 'black list' of island hardliners into a population census, and ordered the confiscation of all short-wave radios – the only form of communication between many isolated farms and houses in Port Stanley. Intelligence officers from a crack commando regiment with a track record in staking out suspected political subversives were specially brought in from the mainland to reinforce protection of military installations and to carry out occasional lightning raids on kelper gatherings of more than two people. Increasingly, as news of the Task Force's approach came through, peppered often with leaked information of secret commando landings by the British, a feeling of paranoia gripped the occupation forces. By the end of May, General Menéndez seems to have been facing distinct difficulties in pacifying the passions of middle-ranking and junior officers who were convinced that the majority of the kelper population were actively engaged in a resistance movement co-ordinated by the Task Force.

The real story of Argentina's relations with the kelpers during the Falklands War was officially suppressed after the war by the Argentine authorities in a clear attempt to minimise its diplomatic fall-out. But the hostile, almost racist, cultural divide which separated the two sides is reflected in the writing of one of the few Argentine journalists present in the islands, himself a close friend of one of the hawks, General Seineldín.

In a chapter called 'The Blind Indians', the journalist says, 'The kelpers were our arch-enemies. I felt from the very first moment that they were fifth columnists and that they would never be won by the Argentine cause. The kelpers were second-class citizens ... very primitive in their way of living. They were hybrids both in character and physique. "Fish" is how we called them. They have a monotonous diet ... sheep night and day. We had that diet for fifty days; the kelpers have the same diet for the whole of their lives ... maybe a psychologist or a sociologist may discover one day a link between this diet and their hybrid character.'[20]

Only a very reduced number of kelpers seem to have been engaged in intelligence work for the British – London appears to have calculated that to have pursued wider and more active links would be to run the risk of a bloodbath. The Argentines themselves hint that at least two kelpers worked clandestinely for them – although I have not been able to establish concrete evidence for this. It is clear, however, that for the majority of kelpers the progress of the war reinforced their anti-Argentine feelings rather than modifying them. One aspect that particularly affected them psychologically was the way the Argentine military officers treated their own men. 'We thought if that's how they treat their own people what's going to happen when they turn on us,' was a comment I heard widely.

In Stanley cemetery ancient mariners and old-age pensioners lie by old moss-covered stone crosses; their tombstones with their tales of shipwrecks and natural deaths are like the chapters of a history book. They are perched on a hill overlooking the bay and the scene is as peaceful as that of any village graveyard in Britain. But when they talked of the graveyards in 1984, the islanders recalled only the mass grave into which the Argentines bundled their dead. (After the war the bodies were dug up by the British and taken to Goose Green, to join other conscripts and officers who had fallen.) Death also emerged in conversation with reference to the 'Old Beever hangar', a shell-ridden building which the Argentines are reported to have used as a secret morgue to hide their casualties from their troops. One islander told me how in the evenings a boat, supposedly filled with bodies, would motor out to sea, before returning empty.

For a community that had scarcely known violence before the 1982 invasion, such images had a traumatic effect. The experience of war entrenched itself deeply into the collective psyche and continued to mould attitudes, making the whole islands question seem at times even more intractable than it was before the war. The legacy of battle moreover was felt on the practical as well as on the psychological level. The islands remained littered with unexploded mines. These were the ones the Argentines laid in a hurry in the last days of the war; they were without metal rings so they could neither be detected nor defused. Whole areas around Port Stanley were declared red zones or 'no-go areas'. Where once they might have had a picnic or gone fishing, kelpers risked being blown to bits.

By contrast, following the war, relations between the British military and the local population were strengthened thanks to a carefully orchestrated 'hearts and minds' campaign built on the cultural legacy of the war. The withdrawal of troops from Port Stanley was principally aimed at avoiding the sense that one occupying army was being replaced by another. However, officers and their men were actively encouraged to build up friendships with islanders by offering free rides in patrol boats or helicopters – much as they do at English country fairs – and joining in communal parties. But the most striking aspect of the campaign was the 'tour of the battle sites'.

Three Sisters and Mount Longdon – stark, unimpressive hills, not mountains at all – were resurrected as part of the 'island heritage' complete with abandoned trenches littered with Argentine toothpaste tubes and morphine bottles, and arms cemeteries with everything from a used bullet to a tangled mass of Pucara. The tour I went on had a group of newly arrived soldiers picking among the debris like excited schoolboys at some prehistoric mausoleum. Clearly, though, it was serving a pre-eminently psychological purpose even as a source of entertainment. As he guided us, the tour operator, a senior officer, gave a potted history of the battle, emphasising the courage, qualities of leadership and general military preparedness which had helped to defeat the Argentines, while at the same time emphasising the extreme bravery of some Argentine troops so as not to give the impression of an amateur contest. It seemed to me that boredom and a potential for losing sight of objectives were the two interconnecting pitfalls for the British armed forces on the islands – even though their hearts and minds campaign reaped a generous political harvest.

On 2 April 1986, the fourth anniversary of the Argentine invasion, an opinion poll published by Marplan on behalf of the Falkland Islands Association, the main British-based support group, showed that more than 94 per cent of adults on the Falkland Islands wanted to live under British sovereignty. The survey of all 1,033 electors in the total Falklands population of 1,956 yielded an 89 per cent response rate – one of the highest in Marplan's experience. It asked the basic question, 'What kind of sovereignty do you want for the Falkland Islands?' Answers were: British sovereignty, 94·5 per cent (869 people); independence, 1·6 per cent (15 people); other solutions, 1·2 per cent (11 people); voters who selected 2 solutions, 1·1 per cent (10 people); United Nations trusteeship, 0·3 per cent (3 people); Argentine sovereignty, 0·3 per cent (3 people).

Between 1982 and 1986 the three main players in the Falklands equation, the Argentine government, the British government, and the islanders, became trapped increasingly by their respective histories. It need not be so in the future. Argentina, if it is to consolidate a genuine collective identification with democracy, should extend its reappraisal of history to correct propagandist and mythological versions of the past. Argentina's political and economic decline this century cannot simply be blamed on British colonialism. It is the result of complex internal as well as external factors; politically an important cause has been the absence of a genuine national identity and the excessive militarisation of the country's political culture. The Falklands conflict undeniably had an underlying nationalist current, part of which rebelled passionately against what was perceived as the vindictive death throes of the British Empire. But the decision to invade and the subsequent euphoria was not so much the ultimate expression of patriotism as the tragic and inevitable product of a regimented society.

George Orwell, trying to explain the emotions generated by the Second World War, wrote in 1945:

> Nationalism is not to be confused with patriotism. Both words are normally used in so vague a way that any definition is liable to be challenged, but one must draw a distinction between them, since two different and even opposing ideas are involved. By 'patriotism' I mean devotion to a particular place and a particular way of life, which one believes to be the best in the world but has no wish to force upon other people. Patriotism is of its nature

defensive, both militarily and culturally. Nationalism, on the other hand, is inseparable from the desire for power. The abiding purpose of every nationalist is to secure more power and more prestige, not for himself but for the nation or other unit in which he has chosen to sink his own individuality.

The invasion of the Falklands on 2 April 1982 was an offensive act spurred by an essentially emotional and irrational concept of nationhood. It brought to the surface Argentina's confused sense of cultural identity, while momentarily giving birth to the myth of national unity. Subsequently the war showed that armed forces that involve themselves in politics are incapable of defending the nation; and that authoritarianism breeds a distorted perception of the rest of the world. The lesson that should be taught in all schools of the new Argentina under Alfonsín is that those who died in the war were not heroes. They were victims of the British and the professional incompetence and political opportunism of Argentina's military regime.

Nevertheless, by the end of 1986, the Alfonsín government seemed willing to reach a solution to the Falklands dispute by peaceful means, and that is a great deal more than could have been said for the junta. In spite of its insistence that the islands belonged by right to Argentina, the Alfonsín government did try to infuse a greater respect for the feelings of the islanders. Democracy has not brought in its wake an acceptance by Argentina of the validity of the islanders' case for self-determination. However, the Argentine government laid increasing emphasis on its readiness to accept the life-style of the kelpers in any future arrangements and to implement full guarantees in this respect.

Before the Falklands War the military also offered the islanders full political and economic guarantees including 'most pampered region' treatment. But the nature of the Alfonsín government should make Argentina's position carry more weight with the islanders than it has done in the past. Arguably, for the kelpers to blame Alfonsín for the trauma they suffered during the occupation is almost as removed from political reality as the relatives of the 'disappeared' blaming their democratic President for the executions and torture that took place following the 1976 coup. The relatives of the 'disappeared' have of course not blamed Alfonsín and yet their suffering was greater than that of the kelpers.

To provide a framework for the preservation of the islanders' interests, Argentine officials were at pains to discover solutions within the existing Argentine constitution – a move essentially aimed at winning over nationalist sectors who believe that a respect for the islanders is synonymous with British sovereignty. The move was also aimed at building a bridge between the British and Argentine administrations. As has been noted by Dr Peter Beck, Articles 104–6 of the Argentine constitution enable provinces to enact their own constitutions, organise local institutions, elect the Governor, legislators, judges and other officers, and establish their own educational system.[21] Significantly, Article 104 stipulates that the 'provinces retain all power not delegated by the Constitution to the Federal Government and those expressly reserved by special covenants at the time of their incorporation'. Between 1984 and 1986 the Alfonsín government consistently emphasised that for the islanders to decide on forms of education and social organisation best suited to their interests was perfectly acceptable to them as long as the unity of any negotiated 'package' was retained through the inclusion of sovereignty.

In November 1986 the Alfonsín government, using its majority in the lower house of the Argentine Congress, passed a Bill to create a self-governing province out of Argentina's southernmost territory of Tierra del Fuego; but significantly the government resisted pressure from the nationalist lobby to include the 'Malvinas' in the Bill, thereby leaving options open for a larger degree of autonomous self-government on the islands.[22]

Alfonsín's decision to move the capital of Argentina to Viedma in Patagonia could eventually pave the way for more genuine economic and physical links between the mainland and the islands than have existed in the past. For, as has been argued, 'It is just possible that if Argentina dangles the prospect of investment and closer links with the outside world, islanders' perceptions of their interests will change.'[23]

Some islanders have argued that in the ten years before the invasion of the Falklands a succession of Argentine governments had ample opportunity to create trust and confidence. The invasion simply confirmed the islanders' earlier suspicions, and the deep-seated hostility the kelpers feel towards Argentina will take generations to heal. Nevertheless, it is Britain that ultimately has to decide what in the long term best serves the islanders' interests and what solution best serves the concept of a stable world, the principles of democracy, and the rule of law – the issues which motivated the British people to back Mrs Thatcher's military reaction in 1982. Following the end of the Falklands War the British government made an effort to make up for its past lack of interest in the islands. It ploughed more money into the islands than it had done in *per capita* terms for any other single community inside the British Isles. Nevertheless, the government has been wary of encouraging 'colonisation' – getting people to settle the land – on any massive scale. Part of the problem has been that settlers cannot be housed cheaply because so much has to be imported and there have been inadequate financial incentives to boost farming. The post-war experience, including the building of the airport, has suggested formidable development problems and considerable cost over-runs of existing civil expenditure.[24]

Lord Shackleton, who has prepared one of the few serious independent studies of the economic prospects of the islands, argued that the key to Britain's future commitment to the Falklands lies in the Antarctic. The current treaty governing the continent was signed by twelve nations in 1959. It froze all territorial claims including the overlapping claims of Britain, Argentina and Chile and paved the way for over twenty years of unprecedented international co-operation. It was agreed that the basis of the treaty should be scientific co-operation and that all measures of a military nature should be prohibited, including the transport, installation or use of nuclear weapons. As a result the Antarctic became a genuinely nuclear-free zone and one of the few areas of the world not to be affected by the Cold War.

Nevertheless the Treaty is up for review in 1991, so pressures to pursue economic interests, given the Antarctic's untapped natural resources, may increase. In an article in *The Times* in April 1985 Shackleton commented, 'While I have always favoured some form of international ownership or administration of the Antarctic, the fact is that if Britain were to give up the Falklands the British position and influence and that of the British Antarctic Survey would be gravely weakened.'[25]

By the end of 1986 it seemed that the Falklands War had turned the South Atlantic, to coin Shackleton's own phrase, into 'a complex regional situation with global implications'. There seemed therefore all the more urgent need for Britain and Argentina to allow diplomatic imagination and political good sense to prevail. Churchill, on whom Thatcher based so much of her political style during the Falklands War, was a historian as well as a Prime Minister. He admired the concept of the 'island race' but he also recognised the advantages in showing magnanimity after victory. If he were alive today he would have no doubt welcomed the peaceful nature of

England's World Cup tie against Argentina in June 1986, but at the same time issued a warning about the future. For before Mexico City, the last time Britain engaged the enemy at football was Christmas 1914. When the match was finished, the shooting began again.

NOTES

Introduction

[1] See Carlos Escudé, 'Not a Clear-cut Case', *Buenos Aires Herald* (18 November 1985). Escudé's series of six articles was a courageous attempt to bring some dispassionate debate to bear on the Malvinas issue; but it had few public repercussions in Argentina.

[2] Anti-British feelings were stirred by the nationalist forces which began to emerge in the 1930s, and which were dominated, initially, by a new generation of historians. These historical revisionists, who made a lasting impression on public opinion, re-examined the nineteenth- and early twentieth-century history of Argentina, concentrating on the British invasions of Buenos Aires in 1806–7 (against the colonial Spanish authorities), Britain's role in the foundation of Uruguay as a buffer state between Argentina and Brazil in the late 1820s, the seizure in 1833 of the Falklands, and the later collaboration between the local oligarchy and British commercial, banking and farming interests during the boom years of the early nineteenth century. *Revisionismo* helped to unearth part of the seamier side of British economic imperialism, such as the collaboration of British farmers in the repression of an anarchist movement in Patagonia, and the corrupt deals governing the British-owned railroads and meat trade. However, its main impact on Argentine political culture was to distort the historical role of figures like the nineteenth-century Juan Manuel Rosas and General Juan Perón. They were depicted as symbols of a great anti-imperialist Argentina, to the exclusion of any other aspect of their rule, such as their contribution to violence and their erosion of democracy as an inseparable factor in Argentine national life.

[3] Max Hastings and Simon Jenkins, *The Battle for the Falklands* (Michael Joseph, 1983).

[4] In 1964 an Argentine civilian landed a light aircraft at Port Stanley, erected an Argentine flag, handed a proclamation to a bystander, and then returned to the mainland. The Argentine government publicly dissociated itself from the incident and there was no major public reaction. In 1966 an armed group of twenty Argentines led by Perónist trade unionists hijacked an Argentine airlines plane on the way to Tierra del Fuego and landed on the racecourse near Port Stanley. The Argentine government again dissociated itself, although there were small isolated demonstrations in Buenos Aires and other towns, and public reaction remained generally subdued.

[5] David Rock, *Argentina, 1516–1982* (I. B. Tauris, 1986).

[6] George Philip, *The Military in South American Politics* (Croom Helm, 1985).

[7] John Simpson and Jana Bennett, *The Disappeared* (Robson Books, 1985).

[8] *Nunca Mas* (Faber & Faber, 1986).

[9] Joseph Page, *Perón* (Random House, 1983) and Eduardo Crawley, *A House Divided* (C. Hurst & Co., 1984).

[10] In particular Anthony Barnett, *Iron Britannia* (Allison & Busby, 1982).

Chapter 1

[1] The Rt Hon. The Lord Franks, *Falkland Islands Review* (HMSO, 1983), p. 1.

[2] According to one of the leading Argentine experts on the Falklands, the journalist Haroldo Foulkes, the officer who was instructed to carry out the feasibility study for the invasion of the Falklands in 1942 was Lieutenant-General Rattenbach, at that time teaching in a military institute. Haroldo Foulkes, *Las Malvinas: Una Causa Nacional* (Corregidor, 1982), pp. 68–9.

The Franks Report has been overtaken by the release of previously secret British government records. These show that it was in 1942 that Britain first became seriously concerned about the military security of the Falklands. In June 1942 Winston Churchill ordered the despatch of a military force to bolster the islands' defences, and about 2,000 men were garrisoned in and around Port Stanley for the rest of the war. Churchill seems to have acted in response to what he saw as the threat of an invasion by pro-Axis sectors of the Argentine armed forces and the large German community in Argentina.

Significantly the decision to despatch the military Task Force was taken in spite of the views of Sir David Kelly, the British Ambassador. Kelly was impressed by the pro-British sentiments of the Argentine Foreign Minister, Enrique Ruiz Guiñazu, who belonged to the traditional land-owning class which had strong trading links with the United Kingdom. Churchill, however, seems to have understood the military's overriding influence on Argentine policy-making. See Alain Rouquié, *Poder Militar y Sociedad Política en la Argentina* (Emecé, 1983): 'For those (self-proclaimed) defenders of territorial integrity, the United Kingdom was both the defeated invader of 1806 and the illegal occupant of the Islas Malvinas, almost an enemy by inheritance.'

[3] Tony Geraghty, *Who Dares Wins: the Story of the SAS, 1950–80* (Fontana, 1981).

[4] The sources for this story are leading Argentinian naval officers involved in the operation who wish to remain anonymous.

[5] During the Falklands War, Captain González Llanos, an electronics expert and fluent English speaker (he was posted as naval attaché to London in the early 1970s) was put in charge of monitoring the movement of British ships in the South Atlantic. He was on board the fishing vessel *Narwal* when it was attacked by the RAF. At the time the Argentine media, under instructions from the junta, painted it as an inhuman attack against an innocent group of fishermen. Britain always insisted that the *Narwal* was carrying sophisticated radar equipment and was a spy ship.

[6] Manuel Mujica Laínez, *Misteriosa Buenos Aires* (Sudamericana, 1985), pp. 9–16.

[7] Bartolomé Mitre, quoted in John Lynch, *The Spanish American Revolutions, 1808–26* (Weidenfeld & Nicolson, 1973).

[8] See Guillermo Makím, *The Military in Argentine Politics, 1880–1982* (Millennium Spring, 1983), pp. 49–51.

[9] Raymond Carr, *Modern Spain, 1875–1980* (Oxford University Press, 1980), p. 18.

[10] General Augustin P. Justo (1932–8) was voted into office, but the elections were far from democratic. The Perónist party was not yet in existence – the working class was therefore denied any political expression. At the same time, polling day was preceded by a military decree banning the candidate for the Radical party, Marcelo Torcuato de Alvear.

[11] S. Lozada, E. Barcesat, C. Iamocaeno and J. Viaggio, *La Ideología de la Seguridad Nacional* (El Cid Editor, 1983), pp. 22–4.

Chapter 2

[1] Timerman had supported the coup of General Juan Carlos Onganía against the Radical government of Arturo Illía in 1966. Ten years later he argued strongly that Congress should give the armed forces emergency powers to deal with terrorism. He seems to have been unconvinced by the argument that to do so would inevitably hand the military the keys to government. Even after the coup took place and some of his own journalists were being kidnapped by the security forces, Timerman still believed that it was possible to distinguish moderates from hard-liners within the military establishment. His own arrest and subsequent torture shattered this illusion. Timerman was typical of an older generation of conservative middle-class Argentines who became politically radicalised as a result of a personal experience. For a moving account of how the Timerman case brought the junta's latent anti-Semitism to the fore see Jacobo Timerman, *Prisoner Without a Name, Cell Without a Number* (Weidenfeld & Nicolson, 1981).

For a critical analysis of Timerman's contribution to Argentine journalism see Andrew Graham-Yooll, 'La Opinion – Not a Word', *Index on Censorship* (June 1977), pp. 8–10. Graham-Yooll comments, 'Timerman backed all governments, at first, then when he saw them failing or that a *coup d'état* was in the making, changed sides to try to back the new winner.' Timerman returned to Argentina after a four-year exile in 1984 to collaborate with President Alfonsín's human rights trial of the juntas. After accusing General Ramón Camps, the head of the Buenos Aires police force, of being responsible for his torture, Timerman became a prime witness for the prosecution. He told me in an interview, 'Like many Argentines, I used to think that backing the military was the only way to change things. Now I know I'm wrong. What Mr Raúl Alfonsín is doing in this country has no precedent anywhere in South America. Even in Germany the bulk of the population had to wait until the screening of *Holocaust* to realise what really happened.' *Financial Times* (4 February 1984).

[2] 'Capital Venture in Argentina', *Financial Times* (16 May 1986).

[3] Ezequiel Martínez Estrada, *La Cabeza de Goliath* (Losada, 1943).

[4] *Falklands, Whose Crisis?* (Latin America Bureau, 1982), p. 75.

[5] Interview with the author and María-Laura Avignolo.

[6] The Propaganda-Due, P-2 for short, Freemasons' Lodge originated in the late nineteenth century and was so named to distinguish it from the existing more open Propaganda Masonic Lodge in Turin. The P-2 had languished for many years, but in the early 1970s was revived with a vengeance by Licio Gelli, an Italian business-man with extreme right-wing political views and ambitions for power on an inter-national scale. An Italian court investigation into the activities of P-2 in 1981 accused Gelli of forming a State within a State with former secret servicemen, serving military officers, businessmen, bankers and politicians, and of having a hand in right-wing terrorist outrages in recent Italian history, from the so-called 'strategy of tension' of the late 1960s to the Bologna station bombing of August 1980. Gelli was also alleged to have given the Lodge a Latin American dimension. When Italian police raided Gelli's villa near Florence in 1981, they found a list of 962 members of the Lodge. The list included senior Argentine military figures and

politicians belonging to a special section of P-2 called Pro-Patria. The section was headed by Admiral Massera, the navy chief, General Guillermo Suarez Mason, the commander of the First Army Corps (who was appointed head of the State oil company, Yacimentos Petroliferos Fiscales in 1981) and two former Ministers of the Perón government, Alberto Vignes (Foreign Minister) and José Lopez Rega (Social Welfare). As a result of the P-2 scandal which subsequently swept Italy, the Italian government fell and the Banco Ambrosiano (the most powerful banking group in Italy, with an office in the same building as Massera's in Buenos Aires) was declared bankrupt. In the early morning of 18 June 1982 the body of Ambrosiano's president, Roberto Calvi, was found hanging from London's Blackfriars Bridge – the only bridge in London to be painted blue and white, the colours of the Argentine national flag. The police suspected suicide. Calvi's family was convinced that it was murder. The Ambrosiano collapse exposed the shady financial dealings of the Vatican, although much of the history of P-2 remains surrounded with mystery and probably always will be. At the end of 1986 Gelli remained a fugitive. For a detailed account of Gelli and the Calvi affair, see Rupert Cornwell, *God's Banker* (Gollancz, 1983), particularly pp. 44–50.

[7] The background for this provided by Martínez de Hoz and María-Laura Avignolo.

[8] According to a private investigation carried out by the Argentine journalist Jesús Iglesias Rouco, the bulk of these funds was held in a New York bank account.

[9] Based on information supplied by the Stockholm International Peace Research Institute (SIPRI).

[10] Max Hastings and Simon Jenkins, *The Battle for the Falklands* (Michael Joseph, 1983), pp. 11–13.

[11] *La Opinión* was taken over by the military in May 1977 and subsequently closed down. By then the newspaper editor Jacobo Timerman had been arrested, along with his deputy editor Enrique Jara. Edgardo Sajón, the production director, had disappeared that April after being abducted by the security forces. See Timerman, *Prisoner Without a Name*. The *Buenos Aires Herald* was not closed down, but its editor, Robert Cox, and the chief news editor, Andrew Graham-Yooll, were forced into exile after receiving death threats. See Graham-Yooll, *A State of Fear* (Eland, 1986). *La Prensa*, editorially the most conservative of the three, survived although some of its journalists, including the columnists Jesús Iglesias Rouco and Manfred Schonfeld, were constantly intimidated by the security forces.

The deference with which the junta treated the *Herald* until the outbreak of the Falklands War was based on the belief that the newspaper's small circulation denied it any real influence outside the Anglo-Argentine community, and that the majority of Englishmen living and working in Argentina were pro-junta after the 1976 coup. *La Prensa* was owned and edited by the Gainza-Paz family, one of Argentina's land-owning élite which, in spite of *La Prensa*'s critical attitude towards human rights violations, maintained friendly relations with General Ramón Camps, the head of the Buenos Aires police and senior members of the Argentine Cabinet.

For the background on the relations of the Argentine media with military governments I am indebted to Andrew Graham-Yooll, who has written several articles on the subject for *Index on Censorship*. See in particular, *The Press in Argentina, 1973–8* (Writers' and Scholars' Educational Trust, 1979) and 'La Opinion – Not a Word', *Index on Censorship* (1977/5), pp. 8–10.

[12] Ernesto Sábato, Introduction to *Nunca Más: a Report by Argentina's National Commission on Disappeared People* (Faber & Faber, 1986).

[13] See Emilio F. Mignone, *Iglesia y Dictadura* (Ediciones de Pensamiento Nacional, 1986), p. 17, and 'Iglesia y Dictadura', *El Periodísta* (28 December 1984), p. 17.

[14] Both these cases are reported in *Nunca Más*, pp. 248–51.

[15] For an interesting anecdotal insight into Galtieri before the Falklands War, see Antonio Cabral, Hugo Martínez, Marcos Wilson and Roberto Godoy, *Guerra Santa nas Malvinas* (EMW Editores, 1982), pp. 114–17.

[16] The 'exile' was Pacho O'Donnell, an Argentine writer, who was put in charge of cultural affairs by President Raúl Alfonsín in 1984. Pacho O'Donnell, 'El Mundial y Otros Mefistos', *Contraseña*, 6 (July 1983).

[17] See Juan José Sebreli, *Los Deseos Imaginarios del Peronismo* (Legasa, 1983).

Chapter 3

[1] Peter Calvocoressi and Guy Wint, *Total War* (Penguin, 1981), p. 9.

[2] *Falklands, Whose Crisis?*, p. 74.

[3] Alejandro Dabat and Luis Lorenzano, *The Malvinas and the End of Military Rule* (Verso, 1984), p. 73.

[4] Dabat and Lorenzano, *The Malvinas and the End of Military Rule*.

[5] Conversation with Alec Betts, a former employee of LADE, the State airline, in Port Stanley who left for the Argentine mainland soon after the war. Betts left behind his wife, two daughters, mother and a brother – General Secretary of the Trade Union Organisation. Betts later testified in support of Argentina at the United Nations.

[6] For an account of the efforts made by Mrs Derian and the US Embassy in Buenos Aires see John Simpson and Jana Bennett, *The Disappeared: Voices from a Secret War* (Robson Books, 1985), pp. 278, 280 and 389.

[7] Interview conducted by author and María-Laura Avignolo with senior naval officer after the Falklands War had ended.

[8] For an account of the US link with Argentina during the Carter and Reagan years, see Horacio Verbitsky, *La Ultima Batalla de la Tercera Guerra Mundial* (Nueva Informacion/Legasa, 1985), pp. 80–110.

[9] Quoted in Hastings and Jenkins, *The Battle for the Falklands*, p. 46.

[10] Interview conducted by author and María-Laura Avignolo with high-ranking navy official following the end of the Falklands War.

[11] My account of the New York talks is based on Argentine diplomatic sources and the Franks Report.

[12] The main source for this is an Argentine General and the official army investigation. Although a slightly different version of these conversations appears in O. Cardoso, R. Kirschbaum and E. Van der Kooy, *Malvinas: la Trama Secreta* (Sudamericana-Planeta, 1983), pp. 67–8, there is no substantial difference. Galtieri himself confirmed after the war that he never really expected a British reaction. An interesting interview with him was published in *Clarín* (2 April 1983).

[13] For a detailed account of Argentine economic policy before and during the Falklands War, see Roberto Alemann, *La Politica Económica durante el Conflicto Austral* (Academie Nacional de Ciencias Economicas, 1983).

Chapter 4

[1] Christian Salvesen & Co. of Leith, Scotland was founded in 1846 as a shipping and whaling firm. Initial interest in whaling was concentrated in the North Atlantic, particularly around Iceland, but soon shifted to the South Atlantic when stocks dwindled. The firm first applied for a lease from the Falkland Islands Government in 1907. Salvesen went on to become the largest whaling group in the world, although its activities in and around the Falklands diminished after the Second World War. When Salvesen was first approached by Davidoff in 1978 it hadn't engaged in commercial activities around the islands for thirteen years.

> From Salvesen's standpoint, the proposal offered an interesting prospect. Although they had no immediate commercial plans in the area, they wished to retain a stake in the future of South Georgia. Ideally, they wished to eliminate any possible future competition ... Davidoff gambled that the value of the scrap would be £7·5 million sterling at current prices. They calculated their direct and indirect costs at £3 million, so the theoretical profit of £4·5 million justified the effort involved. In the event, these figures were always highly optimistic and they became even more suspect when the onset of the world economic recession led to a fall in scrap-metal prices.

I am indebted to Roger Perkins, a naval historian, for details on the Salvesen contract. Roger Perkins, *Operation Paraquat* (Picton Publishing Ltd, 1986).
[2] Interview with high-ranking navy official conducted by author and María-Laura Avignolo.
[3] See Perkins, *Operation Paraquat*, pp. 32–3.
[4] Franks, *Falkland Islands Review*, p. 49.
[5] *Operation Paraquat*, p. 35.

Notes to Chapter 5

[1] For the attitude of the Bank of England, see Anthony Sampson, *The Changing Anatomy of Britain* (Hodder & Stoughton, 1982), pp. 266–8.
[2] Conversations with the author. See also a lecture given to a restricted group of bankers and businessmen, later produced in pamphlet form: Alemann, *La Politica Económica durante el Conflicto Austral: un Testimonio*.
[3] Report published in the Lima magazine, *Oiga,* quoting top-level military and government sources as its sources. See the *Guardian* (5 June 1985).
[4] Details of the links between Chile and Britain during the Falklands War were given in a press conference in Buenos Aires in October 1984 by Admiral Isaac Rojas, in an attempt to boost the 'no' vote during the Alfonsín government's referendum on its peace treaty with Chile. The treaty, confirming Chilean possession of three small islands in the Beagle Channel and granting Argentina increased territorial rights in the South Atlantic, was carried by a massive vote in favour. For further details on the Chilean connection I am indebted to Duncan Campbell. See his articles in the *New Statesman* (7 June 1985, 25 January 1985).
[5] Tomas Eloy Martínez, *La Novela de Perón* (Legasa, 1985), p. 21.
[6] See interview on 'Panorama', quoted in *The Times* (12 May 1986).
[7] See Verbitsky, *La Ultima Batalla*.
[8] See 'Asi Querian Vola la Roca', *Cambio 16* (24 October 1983), pp. 20–4.
[9] Verbitsky, *La Ultima Batalla*, analyses in detail the way the extreme nationalism

of the Montoneros influenced naval thinking on the Malvinas, replacing strategic with ideological considerations. The militarisation of the Montonero organisations is described in Richard Gillespie, *Soldiers of Perón* (Clarendon Press, 1982) and Pablo Giussani, *La Soberbia Armada* (Sudamericana/Planeta, 1984).

Chapter 6

[1] See the Argentine navy's only published account of the invasion, *Operación Rosario* (Editorial Atlántida, 1984), pp. 62–6.

[2] For an example see Juan Carlos Moreno, *La Recuperación de las Malvinas* (Plus Ultra, 1973).

[3] 'Bishops Give Junta's Troops a Sense of Crusade', *Financial Times* (12 May 1982).

[4] See Nicolas Kasanzew, *Malvinas a Sangre y Fuego* (Siete Dias, 1982).

[5] Kasanzew, *Malvinas a Sangre y Fuego*.

[6] The idea of the war against Britain as a holy crusade pervades most semi-official Argentine accounts of the war. For the army's view, see Carlos M. Túrolo, *Así Lucharon* (Sudamericana, 1982). For the air force's, see Pablo Marcos Carballo, *Dios y los Halcones* (Siete Dias/Editorial Abril, 1982).

[7] *Financial Times* (12 May 1982).

[8] See interview with the author, 'Envoy of Peace in Argentina', *Financial Times* (29 April 1982).

[9] Particularly suspicious of Monsignor Spraggon were the so-called 'professionals' – the commandos and intelligence officers in 601 and 602 Companies, who were specifically entrusted with keeping a careful watch on the islanders and the SAS. I. J. Ruiz Moreno, *Comandos en Acción, el Ejército en las Malvinas* (Emecé, 1986).

[10] Quoted in Sergio Cerón, *Malvinas, Gesta Heroica o Derrota Vergonzosa?* (Sudamericana, 1984).

[11] The anti-government magazine, *Humor*, never forgot that it was the junta fighting the war, although it did sympathise with what it believed was an 'anti-imperalist struggle'. Both *La Prensa* and *La Nación* had regular coverage – most of it competent – by their correspondents in London, Maximo Gainzer and Eduardo Crawley.

[12] Jacques Lesigne, correspondent of *Le Figaro*, was expelled from Argentina after being accused by the authorities of contravening the security laws. According to his colleagues, Lesigne had written an article suggesting that there was a growing feeling among Argentines that military defeat was near. For the atmosphere at the time see 'Lies, Damned Lies and Picture Book Heroes', *Financial Times* (4 June 1986).

[13] Interview with the author.

[14] Latin American Newsletters, *Guerra de las Malvinas y del Atlántico sur en Partes Oficiales y Comparativos* (Catálogos, 1983).

[15] Robert Harris, *Gotcha: the Media, the Government and the Falklands Crisis* (Faber & Faber, 1982). Another account of the Ministry of Defence's relationship with the media can be found in Valerie Adams, *The Media and the Falklands Campaign* (Macmillan, 1986).

[16] Cerón, *Malvinas, Gesta Heroica o Derrota Vergonzosa?*

[17] Robert Guareschi, the foreign editor of *Clarín*, predicted with accuracy the

downfall of the junta in a conversation with the author in mid-May 1982 – needless to say, his perceptions were never allowed to appear in print.

[18] Lieutenant-Colonel Herbert Jones, popularly dubbed Colonel 'H', was the commander of the Parachute Regiment on the Falklands. He was mortally wounded while leading an attack on an Argentine machine-gun position during the Battle of Goose Green on 29 May 1982. He was posthumously awarded Britain's highest military distinction, the Victoria Cross, for his gallantry.

Detailed accounts of Lieutenant-Colonel Jones's death were investigated by several well-respected British reporters with the Task Force, including Max Hastings, then of the *Evening Standard*, Patrick Bishop, then of the *Observer*, John Witherow, then of *The Times*, and Robert Fox, BBC, and, after the war, by military historian, Martin Middlebrook (*Operation Corporate, the Story of the Falklands War, 1982* [Viking, 1985]). Journalists and historian confirm that Jones was hit while running towards a fully manned Argentine trench. He was shot in the back of the neck by an Argentine machine post he had outflanked and left to his rear in dead ground. Middlebrook concludes, 'There is a comparison here with Captain Giachino, the commander of the Argentinan commandos who attacked Government House at Stanley on 2 April. Both officers were severely wounded at the head of their men in the first attacking moves made by their respective sides in the Falklands, and both bled to death. Both became national heroes . . .' (pp. 264–5).

After the war, the Argentine military went out of their way to rewrite the history of Colonel 'H' at a time when reports of his heroic death filtered through into the Argentine media and translations of the English Falklands books. Army Lieutenant Juan José Gómez Centurion of 601 Commando Company claimed in a TV documentary on the war that he had personally shot Colonel Jones after the British commando had allegedly tried to trick a group of Argentines into surrendering. Centurion's account, for which he himself was awarded a military distinction, became part of official Argentine history. His account was published in Ruiz Moreno, *Comandoes en Acción*.

[19] The professional and political promiscuity of much of the Argentine media was exposed in Eduardo Varela-Cid, *Los Sofistas y la Prensa Canalla* (El Cid Editor, 1984), a compilation of press cuttings from the period 1976–8. See Verbitsky, *La Ultima Batalla*, for Gente's reporting of the Falklands War.

[20] Quoted by the *Sunday Times* Insight team, *The Falklands War* (Sphere, 1982).

[21] The afternoon briefing was regularly brought to an abrupt halt by a correspondent for the *Daily Express* who insisted on punctuating each question with the word 'Falklands'.

[22] For a light-hearted but well-informed account of *carne podrida*, see Rogelio García Lupo, *Diplomacia Secreta y Rendición Incondicional* (Legasa, 1983).

[23] Graham-Yooll, *A State of Fear*. See also *The Press in Argentina, 1973–1978* by the same author.

Chapter 7

[1] See Sebreli, *Los Deseos Imaginarios del Peronismo*, and an illuminating essay by V. S. Naipaul, *The Return of Eva Perón* (André Deutsch, 1980).

[2] Quoted by Cerón, *Malvinas, Gesta Heroica o Derrota Vergonzosa?*

[3] See Cecil Woolf and Jean Moorcroft Wilson, *Authors Take Sides on the Falklands* (Cecil Woolf, 1982).

[4] Quoted by Cerón, *Malvinas, Gesta Heroica o Derrota Vergonzosa?*

[5] See Dabat and Lorenzano, *Argentina, the Malvinas and the End of Military Rule*.

[6] In 1980 Soriano was forced to publish the first of his three-part trilogy on contemporary Argentine history in Spain because Argentine publishers at the time feared a military reaction: *No Habrá mas Penas ni Olvido* (Bruguera, 1980).

[7] John King has provided some useful background on the élitist nature of Argentine culture and the inability of Borges's generation to understand and explain their country's political culture. See 'Victoria Ocampo, Sur y el Peronismo', *Revista de Occidente* (June 1984).

[8] During the war an original variation on the collective theme was provided by Jim Markham, the *New York Times* correspondent. During a night of revelry in Buenos Aires's sophisticated night club 'Mau Mau', the intrepid hack took to the dance floor, chanting to the many Argentines present, 'El que no baila es un Ingles' ('If you don't dance you're an Englishman').

[9] A thorough if somewhat sympathetic history of the British in Argentina is Andrew Graham-Yooll, *The Forgotten Colony* (Hutchinson, 1981).

[10] 'Los muchachos Peronistas, todos unidos venceremos' ('We the Perónist boys, united we'll win').

[11] Alexander M. Haig, *Memorias* (Editorial Atlántida, 1984). Haig also gives a revealing account of the difficulties of negotiating with a military regime which becomes increasingly divided within itself.

[12] According to highly placed Vatican sources, because of the Pope's sensitivity to the generally pro-Argentine feelings of the Italians and the pressure from his own close advisers, he sent word to the head of the English Catholic Church, Cardinal Basil Hume, that because of the development of the Falklands War he had been left with no choice but to postpone his trip to England. The Cardinal regarded the papal visit – the culmination of years of delicate arrangements – of historic and crucial importance for efforts towards ecumenicism. He promptly consulted a small group of trusted Catholics as to the best way of resurrecting the visit. Tom Burns, the then editor of the influential Catholic weekly, the *Tablet*, and Derek Worlock, the Archbishop of Liverpool, strongly argued that the papal visit should not only go ahead but also be used to good diplomatic ends in the Falklands dispute. It was Worlock who flew to Rome and managed to convince the Vatican to confirm the Pope's visit to Britain, while announcing at the same time that he would follow it up with a trip to Argentina. It was also agreed that during the Pope's visit to England his contacts with government officials should be kept to a minimum. The universality of the Church was further underlined in a jointly celebrated Mass held in Rome, to which English Bishops went rather less reluctantly than their Argentine counterparts.

Chapter 8

[1] Quoted in easily the best-researched and least biased account of the diplomatic and military aspects of the war to be written by Argentines, Cardoso, Kirschbaum and Van der Kooy, *Malvinas: la Trama Secreta*.

[2] *La Prensa* (1 July 1983).

[3] Daniel Kon, *Los Chicos de la Guerra* (Galerna, 1982). In the wake of the war several voluntary aid groups were set up in Argentina to offer medical and

psychological help to returning conscripts. Numerous articles were written on the subject. Perhaps the best summary of the sad fate of *los chicos* was written by the psychologists Ines Ghironzi and María Julia García. They wrote, 'There are six essentials on which a soldier should be able to count before going to war: a morally just war, good training, good equipment, confidence in senior officers, *esprit de corps* and a clear idea about the battle that lies ahead ... when they came back the only thing they still believed in was the justice of their cause. This was a noble sentiment but insufficient to win a war, and, in the end, of little consequence compared to the frustrations the conscripts brought back with them in exchange for their youth and the best part of their lives ...' See 'La Decepción fue peor que la Derrota', *La Voz* (31 October 1982). See also Dalmiro M. Bustos, *El Otro Frente de la Guerra: los Padres de las Malvinas* (Ramos Americana Editora, 1982) for an account written by the parents of the *chicos*, who suffered psychologically as much as their sons.

[4] Secret memorandum, Argentine air force, published in Cardoso, Kirschbaum and Van der Kooy, *Malvinas: la Trama Secreta*.

[5] David Rock, *Argentina, 1516–1982: from Spanish Colonisation to the Falklands War* (I. B. Tauris, 1986), p. 372.

Chapter 9

[1] Interview with the author, December 1983.

[2] See Hastings and Jenkins, *The Battle for the Falklands*.

[3] Yrigoyen gives an account of his ordeal at the hands of the military in *Los Años Crueles* (Bruguera, 1983).

[4] For the background to this I am indebted to supporters of the Uruguayan presidential candidate, Wilson Ferreira.

[5] Alfonsín's human rights record before he became President is not entirely without blemish. He was after all an Argentine not a picture-book saint. The Madres de la Plaza de Mayo recall an occasion in 1980 when a small group of them paid an unexpected visit to Alfonsín while he was spending the weekend in Chascomus. The women had just been to the seaside resort of Mar del Plata to identify some bodies which had been washed ashore. They found Alfonsín reclining in a deck-chair, looking both well fed and well drunk. He seemed visibly upset at having his weekend disturbed, and gave the women only a half-hearted commitment to intercede on their behalf.

In the same year Alfonsín privately considered supporting a project that was then circulating within the military, to declare the 'disappeared' officially 'dead'. Alfonsín appears genuinely to have felt that this would be of psychological help to the relatives of the disappeared. He only changed his mind thanks to a last-minute intervention by Emilio Mignone, the human rights lawyer, himself a parent of a 'disappeared' student. Mignone convinced Alfonsín that the only reason the military wanted to undertake such a project was because they believed that it would provide them with a legal loophole against being forced in the future to declare the whereabouts of their prisoners.

[6] See Alfonsín's two political autobiographies: *La Cuestión Argentina* (Propriesta Argentina, 1981), and *Ahora* (Sudamericana/Planeta, 1983).

[7] See Cardoso, Kirschbaum and Van der Kooy, *Malvinas: la Trama Secreta*.

Chapter 10

[1] For a detailed background history of the Argentine cinema, see *Historia del Cine Argentino* (Centro Editor de America Latina, 1984) by various authors.

[2] 'Argentina: Angels and Demons', *Index of Censorship* (6 December 1985). The article by Alberto Ciria, Professor of Political Science at Simon Fraser University, British Columbia, provides a penetrating insight into the extent to which culture in Argentina has been exploited for political ends, particularly during the Perónist governments.

[3] See Carlos Barulich, *La Listas Negras* (El Cid Editor, 1983). A 'black list', circulated by the junta in April 1981, for example, contained nearly 400 names from the cultural world including journalists, authors, actors and musicians. Among the internationally known Argentine artists unacceptable to the junta were Hector Alterio, Luis Brandoni, Norman Brinski and Norma Aleandro.

[4] For foreign films that managed to find their way to the Argentina of the juntas the year 1979 was perhaps typical. As *La Prensa* reported (13 March, 8 August 1979), two Spanish films, *Grande Vacaciones del '36* and *Carabina Nacional* were banned after being considered too anti-Franco. Bertolucci's *1900* was banned for being too 'offensive to the moral order and to the Christian ethic'; H. Ashby's *Coming Home* was banned for 'undermining family unity'; Leopoldo Torre Nilsson's *Piedra Libre* was banned then passed, before being banned again finally, 'because of its attacks on the family, religion, morality, tradition and other values and pillars of our society'. Woody Allen's *Manhattan* was shown on the condition that all references to lesbianism were cut; Bo Derek's *10* was judged too offensive heterosexually and suffered sixty-five cuts before being approved by the censors.

[5] John King, *Argentine Cinema* (Plymouth Arts Centre, 1986).

[6] *La Prensa* (24 July 1980).

[7] The military's definition of the Ente's role was summarised concisely by one of its directors, Captain Bitleston, 'Authorisation will only be given to films which depict the eternal and everyday struggle of mankind against materialism, egoism, despair, venality and corruption. Authorisation will also be given to films showing man defending his honour, religion or principles, without recourse to violence or scepticism. Only such films will be considered works of art' (*La Prensa*, 8 November 1977).

[8] Interview in the *Financial Times* (27 September 1985). During his first year in office, Antín fostered over fifty new productions and fifteen new directors. He described the renaissance of the cinema as the 'effervescent outpourings of an uncorked bottle of champagne'.

[9] Interview with the author, published in the *Observer* (8 September 1985).

[10] *Observer* (8 September 1985).

[11] The CONANEP official investigation into human rights violations registered 172 cases of children who 'disappeared' after the 1976 coup, most of whom were seized at the time of their mothers' detention or were taken away by the security forces after being born on their way to or inside a prison. Following the inauguration of Alfonsín as President, relatives belonging to the Abuelas de la Plaza de Mayo (Grandmothers of May Square) stepped up legal proceedings to recover more than thirty children whose whereabouts had been traced. The majority of the 'adoptive' parents turned out to belong to the former regime or were members of the police force.

[12] See King, *Argentine Cinema,* and Silvia María Hirsch, 'Argentine Cinema in the Transition to Democracy', *Third World Affairs* (1986), pp. 429–33.

[13] See film review, arts page, *Financial Times* (27 September 1985).

[14] Conversation with the author on location, June 1984.

[15] Eduardo Pavlovsky, *Index on Censorship*, 1 (1985).

[16] Edward Shaw, 'To Be or Not To Be – the Argentine Dilemma', *Buenos Aires Herald* (22 September 1985).

[17] Background based on an interview with the author.

[18] 'If one is to point to a sector of Argentine society that was singled out to be closely watched by the whole repressive and persecutory apparatus of the military government, then, inevitably, one must mention journalists' (CONANEP report). Rodolfo Walsh was perhaps the best-known of the numerous journalists who 'disappeared'. He was kidnapped by the security forces on 25 March 1977 and his body has never been recovered. The day before he disappeared, he wrote an 'open letter' to the junta, including the following, 'Press censorship, the persecution of intellectuals, the police raids on my house, the murder of dear friends, and the loss of a daughter who died fighting the dictatorship are some of the circumstances which oblige me to adopt this form of clandestine expression after having worked openly as a writer and journalist during almost thirty years.' Among the books exhibited in the book fair of the new democracy was Walsh's *Operation Massacre*, a courageous investigation into the circumstances surrounding the death of sixteen guerrillas shot while detained by the navy in the Patagonian town of Trelew in August 1972. During the government of General Alejandro Lanusse, Haroldo Conti won several international prizes for his literature and journalism. He was a regular contributor to the magazine, *Crisis*. He was abducted by the security forces on 4 May 1976.

[19] 'Letter from Argentina', *New Yorker* (21 July 1986).

[20] 'Argentina: the State of Transition, 1983-5', *Third World Quarterly* (July 1985).

[21] The most detailed recent studies on the history of Argentine education have been written by Emilio Mignone. See *Evalución de la Autonomía Universitaria en la Argentina* and *Relaciones entre el Sistema Político y el Sistema Educativo* (Editorial Docenia, 1986).

[22] According to the CONANEP report, of the nearly 9,000 documented cases of 'disappearances' 27 per cent were students and teachers.

[23] See José Pablo Feinman, 'Autoritarismo y Cultura', *Humor* (28 March 1984).

[24] This account is given in Simpson and Bennett, *The Disappeared*, pp. 19-20.

Chapter 11

[1] See Verbitsky, *La Ultima Batalla*.

[2] Verbitsky, *La Ultima Batalla*.

[3] See Dabat and Lorenzo, *Argentina, the Malvinas and the End of Military Rule*.

[4] Quoted to the author in conversation with highly placed military sources.

[5] 'When Is a Coup not a Coup?', *The Economist* (24 April 1985).

[6] *Index on Censorship* (April 1986).

[7] 'Argentina Discovers Its Past and Its Horror', *The Economist* (28 September 1985), pp. 43-4.

Chapter 12

[1] 'Report from Hell', *New York Review of Books* (17 July 1986), pp. 11–16.

[2] One of the most moving personal testimonies of the camps' repression is contained in Timerman, *Prisoner Without a Name, Cell Without a Number*.

[3] General Ramón Camps was appointed Chief of the Buenos Aires police following the 1976 coup. In 1986 he was put on trial by the Alfonsín government.

[4] Quoted in 'Report from Hell', *New York Review of Books*.

[5] Graham-Yooll, *A State of Fear*, pp. 156–7.

[6] Between 1982 and 1986 the navy continued to reap the benefits of ship contracts placed in the run-up to the Beagle Channel dispute in 1978. Acquisitions include a force of four TR-1700 submarines from West Germany, with an attack speed of over twenty knots and a submerged endurance of seventy days, and four MEKO 360-H2 destroyers, also from West Germany. France meanwhile has continued to deliver Superétendards equipped with Exocet missiles.

Re-equipment: number of planes

	Prewar (approx.)	Current (approx.)	Supplier
Air Force	115	120	France, Israel, Peru
Naval Air Force	16	20	Israel, France

Source: General Sir Hugh Beach, 'British Defence Policy and the South Atlantic', *South Atlantic Council Occasional Papers* (May 1986). See also Paul Rogers, 'An Assessment of Argentine Re-armament, *Peace Studies Briefing*, no. 19 (University of Bradford).

[7] Direct State subsidies to the Church are channelled out of the Treasury and represent about 0·27 per cent of the national budget; but the main State support goes to private Catholic schools where the salaries of all teaching staff are paid out of Treasury funds. Local authorities are also reponsible for funding Church-backed schemes considered to be of 'social or cultural interest'. See Emilio Mignone, *Iglesia y Dictadura* (Ediciones de Pensiamento Nacional, 1986), pp. 154–64.

[8] See an article on the Church's influence on Argentine society, 'Iglesia y Dictadura', *El Periodista* (22 September 1984).

[9] 'Ill at Ease with Democracy', *Tablet* (27 April 1985), pp. 421–3.

[10] Elsewhere only Paraguay, Andorra, San Marino and Ireland (Eire) remained as inflexible on the issue of divorce.

[11] For a detailed if now somewhat dated account of the Labour party's links with the TUC, see Robert Taylor, *The Fifth Estate* (Pan, 1980).

[12] Described in Joseph Page, *Perón: a Biography* (Random House, 1983). For a colourful account of Perón's rise to power, see also Félix Luna, *El 45* (Sudamericana, 1982).

[13] See A. Borrini, *Política y Sociedad, Cómo Se Hace un Presidente* (El Coronista Comercial, 1984).

[14] Reported by the author for the *Observer* foreign news service, May 1984.

[15] For the fullest account of the Ezeiza massacre see Horacio Verbitsky, *Ezeiza* (Contrapunto, 1986).

[16] *Observer* foreign news service.

[17] See a report by the author, 'Alfonsín Leads from the Front', *Financial Times* (18 June 1985).

[18] See a report by the author, 'Argentines Put Their Money Behind Alfonsín', *Financial Times* (28 June 1985).

[19] Robert Graham, 'Alfonsín Clears the First Hurdle', *Financial Times* (30 July 1985).

[20] 'Argentina's Union Bosses Take a Turn to the Right', *Guardian* (2 September 1986).

[21] See 'Austerity Boost for Trade Unionists', *Irish Times* (30 July 1986), and 'Argentine Union Crusader Takes on Alfonsín', *Financial Times* (9 October 1986).

[22] Figures on European and US trade-union density were provided by Philip Bassett. See his article, 'At War with a Wasting Disease', *Financial Times* (28 August 1986).

[23] I am indebted to my colleague Tim Coone in Buenos Aires for his research on union elections in Argentina.

[24] *Financial Times* (17 October 1986).

[25] The CGT became increasingly insistent in its demands for a moratorium on all debt payments following the implementation of the 'austral plan'.

[26] For an account of the 'Baring crash', see David Rock, *Argentina, 1516–1982* (I. B. Tauris, 1986).

[27] Deborah Rimer, 'The Future of Banking and Finance in Latin America', *Latin American and Caribbean Review* (World of Information, 1983), p. 19.

[28] The group of military officers jailed by the Alfonsín government soon after it came to power included Brigadier Osvaldo Cacciatore accused of various offences linked mainly to financial corruption. As the newly appointed mayor of Buenos Aires under the juntas, Cacciatore had declared boldly that under him Buenos Aires was to be transformed. And indeed it was. Cacciatore's *projetos faraónicos* (Pharaonic plans) so dubbed by the mayor himself in memory of the Egyptian pyramids, included a massive road-building programme designed to speed traffic out of the capital towards the airport. Over 2,000 houses, among them *fin de siècle* buildings of considerable historic and aesthetic value, were bulldozed, as were the squatter settlements which were dotted around the city. Construction of the project, costing an estimated one billion dollars, was never finished. However, the destruction wrought by Cacciatore in the centre of Buenos Aires was equivalent to the fall-out from a small nuclear bomb. A no less ambitious scheme was the building of an ecological 'green belt' around the capital including a Disney-type amusement park. 'Interama', as the project was called, turned into one of the biggest financial scandals of the military regime when it was discovered that much of it had been used as a front for contraband. The 'green belt' also became shrouded in gruesome rumour. It was widely believed that the rubbish tips over which the grass was sown contained the mangled bodies of many of the 'disappeared'. For more details of Cacciatore's corruption, see Simpson and Bennett, *The Disappeared*.

[29] See Aldo Ferrer, *Poner la Casa en Orden* (El Cid Editor, 1984).

[30] See Ferrer, *Poner la Casa en Orden*.

[31] Based on conversations with several government officials within the Economy Ministry.

[32] Alfonsín's first Cabinet bore the unmistakable stamp of the President. It was picked from an entourage of academics, lawyers, economists and trade union officials who had supported him since 1972 when he first formed 'Renewal and Change', a centre-left faction within the Radical party. One of two surprises was the appoint-

ment of Dante Caputo, a thirty-nine-year-old sociology graduate of the Sorbonne with no previous ministerial or diplomatic experience to head the Foreign Ministry. The other was the choice of sixty-year-old independent print union official, Antonio Mucci, to head the Labour Ministry. Raúl Borras, one of the main strategists, with Caputo, of Alfonsín's election campaign was given the Ministry of Defence. The one exception in an otherwise closely knit clique was Antonio Troccoli, a member of the conservative wing of the Radical party and former rival of Alfonsín, who was given the post of Minister of the Interior to ensure the unity of the party.

[33] I am indebted to my colleague, Peter Montagnon of the *Financial Times*, for his insights into how Grinspún was perceived from the 'other side' of the negotiating table. Montagnon was Euromarkets correspondent throughout the Latin American debt crisis.

[34] See 'Argentina's Creditors Grow Impatient', *Financial Times* (1 February 1984).

[35] On 10 June 1984, Argentina took the step – unprecedented for a major debtor country – of signing a 'letter of intent' to the IMF in open defiance of the recommendations of the Fund's special mission to Buenos Aires headed by Eduardo Weisner, the director for the western hemisphere division. While reaffirming that Argentina was willing to honour its debt obligations, the Alfonsín government issued a statement emphasising that the 'realistic possibilities of payment are rooted in economic recovery and defence of social justice ... the rescheduling of the foreign debt must proceed on the basis of an economic programme which makes it possible to deploy Argentina's full potential without impairing the interests of the country or national dignity.' Both the tone of the letter and the manner in which it was written went against all the known orthodoxies of the IMF and was received with profound shock, if not outrage, by Argentina's commercial bank creditors.

[36] Anatole Kaletsky, 'Debating Debt Default', *Third World Affairs* (August 1986). For a more detailed account of Kaletsky's arguments, see his *The Cost of Default* (Twentieth Century Fund, New York, 1985).

[37] See *Financial Times* (15 September 1986).

[38] Pedro Pablo Kuczynski, 'Latin American Debt: Act Two', *Foreign Affairs* (Autumn 1983).

[39] See Everett Martin, *Wall Street Journal* (5 December 1985).

[40] *Financial Times* (9 November 1985).

[41] *Financial Times* (9 September, 1986).

[42] Another novel approach to the debt issue endorsed by the Alfonsín government was a plan to capitalise part of the debt, along with a tax amnesty on undeclared property and capital sums held by Argentine citizens outside the country. The capitalisation scheme announced by Mario Brodersohn, the Under-Secretary for Finance, would enable holders of Argentinian debt, mainly foreign banks, to sell their outstanding loans to potential investors in existing Argentinian industry or in new ventures. Provided that investors bring at least one extra US dollar of fresh money for every dollar of debt purchased at a discount (at the time running at around 30 per cent in the international money markets), they would have the debt certificates immediately paid off in full in local currency with which they would then be able to invest in Argentina. When first announced, the scheme appeared to be particularly attractive to smaller foreign banks holding Argentine debts, which wished to extricate themselves from the danger of further exposure during each renegotiation cycle of interest payments on Argentina's foreign debt. It was hoped that the capitalisation scheme would create greater opportunity for banks to reduce

their exposure in Argentina at the same time as boosting foreign investment. See *Financial Times* (15 August 1986).

[43] See Kaletsky, 'Debating Debt Default', *Third World Affairs*.

[44] Rock, *Argentina, 1516–1982*.

[45] See Aldo Ferrer, *La Posguerra* (El Cid Editor, 1982), and *Vivir con lo Nuestro* (El Cid Editor, 1983).

[46] A final figure for the number of Argentine military killed has never been established, although the official figure of 1,200 is undoubtedly an underestimate.

[47] Typical of the new optimism generated by the coming of Alfonsín, with its emphasis on Argentina becoming a modern nation through the exploitation of its natural economic potential, is Rodolfo Terragno, *La Argentina del Siglo 21* (Sudamericana/Planeta, 1985), which became a bestseller in Argentina.

[48] *Financial Times* (15 August 1986).

[49] See 'Brazil's Pact with Argentina', *Financial Times* (1 August 1986).

[50] In spite of striking, often divergent views, on issues like regional debt and Central America (where the Alfonsín government has been a strong critic of US military involvement) relations between Buenos Aires and Washington recovered from the tension generated by the Falklands War. Argentine Foreign Minister, Dante Caputo, recognised that the United States could be a useful ally for democracy, keeping the military at bay and exercising some influence on the international banking community, and on Britain over the Falklands. In March 1985 Alfonsín went on a six-day official visit to Washington to improve trade and political relations between his country and what, during the Falklands War, became for many Argentines the 'enemy'. Two-way trade with the United States remained an important factor of economic life in the years 1983–6, although steel, textiles and leather were among the leading Argentine exports affected by US quotas. The Argentines also engaged in a price war with the United States over subsidised grain exports to the Soviet Union. See *Financial Times* (18 March 1985).

Alfonsín paid several official and semi-official visits to Western Europe in the years 1983–6. Cultural and political ties brought Argentina particularly close to Italy and Spain (Argentina has large Spanish and Italian communities, and Alfonsín always felt a strong personal respect for Italian President Sandro Pertini and for Felipe González of Spain). Argentine officials also boasted a strong 'special relationship' with France as a result of the support given to members of the Alfonsín government during exile in Paris. Dante Caputo was for a time one of these 'exiles', and later married a member of the French Foreign Ministry. On the investment side, the Alfonsín government maintained strong ties with companies like Siemens, Kraftwerk Union and Mercedes Benz, which have a considerable stake in Argentina. In April 1985 Siemens – whose interests in Argentina spanned energy installations, electrical hardware, hospital equipment and nuclear power – made a successful bid for Standard Electric, the troubled local ITT subsidiary of Standard Electric. See 'Alfonsín Seeks European Investment', *Financial Times* (16 September 1985).

[51] The feasibility of the 'austral plan' was first considered at the Catholic University (PUC) in Río de Janeiro in 1984, when a group of young economists began to look for models to combat Brazil's chronic inflation. The principal Brazilian academics involved were Perso Arida, Andre Lara Resende and Francisco Lopes. Their ideas were picked up and discussed by visiting Argentine economists, including Robert Frenkel. The cross-fertilisation occurred when Bernardo Grinspún was sacked as Economy Minister in March 1985 and Frenkel was brought on to the staff of the new Minister Juan Sourrouille. For the background to the launching of

the 'austral plan', see 'Brazil and Argentina Swap ideas on Economic Plans', *Financial Times* (2 May 1986). Also 'Latin Surprise', *Wall Street Journal* (5 December 1986).

[52] 'Brazil's Pact with Argentina', *Financial Times*.

[53] Article by author in *Latin American and Caribbean Review* (1986), pp. 33–5.

[54] See *Financial Times* (5 August 1985).

[55] General Suárez Masón was appointed President of YPF following the 1976 coup. Alfonsín ordered his arrest in November 1985 in connection with a plot to destabilise the government. He remained a fugitive from justice, having disappeared soon after the end of the Falklands War.

[56] One important initiative held up was the government's plan to sell off State shares in companies linked to the military–industrial complex, Fabricaciones Militares. The companies chosen by the Economy Minister, Juan Sourrouille, in February 1986 were the steel giant, Somisa, the petrochemical companies, Bahía Blanca, General Mosconi and Río Tercero, and the chemicals group, Antanor. Subsequently the government was faced with complex vested interests, including those spanning three major Ministries – Defence, Economy and Public Works – each of which had shares in the companies and theoretically had a veto on any decision about their futures. See *Financial Times* (26 February 1986). Another reform which was held up was one to correct the distortions in the banking system caused by the military's policies. See 'Argentina Grapples with Banking Reform', *Financial Times* (16 October 1986).

[57] See *Financial Times* (17 April 1986) and *Washington Post* (2 October 1986).

[58] *Washington Post* (2 October 1986).

Chapter 13

[1] The BBC journalist who sailed in HMS *Canberra* and accompanied the first troops ashore at San Carlos when the British moved to recover the islands has provided an interesting account of the threat posed by the *Belgrano* and the vulnerability of the Task Force:

> The first weekend in May, the carrier force was engaged in air battles over the Falklands and ground attacks on Stanley and Goose Green. This would mean little cover for the small force on South Georgia. If the *Belgrano* had eluded the main Task Force and the submarine shadow, she would have flattened Grytwiken and Port Leith on South Georgia with her big guns in a matter of hours. Superficially, the sinking of the cruiser outside the exclusion zone seemed diplomatic ineptitude, but on closer examination it indicates how vulnerable the whole of the British sea operation was at this stage.

Robert Fox, *Eyewitness Falklands* (Methuen, 1982), p. 49.

[2] Interview with high-ranking naval official conducted by author and María-Laura Avignolo.

[3] A British parliamentary inquiry into the sinking of the *Belgrano* conducted in July 1985 concedes that the nuclear submarine *Conqueror* had been in contact with the cruiser's oil tanker auxiliary on 30 April, and was in visual contact with the cruiser *Belgrano* herself on 1 May. When hit, the cruiser had been steaming away from the Task Force and not closing in, as first reported by John Knott, the British Defence Secretary, on 4–5 May 1982. However, the inquiry concludes, 'that there

was no evidence that such a withdrawal would have been intended to achieve anything other than short-term tactical advantage ... there was no reason to suppose that the decision to authorise the sinking of the *Belgrano* was not militarily justified.' 'Events Surrounding the Weekend of 1–2 May', *Foreign Affairs Committee*, House of Commons Papers 11 (HMSO, 1982). Labour MPs dissociated themselves from the conclusions of the inquiry, insisting that the government did mount a cover-up of the events leading to the sinking of the *Belgrano* and the absence of government reaction to warnings about an impending Argentine invasion of the Falklands. See *Financial Times* (25 July 1985).

⁴ In November 1986 Juan Carlos Heinze, a conscript sailor who survived the sinking of the *Belgrano*, sued the British government in a suit filed in Buenos Aires for the psychological and physical injuries he had allegedly suffered as a result. He argued that both the sinking and the injuries he suffered were the product of 'an act that was clearly and unequivocably illegitimate'. The suit concluded that the attack represented 'one of the most unjustifiable violations of the rights of people and of all the ethical and judicial norms erected by mankind to protect the right to life'. *The Times* (11 November 1986).

⁵ Desmond Rice and Arthur Gavshon, *The Sinking of the* Belgrano (Secker & Warburg, 1984).

⁶ Article 756, *Rattenbach Report*. The first detailed official Argentine inquiry into the military conduct of the Falklands War was leaked to *La Voz* and *La Nacion*, two Buenos Aires newspapers, on 24 August 1983, but the report was never published officially by the military.

⁷ Jackson Diehl, 'The Spectre at the Heart of Argentina's Ills', *Washington Post* (10 January 1985).

⁸ The trial on charges of human rights violations of the nine members of the juntas which ruled Argentina between 1976 and 1982 began in April 1985. Verdicts were passed in December 1985. Of the first three-man junta, General Jorge Videla (army) and Admiral Emilio Massera (navy) received life sentences, but General Orlando Agosti (air force) received 4 years. Of the second junta, General Roberto Viola (army) was sentenced to 17 years in prison, Admiral Armando Lambruschini (navy) to 8 years, and General Omar Grafigna was acquitted. The third junta was acquitted of all charges, but its members, General Leopoldo Galtieri (army), Admiral Jorge Anaya (navy) and General Basilio Lami Dozo (air force) were subsequently put on trial before a military court martial board for negligence during the Falklands War. Verdicts were passed in May 1986. Anaya was judged the most guilty and was condemned to 14 years in prison; Galtieri to 12 years; and Lami Dozo to 8 years; the lighter sentence reflecting the good performance of the Argentine air force against the British Task Force. Towards the end of 1986, Galtieri was facing a third trial for his responsibility for human rights violations when he was commander of the Second Army Corps based in Rosario between 1976 and 1979 before becoming army chief.

⁹ Carr, *Modern Spain*.

¹⁰ See the *Observer* (11 December 1983). Alfonsín told me, 'A fundamental argument that used to be held by people in Britain as a reason for not negotiating with us has now disappeared. We are no longer a *de facto* regime, nor are we run by a dictatorship. We Argentines have finally understood that we will always be a tin-pot country if we don't follow a golden rule: the armed forces must come under the firm control of the civilian powers.' In the interview Alfonsín did not specifically declare an end to hostilities, but he indicated that he would take such a move if

Mrs Thatcher agreed to lift the 150-mile exclusion zone around the islands and to freeze the construction of the new airport. The newly elected Argentine President strongly supported Argentina's claim over the Falklands, but suggested that 'lease-back', a British lease of the Falklands after Argentine sovereignty had been recognised, could possibly be a basis for a future deal.

[11] See Dr Peter Gold, *The Liberals and the Falklands/Malvinas*, background paper prepared for the meeting in Madrid between President Alfonsín and David Steel, leader of the British Liberal party on 6 October 1985.

[12] The triumphalism and easy slogans of the past still seemed to permeate Argentine culture – 'Las Malvinas son nuestras' ('The Malvinas are Argentine') – and were shared by political leaders as they had been by the military. Little initial attempt seems to have been made to alter the school texts which represent one of the few bridges built between successive governments since the Second World War. Children were told, 'There they are, our Malvinas/Between foams of water and salt./The wind says [they are] Argentine/[They are] Argentine cries the sea!' And, 'By their location and their history, these islands are Argentine without discussion.' See Alberto Ciria, 'Angels and Demons', *Index on Censorship* (6 December 1985), pp. 46–9.

[13] In July 1984 the British Foreign Office made every effort to meet Argentine officials for the first talks between the two sides since the end of the war in Berne, Switzerland. On the British side in particular weeks of delicate and generally secret diplomatic footwork had gone into the preparation of the talks and it seemed fair to assume that Whitehall would not have acceded to them unless they thought there was a reasonable chance of success. The formula agreed to by both sides was that the Argentine delegation would be allowed to raise the issue of sovereignty and that in reply the British would say simply they were not prepared to discuss it. Then both sides would agree – at least in the opening round – to talk about other items such as the resumption of diplomatic links and the demilitarisation of the South Atlantic. The formula, however, never materialised. Argentine officials insisted from the outset that the British should agree to a discussion of a 'firm and sure' mechanism for the transfer of sovereignty of the islands. Without this, they insisted, there was no point in discussing anything else.

[14] Peter Riddell, *The Thatcher Government* (Basil Blackwell, 1985).

[15] In a television documentary, 'The Englishwoman's Wardrobe', BBC 2, 20 November 1986, Thatcher revealed that her most cherished dress was a 'sombre dark navy creation' which had sustained her through the Falklands conflict.

[16] General Sir Hugh Beach, *British Defence Policy in the South Atlantic*, South Atlantic Occasional Papers, 2 (May 1986).

[17] Anthony Barnett, *Iron Britannia* (Allison & Busby, 1982).

[18] Hastings and Jenkins, *The Battle for the Falklands*.

[19] Interview with the author.

[20] Kasanzew, *Malvinas a Sangre y Fuego*.

[21] *International Affairs* (April 1985).

[22] *Financial Times* (19 November 1986).

[23] R. Harvey, 'A Way Out of the Falklands Jam', *Sunday Times* (24 February 1985).

[24] Robert Graham, 'Economics of the Falklands', *Financial Times* (25 January 1985). For a more detailed account of Falklands policy in the years 1982–6, see Robert Fox, *Antarctica and the South Atlantic: Discovery, Development and Dispute* (BBC, 1985).

[25] 'Why the Falklands Matter', *The Times* (22 April 1985).

SELECT BIBLIOGRAPHY

General

Couseló, Jorge Miguel, *Historia del Cine Argentino* (Centro Editor de America Latina, 1984).

Crawley, Eduardo, *A House Divided: Argentina 1880–1980* (C. Hurst & Co., 1984).

Escudé, Carlos, *La Declinación Argentina* (Editorial Belgrano, 1983).

Ferns, H. S., *Britain and Argentina in the Nineteenth Century* (Oxford University Press, 1960).

—— *La Argentina* (Solar/Hachette 1979).

García, César, *Historia de los Grupos y Partidos Politicos* (Saint Claire, 1983).

Graham-Yooll, Andrew, *The Forgotten Colony* (Hutchinson, 1981).

Imaz, José Luis de, *Los que Mandan* (Eudeba, 1964).

López, Alonso, Gerardo, *Cincuenta Años de Historia Argentina* (Belgrano, 1982).

Luna, Félix, *Buenos Aires y el Pais* (Sudamericana, 1982).

Lynch, John, *The Spanish American Revolutions, 1808–26* (Weidenfeld & Nicolson, 1973).

Martínez Estrada, Ezequiel, *Radiografía de la Pampa* (Losada, 1942).

—— *La Cabeza de Goliath* (Losada, 1943).

Massuh, Victor, *La Argentina Como Sentimiento* (Sudamericana, 1983).

Matamoro, Blas, *La Ciudad del Tango* (Galerna, 1982).

Rock, David, *Argentina 1516–1982: From Spanish Colonisation to the Falklands War* (I. B. Tauris & Co., 1986).

Sarmiento, Domingo F., *Facundo* (Editorial Kapelusz, 1971).

Scobie, James, *Argentina: a City and a Nation* (Oxford University Press, 1971).

Fiction and Travel

Arlt, Roberto, *Los Siete Locos* (Losada, 1973).

Asís, Jorge, *Los Reventados* (Sudamericana, 1982).

Borges, Jorge Luís, *Obras Completas* (Emecé, 1974).

Chatwin, Bruce, *In Patagonia* (Jonathan Cape, 1977).

Cortázar, Julio (trans.), *Cronopios and Famas* (Marion Boyars, 1978).

Cunningham Graham, R. B., *The Horses of the Conquest* (Heinemann, 1930).

Darwin, Charles, *Charles Darwin's Diary of the Voyage of the* HMS Beagle (Cambridge University Press, 1933).

Fogwill, Rodolfo, *Los Pichy-Cyegos* (Ediciones de la Flor, 1983).

SELECT BIBLIOGRAPHY

Hudson, W. H., *Far Away and Long Ago* (Dent, 1962).
Lucas Bridges, E., *Uttermost Limits of the Earth* (Hodder & Stoughton, 1948).
Mujica Laínez, Manuel, *Misteriosa Buenos Aires* (Sudamericana, 1985).
Puig, Manuel, *Boquitas Pintadas* (Sudamericana, 1969).
Sábato, Ernesto, *Sobre Heroes y Tumbas* (Sudamericana, 1984).
Soriano, Osvaldo, *No Habrá más Penas ni Olvido* (Bruguera, 1982).
Theroux, Paul, *The Old Patagonian Express* (Penguin, 1979).

Radicalism

Alfonsín, Raúl, *La Cuestión Argentina* (Propuesta Argentina, 1981).
—— *Ahora* (Sudamericana/Planeta, 1983).
Luna, Felix, *Yrigoyen* (Belgrano, 1981).
Rock, David, *Politics in Argentina: 1890–1930* (Cambridge University Press, 1975).
—— *Radical Populism and the Conservative Elite: Argentina in the Twentieth Century* (Duckworth, 1975).
Snow, Peter G., *El Radicalismo Argentino* (Francisco de Aguirre, 1972).
Solari Yrigoyen, Hipólito, *Los Años Crueles* (Bruguera, 1983).

Perónism

Barnes, John, *Evita – First Lady: a biography of Eva Perón* (Grove Press, 1978).
Di Tella, Guido, *Perón–Perón, 1973–6* (Sudamericana, 1983).
Gillespie, Richard, *Soldiers of Perón: Argentina's Montoneros* (Clarendon Press, 1982).
Giussani, Pablo, *La Soberbia Armada* (Sudamericana/Planeta, 1984).
Graham-Yooll, Andrew, *Tiempo de Violencia* (Granica, 1973).
Horowicz, Alejandro, *Los Cuatro Peronismos* (Legasa, 1985).
Luna, Félix, *El 45* (Sudamericana, 1982).
Naipaul, V. S., *The Return of Eva Perón* (André Deutsch, 1980).
Navarro, Marysa, and Fraser, John, *Eva Perón* (André Deutsch, 1980).
Page, Joseph, *Perón: a Biography* (Random House, 1983).
Pena, Milciades, *El Peronismo* (Fichas, 1973).
Perón, Evita, *La Razón de Mi Vida* (Peuser, 1951).
Perón, Juan Domingo, *Los Estados Unidos de America del Sur* (Corregidor, 1982).
Sábato, Ernesto, *El Otro Rostro del Peronismo* (López, 1956).
Sebreli, Juan José, *Los Deseos Imaginarios del Peronismo* (Legasa, 1983).
Verbitsky, Horacio, *Ezeiza* (Contrapunto, 1986).

SELECT BIBLIOGRAPHY

The Military

Aguinís, Marcos, *Carta Esperanzada a un General* (Sudamericana/Planeta, 1984).

Cantón, Idario, *La Política de los Militares Argentinos: 1900–71* (Siglo-veintiuno, 1971).

Luna, Félix, *Golpes Militares* (Sudamericana, 1983).

O'Brien, Philip, and Cammack, Paul (eds), *Generals in Retreat: the Crisis of Military Rule in Latin America* (Manchester University Press, 1985).

O'Donnell, Guillermo, *El Estado Burocrático Autoritario* (Belgrano, 1982).

Philip, George, *The Military in South American Politics* (Croom Helm, 1985).

Potash, Robert, *The Army and Politics in Argentina*, 2 vols (Stanford University Press, 1969).

Ramos, J. A. (ed.), *El Cordobazo* (Editorial Octubre, 1974).

Rattenbach, Benjamín, *Sobre el País y las Fuerzas Armadas* (Emecé, 1975).

Roth, Roberto, *Los años de Onganía* (La Campana, 1981).

Rouquié, Alain, *Poder Militar y Sociedad Política,* 2 vols (Emecé, 1983).

The Unions

Rotondaro, Ruben, *Realidad y Cambio en el Sindicalismo* (Pleamar, 1971).

Senen González, Santiago, *Diez Años de Sindicalismo Argentino* (Corregidor, 1984).

Torre, Juan Carlos, *Los Sindicatos en el Gobierno 1973–6* (Centro Editor de Americana Latina, 1983).

The Church

Mignone, Emilio, *Iglesia y Dictadura* (Ediciones de Pensamiento Nacional, 1986).

The Process of National Reorganisation

Aldaburu, María Inés (ed.), *Diario Colectivo* (La Campana, 1982).

Barulich, Carlos, *Las listas negras* (El Cid Editor, 1983).

Bonasso, Miguel, *Recuerdos de la Muerte* (Bruguera, 1984).

Bousquet, Jean-Pierre, *Las Locas de la Plaza de Mayo* (El Cid Editor, 1983).

Duhalde, Eduardo, *El Estado Terrorista Argentino* (Argos-Vergara, 1983).

Gabetta, Carlos, *Todos Somos Subversivos* (Bruguera, 1984).

Graham-Yooll, Andrew, *A State of Fear* (Eland, 1986).

Hagelin, Ragnar, *Mi Hija Dagmar* (Sudamericana-Planeta, 1984).

Kirkpatrick, Jeane J., *Dictadura y Contradicción* (Sudamericana, 1982).

SELECT BIBLIOGRAPHY

Lozada, Salvador (ed.), *La Ideología de la Seguridad Nacional* (El Cid Editor, 1983).
Nosiglia, Julio, *Botín de Guerra*, an account of the 'disappeared children' (Tierra fertil, 1985).
Rouquié, Alain (ed.), *Argentina Hoy* (Siglo Veintiuno, 1982).
Sábato, Jorge, *Ensayos de Humor* (Ediciones de la Urraca, 1983).
Timerman, Jacobo, *Prisoner Without a Name, Cell Without a Number* (Weidenfeld & Nicolson, 1981).
Varela Cid, Eduardo (ed.), *Los Sofistas y la Prensa Canalla* (El Cid Editor, 1984).
Vázquez, Enrique, *La Ultima* (Eudeba, 1985).

The Economy

De Pablo, Juan Carlos, *Los Economistas y la Economía Argentina* (Ediciones Macchi, 1977).
Díaz Alejandro, Carlos, *Essays on the Economic History of the Argentine Republic* (Yale University Press, 1970).
Ferrer, Aldo, *The Argentine Economy* (University of California Press, 1967).
—— *La Posguerra* (El Cid Editor, 1982).
—— *Puede Argentina Pagar Su Deuda Externa?* (El Cid Editor, 1983).
—— *Vivir con lo Nuestro* (El Cid Editor, 1983).
—— *Poner la Casa en Orden* (El Cid Editor, 1984).
Randall, Laura, *An Economic History of Argentina in the Twentieth Century* (Columbia University Press, 1973).
Rivas, Armado, *Inflación: La Experiencia Argentina* (El Cronista Comercial, 1980).

Falklands Malvinas

HISTORY

Bennett, Geoffrey, *Colonel and the Falklands* (Pan, 1982).
Foulkes, Haroldo, *Las Malvinas: una Causa Nacional* (Corregidor, 1982).
—— *Los Kelpers* (Galerna, 1983).
Goebel, Julius, *The Struggle for the Falkland Islands,* preface by J. C. Metford (Yale University Press, 1982).
Groussac, Paul, *Las Islas Malvinas* (Lugar Editorial, 1982).
Holmberg, Adolfo, *Cree Usted que los Ingleses nos Devolveran las Malvinas? Yo No* (Grandes Temas, 1977).
Lanus, Juan, *De Chapultepec al Beagle* (Emecé, 1984).
Moreno, Juan Carlos, *La Recuperación de Las Malvinas* (Plus Ultra, 1973).
Moro, Rubén, *La Guerra Ináudita* (Pleamar, 1986).
Ravenal, Eugenio, *Las Islas de la Discordia* (Sudamericana, 1983).

SELECT BIBLIOGRAPHY

Silenzi de Stagni, Adolfo, *Las Malvinas y el Petroleo* vol. I (El Cid Editor, 1982), vol. II (Teoria, 1983).

Solari Yrigoyen, Hipólito, *Asi son las Malvinas* (Hachette, 1959).

Strange, Ian, *The Falkland Islands* (David & Charles, 1983).

THE WAR: BOOKS PUBLISHED IN ARGENTINA

Aliverti, Eduardo, and Montenegro, Nestor, *Los Nombres de la Derrota* (Nemont Ediciones, 1982).

Andrada, B., *Guerra Aérea en las Malvinas* (Emecé Editores, 1983).

Arevalo, Oscar, *Malvinas, Beagle, Atlantico Sur* (Anteo, 1985).

Bustos, Dalmiro, *El Otro Frente de la Guerra: los Padres de las Malvinas* (Ramos Americana Editora, 1982).

Cabral, Antonio (ed.), *Guerra Santa nas Malvinas* (São Paolo EMW Editores, 1982).

Calvi, Mario, *Malvinas el Mito Destruido* (Ediciones Devoto, 1982).

Carballo, Pablo, *Dios y los Halcones* (Siete dias/Editorial Abril, 1982).

Cerón, Sergio, *Malvinas: Gesta Heroica o Derrota Vergonzosa?* (Sudamericana, 1984).

Del Carril, Bonifacio, *El Futuro de las Malvinas* (Emecé, 1982).

Foulkes, Haroldo, *74 Dias Halucinantes en Puerto Argentino* (Corregidor, 1984).

Gamba, Virginia, *El Peón de la Reina* (Sudamericana, 1984).

Gambini, Hugo, *Crónica Documental de las Malvinas* (Redacción/Sánchez Teruelo, 1982).

García Lupo, Rogelio, *Diplomacia Secreta y Rendición Incondicional* (Legasa, 1983).

Haig, Alexander (trans.), *Memorias* (Atlantida, 1984).

Hernández, Pablo, and Chitarroni, Horacio, *Malvinas: Clave Geopolítica* (Castaneda, 1982).

Kasanzew, Nicolas, *Malvinas a Sangre y Fuego* (Editorial Abril, 1982).

Kon, Daniel, *Los Chicos de la Guerra* (Galerna, 1982).

Mafezzini, Ángel, *Días de un Cura Soldado* (Argentine Navy Publication, 1982).

Moreno, Ruiz I. J., *Comandos en Acción: el Ejército en las Malvinas* (Emecé, 1986).

Roth, Roberto, *Después de las Malvinas, Qué?* (La Campana, 1982).

Schonfeld, Manfred, *La Guerra Austral* (Desafíos Editores, 1982).

Simeoni, Hector, *Malvinas: Contrahistoria* (Editorial Inédita, 1984).

Turolo, Carlos, *Así Lucharon* (Sudamericana, 1982).

—— *Malvinas, Testimonio de Su Gobernador* (Sudamericana, 1983).

Verbitsky, Horacio, *La Ultima Batalla de la Tercera Guerra Mundial* (Legasa, 1985).

SELECT BIBLIOGRAPHY

THE WAR: BOOKS PUBLISHED IN BRITAIN

Adams, Valerie, *The Media and the Falklands War* (Macmillan, 1986).

Barnett, Anthony, *Iron Britannia: Why Britain Waged Its Falklands War* (Allison & Busby, 1982).

Bishop, Patrick, and Witherow, John, *The Winter War* (Quartet, 1982).

Calvert, Peter, *The Falklands Crisis: the Rights and the Wrongs* (Frances Pinter, 1983).

Dabat, Alejandro, and Lorenzano, Luís, *Argentina: the Malvinas and the End of Military Rule* (Verso Editions, 1984).

Dalyell, Tam, *One Man's Falklands* (Cecil Woolf, 1983).

Dobson, Christopher, Miller, John and Payne, Ronald, *The Falklands Conflict* (Coronet, 1982).

Ethell, Jeffrey and Price, Alfred, *Air War South Atlantic* (Sidgwick & Jackson, 1983).

Fox, Robert, *Eyewitness Falklands* (Methuen, 1982).

—— *Antarctica and the South Atlantic* (BBC, 1985).

Hands, Jeremy and McGowan, Robert, *Don't Cry for Me, Sergeant-Major* (Futura/Macdonald, 1983).

Hanrahan, Brian and Fox, Robert, *I Counted Them All Out and I Counted Them All Back* (BBC, 1982).

Harris, Robert, *Gotcha: the Media, the Government and the Falkland Crisis* (Faber & Faber, 1983).

Hastings, Max and Jenkins, Simon, *The Battle for the Falklands* (Michael Joseph, 1983).

Latin America Bureau, *Falklands/Malvinas: Whose Crisis?* (Latin America Bureau, 1982).

Latin American Newsletters, *The Falklands War: the Official History, Official Communiqués (English and Spanish)* (Latin American Newsletters, 1983).

Middlebrook, Martin, *Operation Corporate* (Viking/Penguin, 1985).

Perkins, Roger, *Operation Paraquat: the Battle for South Georgia* (Picton Publishing, 1986).

Ponting, Clive, *The Right to Know: the Inside Story of the* Belgrano *Affair* (Sphere, 1985).

Rice, Desmond and Gavshon, Arthur, *The Sinking of the* Belgrano (Secker & Warburg, 1984).

Smith, John, *74 Days: An Islander's Diary of the Falklands' Occupation* (Century, 1984).

Sunday Times 'Insight' Team, *The Falklands War* (André Deutsch, 1982).

Thompson, Julian, *No Picnic: the Story of 3 Commando Brigade in the Falklands War* (Fontana, 1983).

Tinker, David, *A Message from the Falklands* (Junction Books, 1982).

Winchester, Simon, *Prison Diary, Argentina* (Chatto & Windus, 1983).

Woolf, Cecil and Moorcroft Wilson, Jean (eds), *Authors Take Sides on the Falklands* (Cecil Woolf, 1982).

Transition to Democracy

Borrini, A., *Política y Publicidad: Como Se Hace un Presidente* (El Cronista Comercial, 1984).

Camarasa, J., Felice, R. and González, D., *El Juicio: Proceso al Horror* (Sudamericana/Planeta, 1985).

Gilobert, Isidoro, *La Ilusión del Progreso Apolítico* (Legasa, 1986).

Giussani, Pablo, *Los Días de Alfonsín* (Legasa, 1986).

King, John, *Argentine Cinema* (Plymouth Arts Centre, 1986).

Moneta, C., López, F. and Romero, A., *La Reforma Militar* (Legasa, 1985).

Terragno, Rodolfo, *Memorias del Presente* (Legasa, 1984).

—— *La Argentina del Siglo 21* (Sudamericana/Planeta, 1985).

Various authors (including Raúl Alfonsín) *Argentina: de la Transición al Despegue* (Fundacion Eugenio A. Blanco, 1986).

Verbitsky, Horacio, *La Posguerra Sucia* (Legasa, 1985).

Comparative Studies

Although not directly about Argentina, the following books provide an interesting point of reference.

Agee, Philip, *Inside the Company: CIA Diary* (Penguin, 1983).

Ardagh, John, *France in the 1980s* (Penguin, 1982).

Calvocoressi, Peter and Wint, Guy, *Total War* (Penguin, 1981).

Carr, Raymond, *Modern Spain* (Oxford University Press, 1980).

Cooley, John, *The Eye of the Storm* (Croom Helm, 1983).

Cornwell, Rupert, *God's Banker: an Account of the Life and Death of Roberto Calvi* (Victor Gollancz, 1983).

Galbraith, J. K., *Money* (Penguin, 1976).

Graham, Robert, *Spain: Change of a Nation* (Michael Joseph, 1984).

Grunberger, Richard, *A Social History of the Third Reich* (Penguin, 1979).

Knightley, Philip, *The First Casualty* (Quartet, 1982).

Nichols, Peter, *The Pope's Divisions* (Faber & Faber, 1981).

Orwell, George, *Decline of the English Murder and Other Essays* (Penguin, 1984).

Riddell, Peter, *The Thatcher Government* (Basil Blackwell, 1985).

Sampson, Anthony, *The Changing Anatomy of Britain* (Hodder & Stoughton, 1982).

Taylor, Robert, *The Fifth Estate: Britain's Unions in the Modern World* (Pan, 1980).

Reports, Documents and Pamphlets

Alemann, Roberto, *La Política Económica Durante el Conflicto Austral. un Testimonio* ('Economic background to the Falklands War') (Academia Nacional de Ciencias Económicas, 1982).

SELECT BIBLIOGRAPHY

Amnesty International, *Report of an Amnesty International Mission to Argentina* (London, 1977).
—— *The Disappeared of Argentina* (London, 1979).
—— *Testimony on Secret Detention Camps in Argentina* (London, 1979).
Catholic Institute for International Relations, *Death and Violence in Argentina* (London, 1976).
Comisión Argentina de Derechos Humanos, *Testimonio del Inspector de la Policía Federal Argentina, Rodolfo Peregrino Fernández* (Madrid, 1983).
Comisión Permanente en Defensa de La Educación, *Elecciones y Participación* (Analysis of 1983 elections results) (COPEDE, 1984).
CONANEP, *Nunca Más: a Report by Argentina's National Commission on Disappeared People* (Faber & Faber, 1986).
Conferencia Episcopal Argentina, *La Iglesia y los Derechos Humanos* (Church's documents on human rights) (Conferencia Episcopal, 1984).
Congreso Pedagogico, *Evolución de la Autonomía Universitaria en la Argentina* (several academic pamphlets providing details of the educational system) (Editorial Docencia, 1986).
El Libro de El Diario del Juicio (Documentation on trial of the juntas) (Editorial Perfil, 1985).
El Terrorismo en la Argentina (Argentine military propaganda on war against subversion) (1980).
Falkland Islands Review, *Report of a Committee of Privy Councillors (Franks Report)* (HMSO, 1983).
House of Commons, *The Falklands Campaign: A Digest of Debates* (HMSO, 1982).
Informe Oficial Ejército Argentino, *Conflicto Malvinas* (Official army report on the Falklands War) (1983).
La Constitución Nacional y Los Derechos Humanos, ed. Jorge Vanossi (the Argentine Constitution) (Eudeba, 1985).
Organisation of American States, *Informe Sobre los Derechos Humanos en la Argentina* (Washington, 1979).
Viaje Apostólico a Gran Bretaña y Argentina (Documentation on Pope's visit to Britain and Argentina) (BAC popular, 1982).

Periodicals, Magazines and Newspapers

ARGENTINA

Aerospacio, Ámbito Financiero, Buenos Aires Herald, Clarín, Criterio, Crónica, Cronista Comercial, Contraseña, El Periodista, El Porteño, Esquiu, Estrategia, Gente, Humor, La Prensa, La Nación, La Nueva Provincia, La Opinión, La Razón, La Voz, Quorum, Siete Dias

SELECT BIBLIOGRAPHY

BRITAIN

Contemporary Review, Daily Telegraph, The Economist, Financial Times, Guardian, Index on Censorship, International Affairs, Irish Times, Millennium: Journal of International Studies, New Statesman, Observer, South Atlantic Council Occasional Papers, Sunday Times, The Times, Third World Affairs, Third World Quarterly

UNITED STATES

Newsweek, New York Times, Time Magazine, Wall Street Journal, Washington Post

INDEX

279

INDEX

Argentine army – *contd.*
  107–8; and the human rights issue, 110;
  under Alfonsín, 178
Argentine Central Bank, 129
Argentine navy: arms build-up, 17; 1981
  coup, 30; plans for occupation of
  Falklands, 30–2, 35, 42; UNITAS exercises,
  33–5; *buzos tacticos*, 65; and the collapse
  of the junta, 102, 106, 109; nuclear
  submarines, 175–6; under Alfonsín, 178;
  Falklands War, 227–9
Arguindeguy, General, 165
Arosa, Admiral Ramón, 175
Asesinato en el Senado de la Nación, 142
Asís, Jorge, 151–2
Astiz, Lieutenant Alfredo, 46–7, 80, 87, 160,
  173
ATC, 82
Atomic Energy Commission, 16
Austria, 18

Bahía Buen Suceso, 41, 47–8
Bahía Paraíso, 46
BAI Press, 82, 85
Baker, James, 217–18, 223
Balbín, Ricardo, 119–20, 122, 123
Banco de Intercambio Regional, 113
Bank of England, 52
Bank of London and South America, 51
Baring Brothers, 210
Barker, Captain, 46, 48
Barnett, Anthony, 239, 240
Barrionuevo, Ruben, 179
Bayer, Osvaldo, 90
Beagle Channel, 17, 54, 63, 72–3, 98, 181,
  185, 202, 236, 238
Beck, Dr Peter, 248
Belaunde Terry, Fernando, 53, 230
Belize, 237
Bemberg, María Luisa, 87, 137, 139, 141,
  143, 144
Benitez, General Aguado, 165
Berreneche, María Lorenza, 116–17
Bignone, General Reynaldo, 109, 129, 137,
  140, 147, 160, 164, 170, 183; background,
  106; and the transition to civilian rule, 105,
  106–8, 123–4, 134; excluded from
  Alfonsín's inauguration, 172
Bittel, Deolindo, 89, 125
Bloomer Reeve, Brigadier, 242–3
Bluff Cove, 96
Boado, 7–8
Boffi, Admiral, 4
Bolivia, 25, 227

Borges, Jorge Luís, 90–1, 147, 151, 199
Borras, Raúl, 165–6, 179
Bossano, Miguel, 151
Brando, Lusiana, 144–5
Bravo, Alfredo, 155
Brazil, 7, 125, 181, 208, 211, 227, 233;
  reaction to invasion of Falklands, 54, 55;
  debt crisis, 219; economic co-operation
  with Argentina, 221–2; human rights
  issue, 232
Briatore, Captain, 48
BRIDAS, 15
Brinski, Norman, 146
Britain: World Cup, 1; Franks Report, 2–6;
  and Argentina's *Santiago* operation
  against Falklands, 4–5; media reactions to
  war, 74, 78–9, 85; Alfonsín visits, 122;
  trade unions, 207; and the sinking of the
  Belgrano, 227–30; post-war relations with
  Argentina, 233–8; and the future of the
  Falklands, 233–5, 237–8, 247–50; arms
  sales to Chile, 236
British Antarctic Survey, 2, 41, 44, 47, 48,
  249
British Broadcasting Corporation (BBC), 74,
  78, 242
Buenos Aires, 7, 8, 13, 111, 136, 176–7,
  204–5, 220, 225
Buenos Aires Herald, 1, 19, 75–7
Buenos Aires Military Academy, 6
Buenos Aires University, 153, 155, 185
bureaucracy, 224–5
Busser, Rear-Admiral Carlos, 68
buzos tacticos, 65

Cagliari, Lieutenant Luís, 179
Calabresi, Monsignor Ubaldo, 73
Calvocoressi, Peter, 28
Camila, 139, 141
'Campaign of the Desert', 7
Camps, General Ramón, 173
Canale, Brigadier-General Hector, 173–4
Capaglio, Captain, 32
Caputo, Dante, 122, 133, 181, 212, 215, 235
Carr, Raymond, 233
Carranza, Roque, 122, 179
Carrington, Lord, 237
Cartagena group, 215, 218–19, 220, 222
Carter, Jimmy, 33–4, 52, 102–3, 157
Casado, Arsenio, Bishop of Jujuy, 186
Casella, Juan Manuel, 199
Castro, Fidel, 103, 159
Castro Madero, Admiral Carlos, 175
Catholic Action, 22

INDEX

INDEX

INDEX

INDEX